THE ANIMATED RAGGEDY ANN & ANDY

THE ANIMATED

RAGGEDY ANN & ANDY

An Intimate Look at the Art of Animation:
Its History, Techniques, and Artists

BY JOHN CANEMAKER

DESIGNED BY JACQUES CHAZAUD

BOBBS-MERRILL

INDIANAPOLIS / NEW YORK

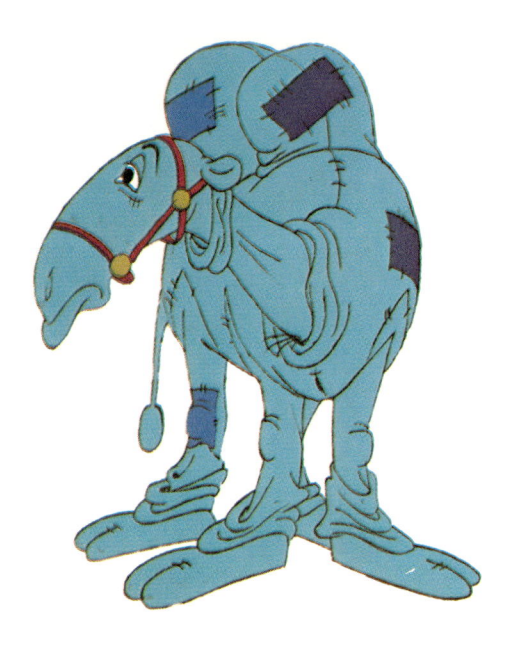

Copyright © 1977 by The Bobbs-Merrill Company, Inc.
All rights reserved, including the right of reproduction in whole or in part in any form
Published by The Bobbs-Merrill Company, Inc.
Indianapolis   New York

Manufactured in the United States of America

First printing

> **Library of Congress Cataloging in Publication Data**
> Canemaker, John.
>   The Animated Raggedy Ann & Andy
>
>   1. Raggedy Ann and Andy. [Motion picture]
> 2. Moving-picture cartoons—United States.   I. Title.
> NC1766.U53R343   791.43'7   76-53289
> ISBN 0-672-52329-9 cloth
> ISBN 0-672-52330-2 paper

CONTENTS

ACKNOWLEDGMENTS   7

INTRODUCTION   9

PART ONE.   BACKGROUND
CHAPTER I —From Storyboard to Screen   15
CHAPTER II —Personality Animation: Its History and Techniques   45
CHAPTER III—Johnny Gruelle and His Million-Dollar Dolly   63

PART TWO.   GETTING STARTED
CHAPTER IV —Setting the Gears in Motion   79
CHAPTER V —The Richard Williams Story   91
CHAPTER VI —Designing the Production   109
CHAPTER VII—Auditioning for Bobbs-Merrill/ITT   125

PART THREE.   COMING TO LIFE
CHAPTER VIII—Recording the Soundtrack   135
CHAPTER IX —Animation   145
    Summit Meeting in New York   145
    Tissa David—The Loneliness of the
        Long-Distance Animator   157
    Art Babbitt—The Animator as Legend   175
    Emery Hawkins—The Restless Cowpoke   193
CHAPTER X —Notes at the Halfway Point   207
    Shooting the Live-Action   207
    The Leica Reel Race   210

PART FOUR. A CLOSER LOOK

CHAPTER XI—Raggedy Ann West—The Hollywood Studio   219

CHAPTER XII—Raggedy Ann East—The New York City Studio   241

         Assistants and Inbetweeners   244

         Xeroxing   250

         Checking and Opaquing   254

         Backgrounds   266

         Camera and Sound Effects   275

EPILOGUE: From Rags to Riches   283

ACKNOWLEDGMENTS

I would like to thank the following individuals for their help in making this book a reality:

First, I want to express my gratitude to my parents, Rose and John Cannizzaro, and all of my family, for their continued love, support and encouragement of all of my interests through the years, especially animation. I am also indebted to Sr. Dymphna Leonard, Ph.D., for her dynamic guidance, continued interest and valued advice.

Next, I wish to thank Terry Ork for introducing me to my terrific literary agent, Susan Ann Protter, and I thank Susan for her encouragement and hard work on my behalf.

I am especially indebted to Worth and Sue Gruelle for their patience in answering all my letters inquiring about Johnny Gruelle, and for going out of their way to find two rare photos of the artist in their family collection and allowing me to use them in this book.

I am grateful to Greg Shelton of Indianapolis for his enthusiastic and helpful search for historical material about Johnny Gruelle, and I thank Tom Rumer, Reference Librarian at the Indiana Historical Society, for researching and photographing an old newspaper photo of the young Gruelle.

I owe appreciation to David R. Smith, the kind and patient Archivist at the Walt Disney Archives, for his help in gathering information on Gruelle's contact with the Disney studio, and for his continued interest in and support of all my animation projects.

All the black and white production photos of the *Raggedy Ann* studios were taken by me with my trusty Minolta; I acknowledge with gratitude the following people and organizations for permission to use other photographs: Kathleen Williams, the mother of Richard Williams, for searching out some early photos of her remarkable son; Anthony Farinacci and Charles E. Kent of ABC-TV for permission to use photos from *A Christmas Carol*, ©1971 ABC, Inc.; Riad Traboulsi for a photo of Tissa David on page 158; Martin Lasky, with the assistance of Maryann Paliema, for the Knickerbocker Toy photos; Carol Stallings, Executive Administrator of the Richard Williams Studio, London; Edward Oldman, Tony Richardson and Woodfall Films for permission to publish a still from *The Charge of the Light Brigade*; Ron Perkins of United Artists and Tony Adams of 20th Century-Fox; Carol Millican for use of her personal photos; Wide World Photos for the photo of Johnny Gruelle on page 74; and Culver Pictures for the photo of Walt Disney. The photo of Dick Williams receiving the Academy Award is by Sheedy & Long.

Thanks to Lou Appet and Jim Carmichael for permission to quote *The Peg-Board*.

I owe a special debt to the following people: Louise Beaudet, Directrice of the Animation Division of La Cinémathèque Québècoise, a valuable friend to the art of animation and to me, who provided many of the Winsor McCay stills and two Emile Cohl stills; Joe Oriolo of Oriolo Film Studios, Inc., for permission to use drawings of Felix the Cat; Marilyn Giardina, Joe Raposo's secretary, for her prompt reply to all of my requests for recording dates, photos of Joe, and original sheet music and lyrics, for which the proper copyright notice is © copyright 1976, Jonico Music Inc., The Bobbs-Merrill Company, Inc.

Thanks also to Ward Kimball for permission to use his marvelous caricature of the Disney animators, and to Woody Gelman for permission to use a Winsor McCay comic strip of *Little Nemo in Slumberland*.

I am grateful to Herbert J. Jacobi, Eugene Winick, Evva Joan Pryor, Leslie Cabarga, Charles Samu, Mark Kausler, Harold Feuer, Martin D. Williams, Leonard Maltin, Chuck Jones, Frank Thomas, and the gang at *Millimeter*.

Special thanks goes to Les V. Perkins for patiently putting me up during a hectic visit to Hollywood last summer. For reading and criticizing parts of the original manuscript, I want to thank Patrick Agan; William Williams; Conn Fleming; and the spelling bee champ from Jackson Heights, my friend and advisor Joseph Kennedy.

And thanks to Linda Holiday, art director at Bobbs-Merrill, and Jacques Chazaud, designer, for making this book so beautiful. Thanks, too, to Gene Rachlis for his suggestions, and to Diane Giddis, my editor, for her terrific help.

Finally, I would like to thank all the artists and technicians connected with the film *Raggedy Ann & Andy* for taking time out of their extremely busy schedules to talk with me and for answering my endless questions. For opening up the production to me I am grateful to Stanley S. Sills, Richard Horner, Joe Raposo and Richard Williams.

INTRODUCTION

Here's a recipe I dare you to try:

Take one multinational corporation eager to enter the lucrative entertainment field. Add two Broadway producers who have never made a film, let alone an animated feature, and a young animation director who has directed only shorts and movie titles. Drop in a set of extraordinary older animators who have had little opportunity of late to use the full range of their skills, plus a group of youngsters just starting out in the cartoon industry who must be trained on the job.

Set up a studio in New York City as the base of operations, although no animated feature has ever been completed in that city. Set up a second studio in Hollywood, and try to coordinate the work by having the director fly back and forth between the two studios.

Finally, insist on a "Disney-quality" film, but add a pressing deadline and a preliminary budget that Disney wouldn't have touched forty years ago.

Mix for a couple of years, and what have you got?

You have *Raggedy Ann & Andy*, a feature-length animated musical, the first to equal those of the Disney studio in the high quality of its animation, and in the excellence of its production techniques. "A miracle production," "a freak production," "a lucky film," were comments I often heard from the artisans working on the film in the course of almost sixty interviews I conducted.

The main intent of this book is to present in detail the fascinating people and processes involved in bringing the famous and beloved Raggedy Ann and Raggedy Andy to the screen. To the general public the great and new art of animation remains largely a mystery; it is hoped that this text will clear up most of that mystery and reveal the hard work, dedication and amazing skill necessary to bring drawings to life. To make this possible, the entire *Raggedy Ann & Andy* staff gave me their full cooperation, and the studios in New York and Hollywood placed their resources at my disposal.

As a result of this generous help, the illustrations for the book feature photographs and art work that provide a unique, intimate glimpse at the procedures involved in making an animated feature. The preparatory sketches and preliminary drawings necessary for defining and controlling what is at last released on the screen are as exciting, artistic and beautiful in their own way as the final color Panavision result.

Because of the collaborative nature of the production of animated features and the process of distillation that makes the work of many hands look like the accomplishment of one person, individual animators have often gone unsung and therefore unappreciated by general audiences and by art and film critics. The detailed portraits of some of this film's key animators—their lives and careers, their individual talents, their working methods, and the problems they encounter in their work—will, I hope, illuminate the significance of their contribution to what many believe is the most exciting new art form of this century: the animated film.

It is to all of the animators and other craftspeople who have made *Raggedy Ann & Andy* a thing of joy and wonder that this book is dedicated.

PART ONE:

BACKGROUND

January 26, 1976
To: Mike and All!
From: Dick Williams

Regularly, and without exception, there will be a Monday morning screening of the previous week's material—all of it. All the filmed material of the previous week. This should have happened three months ago, and it will now happen every Monday morning at 9:00 A.M.

This is obviously vital to all the artists concerned as they must be able to see their work and the work of others if this production is going to be coherent and interesting.

Should any assistant or painter or any artist wish to see any section of the film at any time, they must be granted access to the footage, starting *today* until the end of production.

Thank you.

Dick

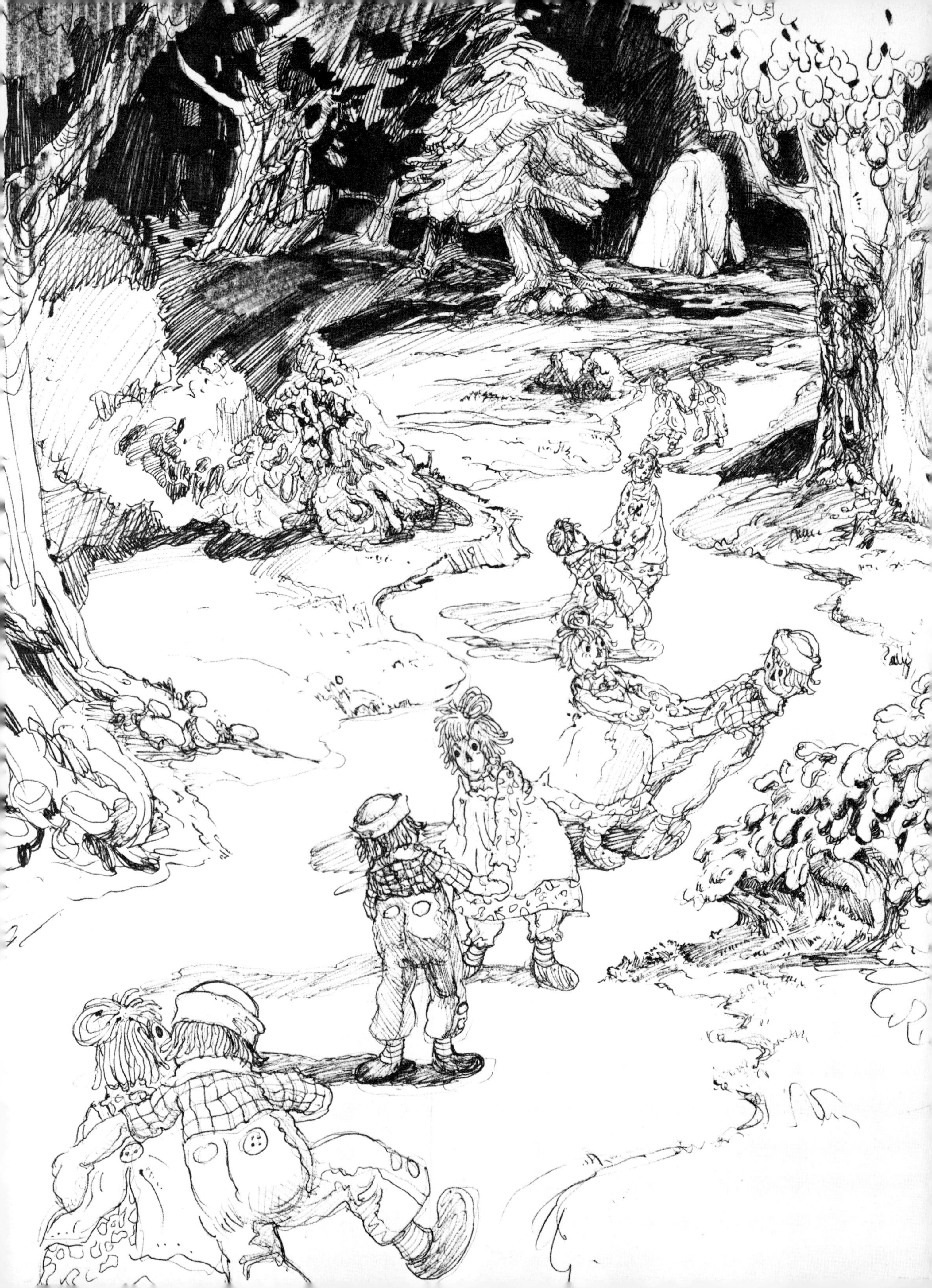

CHAPTER I

From Storyboard to Screen

Raggedy Ann & Andy is a unique production . . . an all-star "jazz band" playing in all parts of the country with the rhythm section in New York. I don't think any of us could do it again working this way.
—*Richard Williams*

The demand in director Richard Williams's memo that his creative staff have access to all of the *Raggedy Ann & Andy* film shot each week points up the unique nature of the art of animation. For it is a truism that the great number of carefully hand-rendered consecutive drawings (sometimes twenty-four to make up one second of action) come to life only when they are photographed frame by frame by a movie camera and projected onto a screen. Only at that moment do the sketches achieve the imitation of life that artists have sought for centuries, beginning with the Altamira caveman who painted six legs on a running boar.

The technology of the twentieth century has made possible the new art of animation. The practitioners of this art, the animators, may flip their drawings back and forth on their lightboards to check the vitality of the creatures

Finished sequential cels of Raggedy Andy and Queasy the Parrot.

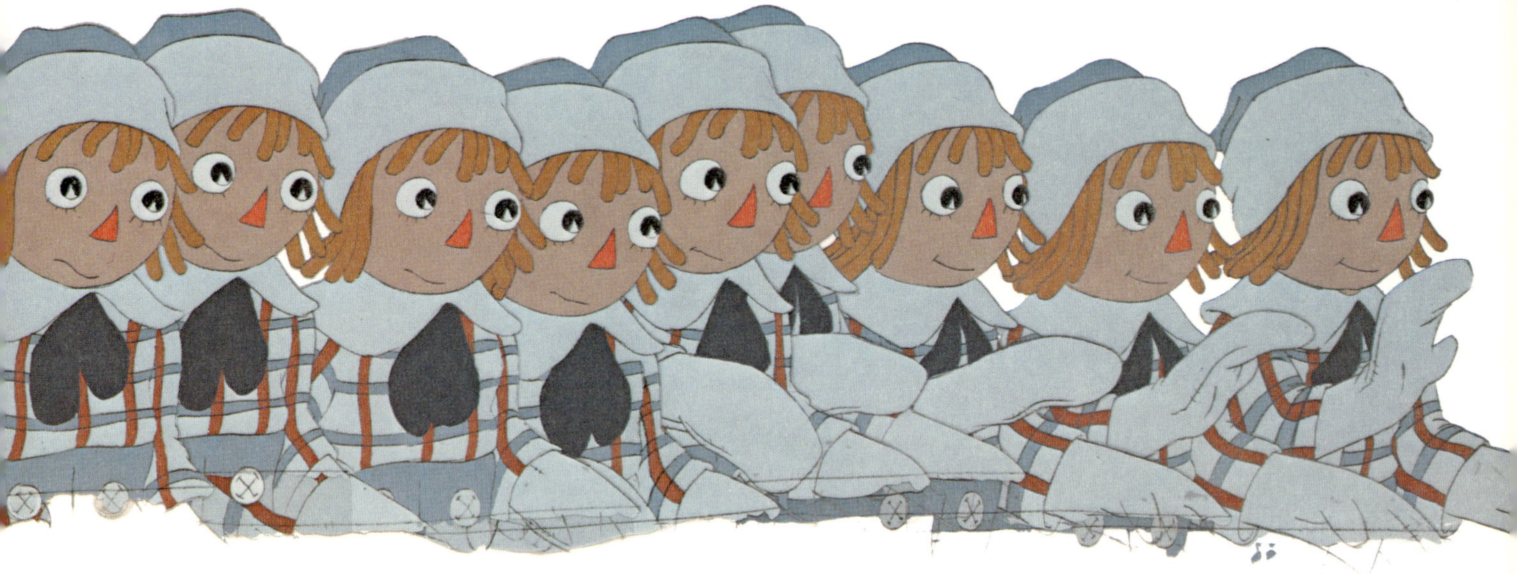

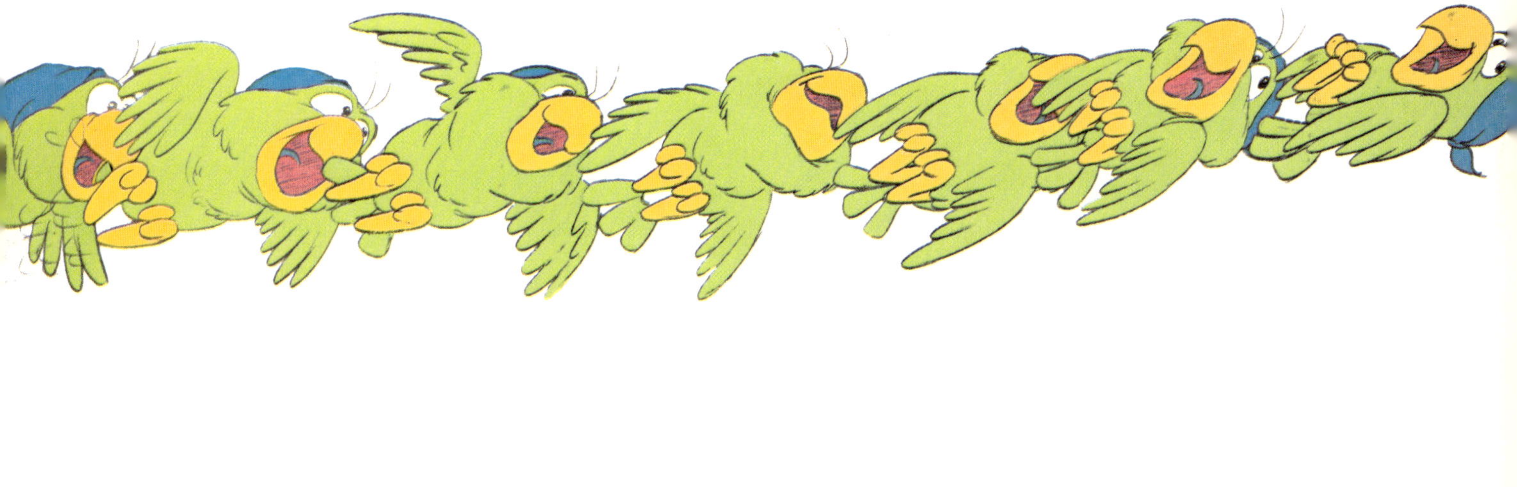

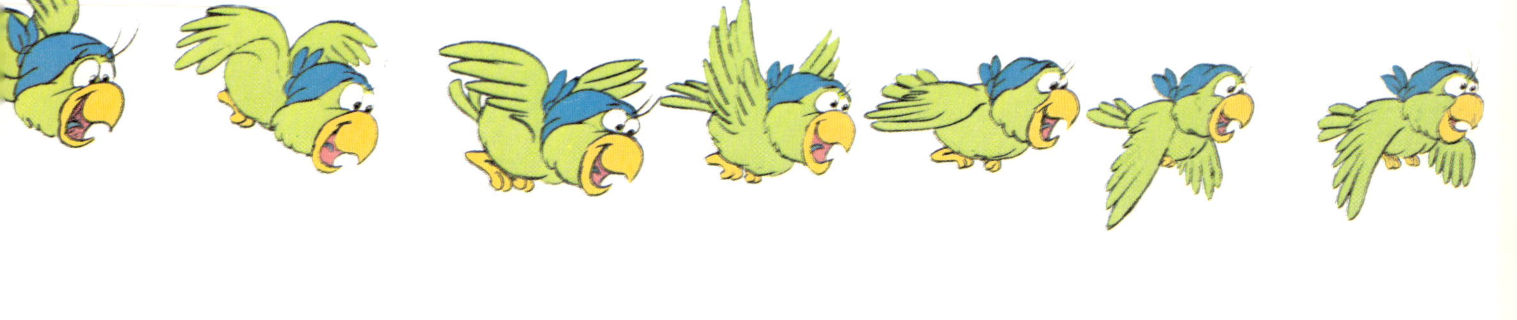

(*Top*) A Monday morning staff screening of pencil tests at the New York Raggedy studio. (*Left to right*) Assistant director Fred Berner; associate director Cosmo Anzilotti; behind him, an unidentified inbetweener; director Richard Williams, hand on head; animator Tissa David; supervisor of assistants and inbetweeners Mike Sporn. Editor Harry Chang, back to camera, operates the flatbed Moviola. (*Bottom*) Actors with a pencil: Director Richard Williams (*left*) demonstrates for New York animator Willis Pyle how and why Raggedy Andy helps boost Raggedy Ann up to the playroom window.

(Top) At the Hollywood Raggedy Ann studio, director Williams flips animator Gerry Chiniquy's drawings to test the approximate smoothness of the animation action. *(Bottom)* In the New York studio's ink and paint department, *(left to right)* assistant animator Dan Haskett, background artist Sue Butterworth, director Williams, and head of ink and paint Ida Greenberg choose colors for the Greedy's taffy.

they are bringing to life, but they must wait to see the creatures gamboling on the screen before they can truly assess their art. Only then can they decide whether they have created characters that appear to think and act and react as real personalities, whether they have instilled the proper motivation in the characters, and whether the complete scene has been brought across to the audience in the best possible way. "Actors with a pencil" is a cliché description of animators, but it is very apt.

Animators, of course, are an essential part of the behemoth that is a feature-length animated production, but nearly twenty other specialized crafts and processes with a couple of hundred people are involved in getting animation off the drawing boards and onto the screen. Williams's *Raggedy Ann & Andy* memo alludes to this intricate group effort.

Most of the production steps involved with animated features were either invented or refined at the Walt Disney studio between 1928 and 1940, a remarkable period often referred to by film historians as animation's "Golden Age." In search of better-quality animation to define his cartoon characters' personalities, Disney took the old methods of the assembly-line cartoon factories of the first two decades of this century and substituted new formulas. He created an assembly-line cartoon factory of his own, but with a difference: it was streamlined to allow flexibility and creativity to flourish. As a result, Walt Disney was able to profoundly develop animation as an art form as well as an industry.

All films begin with an idea that is first worked up as a script; in animation the script is always a visual one. Countless preliminary sketches explore the possibilities in a cartoon idea. For *Raggedy Ann & Andy* approximately half a million idea and story sketches were drawn, and another half million finished drawings were used in the final film.

The Disney studio created a device to enable changes in the story or character development to be made with flexibility and time-saving convenience. It is called the storyboard, and it is simply a series of sketches pinned up in sequence on a cork board in the manner of a large comic strip, a perfect way of graphically telling a cartoon story as the camera will see it. (Over the years the storyboard has also been used by certain live-action directors, e.g., Alfred Hitchcock and Stanley Kubrick.)

The *Raggedy Ann & Andy* storyboard is drawn in a loose, free style, mostly in black and white; but it presents all the essential plot points, songs, and nuances of action of the story. In great detail we learn about Marcella, the little girl who owns Raggedy Ann and Raggedy Andy and a new French doll, Babette, which she has received for her birthday. The storyboard shows Babette being abducted by a love-mad Pirate (another of Marcella's toys) and Raggedy Ann and Andy leaving the safety of the nursery to rescue her. In the Deep Deep Woods they encounter The Camel with the Wrinkled Knees—a discarded toy—who joins them in their search.

At the Hollywood studio, story sketches for a scene from the Greedy sequence are pinned loosely to a cork board so that one visual idea can easily be replaced with a newer and perhaps better one.

Corny Cole, *Raggedy Ann & Andy*'s production designer, drew hundreds of ornate story sketches and created the lush visual concept of the film. (Opposite) Cole's storyboard richly illustrates how the doll Babette is kidnapped from the playroom by Pirates.

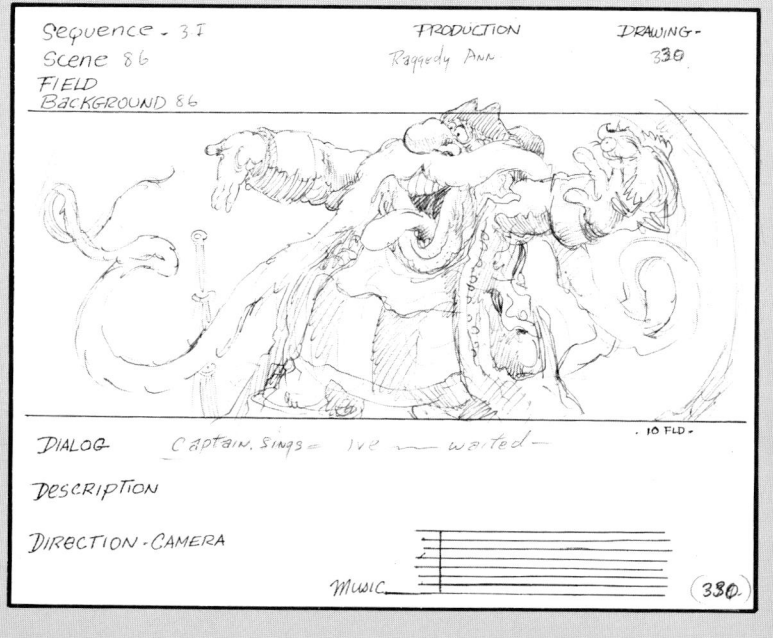

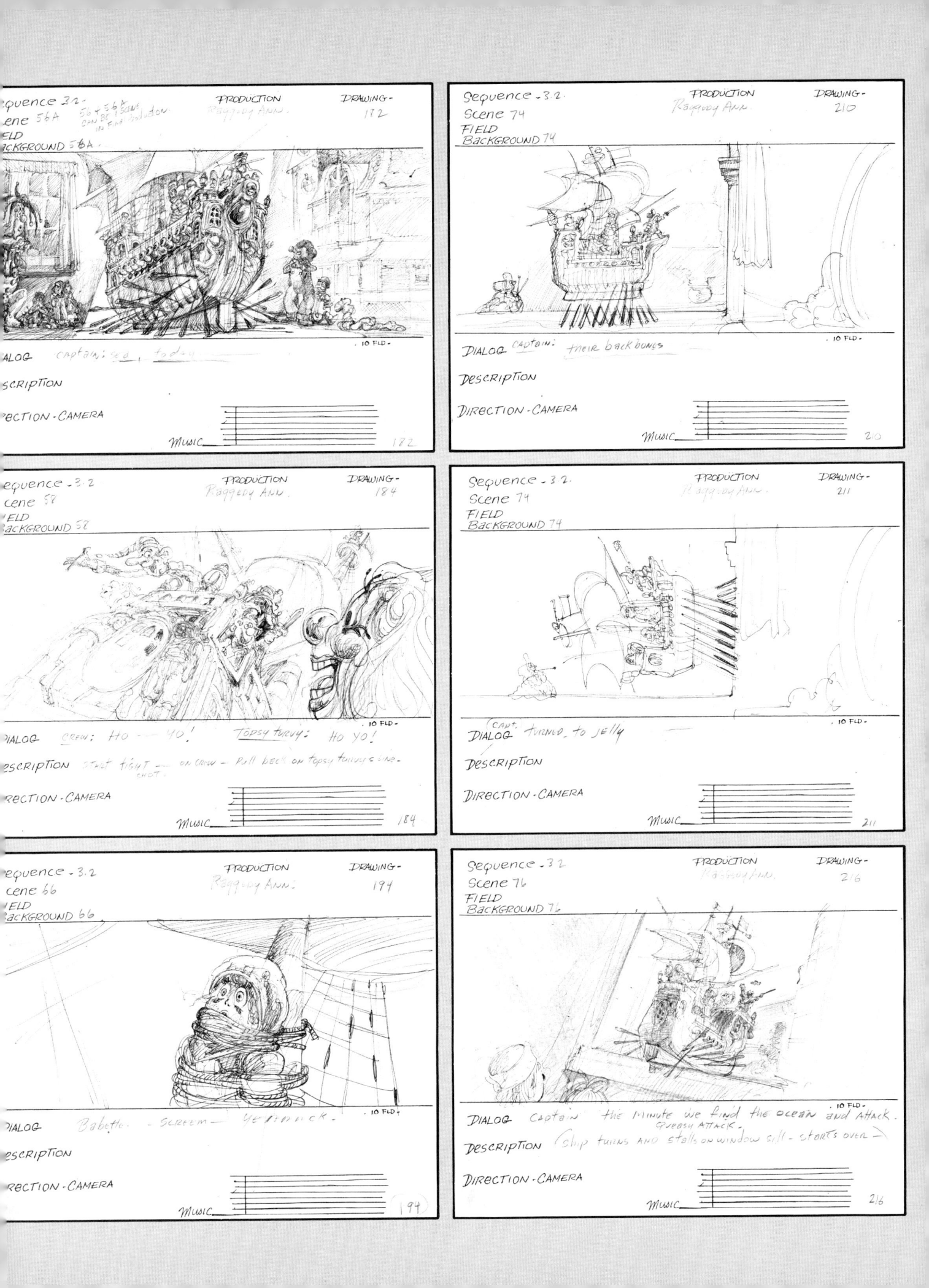

Sequence 3.2 **Scene** 56A (56+56z can be 1 scene in the solution) **Field** **Background** 56A **Production** Raggedy Ann **Drawing** 182	**Sequence** 3.2 **Scene** 74 **Field** **Background** 74 **Production** Raggedy Ann **Drawing** 210
Dialog captain: go, today **Description** **Direction · Camera** **Music** 182	**Dialog** captain: their backbones **Description** **Direction · Camera** **Music** 210
Sequence 3.2 **Scene** 58 **Field** **Background** 58 **Production** Raggedy Ann **Drawing** 184	**Sequence** 3.2 **Scene** 74 **Field** **Background** 74 **Production** Raggedy Ann **Drawing** 211
Dialog CREW: HO — YO! TOPSY TURVY: HO YO! **Description** start fight — on crew — Pull back on topsy turvy's line shot. **Direction · Camera** **Music** 184	**Dialog** (Capt.) turned to jelly **Description** **Direction · Camera** **Music** 211
Sequence 3.2 **Scene** 66 **Field** **Background** 66 **Production** Raggedy Ann **Drawing** 194	**Sequence** 3.2 **Scene** 76 **Field** **Background** 76 **Production** Raggedy Ann **Drawing** 216
Dialog Babette — screem — yermnick **Description** **Direction · Camera** **Music** 194	**Dialog** captain: the minute we find the ocean and attack. queasy attack. **Description** (ship turns and stalls on window sill - starts over -) **Direction · Camera** **Music** 216

Gerry Potterton, responsible for storyboarding the Loonie Knight and King Koo Koo sequences, has a simple and direct drawing style that contrasts sharply with Cole's subtle rococo draftsmanship.

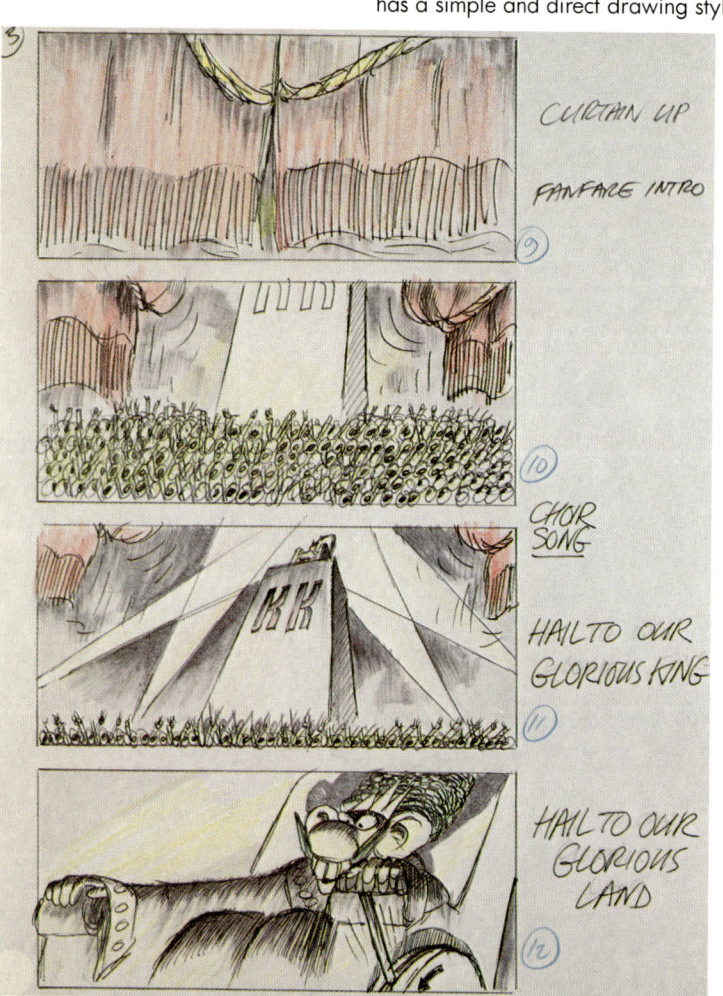

5
(GENERAL NOISE
17
18
REPRISE
HAIL TO OUR GLORIOUS KING
19
HAIL TO OUR-
20

7
LOONEY NOISE
25
SPROING
26
27
KING
SILENCE!
SILENCE
28

9
KING
-ALL OF THEM ARE IDIOTS!
33
LOONEY F/A
34
ANN
YOUR HIGHNESS-
35
SHE PUSHES THRU CROWD
-YOUR HIGHNESS
36

11
SILENCE
KING
SILENCE-
41
THIS IS NOT COMEDY-
42
-THIS IS TRAGEDY!
43
-FOR A MA
OF MY STATURE
44

Director Williams allowed animator Tissa David to develop her own storyboard for the Deep Deep Woods sequence she animated, and her sensitive drawings are an eloquent graphic shorthand, full of life and movement.

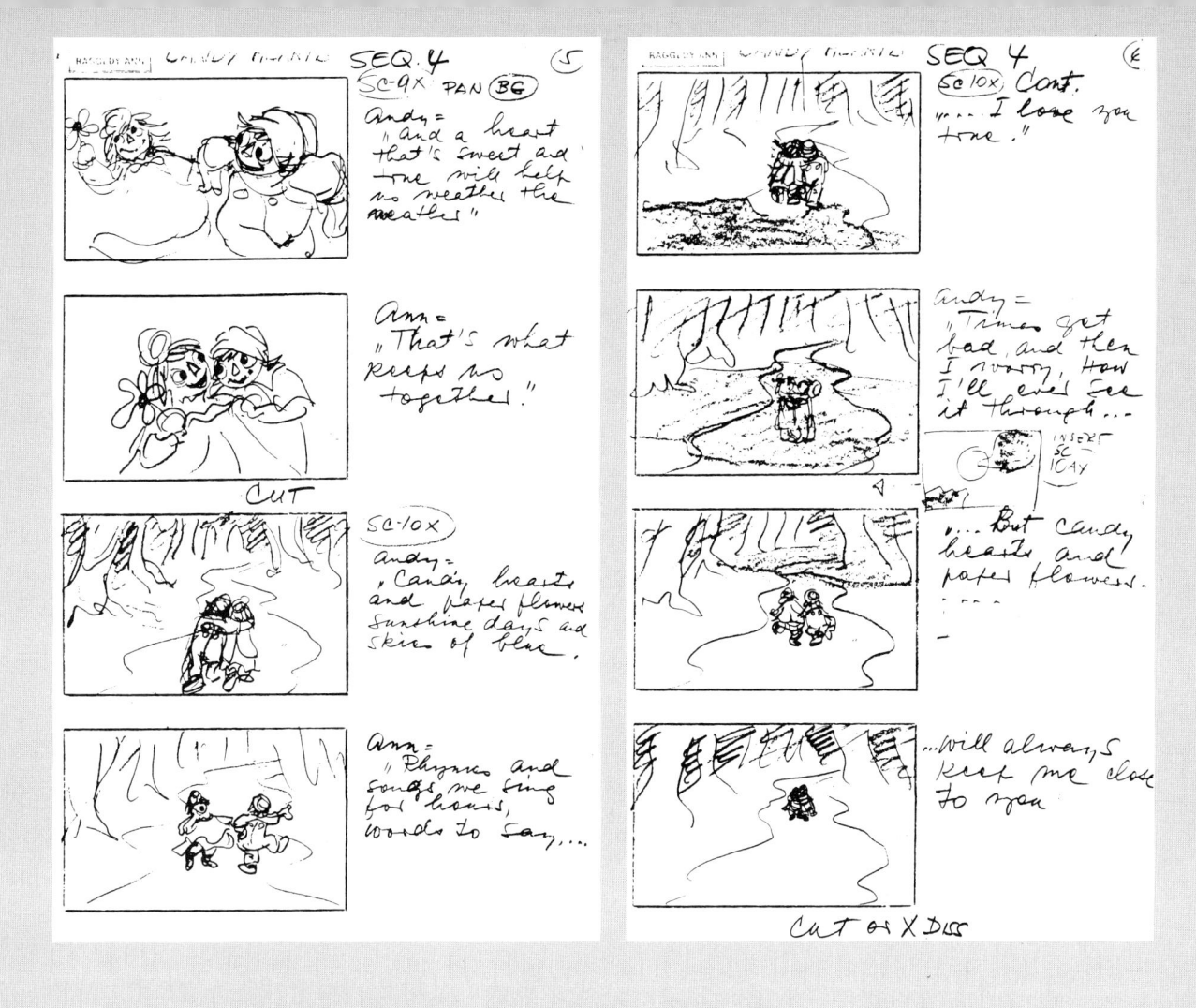

SEQ. 4 — Page 5

SC-9X PAN BG
Andy: "And a heart that's sweet and true will help us weather the weather."

Ann: "That's what keeps us together."
CUT

SC-10X
Andy: "Candy hearts and paper flowers, sunshine days and skies of blue,"

Ann: "Rhymes and songs we sing for hours, words to say,..."

SEQ. 4 — Page 6

SC-10X Cont.
"... I love you true."

Andy: "Times get bad and then I worry, how I'll ever see it through..."
INSERT SC 10AX

"...But candy hearts and paper flowers..."

"...will always keep me close to you"
CUT or X DISS

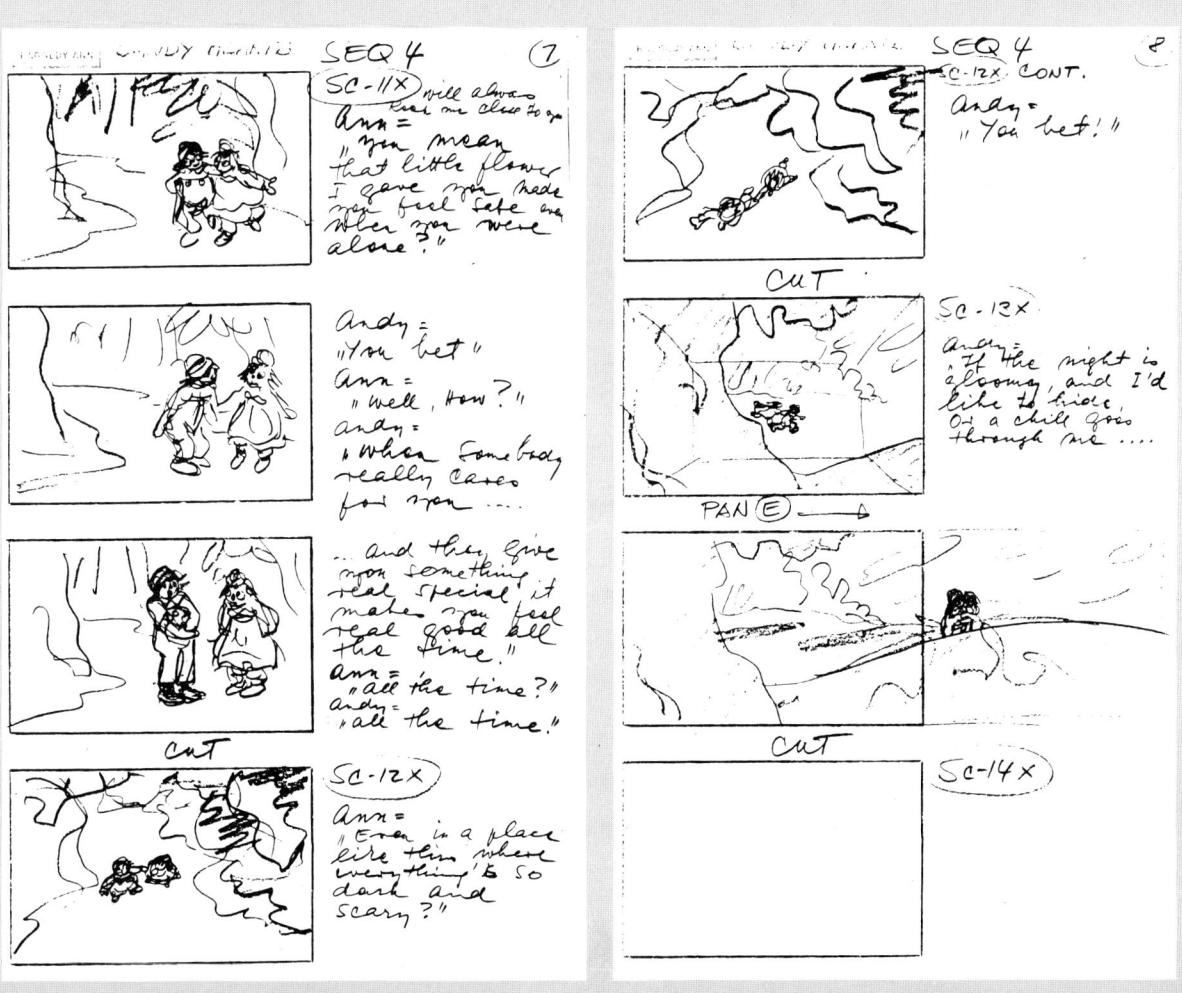

SEQ. 4 — Page 7

SC-11X "will always keep me close to you"
Ann: "You mean that little flower I gave you made you feel like me when you were alone?"

Andy: "You bet"
Ann: "Well, how?"
Andy: "When somebody really cares for you ..."

"... and they give you something real special, it makes you feel real good all the time."
Ann: "All the time?"
Andy: "All the time."
CUT

SC-12X
Ann: "Even in a place like this where everything's so dark and scary?"

SEQ. 4 — Page 8

SC-12X CONT.
Andy: "You bet!"
CUT

SC-12X
Andy: "If the night is gloomy, and I'd like to hide, or a chill goes through me...."
PAN E →

CUT

SC-14X

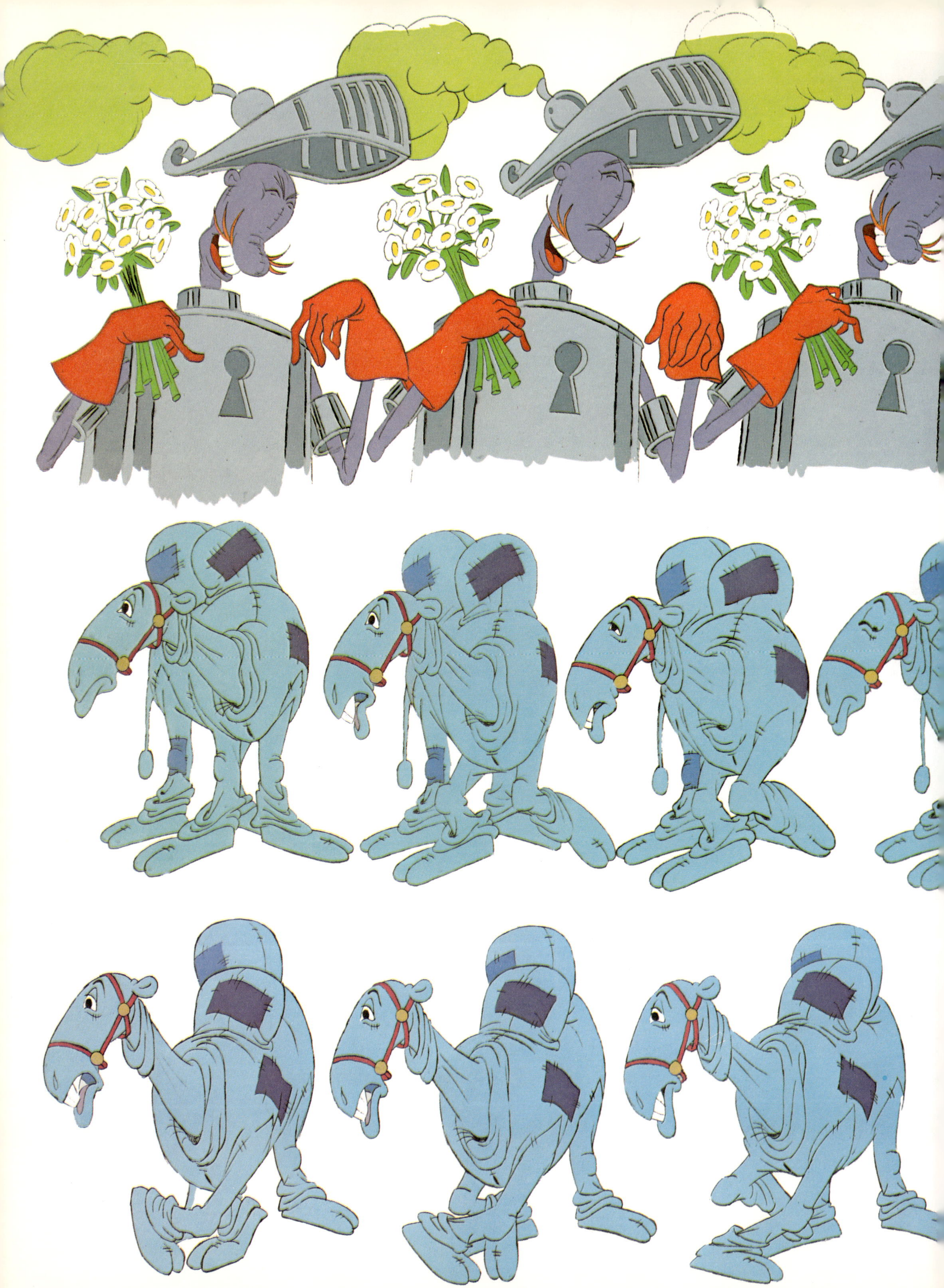

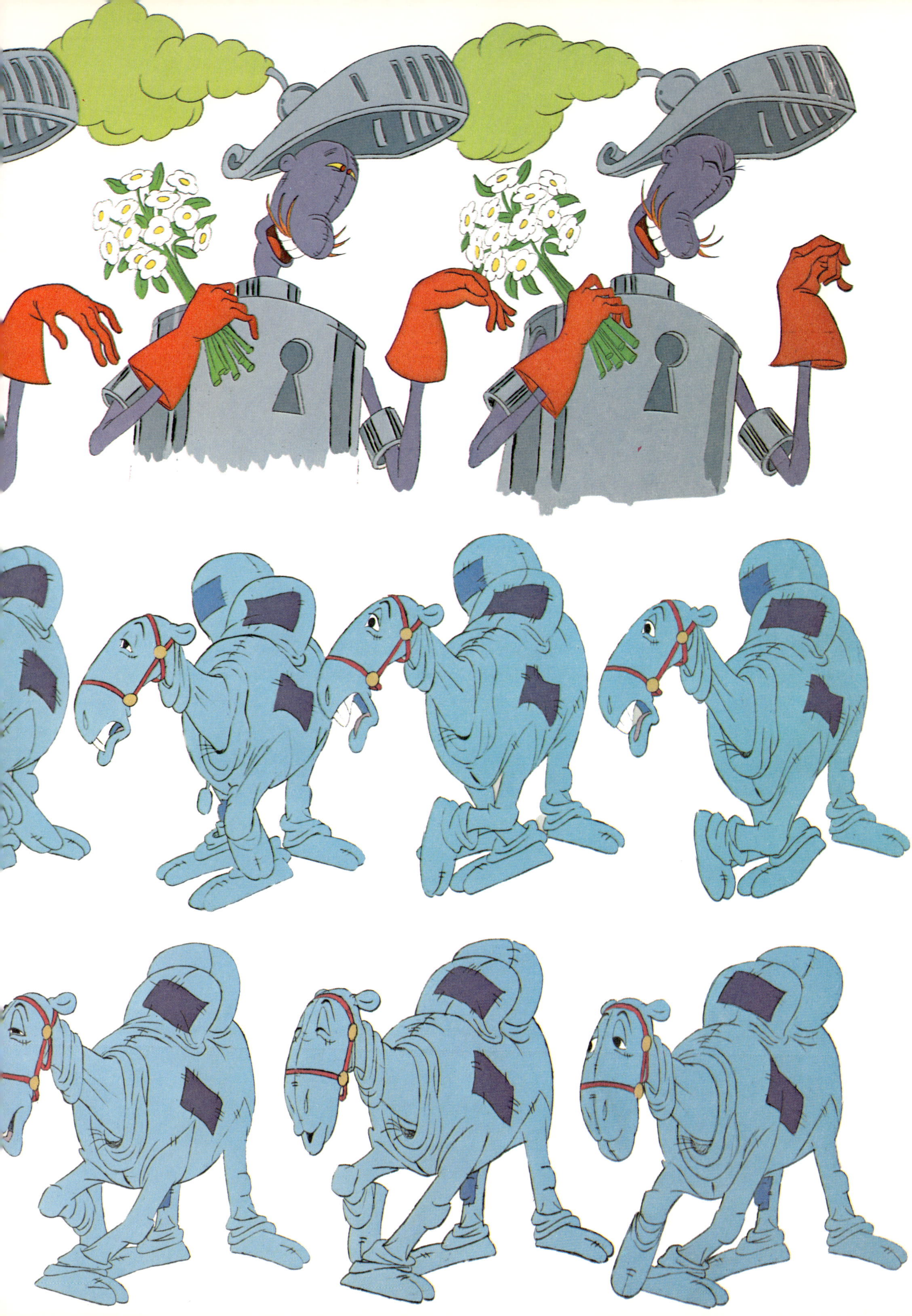

They also encounter, among others, the Greedy, a gigantic taffy pit, fated to eat and regurgitate itself eternally; the Loonie Knight and Loonie King; and the Gazooks, a deep-sea monster. The storyboard chronicles their capture on the Pirate Captain's ship, their eventual escape, and their return to the nursery, where the other dolls make the Camel a part of their home.

Design and layout usually follow on the heels of the storyboard and are often done by the same person or persons who developed the board. Layout sketches in animation help determine the relation of the cartoon actors to their backgrounds or settings—the visual concept of the film as a whole.

The conference technique, another Disney development, subjects storyboards and other cartoon ideas to intense critical analysis. Minor and major points that make up an individual character's personality are discussed and thrashed out. In Bob Thomas's *The Art of Animation*, an excerpt from one of the many conferences on *Snow White* gives a good idea of the detail the Disney artists strove for in devising distinct characters for the screen:

HAM LUSKE: I would like to get an expression of opinion whether we should drive toward the human angle of the dwarfs walking, or whether they should swing from side to side, working with their hips and legs.

BILL TYTLA: On account of pelvis condition, dwarfs are inclined to walk with a swing of the body.

FRED SPENCER: Dwarfs seem to walk with a little waddle. I think we should establish some kind of walk but not make it repulsive.

FRED MOORE: I think we should use a quick little walk, try to work out some pattern where we could get away from the usual way of covering ground.

HAM LUSKE: Take Dopey's walk. He could walk in a shuffle with his toes out and looking around.

DAVE HAND: I don't think Sleepy would walk as fast.

Soundtrack recordings of dialogue, songs and any music that must be in synchronization with the animation are done before the animation is drawn. The tracks are then analyzed ("read") by a film editor, and the sound is written frame by frame onto charts called exposure sheets. Animators can tell from looking at an exposure sheet how many frames (drawings) are needed for words, sound effects and music. "X-sheets" follow the film through all the stages of its creation, and several people, from the director to the cameraman, add to them or act on their instructions. They are a unifying element in coordinating an animated film.

The animator, according to a Disney description, "makes the key or 'extreme' drawings for a particular cartoon character. When the action is slow, he makes only a few drawings and leaves the rest to his staff. When the

Layout sketches suggest where the subject will move and how it will look in relation to the background. In these layouts of the inflated King Koo Koo from the film's finale, Corny Cole treats movement as an element of compositional balance.

Emery Hawkins's rough animation drawing #311 of the Greedy and Dan Haskett's clean-up of the same drawing. On the facing page is the final Xeroxed and opaqued cel of drawing #310. Note the slight variations in spacing and drawing between #310 and #311.

action is fast, he may do all the drawings in a short sequence." It was at the Disney studio that the "key" or "pose" method of animating was perfected. The pose method sets up certain key drawings that tell the story of an action first; the other "in between" drawings are filled in later to smooth out the action.

For years most animators preferred to work "straight ahead," which meant going from drawing A at the beginning of an action to drawing Z, taking each drawing as it came along. The result was a smooth, overlapping animation which, because of its too-even timing, often failed to emphasize the main points of action. The pose method of animating is a quick, expressive way to work, and since the introduction of a soundtrack it has proved to be the best way of synchronizing action to musical beats and dialogue.

Animators put their first impressions on paper in a series of action poses known as rough (or "ruff") drawings. The roughs contain life-giving elements and are an eloquent graphic shorthand that gets to the heart of an action or character without bothering with nonessential details.

Details are the responsibility of the assistant animator, who "cleans up" the animator's rough sketches and makes the production look like the work of one artist. To do this, the assistant constantly refers to a character model sheet, a sheet of drawings showing the feature's characters in their relative sizes and proportions.

THE SUSIE PINCUSHION MODEL SHEET

"RAGGEDY ANN & ANDY
© COPYRIGHT 1976
THE BOBBS-MERRILL CO. INC.

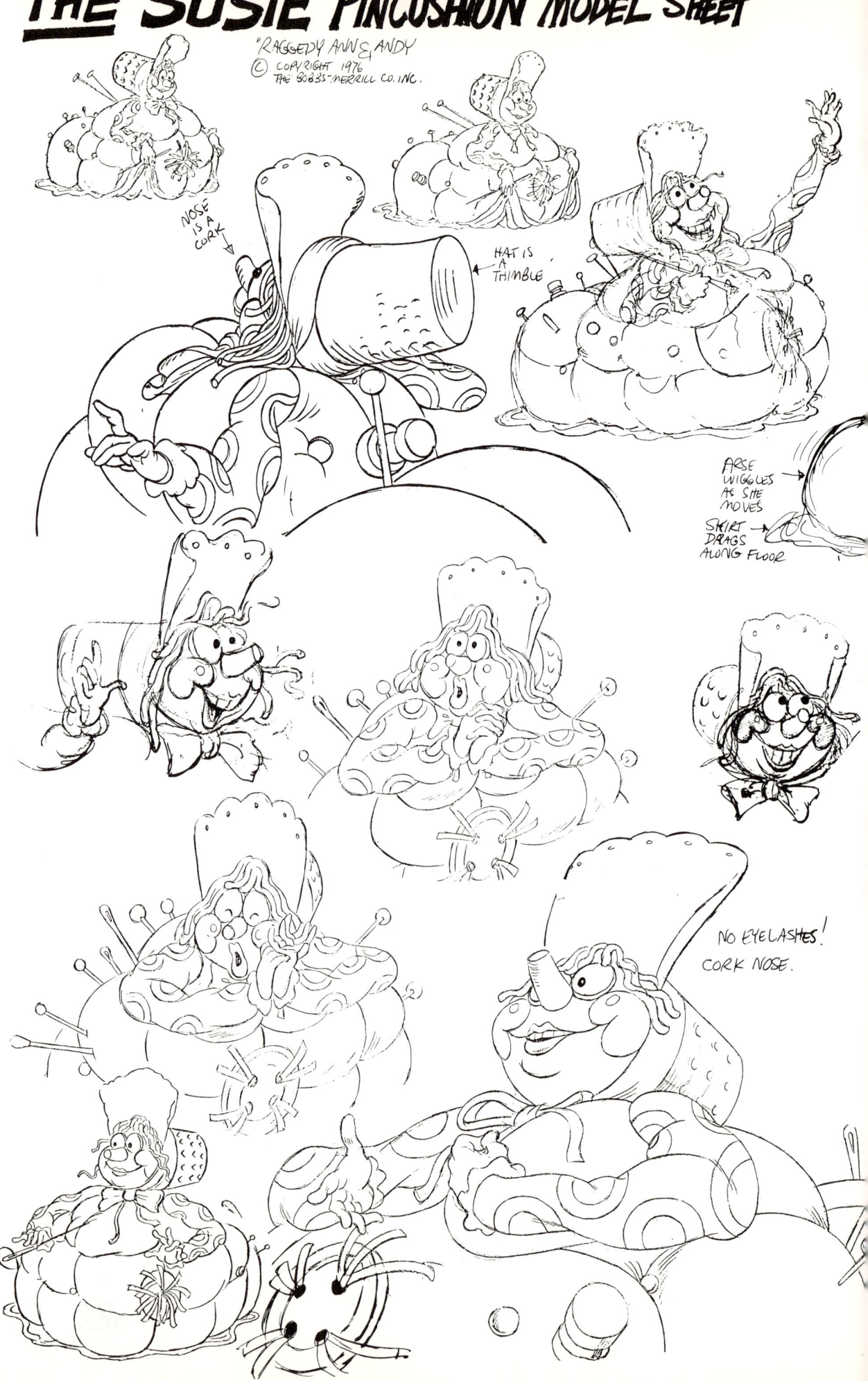

NOSE IS A CORK

HAT IS A THIMBLE

ARSE WIGGLES AS SHE MOVES

SKIRT DRAGS ALONG FLOOR

NO EYELASHES!
CORK NOSE.

The model sheet for Susie Pincushion, illustrating the proportions and detail of the bizarre but motherly doll.

A test cel for determining the line quality, after Xeroxing, of drawings made with various pencils (Staedtler B, 2B, etc.) and ball-point pens (Bic Fine Point F29, etc.).

Lowest in the animation hierarchy is the inbetweener. Inbetweening is the traditional starting spot for most beginning animators who join a cartoon factory; they sketch the animation drawings between the key poses of the animator.

Pencil tests, another Disney innovation, is the process of photographing and projecting the penciled animation drawings to determine the correctness of the animation before proceeding to other, more expensive processes. Disney's also developed the Leica reel, a film of the entire feature in all its stages of development, in synchronization with the soundtrack. The images appear on the Leica reel in four forms: still story sketches; rough animation full of motion and characterization but few details; clean-up animation, which is approved rough animation that has been traced with careful attention to detail and style consistency; and finished full-color animation on backgrounds. The Leica is a sort of jigsaw puzzle that allows the director an overall view of the progress of the production.

If approved in pencil test, the clean-up drawings are sent to the ink and paint department. Before 1961, all the drawings were hand-inked onto transparent celluloid (cels) by a small army of inkers. But in Walt Disney's feature *101 Dalmatians* (1961) the drawings were photographed by a Xerox camera directly onto cels, thus eliminating the time-consuming task of the inkers. The Xeroxed cels retain much of the spirit of the animator's line and the lively, rough quality of the original paper drawings.

The cels are now painted on the reverse side by a staff of opaquers, who literally push opaque paint with a brush into the proper places on the cels; in the meantime the background department, working with design and layout, has been rendering full-color watercolor backgrounds—the "sets" against which the characters will perform. (In *Raggedy Ann & Andy* almost 1,000 backgrounds are used.)

(Above) A specimen cel of Maxi Fix-It with the various colors numbered as a guide for the opaquers. In this playroom scene Maxi requires seventeen separate colors.

(Left) Sue Butterworth brings a problem playroom background to Dick Williams for advice. Williams usually suggested darkening the playroom settings to enable the characters on cels to "read" more clearly when placed on top of the backgrounds.

THE GAZOOKS — FIRST ANIMATION ROUGHS

RAGGEDY ANN & ANDY
© COPYRIGHT 1976
THE BOBBS-MERRILL COMPANY INC.

RAGGEDY ANN + ANDY © COPYRIGHT 1976
THE BOBBS-MERRILL COMPANY INC.

GRAMPA
LASTEST CLEAN-UPS
MAY 24 76

(Above) Animator Spencer Peel's model chart of Grandpa's walk, a twenty-drawing "cycle" that hooks up drawing #20 with drawing #1 for repetition of the action. The slight limp on drawings #10 and #11 is an excellent personality touch.

(Opposite, top) This model sheet of the Gazooks was derived directly from animator George Bakes's first animation roughs of the character.

(Opposite, bottom) Richard Williams's clean-ups of his own animation of Grandpa. Notice the free use of exaggeration and distortion, the key to supple personality animation.

39

A final set-up of three cels and a background, with a camera move ("truck") indicated on a separate cel. The "field" is the area actually photographed by the camera. Field "A" (in blue) concentrates on the Camel's fancy footwork. The camera then moves diagonally up to Field "B" (in red), to take in both the Camel's and Raggedy Ann's facial expressions. Raggedy Andy will not appear in this scene; he is far outside the camera field in this set-up.

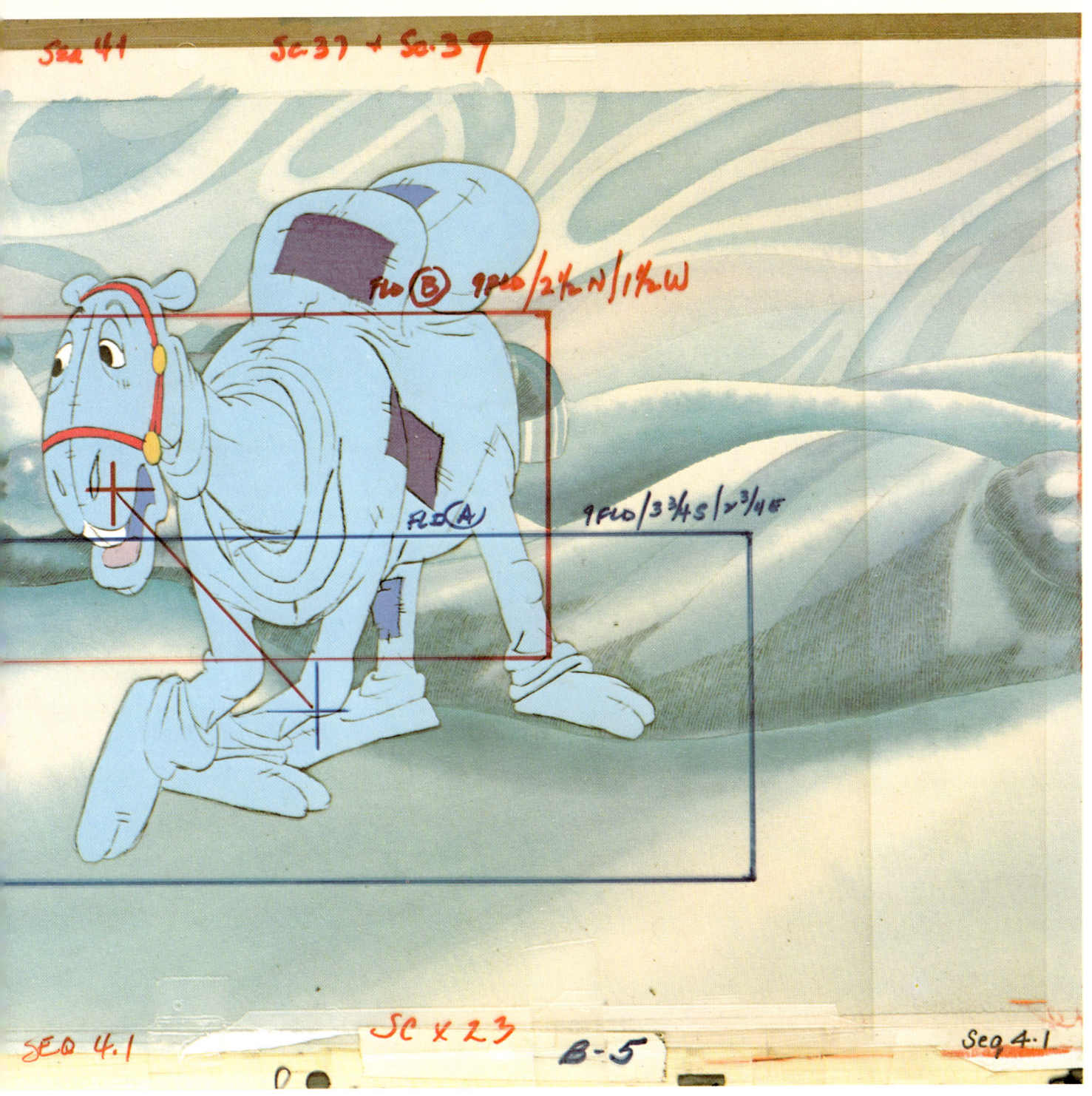

Before the drawings are Xeroxed and after the cels are painted, a keen-eyed group of checkers scrutinize all aspects of the visuals to make sure everything is as it should be before the cels and backgrounds are bundled together and are sent with their X-sheets to their last stop, the camera department. There the cels are matched to their backgrounds and shot one frame at a time. The area being photographed is called the "field." Standard size is a 12 (-inch) field; wide-screen (Panavision) requires the larger, more rectangular 18-field size in paper and cels. *Raggedy Ann's* cels were shot onto 35-mm color film.

41

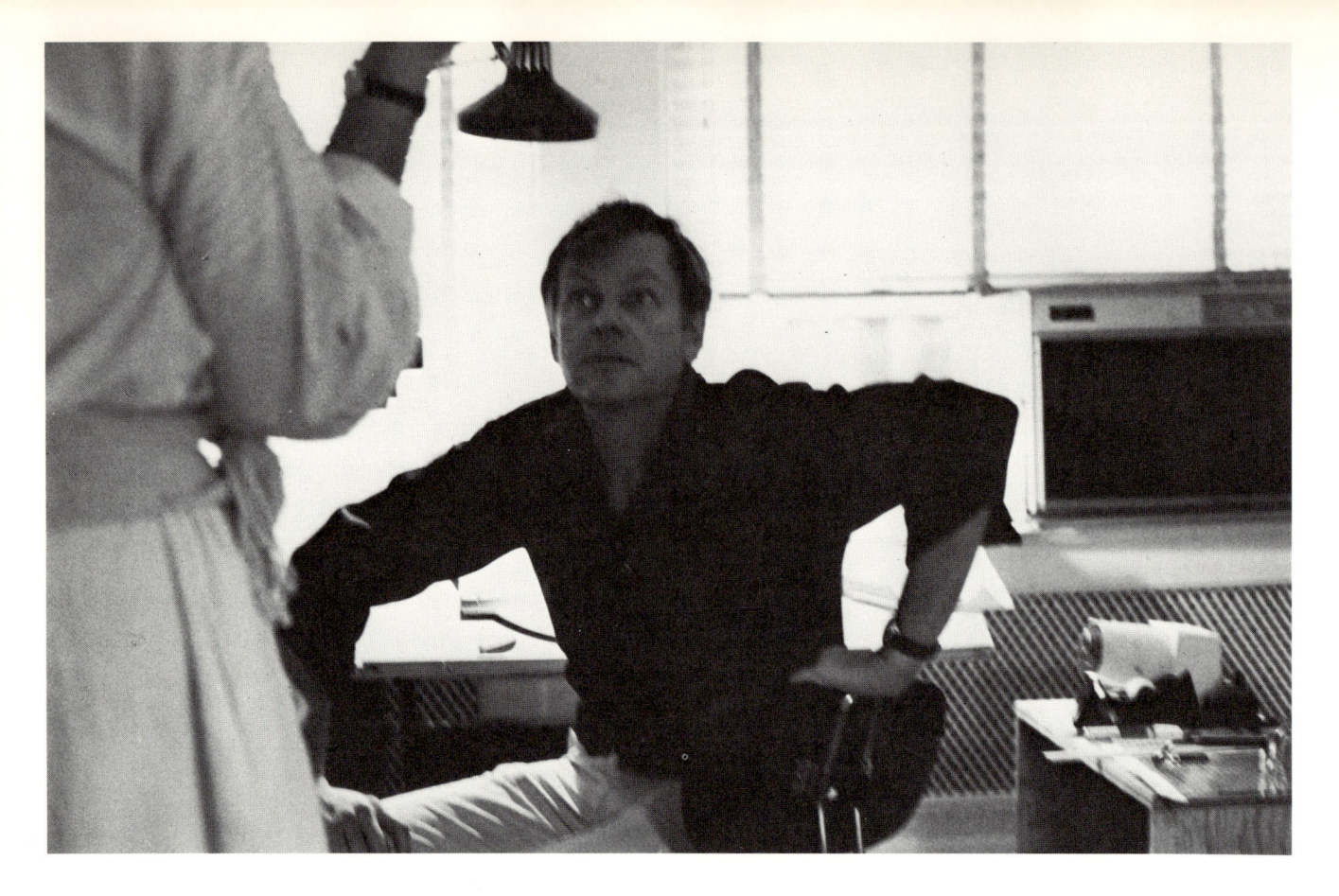

Richard Williams listening to Tissa David.

There are still more steps in the production before the finished animated feature is seen by the public. For example, the composer arranges and records incidental music that fits the songs and dialogue; a sound-effects man works out various noises to enhance the action of the characters; all the various music, dialogue and sound-effects soundtracks are "mixed" onto one balanced soundtrack in a recording studio; the final cut picture and mixed track are "married" in a lab; and a "first-answer print" emerges for final approval. If this first-answer print is approved, the lab turns out hundreds of copies of the film for showing in local theaters around the world.

The one constant in the entire animation production is the director. He is the pace setter and the decision maker. During *Raggedy Ann & Andy*, Richard Williams, with his fierce perfectionism and seemingly inexhaustible energy, sometimes worked a frantic eighteen-hour day, running from one department to another at the studios on both coasts. Encouraging some animators with pep talks, cajoling others, explaining technical details to the producers, attending to the myriad problems involved in producing a picture in New York and California, he was the unifying force from the beginning to the end.

Taped to the cover of Williams's battered red script was a slip of paper from a fortune cookie: "Success depends upon hard work." And success in making *Raggedy Ann & Andy* come alive required lots of hard work plus the skill and dedication of the animators in creating the special magic known as "personality animation."

FOOTAGE WEEK ENDING - JULY 2				
ANIMATOR	# WKS	WK FTG	FOOTAGE	WK AVER
HAL AMBRO	23	11¹³	128⁰²	13⁰⁸
GEORGE BAKES				
ART BABBITT	48	—	704⁰⁴	8⁰⁸
WARREN BATCHELLER	6	—	18²	3²
JOHN BRUNO	15	—	67⁰²	4²
GERRY CHINIQUY	18	5¹⁵	333⁰¹	40²
DOUG CRANE	14	—	100²	6⁰⁸
TISSA DAVID	35	17⁰⁸	556¹⁵	21⁰⁵
CHARLIE DOWNS	29	13¹²	156¹¹	10⁰⁸
EMERY HAWKINS	35	—	336⁰³	9⁰⁸
JOHN KIMBALL	48	17⁰⁹	316¹⁴	11²
GRIM NATWICK	17	—	29⁰²	2⁰
SPENCE PEEL	26	—	136⁰²	1²
WILLIS PYLE	10	9²	123¹⁴	12²
CHRYSTAL RUSSELL	12	19⁰⁴	99⁰³	8²
JACK SCHNERK	17	7⁰⁸	142¹⁴	8²
DICK WILLIAMS + MISC.			207⁰²	
		148²	3926⁰⁴	9²

WEEKLY FOOTAGE - JULY 5-9

MON JULY 5 - HOLIDAY
TUES JULY 6 -

JUNE 25
LIVE ACTION   8 MIN. APPER
CALIF ANIM.   7 MIN. 36 SEC.
N.Y. ANIM.   37 MIN. 36 SEC.
                 53 MIN. 12 SEC.

FINAL COLOR 8635 - 9 MIN 36 SEC

REMAINING TO ANIMATE 3852 - 13 WKS - 295² PER WK.

(*Above*) The animator's film footage chart for the week ending July 2, 1976. One foot of 35-mm film contains sixteen frames, or less than one second of screen time. (*Below*) The film editor's work bench.

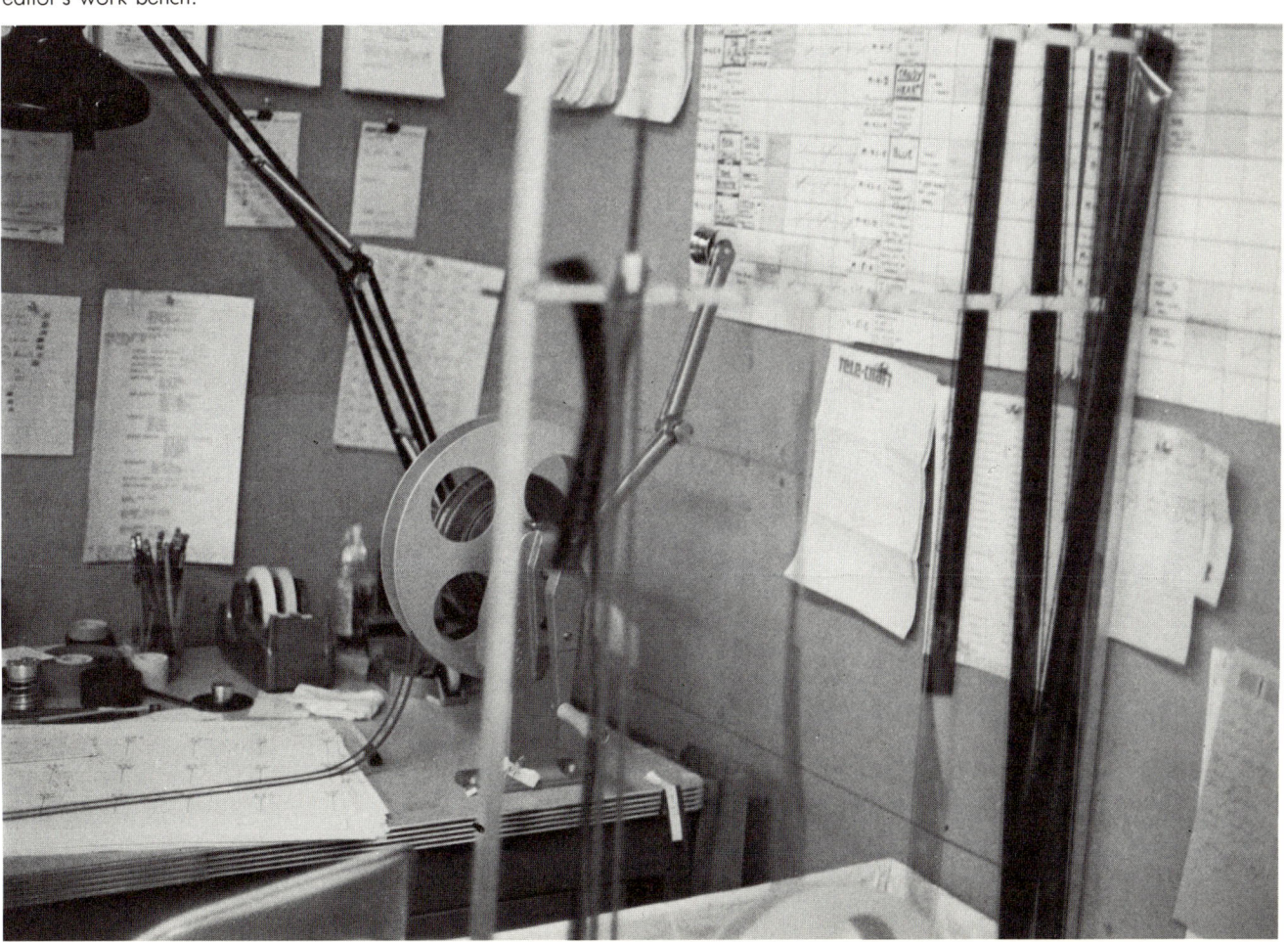

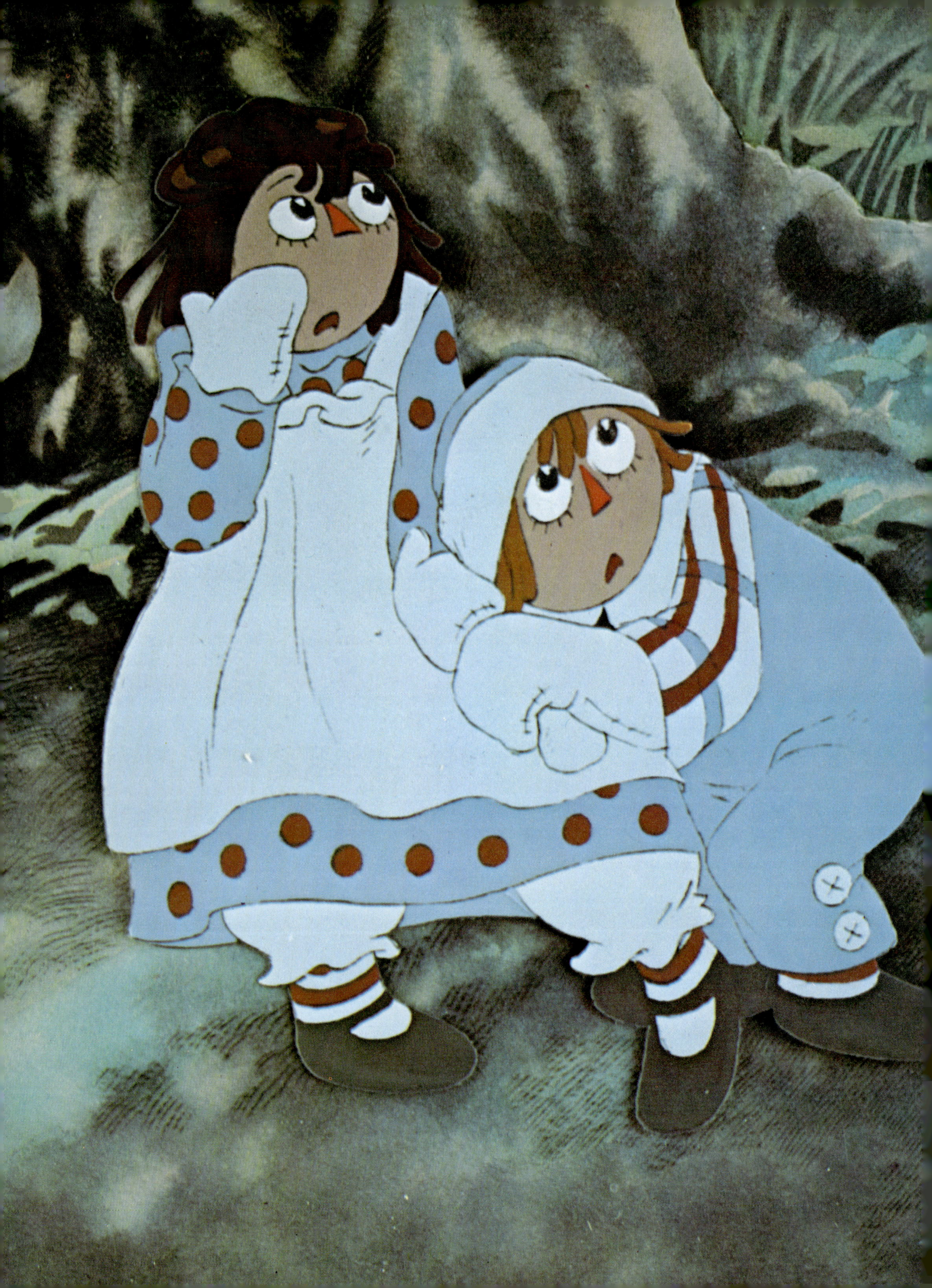

CHAPTER II
Personality Animation: Its History and Techniques

Until a character becomes a personality, it cannot be believed. Without personality, the character may do funny or interesting things, but unless people are able to identify themselves with the character, its actions will seem unreal. And without personality, a story cannot ring true to the audience.
—Walt Disney

Chaplin had a great influence on us.
—Otto Messmer

Outside the cottage of the seven dwarfs, in the dripping aftermath of a violent rainstorm, the forest animals keep a silent vigil. Inside lies the body of the young princess Snow White, felled by a witch's poisoned apple. Around the bedside, candles drip as if in sympathy with the rainy sky and the weeping eyes of the little men surrounding the dead princess.

Happy, Sneezy, Sleepy and Bashful stare absently, holding their hats and occasionally wiping an eye or a nose. Dopey, the youngest of the seven, weeps loudly into Doc's chest as Doc tries mightily to keep himself from breaking down. Grumpy, the dwarf who pretended aloofness from Snow White's charms but secretly adored her, is devastated by her death. He turns his back, heaving deep sobs, unable to face the lifeless girl.

This remarkable scene from Walt Disney's first animated feature, *Snow White and the Seven Dwarfs* (1937), was a daring attempt to introduce a new element to animation's emotional spectrum: the serious and completely realistic depiction of the grief that follows the death of a loved one.

It could have been ludicrous. Rubbery little cartoon characters who throughout the film had made us roar with laughter at their quaint mannerisms, peculiar walks, and weird voices were now supposed to make us believe they were actually grieving over the loss of another cartoon character.

But Disney's gamble paid off, and at every screening of the film in any corner of the world, Disney's cartoon deeply touches the emotions of the audience. The secret lies in the emphasis placed throughout *Snow White* on the very qualities that make us laugh: the details of personality mentioned above—walks, voices, mannerisms—and of anatomical design and clothing. This individualization of each character produces audience identification, an emotional attachment to all the dwarfs and to Snow White. We believed them when they were happy, and consequently we believe them when they are sad.

Frank Thomas, a top animator at the Disney studio for more than forty years and the man who animated the funeral scene described above, says, "It is certainly possible to make strong pictures without much character development, and there are many exciting visual effects that are dazzling and unforgettable. I just feel that they are more dazzling if they are happening *to* me instead of merely in front of me, and this can only be accomplished if I feel that I am living through this film with the cast of characters. As long as I just sit and watch, I am not involved, and I know of no other way to become involved than through identification with characters."

A 1953 caricature by Ward Kimball in which some of Walt Disney's favorite animators are portrayed as Captain Hook (Disney's *Peter Pan* was released that year).

(FRANK THOMAS)   (WARD KIMBALL)   (MILT KAHL)   (MARK DAVIS)   (OLLIE JOHNSTON)

TOOK   FOOK   SHOOK   NOOK   SMOOK

(*Above*) James Stuart Blackton sketching *The Enchanted Drawing* for Edison's camera in 1900. (*Right*) *Humorous Phases of Funny Faces*, created in 1906 by Blackton for his own company, Vitagraph.

The history of personality animation is even shorter than the brief history of animation itself. *The Enchanted Drawing*, made in 1900 by James Stuart Blackton (1875–1941), is generally considered the earliest example of an animated film, but it is more accurately a trick film, as were all of the earliest cartoon experiments. (*Trickfilme* is a German term used in the 1920s in Europe to describe a genre that encompasses techniques which create movie events and effects impossible in live-action filming.) It was Blackton, an ambitious cartoonist-reporter for the *New York Evening World*, who established the graphic style of the early animated films: they were derived from the vigorous popular comic strips found in the mass-circulation newspapers. In his first film, Blackton himself appeared and sketched the face of a sad tramp on an easel outdoors. When he drew a hat on the head of the tramp, the camera was apparently stopped and a real hat substituted, which Blackton jauntily placed on his own head. In Blackton's *Humorous Phases of Funny Faces* (1906), this stop-frame technique is taken even further: the face of a man drawn on a blackboard blows cigar smoke into a cartoon woman's face; a dog jumps through a hoop; words metamorphose into caricatures which are, unfortunately, based on cruel racial stereotypes.

To early movie audiences, the tricks of animation, and indeed the live-action motion pictures, were little more than a novelty; the public demanded nothing but movement from the first films. Soon, however, directors like Méliès and Griffith were developing the potential of the cinema and forging a cinematic "language," producing live-action films that told stories and involved the audience emotionally.

Le Cauchemar du Fantoche (Fantoche's Nightmare), animated and filmed by Emile Cohl in France in 1908.

Animation remained a bit behind in this respect. The white-on-black stick figures of French animator Emile Cohl (1857–1938) remain an entertaining marvel of the metamorphosis technique; but even his "Everyman" character, Fantoche, the first consistent character used in a series (begun in 1908), is memorable because of his design and tricks, not for any intrinsic personality traits.

The first glimmerings of true personality animation came from one of the giants of American popular art and the greatest of the early animators, Winsor McCay (1871?–1934). McCay, a superb self-taught draftsman, started experimenting with progressive movements of characters and backgrounds in his famous epic comic strip, *Little Nemo in Slumberland*, which began in the *New York Herald* on October 15, 1905. McCay's energy, drive, and worldwide fame allowed him to perform from 1906 to 1917 in vaudeville, where he demonstrated the "Seven Ages of Man" by rapidly sketching a series of chalk drawings showing a man and a woman progressing from youth to old age in less than fifteen minutes. He began working with animated films around 1910, and in 1911 he completed his first, *Little Nemo*.

This film features characters from his comic strip, animated with a smoothly flowing motion and a realistic timing that McCay painstakingly worked out with a stopwatch. When he exhibited the film during his vaudeville act, a curious thing happened: the audiences didn't believe the figures on the screen were cartoons! They thought they were either puppets or humans dressed up to resemble Nemo and his gang.

The same thing happened when McCay unveiled his next cartoon film, *How a Mosquito Operates*, in 1912. "While these made a big hit," McCay wrote years later, "the theatre patrons suspected some trick with wires. Not until I drew *Gertie the Dinosaur* [in 1914] did the audience understand that I was making the drawings move. I lectured in connection with the screen presentation, inviting 'Gertie' to eat an apple, which I held up to her. 'Gertie' would lower her long neck and swallow the fruit, much to the delight of the audience. . . ." (McCay, of course, palmed the apple.)

In the film, the gigantic Gertie is as playful as a little girl; when admonished, she cries huge tears, and it is this amusing juxtaposition of the physical size of the dinosaur with her childlike personality that makes her truly memorable, the first animated character with the beginnings of a distinctive identity.

McCay also happened on a truth about the nature of animation itself in his search for an audience-pleasing film: simply that animation should be used to make the impossible seem plausible. It is in the realm of fantasy that the medium functions best, a lesson too often ignored in the seventy-seven-year history of the art.

McCay became a one-man crusade, spreading information about "the most fascinating work I have ever done—this business of making cartoons

(*Left, top to bottom*) Winsor McCay, c. 1925; a film frame from *How a Mosquito Operates* (1912); an original animation drawing of *Gertie the Dinosaur* (1914).
(*Right*) A series of film frames from McCay's first animated film, *Little Nemo* (1911).

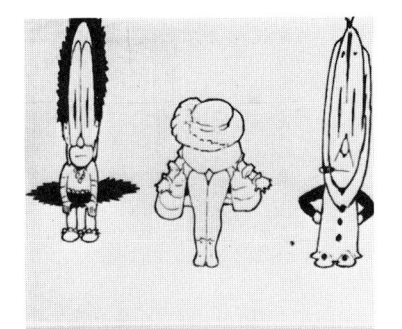

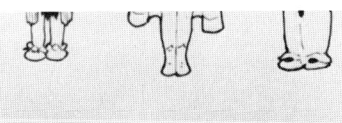

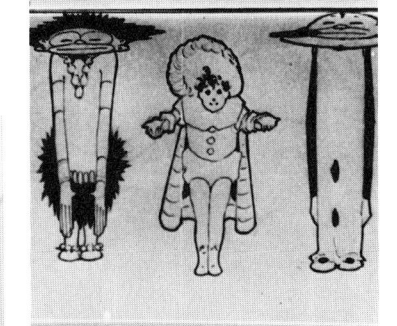

J. R. Bray's *Col. Heeza Liar in Africa*, released by Pathé in December 1913. A lampoon on Teddy Roosevelt, this film gave birth to a series which ran until 1919, then was revived in 1922.

live on the screen." He inspired a generation of future animators by predicting, "People will not be satisfied with going to a gallery and viewing great paintings of people and animals standing still. They will demand action. . . . And to meet this demand, the artists of that time will look to the motion picture people for help; and the artist, working hand in hand with science, will revolutionize the entire field!" McCay was the first artist to view animated films as a new art form; he longed to see the cherubs of Raphael "actually fly and Bonheur horses that gallop and Whistler rivers that flow!"

McCay never fully explored the commercial possibilities of animation, but others did. In 1913, Canadian Raoul Barre (1874–1932) organized in New York the first animation studio, with a staff of cartoonists able to turn out a series of films on demand. The next year a second studio was founded in New York, this one by John Randolph Bray, who at this writing is a spry ninety-seven years old. It was Bray who streamlined the process and paved the way for mass distribution of cartoons; he made them a practical and profitable form of entertainment.

One of Bray's many innovations was the use of sheets of transparent celluloid on which the cartoon characters were drawn; these cels were placed over opaque backgrounds, thus eliminating the necessity of redrawing the entire background each time. Winsor McCay's first three films had been drawn on rice paper, so that the stationary background had to be redrawn on every one of the thousands of drawings. The cel method, patented by Bray and Earl Hurd on June 15, 1915, revolutionized the fledgling cartoon industry. Even McCay adopted the cel method and paid Bray for a license to use the system, as did everyone in animation for seventeen years, until the patent ran out.

The new mass-produced films of the early cartoon factories were similar in their static graphics and vulgar presentation, much like the limited-animation programs seen on most television kids' shows today. No attempt was made to explore the possibilities in the medium: the newspaper comic-strip figures of Mutt and Jeff, for example, were merely moving figures on the screen. The same can be said of Bray's bumptious Colonel Heeza Liar and Dinky Doodle, Paul Terry's *Aesop's Fables* and Max Fleischer's KoKo the Clown. None of them really belonged on the screen; movement was as minimal as in the strips, and when they did move it was usually without motivation.

The first cartoon character to fully express an individual personality in drawings that moved was Felix the Cat. At the height of his movie fame in the mid-1920s, Felix was as popular with audiences as his flesh-and-blood comedic counterparts Charlie Chaplin, Harold Lloyd, and Buster Keaton.

"He has escaped the reality of the cat; he is made up of an extraordinary personality," Marcel Brion of the Académie Française wrote about Felix in 1928. "When he is walking like a man preoccupied, with his head buried in

Otto Messmer (*standing, left*) and Pat Sullivan in the mid-1920s. (*Below*) Inside the Pat Sullivan studio at 47 West 63rd Street, New York City, in 1925. Sullivan, whose private office was behind the doors at right, is sitting at the first animation desk, which was normally Otto Messmer's. Behind Sullivan are a pensive Messmer; animators Raoul Barre, Dana Parker, Hal Walker, Al Eugster, Jack Boyle, George Cannata and Tom Byrne; and Alfred Thurber, the staff cameraman. (*Far right*) Otto Messmer's drawings of Felix the Cat from 1919 and from 1925. Notice the design refinements the character underwent over a period of years.

1919

1925

his shoulders, his paws behind his back, he becomes the impossible in cats, the unreal in man. Felix constructs a universe using two properties, both originating in him, material signs of the state of his own soul: the exclamation point and the question mark. Nothing more is needed for building a world."

In his *Theory of the Film*, Bela Balazs wrote, "Felix loses his tail. He wonders what to do about it. This anxious question grows out of his head in the shape of a large question mark, demonstrating by graphic means that he is torn by doubts. Felix now gazes pensively at the beautifully curved question mark. He has a bright idea, grabs the question mark and sticks it to his rump for a new tail. The problem is solved . . . the question mark was a line, just like Felix's body; their substance was the same. In the world of creatures consisting only of lines the only impossible things are those which cannot be drawn."

Pat Sullivan (1887–1933) produced the Felix films and successfully promoted the character; indeed, it is Sullivan's name and *only* his name that appears on the screen credits. Recently, however, a fact that had been common knowledge within the animation industry for fifty years has come to light: it was Otto Messmer, Sullivan's production manager, who actually created Felix, animated him, and, most important, developed his unique personality. In 1976, with Messmer as guest of honor, two retrospectives of Felix cartoons were held, one at the Museum of Modern Art and the other at the Whitney Museum of American Art.

The easygoing artist, now in his eighties, spoke about his debt to Chaplin in creating a personality for Felix the Cat. It seems that when Messmer joined the Sullivan studio in 1916 (three years before Felix was "born"), he was assigned to work on a series of Charlie Chaplin cartoons. Chaplin viewed the animated films as a means of publicizing his live-action films and himself, and he eagerly cooperated by sending photographs of himself in a variety of poses to the Sullivan studio. "We copied every little movement that he did," recalled Messmer. "Later on, that rubbed off, and we used a lot of that kind of action in Felix. We thought a funny walk sometimes would get a laugh without a script idea. Or the wiggling of the tail, things of that type. But Chaplin had a great influence on us.

"So did Buster Keaton. Keaton paid Sullivan for copying *the walk* [Felix's trademark walk—back and forth, hands behind his back—when trying to solve a problem]. We made a special animation for him which he studied and copied. He then used that. And so between Chaplin and Keaton and Mack Sennett's Keystone Cops . . . they would gain a little and we would gain a little."

Animator Frank Thomas comments, "Felix was great because the audience understood how he felt, what he was thinking, and what he was trying to do. Felix could have been much more interesting visually and the films could have been much more 'artistic,' but what Otto did with his animation is still the type of thing I like to shoot for."

Felix dances! Over three-quarters of the world's population either saw Felix the Cat on the screen or knew him by name. His hundreds of film shorts were the keystone of a million-dollar industry of toys, mascots, phonograph records and sheet music ("Felix Kept on Walking") that foreshadowed Walt Disney's later success in marketing *his* fantasies. (Above) Otto Messmer at age eighty-four in 1976, as photographed by Carol Millican.

Walt Disney and Mickey Mouse, c. 1935.

WDP

Out in Kansas City, a young go-getter named Walt Disney saw Felix the Cat and was impressed. Some of Disney's earliest films—the 1922 Kansas *Laugh-O-Grams* and the *Alice in Cartoonland* series he made in Hollywood, starting in 1923—feature a most Felix-like cat. Likewise, the design of his 1927 series starring Oswald the Rabbit—and even Mickey Mouse, first introduced to the public in 1928—had its roots in Otto Messmer's design concepts for Felix. Messmer found that circles were easier to animate than angles (the first Felix looked like a square dog, but became rounder and cuter over a period of years) and that solid black "saved making a lot of outlines" and "moved better."

It was Felix's famous personality that most impressed young Disney. Under Disney's guidance his studio made many technological advances, but his most important accomplishment was to develop personality animation to its highest degree. To do this, Disney drove his artists to create a new style of animation. The elements of this style are fine draftsmanship, a caricatured impression of reality, and a flexibility of form and kinetic energy unique in the history of art. It is this achievement that makes Walt Disney the single most important influence in the history of the animated film.

In 1932 Disney sought to improve the quality of the animation in the films he was making. He decided to bound ahead of his competitors by setting up his own art school. "We had enough revenue coming in so we could plan ahead," Disney once said, "so I laid out a schedule of what I wanted to accomplish over the years. . . . It was costly, but I had to have the men ready for the things we would eventually do."

Don Graham, an instructor at the Chouinard Art Institute, Los Angeles, was put in charge of Disney's school; he coordinated and supervised training suitable to each individual studio artist in relation to current and future productions. The cartoonists studied anatomy and sketched human and animal models in life classes; Graham brought in guest lecturers from every field, including Frank Lloyd Wright, Rico LeBrun, Alexander Woollcott and Robert Benchley. In "Action Analysis" class, the artists studied slow-motion films of everything from water splashing and glass breaking to Chaplin and Laurel and Hardy going through their paces. There were constant screenings of every type of film, from the latest Hollywood epic *(Gone with the Wind)* to German Expressionist classics *(The Cabinet of Dr. Caligari, Nosferatu)* and the abstract animation in the films of Oskar Fischinger, who also worked briefly on *Fantasia* (1940).

The lessons learned from the intense classwork were incorporated into the animation. Little by little the films became more subtle and expressive. One of these precepts—a natural action must be caricatured to constitute acting—was expounded upon by Don Graham in the December 1940 issue of *American Artist:*

A-27 LINEN

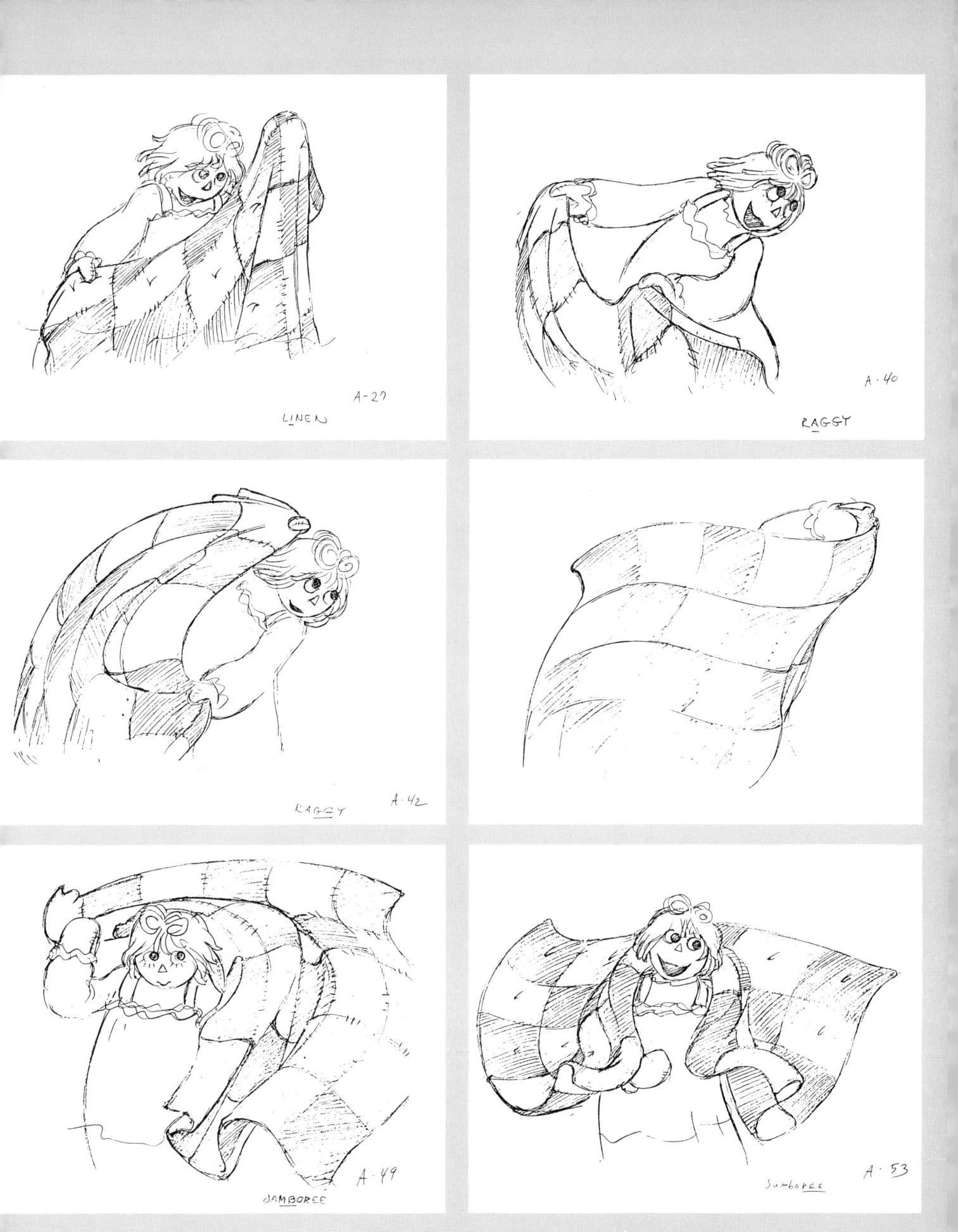

A-40 RAGGY

A-42 RAGGY

A-49 JAMBOREE

A-53 JAMBOREE

Six animation drawings by Chrystal Russell. An example of *anticipation*: Raggedy Ann pulls the quilt backwards before whipping it around her shoulders. This prepares the audience's eye for the major movement in this scene and reinforces the feeling of the weight of the heavy quilt. Anticipation gives an action its full visual value.

Two extreme poses of the Greedy (drawings #1 and #35) demonstrate the principle of *stretch and squash:* exaggerating the natural resilience of figures under duress adds strength to an action and a feeling of weight to the characters. Thirty-three inbetween drawings will smooth out this gesture.

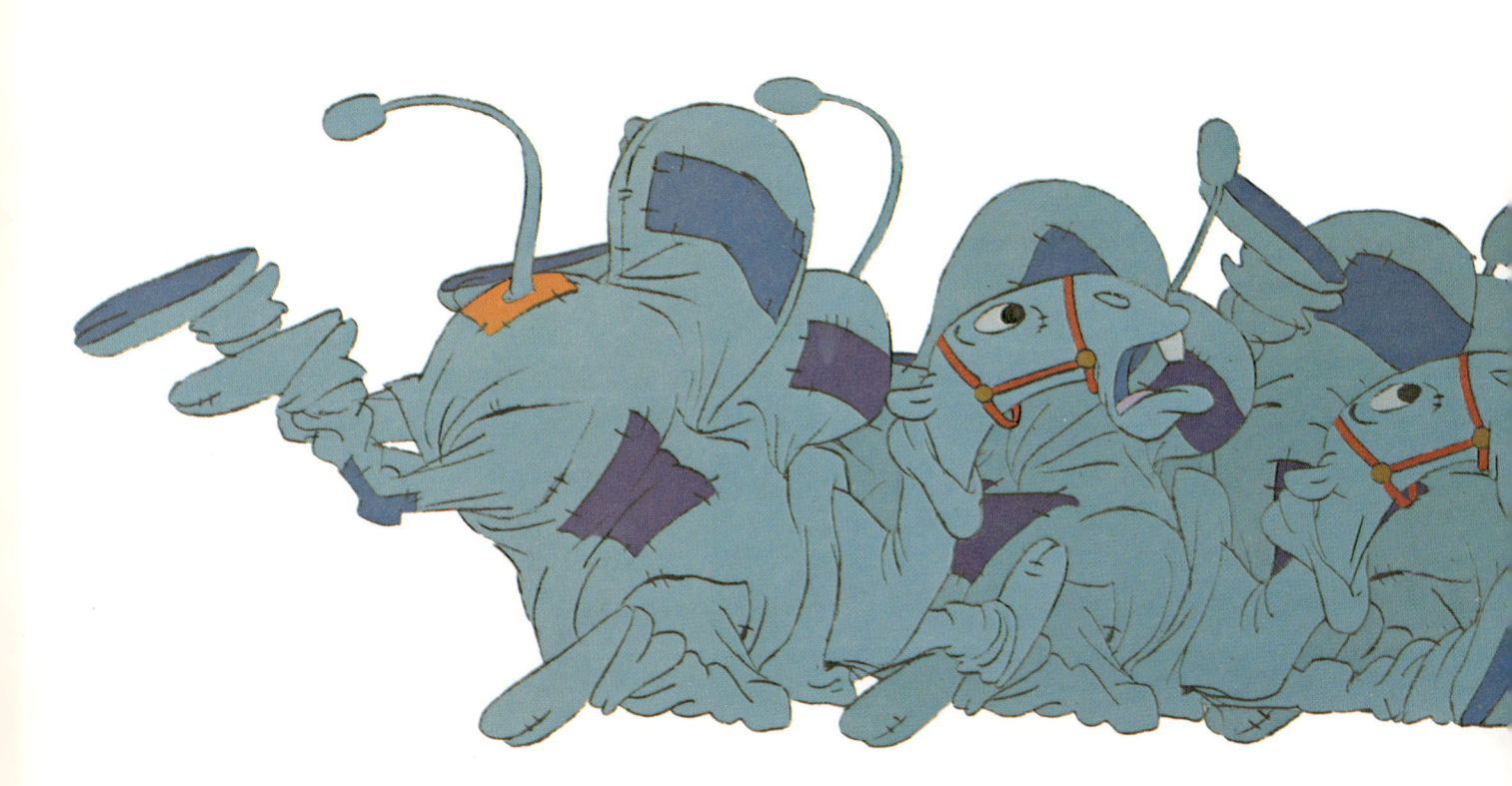

The falling Camel's face *squashes* slightly as it *contacts* the ground. Note the *follow-through* of the Camel's tail.

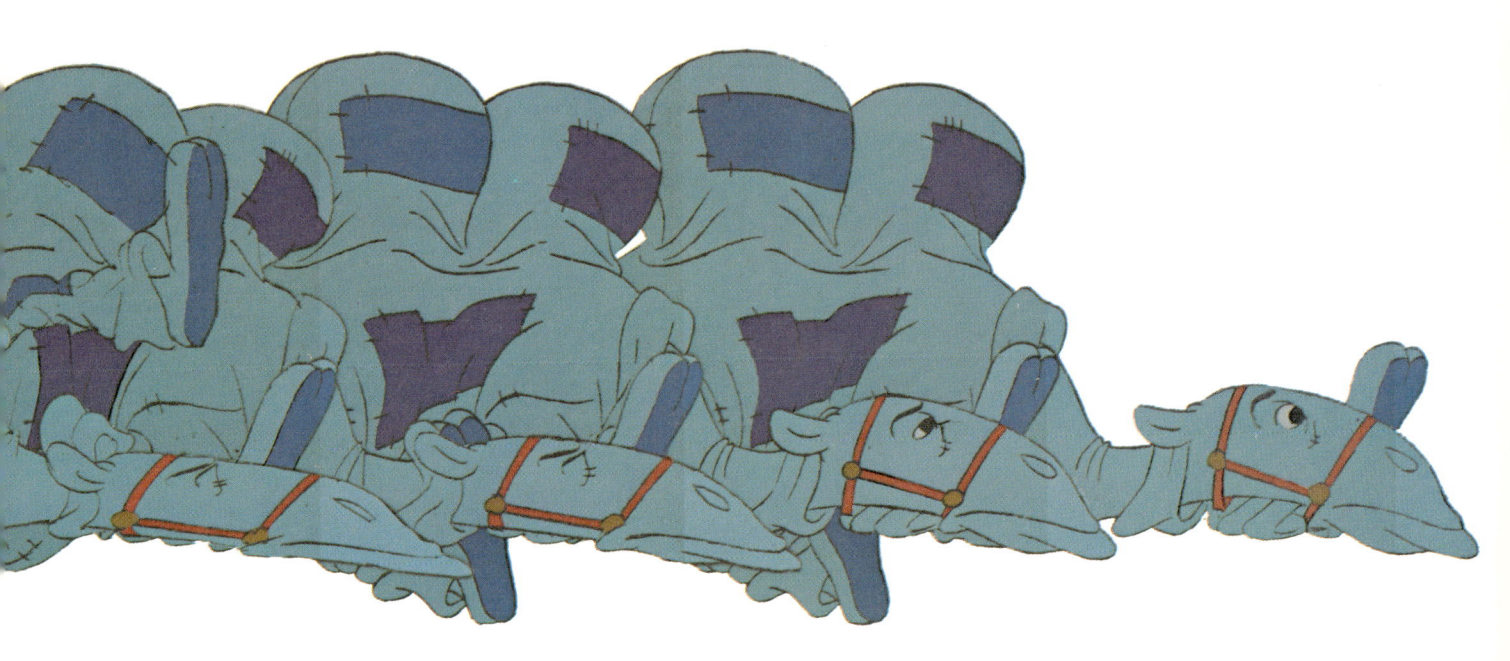

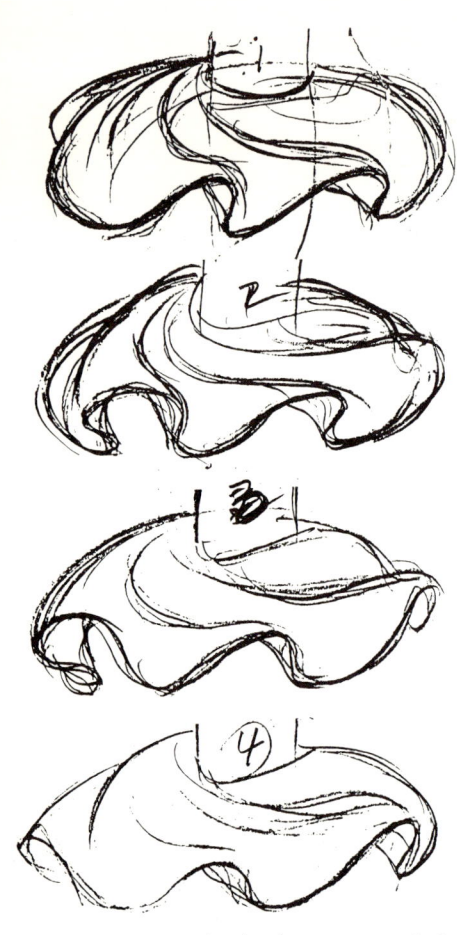

Four sketches by Tissa David of Raggedy Ann's skirt action demonstrate the principle of *follow-through*. "I wanted to find a very simple way to turn a skirt around, so I did this before I animated the scene," David wrote on the drawing. The skirt trails the main action of the character's body, adding quality of detail to the animation.

Action as a thing in itself has little sustaining interest for an audience. When action, portrayed graphically, is ordered—caricatured—it becomes a new form of acting. Caricature and acting then are the foundations upon which animation is built.

Because a great number of drawings are necessary to portray an idea or story, economy must be exercised in the number of lines or shapes utilized. The drawings must be functional, both optically and structurally. Every line must be rhythmic to preserve the continuity or flow of one form into another.

Examples of caricatured actions discovered at the Disney school include: "stretch and squash," an exaggeration of the physical laws of expansion and contraction and of the effect of gravity on objects; "anticipation," a means of preparing an audience for an action and emphasizing an action—e.g., a ballplayer winding up before the pitch; "follow-through," a secondary action working in conjunction with the main action, adding texture to the animation—e.g., a man comes to a sudden stop, but his coattails, necktie and pants cuffs continue to move in the direction the man was running.

The school devised a "silhouette test" to train their animators to draw strong, storytelling poses: when you blackened in a pose, if you could still understand what the character was doing, it was a good information-giving drawing.

All of these disciplines and many more opened up areas of expression "never dreamed of before by the artist," wrote Graham. "Sensations and emotions, gestures and expressions become everyday problems. A character can now be hot, or shiver, become frightened or angry, deliver a speech, laugh and then cry and wipe the rolling tears away."

Aiding the development of personality animation in various ways was the Disney studio's pioneering efforts in the technical areas of animated film production: e.g., the innovative use of sound effects and music (*Steamboat Willie* starring Mickey Mouse in 1928); the first use of Technicolor's three-color process in an animated film (*Flowers and Trees* [1932]); and the multiplane camera, which gave a three-dimensional depth to the cartoon settings and added a stronger semblance of reality to the animated fantasies (first used in *The Old Mill* in 1937).

The Disney studio style—creating the illusion of reality to support impossible characters and situations—can backfire when it attempts merely to re-create reality as a live-action camera does. *Bambi* (1941) is an example of the misguided use of this style, with its ultra-real deer in lifelike woodland settings. In contrast, the dancing hippos and ostriches in "The Dance of the Hours" ballet in *Fantasia* are marvelous examples of the perfect use of caricatured reality. The animals resemble real animals in form and weight, but their anthropomorphized antics are something no live-action animal could ever do.

The Disney style dominated the other studios at first as they all tried to imitate it, usually with overstudied, labored results. However, at Warner

(*Above*) Raggedy Andy slips on a banana peel: two pose drawings that, if blackened in, would still convey the essence of the action. (*Below*) Exaggerated use of *stretch* in the Camel's body.

Brothers, Tex Avery used Bugs Bunny and Daffy Duck to move into areas of wild surrealism that Disney had not explored. Likewise, Bob Clampett and Chuck Jones, also at Warners, introduced new emotional shadings to personality animation. Clampett used extreme elasticity and distortion to depict in his characters what they felt inside; Jones's cartoons, such as the brilliant Roadrunner and Coyote series, are more subtle, making use of irony to provide precisely the desired degree of emotion in the characters.

United Productions of America (UPA) was formed in the late forties by a group of dissident Disney artists who discarded the Disney formula. Instead, the movement in their cartoons was purposely two-dimensional, in keeping with the flat graphic style of Matisse, Picasso, and the other modern artists and illustrators UPA used as inspiration.

The short films are for the most part refreshing in their imaginative use of color, sound and music (*Gerald McBoing Boing* [1950], *Madeline* [1952], the earliest Mr. Magoos, and a chilling depiction of madness in an adaptation of Poe's *The Telltale Heart* [1953]). However, UPA's attempt at a feature-length cartoon, *Magoo's Arabian Nights* (1959), did not sustain audience interest, mainly because of the lack of full personality animation and the absence of any illusion of reality. Feature films from several other studios through the years have failed for the same reasons—the animated characters do not reach an audience emotionally because they have no grounding in reality and no definite personalities.

The recent success of Ralph Bakshi with his feature-length cartoons *Fritz the Cat* (1972) and *Heavy Traffic* (1973) is attributable not only to his exploration of new subject matter and story content suitable for animation (stunning, and convincing, surreal presentations of murder, lust, sex, and abstract thought) but also to his decision to utilize the traditions of personality animation in putting across his characters and their stories.

Use of *anticipation* and *stretch* and *squash*: Raggedy Andy gets his thumb caught in a mousetrap. His head *anticipates* his wail of pain by slightly *squashing* into his shoulders and then *stretching* in the opposite direction.

The familiar Raggedy Ann and Andy characters already have a strong built-in audience identification. The challenge facing director Richard Williams was to be true to the audience's expectations and to present these beloved fantasy characters as realistically as possible. The solution was to employ the full range of personality animation techniques without "Disneyfying" the design of the characters.

To avoid making *Raggedy Ann & Andy* look like a Disney film, Williams based its design on the original detailed Johnny Gruelle illustrations, but the techniques of animation are those of the Disney studio: lush, full movement and the caricatured reality that allows subtle and unique animation performances—even virtuoso turns.

Richard Williams has often been called "the new Disney" by film critics; in the Disney tradition, he is a perfectionist who gives the best of himself in whatever he does. "Do a good job of everything" is, he says, his motto and the secret of his success.

With *Raggedy Ann & Andy*, Williams has come up with a quality feature-length animated musical that, for the first time, seriously challenges the Disney studio expertise on its own ground: the family entertainment film. Its full, personality animation in some areas hits new highs in mastery of technique, a small miracle in these days of lackluster, limited animation.

Our story begins as all truly miraculous tales do. . . .

Once upon a time, there was an unassuming newspaper cartoonist named Johnny Gruelle. One day his daughter Marcella found in the attic an old toy that had belonged to her grandmother.

It was a simple, lovable little rag doll. . . .

Johnny Gruelle in 1929.

CHAPTER III

Johnny Gruelle and His Million-Dollar Dolly

It does pay to do more work than you are paid for after all. Someone usually sees it sometime and appreciates it.

—*Johnny Gruelle*

The search for information about the distinctly American career and life of Johnny Gruelle (1880–1938), the creator of the stories and illustrations of Raggedy Ann and Andy, is not an easy task. Considering that he was such a prolific and famous artist, there is amazingly little reliable information; instead, legends have sprung up and grown into the gaps in the truth.

Martin D. Williams, Director of Jazz Programs at the Smithsonian Institution and an authority on Gruelle's work, once wrote in *Book World* his opinion as to why Johnny Gruelle is so elusive: "He turned out a vast quantity of children's stories and illustrations during his lifetime. . . . Our critics and literary historians are apt to suspect anyone as prolific, and as frankly uneven, as Johnny Gruelle. At his rare best, however, I think that Johnny Gruelle was an exceptional children's author, and his work has qualities found nowhere else that I know of in writing for children."

Sixty-five-year-old Worth Gruelle, one of Johnny Gruelle's two sons and a valuable source of information about his father, agreed with the above opinion in a letter written in 1976:

[Johnny Gruelle] would work mostly at night either on illustrations or an old typewriter—he could get more beautiful work done in the shortest time! He never had to do any art work over. It was always approved and accepted the first time.

Worth gives us a thumbnail description of life with his father:

My dad and I were great buddies. Everyone loved him and he loved everybody. . . . When he was able in the '20's and '30's to have a good sized boat [there] would be

63

firemen, police, the mayor, the governor, actors, artists, singers, truckdrivers, prizefighters all in a heap. No class problems as long as they were with my father. . . . He was 5' 8", slight but supple—played baseball and was a great pitcher. . . .

The myths [and] conflicting stories of course are typical [of] famous people who didn't intend or expect to be famous—their lives could have been calm, peaceful, happy and maybe even uneventful and mediocre. However, most of this was true in our family—except for uneventful and mediocre—it was a happy family!

Johnny Gruelle was born in Arcola, Illinois, in 1880, the son of Richard B. and Alice Benton Gruelle. Johnny and his sister and brother, Prudence and Justin, were raised in Indianapolis, Indiana.

Worth says:

He was born into a family of writers and artists. His father, Richard B. Gruelle, was one of the originators of the famous "Hoosier" group of artists. James Whitcomb Riley was among the friends that swarmed into grandfather's studio—he wrote a poem about my dad, "The Funny Picture Man," so of course he was right in the middle of all sorts of art and must have loved every minute of it. As Grandmother Gruelle said, he was never without a pencil.

My grandmother (who lived with us most of the time) said my dad as a very young boy drew pictures, wrote verse, prose, etc., usually disrupting his studies.

When Johnny Gruelle was fourteen he and a friend hopped a boxcar and ran away to Cleveland. Broke and hungry, Gruelle got a job, it is said, playing piano in a saloon where he met a police officer named McGinty, a character he used in some later cartoons. Johnny drew the cop's picture with soap on the window of a back bar.

McGinty told the kid he thought he had "the makings of a good cartoonist" and offered to stake him until he could get a job on a newspaper. Gruelle appreciated the encouragement, thanked the policeman and returned home. A few years later, when he was a cartoonist on *The Cleveland Press*, Gruelle became good friends with Officer McGinty and his family.

Gruelle began working for the *Indianapolis Sun-Star and Sentinel* (later shortened to the *Star*) in 1903; he drew weather cartoons and political cartoons and illustrated news articles when there were no photographs available.

Some of his fellow artists on the newspaper resented Gruelle's quick ease with a pencil; William F. Heitman, a veteran *Star* staff artist, once recalled, "Johnny loved to fish. He'd even have the gall to show up at the office in old clothes and fishing boots, draw his cartoon for the day in less than an hour, then tip his fishing hat to the rest of us as he left for the day."

He married Myrtle Swann in Indianapolis in 1900, and two years later a daughter was born. They named her Marcella. Around 1909 Gruelle worked as a staff cartoonist on the *Cleveland Press*.

A photo of the young Johnny Gruelle (*left*) and William H. Woodin, Secretary of the Treasury under Franklin D. Roosevelt. Woodin composed the music for the songbook *Raggedy Ann's Sunny Songs*.

An early Gruelle illustration: "The June Bride—Off for the Honeymoon."

In 1910, while on vacation visiting his parents, who were then living in Connecticut, Gruelle learned that the *New York Herald* was conducting a contest to select a new comic page; his mother suggested he submit one. Along with five hundred other applicants, Gruelle entered the contest. The judges eliminated all but a hundred, then narrowed these down to two. It was a tie, and both winners turned out to be—Johnny Gruelle! His "Mr. Twee Deedle" won first prize, and his "Jack the Giant Killer" won second.

"Mr. Twee Deedle" ran as a Sunday comic strip for four years, then was suddenly discontinued by a new Sunday editor. The *Herald* publisher, James Gordon Bennett, noticed the omission while traveling in Europe.

"What became of Twee Deedle?" cabled Bennett.

"Discontinued by Sunday editor," was cabled back.

"Discontinue Sunday editor," was Bennett's succinct reply. "Mr. Twee Deedle" lived another four years.

According to Worth Gruelle,

The *Herald* was just one of his regular jobs. At the same time he had dailies in the *New York World, Women's World, Cleveland Press*. He had a studio in N.Y.C.—did daily juvenile publications—stories and illustrations. "Yapps Crossing" was in *Judge* around 1911, also ran as a monthly for years—then "Yahoo Center" in the old *Life*, then "Punkin Center" in *College Humor* until 1938. "Brutus" in [the] *Herald* ran from 1932–38 and stopped at his death in 1938.

Gruelle moved his wife and daughter East, and in either late 1910 or early 1911 he built a house in Silvermine, Connecticut, where they lived for six years. Worth was born there in 1912, and another son, Richard, was born in Norwalk, Connecticut, in 1917.

Worth Gruelle remembers his sister Marcella:

She was quite ill and rested a great deal, but at times seemed to get a bit of energy, and we played in our large back yard in Silvermine—ran around and even swam in our (then clean) little river. Naturally we were supervised, and Marcella's illness was a very sad time for my parents. Due to a vaccination—when they lived in N.Y.C.—Marcella developed an infection which affected her heart and caused her untimely death. It was a lingering, deteriorating illness and cause[d by an] unsterile needle or vaccine. . . . She died at 14 and had been a healthy girl prior to the vaccination—there was *no* TB.

Marcella's death [on March 21, 1916] was the reason for selling the Silvermine House and they moved to Norwalk. . . . It was closer to the R.R. Station for N.Y.C. also.

I feel Marcella was a very little (young) girl when "Raggedy" stories began. The illustrations for the book (using them as a guide) showed her as maybe 6 or 7 years of age. The folks were very, very busy throughout my younger years of age. But [they] hid their sadness [over Marcella's death] and bitterness, too, quite well, I remember.

Regarding the legend that Marcella started the whole thing by discovering her grandmother's old rag doll, Worth believes:

It's true. I remember an old stringy rag doll—but it must have been found before my folks actually moved to Conn. Maybe on a visit to their folks.

He also thinks Johnny Gruelle made up the Raggedy Ann stories to amuse his ill daughter.

In the preface to the first Raggedy Ann book, titled *Raggedy Ann Stories* and published on September 10, 1918, by P. F. Volland, Johnny Gruelle writes: "I have before me on my desk, propped up against the telephone, an old rag doll. Dear old Raggedy Ann!

"The same Raggedy Ann with which my mother played when a child . . . what lessons of kindness and fortitude you might teach could you but talk, you with your wisdom of fifty-nine years. . . ."

Raggedy Andy Stories appeared in 1920 and was dedicated to "Marcella's Mama." In the preface to this book, Gruelle's mother has supposedly written a letter dated January 12, 1919, from Wilton, Connecticut: "Living next door to us, when I was about four years old, was a little girl named Bessie; I cannot recall her last name. When my mother made Raggedy Ann for me, Bessie's mother made a rag doll for her, for we two always played together. . . . Bessie's doll was made a day or so after Raggedy Ann, I think, though I am not quite certain which of the two dolls was made first. However, Bessie's doll was given the name of Raggedy Andy, and one of the two dolls was named after the other, so that their names would sound alike."

Other accounts suggest that Johnny Gruelle named his mother's doll after the James Whitcomb Riley poem "The Raggedy Man," for which his father had done the illustrations. (Harold Gray worked briefly for the *Star* before he moved to the *Chicago Tribune*, where he launched his "Little Orphan Annie" comic strip, which was based on a Riley poem.)

In the May 13, 1923, *Indianapolis Star*, Gruelle spoke of how he came to put the Raggedy stories into writing:

It was in a room with fourteen other artists, and I only had to draw this one picture, and was generally through by noon, and when I'd start to go out the other artists would look at me, and I'd feel kind of ashamed and decide to stay around a while longer. So I got to doing things to take up the time—writing sketches and bum verses—you know the kind—and finally got to writing Raggedy Ann in verse, and making pictures for it. Raggedy Andy came later. P. F. Volland, the publisher, suggested I do it in prose, so I did, and it's been in prose ever since. Ann is in some of Andy's books but Andy doesn't get into any of her books. The stories write themselves; I've written as many as seventeen in one morning.

ANN & ANDY — ORIGINAL JOHNNY GRUELLE REFERENCE MATERIAL

© COPYRIGHT 1975
THE BOBBS-MERRILL CO. INC.

VERY EARLY ANDY

Richard Williams's drawings of Raggedy Ann and Andy, which he based on Johnny Gruelle's original sketches, were used as reference material for the film.

Worth Gruelle helped his father illustrate the Raggedy books from "around 1922," and in 1940, "when Donahue [which followed Volland as publisher] stopped printing the books and the Johnny Gruelle Company [had] formed, I illustrated all of the books except a couple that my Uncle Justin did.

"I worked with my father for years. I helped first with coloring, then inking, then layouts, etc. I had my own column with George Matthew Adams. I did the 'Raggedy' column also for Adams Syndicate . . . of course with [the] Johnny Gruelle sig[nature]."

Publishers Weekly, October 26, 1940, reported that the original *Raggedy Ann* sold 750,000 copies in fifteen editions, and "all the Gruelle books together have sold more than 5,000,000 copies."

Paul Volland, the original publisher of *Raggedy Ann Stories*, was not initially enthusiastic about the book, but he wanted to keep the good will of writer-illustrator Gruelle, whose earlier work, in 1917, *My Very Own Fairy Stories*, had been an immediate success.

"The book no sooner reached the retail counters than reorders began to pour in, and for the rest of the year every printer in Chicago with an idle press was printing *Raggedy Ann Stories*," recalled Richard L. Cox, publisher of the books from 1939 to 1960.

After the books came the Raggedy dolls, which became perhaps even more popular than the books. One story suggests that the demand for the doll began at Christmastime in 1920 when Marshall Field & Company in Chicago made up a special Raggedy Andy doll for a window display. Supposedly an insistent customer bought it the second day it was in the window, and the rush for the huggable dolls was on.

Gruelle then turned most of his attention to writing and illustrating children's books. Before his death, more than twenty-seven of those books had been published, eighteen of which were Raggedy Ann and Andy books, including two songbooks. Jerome Kern composed a song called "Raggedy Ann" that was showcased in a Broadway musical of 1923, *Stepping Stones*. At the peak of popularity there were Raggedy Ann mother and daughter dresses, Raggedy Ann haircuts, and Raggedy Ann salads. By the mid-twenties, Johnny Gruelle was both famous and wealthy.

The Gruelles moved to Miami Springs, Florida, and it was here that Johnny Gruelle died on January 9, 1938, of heart disease. His death was unexpected, although he had been in ill health for three years. The *Star*, where he first worked professionally as a cartoonist, described him as "a jovial companion, enthusiastic, venturesome and popular among all who knew him. . . . It is unfortunate that a man who brought so much gladness into the world should succumb at the age of fifty-seven."

In 1939 Johnny Gruelle's widow, Myrtle; his son Richard; and Howard

Cox, formerly of Volland, formed the Johnny Gruelle Company. They owned all Raggedy Ann publication rights, as well as motion picture and commercial rights. According to *Publishers Weekly*, Volland had handled almost all of Gruelle's work until 1934, when they liquidated their book publishing division. Publisher M. A. Donahue acquired the Volland plates and by arrangement with Gruelle continued to publish most of the Raggedy Ann titles.

David R. Smith, Archivist at the Walt Disney Archives, recently researched some correspondence between Mrs. Johnny Gruelle and the Walt Disney studio:

Mrs. Gruelle contacted our story department by telegram in May, 1938. She was answered by John C. Rose, who wrote, in part, on May 27: ". . . although we have never considered the possibility of developing an animated cartoon based on Raggedy Ann, we would be happy to talk with you during the course of your visit in Hollywood this coming July."

Worth Gruelle corroborates the above: "After my father died, my mother took material to Disney in California and of course was ushered in royally. [Worth mentions that Disney and his father were "good friends."] But he told her, quote: 'Myrtle, we won't pay a cent for Raggedy Ann, as someday it'll become public domain and we'll have it for nothing.' Unquote."

Motion picture rights to numerous Raggedy Ann stories were assigned to the Max Fleischer studios on April 18, 1940; Fleischer, an animation pioneer whose studio had created Betty Boop and two feature-length animated films, released a two-reel (twenty-minute) short called *Raggedy Ann and Raggedy Andy* on December 6, 1940.

One of the animators of this film recently commented that it lacked the "directness" of today's animation, "but back then that was the style." This is as good a description as any of the Fleischer studio style at that point—unfocused characterizations, and sequences that were overembellished in nonessential areas and impoverished in others. Leslie Cabarga, author of *The Fleischer Story*, puts it this way: "The Fleischer animators were striving to achieve the brightness and tidiness of Disney's cartoons. . . . So, whereas the Fleischer cartoons were once unique in style, they became very standard. . . ."

Animation expert Mark Kausler notes that there were two other presentations of Raggedy Ann and company on the screen before Bobbs-Merrill/ITT's presentation: *Suddenly It's Spring* in 1944 and *The Enchanted Square* in 1947. Both films were directed by Seymour Kneitel, a former member of the Fleischer studio.

Rare copies of the original *Raggedy Ann Stories* (1918) and *Raggedy Andy Stories* (1920).

Dolls by the Knickerbocker Toy Company: the Camel with the Wrinkled Knees, Raggedy Ann and Raggedy Andy.

Worth Gruelle blames a temporary decline in the popularity of the dolls and books on

an infringement suit we had to put into effect due to a Philly doll concern which started manufacturing Raddys [sic] by the thousands. We won this suit, of course, but it took about 5 years to do so, I believe. At the same time, Gerlach died [Gerlach-Barklow, who were publishing the books].

Donahue took several years to start publishing again, slowly but successfully. Then Mr. Donahue passed on.

My mother, brother Richard and Howard Cox started the Johnny Gruelle Co. with only one book—mine—*Raggedy Ann and Andy in the Magic Book*. Through the years they were able to get one book at a time from Donahue and Co. My mother became ill and [in 1960] Cox sold to Bobbs-Merrill [then owned by Howard Sams, later a subsidiary of ITT].

73

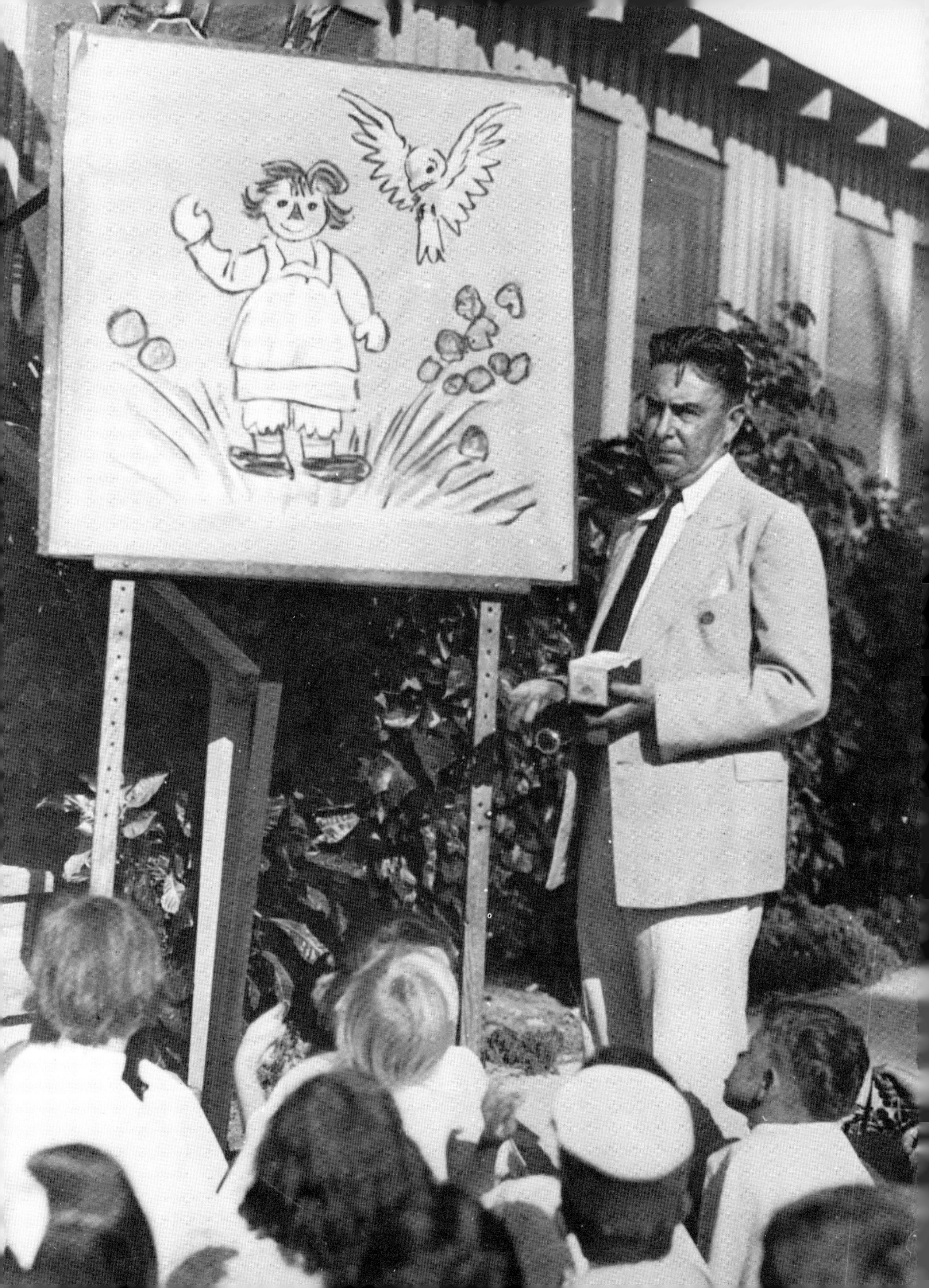

In 1962 the Knickerbocker Toy Company acquired exclusive rights to manufacture the Raggedy Ann and Andy stuffed rag dolls.

The licensing of more than five hundred Raggedy Ann products in the past ten years has helped Ann and Andy stage a spectacular comeback and paved the way for the feature-length film about them.

What are the qualities in Raggedy Ann and Andy and their stories that have made them so popular for so long? Martin D. Williams feels that Gruelle is the only writer to make conscious use of a "great natural resource of childhood"—namely, "Let's pretend."

Williams explains, "Gruelle himself spins out his best tales in a kind of rambling but controlled literary extension of the same breathless uncomplicated what-happens-next that children use when they improvise their own story games."

The first two books contain short domestic adventures that take place in and around Marcella's house; the tales are based on the ancient notion that inanimate dolls have a secret life and can have taffy pulls, rescue a puppy, adopt kittens, enjoy a picnic or a dance as much as "real-for-sure" children do.

Beginning with the book *The Camel with the Wrinkled Knees*, Gruelle introduced his own version of fairyland, which he named "the Deep Deep Woods." It is a place full of witches, elves, and strange wonderful creatures like the Snicksnapper, the Hungry Howloon, the Snarleyboodle. In these tales Gruelle's work takes on classical dimensions. Child psychologist Bruno Bettelheim has explained that all children "fear being deserted by their parents and lost in the deep dark woods like Hansel and Gretel [or Raggedy Ann and Andy], or being swallowed by wild animals [or, as in the film, a Greedy?] like Red Riding Hood. On their own these childhood nightmares have no solutions. Fairy tales tell the child he is not alone in having such anxieties and that he has nothing to be ashamed of."

A child's identification with Raggedy Ann and Andy and their simple adventures may be one of the secrets to the dolls' durable appeal. Williams mentions that the silly character names in the Deep Deep Woods are "extensions of the kinds of names that little children make up for themselves." Such names prove, to Williams, that this "seemingly style-less man had real style."

Williams points further to Gruelle's "elaborate verbal repetitions": "The Tired Old Horse may be The Old Tired Horse or, less often, The Old Horse or The Tired Horse, but he is never simply The Horse. Children love such elegant verbal ritual, and Gruelle used that love in his writing."

"I don't think he wrote just for Marcella alone," sums up Worth Gruelle, "or for Worth and Dick either, but for children of all ages."

(*Opposite*) Johnny Gruelle drawing Raggedy Ann in chalk for the pupils of St. Patrick's School in Miami Beach in 1933. (Wide World Photos)

PART TWO:

GETTING STARTED

HELPFUL WHEN ITT SUGAR BACKS ANIMATED FEATURE
"RAGGEDY ANN"
by Robert B. Frederick

There are plenty of people in the film industry who'd tell you that anyone setting out, in today's inflated situation, to make a full-length animated feature had to be out of his business mind, unless, of course, it was the huge Disney complex with its assembly-line production methods. Because of this, it is always interesting when one of these "demented" characters crosses one's path, and when it's a pair, doubly so.

    Canadian animator Richard Williams and composer Joe Raboso [sic] are well into the production of their "Raggedy Ann and Andy," an animated musical comedy being produced by Broadway producers Lester Osterman and Richard Horner, in association with Bobbs-Merrill. Animated features take a long time to complete, as anyone familiar with *Variety*'s production charts will bear witness. And the longest, hardest, most complicated portion of the work is the month after month of completing drawings. So how did these two get into such a situation? . . .

—*Variety*, November 19, 1975

M-4-D
— CANDY HEARTS —
EV-RY LONE-LY PLACE YOU GO
THERE'S A WAY I AL-WAYS KNOW
WE'RE AL-WAYS TO-GETH-ER
PA-PER DAI-SIES HELP EX-PLAIN
SUN-SHINE AL-WAYS FOL-LOWS RAIN
AND A HEART THAT'S SWEET AND TRUE WILL HELP US WEA-THER THE WEA-THER
TO-KENS PA-PER DAI-SIES
US STRONG-ER KEEP US CLO-SER
E-VEN WHEN WE'RE FAR A-PART SO
(REFRAIN) CANDY
COUNTRY WESTERN RAGTIME
CAN-DY HEARTS AND PA-PER FLOW-ERS
SUN-SHINE DAYS AND SKIES OF
E-7
A9
No. M1D 12 STAVE
MADE IN U.S.A.

CHAPTER IV
Setting the Gears in Motion

I knew nothing about animation before I started this, but one thing I did know was that we wanted to try to achieve the same quality that Disney achieved in his early films.

—*Richard Horner*

I'm a relentlessly Renaissance human being. I just believe in tasting flavors of all kinds of things.

—Joe Raposo

Richard Horner has spent over thirty of his fifty-six years working successfully in that savage, competitive arena of entertainment known as The Theater. He survived and thrived first as an actor, then behind the scenes as a stage manager, as a company manager, and as an independent producer. Today, as a partner with Lester Osterman in Lester Osterman Productions, he co-produces such quality Broadway shows as the 1973 revival of Eugene O'Neill's *A Moon for the Misbegotten;* *Butley;* *Hadrian the Seventh;* and the musicals *High Spirits* and *The Rothschilds.*

The legitimate stage is the milieu in which Richard Horner feels most comfortable; it is familiar turf, a medium that since his earliest years he has pursued with a tenacity and a passion that belie his seemingly unflappable exterior.

Tall, trim, with close-cropped graying hair, Horner is a study of a lifetime invested in emotional control. His low, quiet voice carefully doles out information about how he got involved in the odd and often maddening world of feature-length animated films. Especially this film—*Raggedy Ann & Andy*—which ballooned before his eyes into the most elusive, overwhelming entertainment project of his career. In an unguarded moment, Horner reportedly said mock-angrily to a producer of animation for television, "Why didn't you tell me making animated cartoons is hard as hell?!"

Born in Portland, Oregon, Horner made his stage debut as a walk-on in the Passion Play in Corvallis, Oregon, in 1934 and was stung by the theater bug. He was educated at the University of Washington in Seattle and spent five years in the Navy during World War II, which he says gave him time to think. What he thought about was that "life is just too short not to do what one wanted to do, so I came to New York to be in the theater. Today you can go to a lot of places and be in the theater, because there are resident companies and repertory theaters, but in those days if you wanted to be a professional you either had to go to New York where the theater was or go to Los Angeles where the movies were."

He was an actor for a couple of years "just as an expediency. I didn't know anyone in New York, and I had to make a living, so I felt there would be more jobs for actors than anything else." But Horner was interested in production, so he became a stage manager for the Theatre Guild in 1950 and worked with Cornelia Otis Skinner, Katharine Cornell, Martha Graham, and Agnes DeMille.

"I really felt I'd gone as far as I could as a stage manager and learned as much as I could," he says, "so I went to the other side, the business as opposed to the technical side of the theater." Horner was company manager for Sol Hurok and worked on such shows as *The Pajama Game*, *West Side Story* and *Fiorello*.

"Then I became a general manager, and about twenty years ago I started producing while I was managing."

His first production, *Debut*, a comedy about the old South, starred Inger Stevens and was not a success ("One more play like *Debut* and the North will secede," said Brooks Atkinson in *The New York Times*). In the mid-1950s Horner began to buy rights to Broadway musicals and produce road company versions of them.

Lester Osterman, sixty-two, a native New Yorker, was a partner in a stock-brokerage firm when he went into the theater on a part-time basis as an investor; he has been producing since *Mr. Wonderful* in 1956.

"After I came with him as his general manager [in 1959]," Horner explains, "Lester became interested in the theater more and more. Then we bought the Alvin Theater and what is now the Eugene O'Neill Theater. At present we have the 46th Street Theater, and we operate the Hayes and Morosco Theaters—as well as producing."

In 1969 Horner and Osterman bought the rights to a children's story called *The Littlest Angel* which they made into a ninety-minute live-action television special and sold to NBC's *Hallmark Hall of Fame*. They had never produced for television before but decided, "after watching a lot of television, that it should be easy to do something better than what we were seeing."

Horner admits now, "That's usually mistake number one. I discovered as we were making it that it's not as easy as it looks, but it got the highest rating Hallmark had ever gotten; they repeated the show for two years subsequently, so it then became a good venture for us."

Producer Richard Horner.

Encouraged by this success, Horner looked around for a similar property; that is, "a story that would be a family story that could be musicalized." One day Horner was lunching with an independent merchandiser of children's products that use identifiable characters, such as The Lone Ranger and Raggedy Ann, in their promotions.

"Raggedy Ann came up in our conversation," Horner recalls, "and I said, 'Gee, that would be a great thing for what we have in mind.' Like *The Littlest Angel*, the Raggedy Ann and Andy stories had a wide readership and great popular acceptance."

Horner acquired permission from Bobbs-Merrill to begin work on the project. His idea for a live-action Raggedy Ann and Andy TV show got an enormous boost during a Friars Club "roast" for Johnny Carson. Seated at the same table with Horner and Osterman was the young composer Joe Raposo, who had just won an Emmy Award for his music and lyrics on TV's highly successful children's series, *Sesame Street*. Horner thought, "Well, Joe is *just* the right kind of person for this project." "And I mentioned it to him, asked him if he'd be interested, and he said, 'Oh, that sounds like a great idea!' So he started to work."

Musical director/composer Joe Raposo.

Dark, stout, and direct of manner, Joe Raposo looks and sounds like a tough Italian street fighter from an urban ghetto. This impression is totally erroneous because, first of all, Raposo is not Italian—he is Brazilian, Portuguese and Azorean. He was born in 1937 not in a ghetto but in Fall River, Massachusetts, and went to Harvard (class of '58). And the only fighting he does is with his musical muse and with people who insist he is a genius.

Frank Sinatra, at a recent Carnegie Hall concert, called Raposo "the young genius from New York," and although Joe was flattered by the praise, considering the source, he insists, quite rightly, that the word "genius" is "so overused. It's used about twice each Sunday in the *New York Times* entertainment section. People don't have a concept of someone who is so steeped in his profession that he doesn't have to pose, he doesn't have to put on airs, disguises, crazinesses!"

For Joe Raposo, writing popular songs is easy. "This thing that I do has been a part of my life ever since the day I was born. It's like breathing to me, so I never developed any conceits about it. It's a craft, not genius," he insists. "It's like building cabinets."

It all began with Joe's father, a music teacher and conductor, who gave his son musical instruments instead of toys to play with. Helping his father teach, Joe learned the value of simplicity in composing: "It was an economic necessity. If the music was too complicated, the kids couldn't play it; if they sounded lousy, the parents didn't want them to study any more with you, and you didn't eat!"

A self-described "closet lawyer," Raposo majored in law at college but slipped away often to play the piano as accompanist to great jazz performers at Boston's famed Storyville; summers were spent directing the music at large summer-stock theaters across the country. At eighteen Raposo had conducted his first pre-Broadway tryout of a musical.

After college Raposo studied for two years in Europe under the great French musical theoretician Nadia Boulanger. "I got a fellowship," he says. "At that time I thought I was going to conduct symphony orchestras and write symphonic pieces of music—just prior to going into law school. I figured I was always going to be Ignace Paderewski: I'd be the great musical talent who became the president of his country."

Raposo instead went on to conduct and compose music for several stage productions on and off Broadway, including *You're a Good Man, Charlie Brown* and *Play It Again, Sam.* He has scored films *(The Possession of Joel Delaney, Savages)* and was musical director of the Experimental Theater at Lincoln Center, the Jerome Robbins American Theater Laboratory, the New Theater, and Metromedia Television in New York.

The source of Joe Raposo's most widespread fame, *Sesame Street,* "just came along," in his words. "It didn't have a name. It was a bunch of people meandering around trying to do a show for Public Television." He was with them for five years until 1974, and during that period he became a lyricist as well as a composer. The first song to utilize both talents was "It's Not Easy Being Green," which Sinatra recorded. "And then I became famous," he says matter-of-factly.

Raposo went on to direct the music for another Children's Television Workshop program, *The Electric Company,* and to write more songs, including, among others, "Sing," that were recorded by such performers as Barbara Streisand, Lena Horne and the Carpenters.

When Horner and Osterman approached him about the Raggedy Ann TV special, Raposo said, "Sure, why not? I'm a writer. I look for interesting projects. It seemed to be okay. I was then presented with about two dozen books of Raggedy Ann and Andy."

Raposo studied the Gruelle material and then began a process he calls "psychological dress-up." He explains, "When you write songs, music and lyrics, you're always putting on somebody else's clothes. The degree to which you're able to dress up and counterfeit yourself as this person, that's as good as you are as a writer. And I'm pretty good at it, which leaves me tremendous doubts about my own personality."

Joe Raposo conducting a recording session of incidental music for *Raggedy Ann & Andy*.

Joe Raposo, in the control booth, speaking over an intercom to the sixty-piece orchestra during a playback. Jim Tyler, music arranger (*left*), listens intently.

The first song Raposo wrote for the Raggedy Ann project was "I Look and What Do I See," the first song sung in the film. "The thing I liked most," he explains, "is the innocence of Raggedy Ann. I tried to put my own ideas about Raggedy Ann into that song—what that person is, who is inside that stuffed doll—and came up with the philosophy that's in that lyric."

> I look and what do I see,
> Looking out with two brand-new shoebutton eyes?
> Here's what appears to me:
> I see lots of pretty
> And a lot of happy
> And a bit of everything that's there inside of me.*

In Broadway-musical parlance, this song would be known as "the girl's first number"; it sets up for the audience the personality, philosophy, and desires of the story's heroine and motivates her future actions in the plot. In *South Pacific,* for instance, Nellie Forbush tells us exactly what her outlook on life is when she belts out "A Cockeyed Optimist." In *My Fair Lady,* Eliza Doolittle, the Cockney flower-girl, shares her dreams and diamond-in-the-rough qualities with us in "Wouldn't It Be Loverly?"

With her first number, Raggedy Ann, the homely cotton-stuffed rag doll, shows us her sunny, childlike disposition and her determination to see only the good and "pretty" things in life. In its final version in the film, the song introduces Raggedy Ann to the audience, lets them look her over and become familiar with her personality:

> I look and what do I see?
> From a head all filled with thread and linen
> In a raggy jamboree,
> I see lots of smiling
> And a lot of singing
> And a lot of something else that no one else can see.*

Walt Disney understood the value of firmly establishing major characters in the mind of the audience. In *Snow White* he insisted on lengthening the scene where Snow White wakes up to find the dwarfs around her. "We've got to take the time to have her meet each dwarf individually, so the audience will get acquainted with them," Disney said. "Even if we bore the audience a little, they'll forget it later because they'll be interested in each individual dwarf."

"I Look and What Do I See," as animated principally by Chrystal Russell, gives us a Raggedy Ann of varied and charming accomplishments. She can

---

*© copyright 1976, Jonico Music Inc., The Bobbs-Merrill Company, Inc.

play the toy piano as well as sing and dance in her own loopy, unpretentious way. When she whips a quilt around her shoulders as the music builds in tempo, she resembles a little girl playing grown-up, and by this time, totally enchanted, we begin to love her. We are hooked, and we will care what happens to her for the rest of the movie.

Raposo wrote a song for Raggedy Andy entitled "I Like Rasslin'," which expressed his particular rambunctious little-boy personality. The song was not used in the film; however, "No Girl's Toy," a song with similar intentions, was:

> *You may not like it much,*
> *But I'm my own best boy,*
> *And not some*
> *Sugar and spicey,*
> *Lacey and nicey*
> *Sissy you're gonna enjoy.*
> *No, I'm no girl's toy!* *

Sixteen songs eventually made it into the film, but there were at least ten other numbers that the prolific Raposo rejected before they were recorded. These include a song for Raggedy Ann and Marcella; a dance called "The Raggedy Rag"; a song about "Fifi," as the French doll was first named.

Another song Raposo wrote was the duet "Candy Hearts and Paper Flowers." It is tenderly performed by Ann and Andy as they venture into the "Deep Deep Woods," and as principally animated by the incomparable Tissa David, it puts into words, music and pictures the essence of the two dolls' personalities and their relationship to each other.

> *Times get bad and then I worry*
> *How I'll ever see it through;*
> *But candy hearts and paper flowers*
> *Will always keep me close to you.* *

At an early stage in the development of the Raggedy Ann project, producer Horner brought in Pat Thackray, who was one of the writers of the TV version of *The Littlest Angel* and is the daughter of Lester Osterman. Ms. Thackray, a New Yorker who specializes in writing books for children, was asked to research the Gruelle material and to write a treatment as a basis for a live-action script. Max Wilk, who had written a number of comic novels and films, was then brought in to write the script, which was in turn reworked by Raposo and Williams.

Time went by; nothing happened. Raposo recalls: "One day I said to myself, 'This is not going to work with live-action people at all.'" He decided

*© copyright 1976, Jonico Music Inc., The Bobbs-Merrill Company, Inc.

to start presenting the Raggedy Ann stories as a plan for an animated film, "because when you dress up a pretty young woman in that red fright wig and triangular nose and funny bow mouth with black lines around it, she's gonna look like a circus clown! You're not going to believe what she says.

"I said, 'Why shouldn't this be animation as fanciful and wonderful as all the great Disney musicals'—uh, pictures, because Disney never actually did a musical. He did shows with songs, like *Pinocchio*. *This* is a musical. Nobody's ever done an animated musical, and that is what this is."

(Raposo's opinion about animated musicals is debatable; although *Raggedy Ann & Andy* is the first animated film to utilize a majority of talents with Broadway experience in producing, composing, and performing a soundtrack, it is incorrect to discredit Disney's major role in smoothly integrating a cartoon plot with music. Christopher Finch, in his program notes, "Music in the Disney Films," written for Lincoln Center's 1973 Disney retrospective, wrote: "The way that songs were woven into the fabric of *Snow White* anticipates the technique that was considered revolutionary when it was applied to the Broadway production of *Oklahoma!* which was staged several years later. Perhaps the most remarkable thing about *Snow White*, considered as a musical, is not the intrinsic quality of the songs but the way in which they were used to advance the story.")

The Raggedy group began to get more excited and more convinced that the animation technique was the right path to follow. "Then," says Richard Horner, "as we got further and further into the project, we realized that it had wider possibilities for acceptance than just as a television special. So we thought we should do it as a movie for theaters.

"At that point we went to Bobbs-Merrill, who owns the rights to Raggedy Ann, and said we wanted to do it as an animated feature. We suggested that they be partners in the venture, and we would give Bobbs-Merrill first chance to finance it if they wanted to. So they said okay. It wasn't that simple, but 'okay' was the answer."

Two early concepts of the Gazooks drawn in 1974 by illustrator Carol Nicklaus.

Joe Raposo was very impressed with ITT and its chairman, Harold Geneen. "Geneen is a man with an enormous set of responsibilities, enormous commitments in terms of time. His dedication to his work, which is an art in itself, is manifold. And I think that every once in a while there might be just one minute of a little fun. . . . I think he is interested in using the power of that company and his office to encourage things that will enrich people's lives.

"This picture is going to make a lot of people happy. And I think along with running a multinational corporation brilliantly comes the social consciousness that would say, 'Why don't we make a nice movie for families around the world to see?' "

Geneen himself commented at a reception unveiling the new production that "in the context of our worldwide operations, this movie frankly could not be realistically ranked as a major business venture. But in terms of its impact upon young people in bringing them bright, wholesome entertainment, we consider it a project of major proportions."

And so our intrepid band of Raggedy Ann mythmakers had the assurance of financial backing for the feature. Now they began to look at animation studios to see, in Horner's words, "where and how we could do it—and finally we came upon the idea of Dick Williams, who has his own studio in London and who had won an Oscar a couple of years before for *A Christmas Carol*. He seemed the only person we could hit upon who was capable artistically of equaling the early Disney things."

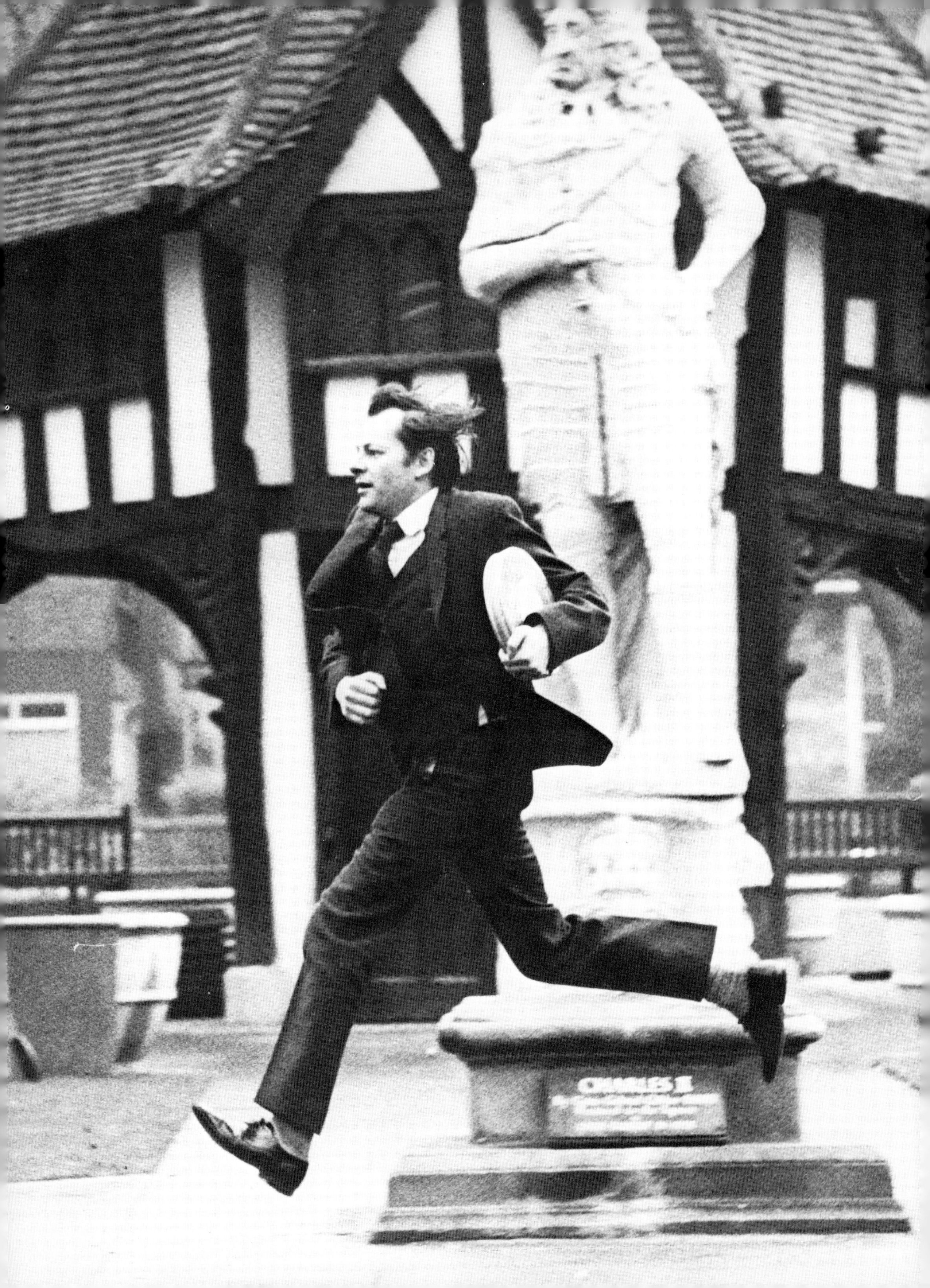

CHAPTER V
The Richard Williams Story

Richard Williams is a potential genius, but he will never be so in his own eyes. He will live and die in uncertainty. So there is great hope for him. We need more and more and more.

—*Chuck Jones*

Midway in the *Raggedy Ann* production, Richard Williams spoke about his remarkable career:

"When I was twenty I saw the possibilities in the medium. *All* the possibilities. Jesus Christ! There are so many things animation can go into. It can be funny, crazy, sad, terrifying, psychological, metaphysical. And I realized that I was uniquely qualified to do it. I had a technical art background, a fine arts training; I played a musical instrument, I could organize and plan, I was a young man and energetic. What I didn't know, I could learn.

"No one else was doing it. On the one hand, you had Disney doing big theatrical things with full animation, and on the other you had people like Norman McLaren, George Dunning and John Hubley doing personal, experimental things. Now, I didn't and still don't want to put the two together, but I want to use the whole palette of all the discoveries—go forward and take the medium a stage further. As Art Babbitt says, 'We have to advance backwards to 1940 (when Disney developed the craft) and start forward from there.' "

Williams is a likable fellow with the infectious energy of a schoolboy. His gestures are those of Pinocchio while he was still on strings, sudden and choppy, and his intelligent blue eyes gaze steadily into yours, full of intensity. The effect is hypnotic.

"I had a master plan," he said. "I decided to become the very best at the commercial side, then master the techniques of the art of personality animation. I wanted it all."

ARDENT "Y" ENTHUSIAST'S AMBITION IS TO GIVE DISNEY IDEAS

TYPICAL OF YOUTHS enjoying Y.M.C.A. activities is Richard Williams, 14, of Toronto, a cartoonist who hopes to be a "top" idea man for Walt Disney. Williams is on a "Y" swimming team, competes in inter-"Y" meets and is painting a mural at Central "Y" pool. The Y.M.C.A.-Y.W.C.A. drive for $2,121,000 will provide facilities for others

Y.M.C.A. ARTIST, 14, PAINTING MERMAID PIN-UP ON 'Y' POOL

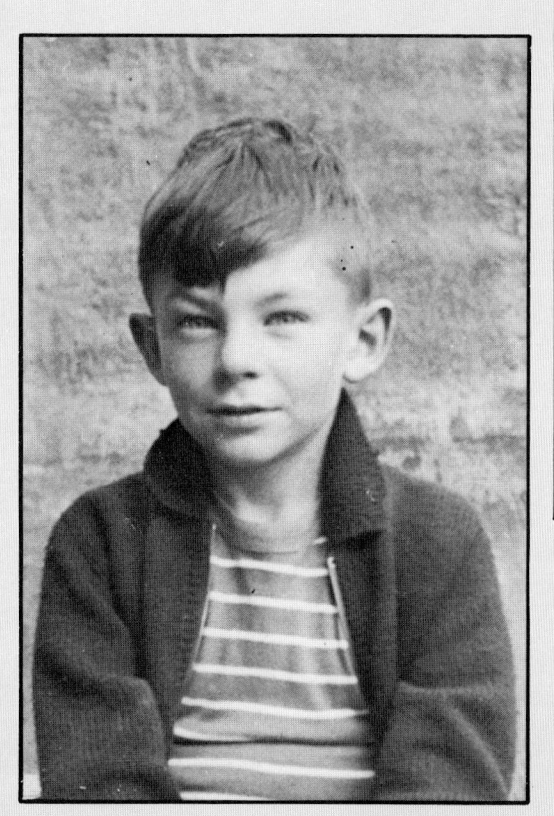

For a young fellow who has a consuming ambition to be a "top" idea man for Walt Disney, 14-year-old Richard Williams has a remarkable streak of modesty.

"Maybe," he says during a thoughtful pause, "my stuff will smell—maybe."

Young Dick Williams, who lives on Golfdale Rd., is a cartoonist. He paints murals. He makes puppets and puts on puppet shows at churches and schools at $7.50 a show. He is on a Y.M.C.A. swimming team and competes in inter-Y meets. Dick is a husky lad and with his bubbling energy and unchanged voice he gives the impression of a tea-kettle at the full boil.

Now conducting a class in cartooning at Central Y.M.C.A., Dick, for the most part, refers to himself as "we." He and his pal, Richard Brown, aged 16, are inseparable and the puppet business is a joint project. Both are in first form at Northern Vocational school.

Dick is in the news at this particular time because of the Y.M.C.A.-Y.W.C.A. drive for $2,121,000. He is typical of many youths who are devoting much of their spare time to Y.M.C.A. activities—lads with talent, ability, energy and enthusiasm. Through its decentralization plan, building branch Y.M.'s and Y.W.'s in Toornto's communities, officials hope to provide facilities where thousands of other young people may expend usefully their talents and energies.

Down on the tile walls of Central Y's big swimming pool, Dick has one large panel of murals nearly completed. The first mural is a sort of pin-up mermaid. A blue-eyed underwater beauty enfolded in her long blonde tresses and perched gracefully on a rock. She is followed by some subterranean foliage, a dolphin, smaller fish and finally a swordfish.

Richard Williams, age six.

(*Left*) A 1947 Toronto newspaper item about fourteen-year-old Richard Williams and his "consuming ambition."

This example of teenager Williams's drawing skill (spoofing his art teachers) shows why schoolmate Carl Bell described him as "the envy of the entire Ontario College of Art."

The Little Island (1958).

And Richard Williams got it all. An Oscar (for Best Animated Short) is prominently displayed in his studio at 13 Soho Square, London, among some eighty other prizes from forty-six international film festivals. But with the impatience of a thirsty man in the Mojave, Williams moans, "I really feel I've spent an awfully long time in school and I haven't done anything yet."

This restless soul was born March 19, 1933, in Toronto; his mother was an illustrator and his father "an all-purpose commercial artist." His parents were divorced when Richard was five, and his mother married Kenneth Williams, then an advertising salesman. Surrounded by a family of artists and craftsmen—his grandfather, with whom he lived "a lot," was a carpenter, and various uncles were photographers and furniture makers—Williams was encouraged to draw, which he began to do at the age of two.

Williams saw *Snow White* and decided, "That's it, I'm going to animate. I just drew Disney stuff when I was a little kid. I remember doing a piece of animation when I was twelve that I filmed when I was eighteen, and it worked very well. It's a bird walking. But it's good, looks like a piece of Disney. The timing in it was good, strangely enough."

At fifteen, Williams took his savings and traveled to Burbank, California, to the Disney studio. "My mother allowed it because it was so important to me. That's all I ever wanted to do," he recalls.

The chubby teenager stayed at the YMCA for five weeks and walked up and down in front of the gates at Disney's. Finally his mother called a friend in advertising, who contacted the Disney publicity department, and they "decided to do a bunch of stories on me as a kid-number-one-Disney-fan who could also draw the stuff."

The number one fan was on cloud nine. He was given a grand tour, met most of the animators and designers working on *Alice in Wonderland* (released in 1951), and received excellent advice from one of them: "I kept raving about animation, and Dick Kelsey said, 'Forget animation—just learn to draw.' It really burned through."

Young Williams returned to Disney's the next year, but six months later he entered a room in the Toronto Art Gallery containing paintings by Rembrandt. "I didn't know anything about fine art, but I saw these Rembrandts and I went to pieces. It made such an impact on me that I immediately dropped anything to do with animation or cartoons."

He did return once more to the Disney Studio the following summer with his art school pal Carl Bell. Williams was paying his way through the Ontario College of Art and made so much money drawing advertisements that he was able to buy a small convertible in which the two students drove down to California. They saw *Peter Pan* (1953 release) in pencil test, and Williams caught his first and only glimpse of Walt Disney himself. "He was out in the hall chatting up this girl from *Look*, telling her about the dog going upstairs in his next feature, *Lady and the Tramp* [released in 1955]. He was really doing a number on her: 'And then we get a little tug on the heart. Dog goes upstairs and we think it's going after the baby.' I was appalled. All he was doing was promoting his movie in an honest way. But the hell with this, I thought. I don't want to do that; I just want to do the work. I kept painting."

He took off for Spain and stayed on the island of Ibiza for two years of painting, swimming, sleeping on the beach, playing the same Bix Beiderbecke choruses on his cornet over and over. "Bix had the same effect on me as Rembrandt," explained Williams. "I hated the sound of the trumpet because of Harry James; hated jazz. Then I heard Bix, then Louis, and then I went bananas."

Today whenever anyone suggests he might be a "workaholic," Williams points to his twenty-four months as a "beach bum" and claims he had "two idyllic years," so he doesn't mind working now. "But I could easily switch right off again," he threatens.

The idea for *The Little Island,* an allegory about Truth, Beauty, and Good living together on a desert isle, came to Williams "right out of the blue" while on Ibiza. At first he fought the idea that was to change the course of his life.

"I started making tiny little drawings, sort of storyboards. I thought, 'Oh God, I don't want to make an animated film—it's too much work. I'll do it when I'm forty.' Then I started to act it out, and I thought, 'That's it!' And I saw the medium that combined everything I was interested in. I decided to go to England because television was opening up." He was twenty-two.

For three and a half years Williams supported himself by animating TV commercials in London while he worked on *The Little Island* at night. Director George Dunning often hired Williams during this time. Impressed by the young man's ferocious energy, determination, and ability to work almost eighteen hours a day, Dunning dubbed him "The Creature from Another Planet."

Gerry Potterton, who had a tiny studio then, recalls, "One day this crazy guy came in. Dropped his drawings on the floor. 'I want to do a feature, and I need help,' he said. Any experience? 'Nope,' he said. 'I'm gonna do it!' 'Course we all looked at each other and laughed. Three years later he sent cards inviting everyone in London to screenings of his thirty-five-minute film and knocked everyone out."

The Little Island, released in 1958, proved a critical success (*Time* reported that "London's prickly movie critics were uniformly delighted") if not a financial one. Soured on commercial animation, depressed by money problems and feeling he "wasn't good enough" because his film "somehow hadn't quite come off," Williams played in a Dixieland band for a couple of years; it eventually became "Dick Williams' Band." "It was my band because of my organizational, not my musical, ability," he comments.

While he was waiting for a tax rebate, Williams decided to make a short cartoon film, *Love Me, Love Me, Love Me,* "for a lark." This 1962 spoof

Love Me, Love Me, Love Me (1962).

Scene from one of the animated sequences produced by Richard Williams and his studio for Tony Richardson's *Charge of the Light Brigade*.

(*Right*) Two stills from *A Christmas Carol* (1971).

about morality, self-image and love featured Squidgy Bod, unkempt but loved by everyone; Thermos Fortitude, whom everyone hated; and a stuffed alligator named Charlie. To Williams's surprise the short was a big success. It cost 1,500 pounds and made back 9,000. "I'd made it as a private joke. The audiences laughed at everything I'd put in for myself. I thought, 'There's a market for my stuff,' and I started digging in."

Publicity resulting from the film helped him establish his own studio, Richard Williams Animation Limited, which produced commercials. It also led to a job creating the animated titles for *What's New, Pussycat?* in 1966, of which "Atticus" of the *Sunday Times* remarked: "One of the best things about the film *What's New, Pussycat?* were the titles. One American reviewer was unkind enough to say *the* best thing."

In the next several years Williams went on to earn praise from critics for his animated titles on a number of live-action features, including *A Funny Thing Happened on the Way to the Forum* (1966), *The Charge of the Light Brigade* (1968), and *The Return of the Pink Panther* (1975). Most important, he won an Oscar for his own twenty-six-minute animated cartoon, *A Christmas Carol*, in 1972.

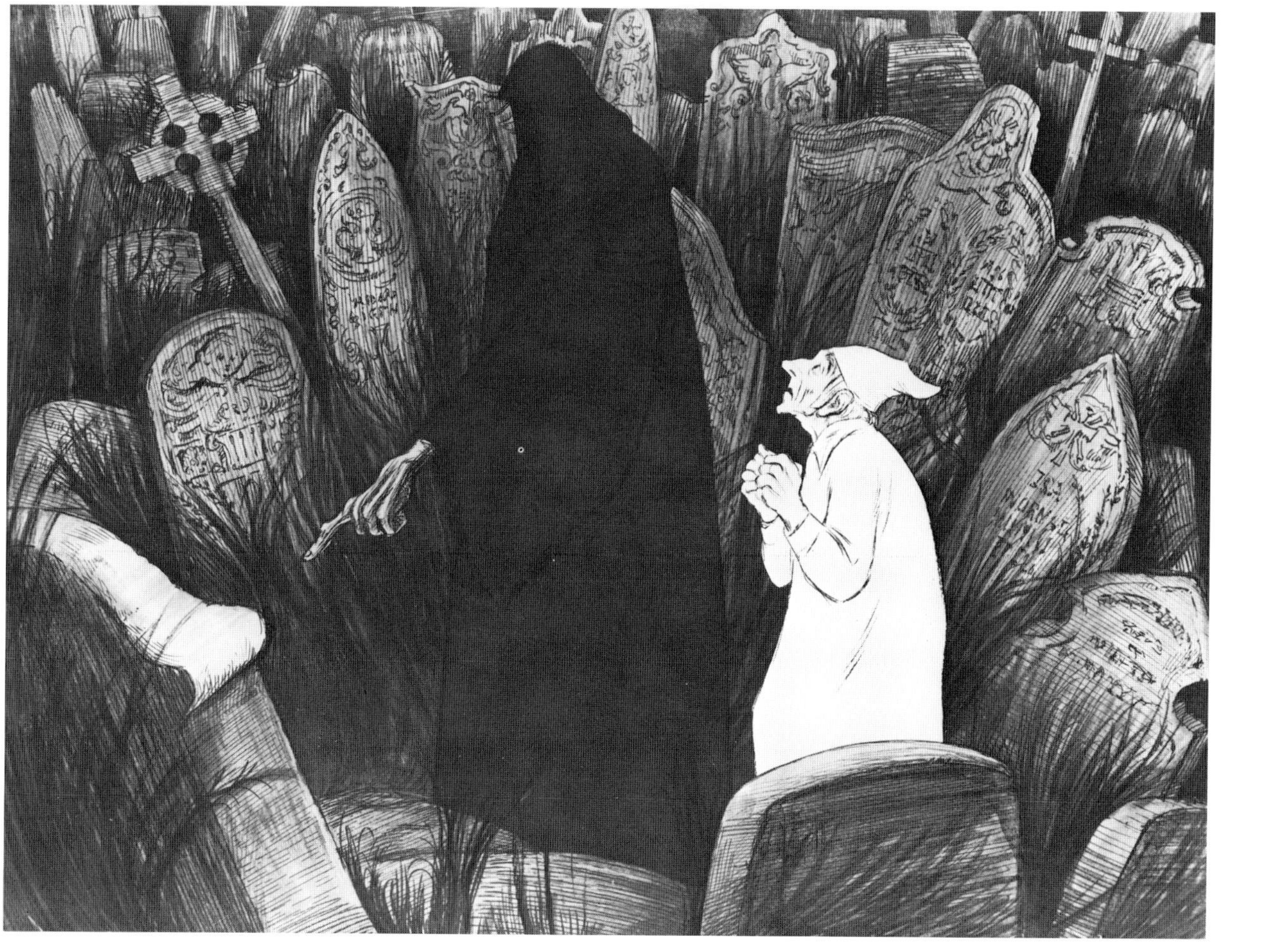

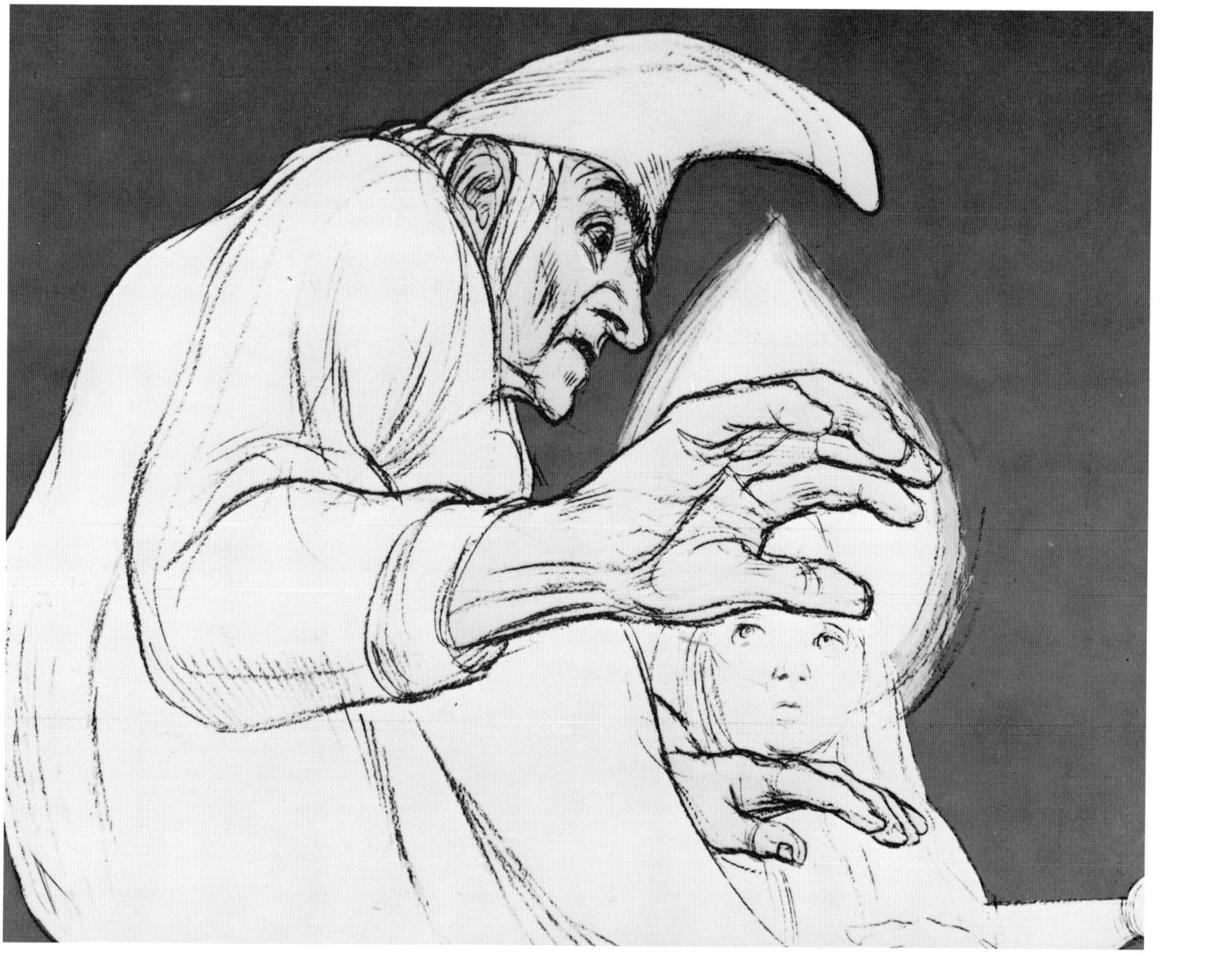

"Dick Williams—the best cartoon director in Britain."

Kenneth Tynan

"The credits to *A Funny Thing Happened on the Way to the Forum* are animated too. . . . Neither innocent nor corrupt. Just splendid."

Jules Feiffer, *Life*

"The rulers and military leaders [in *The Charge of the Light Brigade*] actually blend into interpolated animation (by Richard Williams) that is remarkably witty and effective in itself. The animation provides the only clear exposition we get of what's going on in the movie. It's too bad Richardson didn't leave the *Charge* itself to Williams."

Pauline Kael, *The New Yorker*

"[*The Return of the Pink Panther*] is again introduced by the marvelous Richard Williams cartoon character who upstages all of the title credits and is, in effect, everything that Clouseau is not—urbane, witty, sly, quick-witted, graceful."

Vincent Canby, *The New York Times*

"Star attraction [at the Zagreb International Festival of Animated Films] was the animated version of *A Christmas Carol* made by Dick Williams—who is seriously compared in the film world to Disney, Picasso, and sometimes Charles Dickens himself."

The Guardian

Williams considered the Oscar important to his studio not only for the obvious reasons of prestige and power, but because it was a first inkling that phase two of his "master plan" was now operative. "I feel certain," he says, "that we won the Oscar because we now had the ability to develop Scrooge as a personality.

"When we completed our work on *The Charge of the Light Brigade* we were a highly acclaimed animation studio, but I knew there were severe limitations to our individual 'artistic' and 'stylistic' approach," says Williams. "Flashy titles and TV commercials might make critics rave and might hold an audience's attention for a few minutes, but they would not support characters and a story for, say, twenty minutes. And certainly not a feature-length cartoon." He decided the whole studio needed to "go back to school" and "do post-graduate work on the Disney craft of 'character animation.' "

Williams screened the Beatles cartoon *Yellow Submarine* (1968) and Walt Disney's *The Jungle Book* (1967) for his collaborators. "*Yellow Submarine* convinced us we wanted to be finished with the kind of animation that is based on graphic tricks," Williams told writer David Robinson. "*The Jungle Book*—leaving aside anything you may feel about its aesthetics or narrative methods—was a revelation. We realized how much Disney's techniques and discoveries still had to teach us, and we wanted to go back to school, to grade one, to learn how to make a character live and walk and talk

Richard Williams and the 1972 Oscar for "Best Short."

convincingly. The graphic tricks that had done service for twenty years—the little figures that scuttle about on mechanical legs and move in restricted, stylized ways—won't get you through an hour."

Williams solicited and received "enthusiastic cooperation" from Disney greats, including Milt Kahl, Frank Thomas, Ollie Johnson, Wolfgang Reitherman and Ken Anderson. "I am enormously indebted to them," Williams says, "and feel I'd be letting them down if I didn't do something different or even better than they have done."

He began importing master animators from the golden age of Hollywood animation in the 1930s and '40s: Chuck Jones lectured and helped "in numerous ways," as did the continually innovative artist-director John Hubley. Now in his eighties, Grim Natwick, the creator of Betty Boop and the main animator of Disney's Snow White, was tutor-in-residence for nine months in 1975. Ken Harris, seventy-seven, the top Warner Brothers animator and an acknowledged master of comic timing, joined Williams eight years ago. The great animator and teacher Art Babbitt conducted "intense seminars," and Williams closed the studio down completely for a month in order to allow his staff to concentrate on Babbitt's teaching.

"Technique first, art second," says Williams. "Or I guess they go together. But if you haven't got technique, you better get it!

"When I first worked with Ken Harris, I was amazed at what he could do. I've since learned there are principles that he's using. A lot of it is knack. But a lot of it, as Milt Kahl says, is so simple. The basic things are simple, but nobody knows them. I think it takes two to five years to learn."

Williams's reputation for manic energy and constant pressure for a perhaps unattainable perfection makes him the subject of envy and fear on the part of certain animators and animation directors.

Williams admits, "I can't stand loafing on the job." With keen self-awareness he admits, "What makes me difficult to work with is that I find everyone's Achilles' heel and go around kicking it! If you can get through that with me, you're okay."

He explains further, "I do have violent enthusiasms, pro and anti. My enthusiasms are tremendous in order to bring out the part that's alive—the creativity of the artists. We excite each other—'Yes! Yes! Now go!' But then I find where the person is weak—or weaker, the blank spots. So I tell him, 'Now that's wrong, and *that,* and that's not working right.' Gerry Potterton says I turn on them: 'But you said I was wonderful!' they say. 'You are—but *that* is not good.' Then they get over that and it's okay again."

Williams is also starring in a new version of an old game retitled "What Makes Richard Run?" Chuck Jones writes, "I think Dick suspects that he is better than any director around, but he knows too that he is not and will never become as great an animator as Grim Natwick or Art Babbitt or Milt Kahl or Frank Thomas. What he does not know—or will not admit—is that he could

Williams with Chuck Jones.

Williams with Ken Harris and Roy Naisbitt.

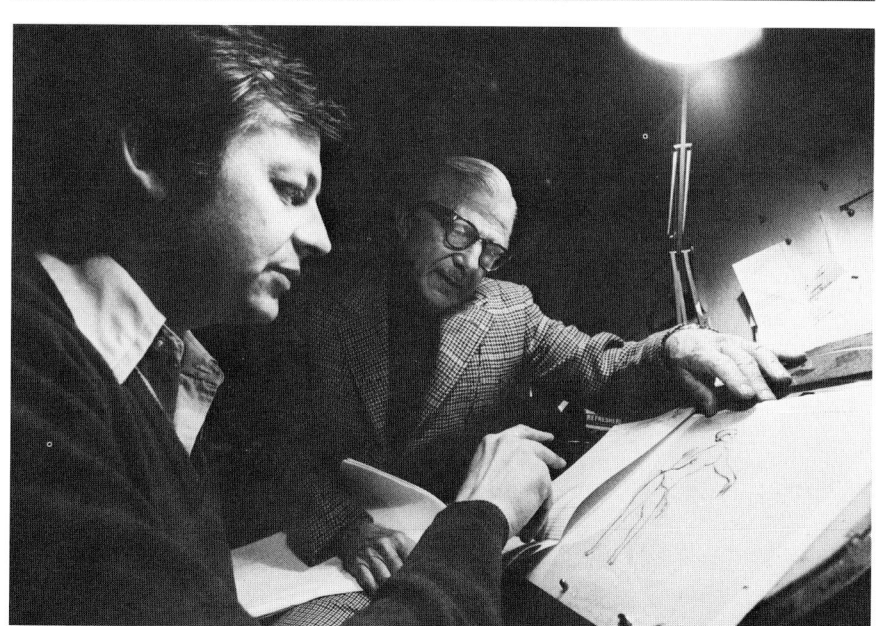

Williams with Art Babbitt.

be if he were willing to spend the time—but he does not want to be a great animator; he wants to be a great animation director, perhaps the greatest, and he has an uncertain suspicion that there is no such thing.

"Now this suspicion is in itself a mark of greatness, not of weakness. This agony of uncertainty is more a part of the creative hunger of Dick Williams than of any other director I have ever known. He not only needs to make fine films, he must also *succeed*."

Williams insists that only animating turns him on. He claims he directs "by default," just as he once had to take over the direction of a Dixieland band. He admits, "I do get vicarious kicks seeing a picture come together. There are two kinds of power: manipulative and creative. Executives and producers use manipulative power on people, and so do I, but I'm not into it. I use it to get creative power.

"There are two kinds of people in the world: those who want to be something (and they should be avoided) and those who want to *do* something." Williams makes it clear which camp he is in. "I never wanted to be a director. I wanted to do the job. In order to get the job done, I had to become a director and producer."

When Williams began his personal crusade to advance the art of animation, George Dunning told him, "You know you'll have to get off the [drawing] board." But Williams refuses to give up the board and become a managerial seer. If he were granted an eternal lifetime, he would love nothing more than to make an animated feature all by himself: he would—and could—design it, write it, do all the voices for it, animate it, paint it, shoot it, and probably run the projector and sell the popcorn.

In *Raggedy Ann* he kept his hand in by doing "repair work," which meant that he redrew other animators' work; he also animated with undeniable mastery most of Raggedy Andy's song, "No Girl's Toy." Was this a manifestation of Williams's quest for perfection or an example of his egocentricity? Does he perhaps sense that in attempting to gain so much for the art of animation, there's a big chance that Dick Williams might get lost?

Although he has dismissed his earliest films as "not very good," there are indications that he misses the one-to-one relationship of an artist to his medium that a small film offers. He suspects, he has said, that someday he'll go "very personal" when he has achieved his other goals in animated features. Three such intimate films have been on and off the burner for years: *I. Vor Pittfalks, the Universal Confidence Man; Circus Drawings*, inspired by his days in Spain; and *My Pretty Girl*, based on a Bix Beiderbecke recording.

Williams's magnum opus, the ultimate synthesis of the skill of the Disney studio and the style of the independents, has been in preparation for twelve years and has, he figures, two and a half more years to go. This is the feature-length animated cartoon called *The Thief and the Cobbler*, which Williams once promised will be "the *War and Peace* of animation!" He has

Williams draws the "Laffing Camel," a character in his forthcoming feature *The Thief and the Cobbler*. (*Below*) Two completed scenes from this long-awaited film.

also claimed that *The Thief* is "going to be the greatest animated film ever made."

There is a bit of Barnum in Williams, who admits, "I am shameless when it comes to publicity," but this is phase three of Williams's master plan. He truly believes the film will "redefine the medium," and he has been pouring every cent of profit from his studio's TV commercial revenue into it.

There is hardly a conversation shared with the man in which *The Thief* is not mentioned, at least in passing. Williams excitedly tries to explain why this will be *the one*:

"*The Thief* is not following the Disney route. It's to my knowledge the first animated film with a real plot that locks together like a detective story at the end. It has no sentimentality, and the two main characters don't speak. It's like a silent movie with a lot of sound."

Dick Williams was still trying to attract financial backers for his masterwork, while his staff of forty experimented with different techniques and approaches to characters on the approximately one hundred forty TV commercials they produce each year, when, three years ago, Raggedy Ann reared her charming little head and offered Williams the opportunity to use his hard-earned directorial expertise in Bobbs-Merrill/ITT's multimillion-dollar venture.

In the winter of 1973, Lester Osterman was in London on business; he called on Richard Williams at his studio to ask him to consider directing an animated feature based on the Raggedy Ann and Andy stories. Williams's first impulse was to answer No, and he recommended John Hubley. He'd never heard of Osterman. But Osterman left a script and a tape of music with Williams overnight.

Williams immediately rang up his friend Tony Walton, the famed set and costume designer, who informed him that Osterman was indeed a legitimate Broadway producer/theater owner "who was always solid for money." Still wary, Williams read the script. He found, to his surprise, that he "couldn't find anything wrong with it! I kept looking for the terrible things, and there weren't any."

The script was deliberately left loose to allow for visual development. Williams took it around to Walton, who was working as art director on *Murder on the Orient Express*, a feature Williams was providing titles for. Walton thought the same thing: the script wasn't really there, but there was nothing wrong with it! It was two in the morning when Williams, preparing to go to bed, flipped on his tape machine to listen to the Raposo score.

"I played the music and was quite taken aback," he later recalled. "I thought, 'This could be extremely good!' "

Negotiations soon began between the Williams studio and the Osterman office. Dickering went on and on, until it was eventually decided not to use the Williams studio. Exit Richard Williams.

Richard Williams's animation
drawings of Raggedy Andy singing
"No Girl's Toy."

But not quite. "Lester would phone me all the time and say, 'Come and supervise it for a week every month,' " says Williams. "I said, 'You're crazy, it's a full-time job!' He rang me for a year saying this."

Once again Horner and Osterman began to cast about for a cartoon studio capable of taking their Raggedy idea and turning it into a "quality" feature—an "early" Disney feature, no less. It has been noted that the two producers are shrewd men of the theater but tyros when it comes to producing films, let alone an animated feature film. Even so, it is curious that for all their talk of "quality" à la Disney, they spent some time looking at West Coast TV kiddie cartoon factories whose relation to Disney animation is that of Woolworth to Cartier.

At an audition in the spring of 1974 three former Disney staffers, one an animator and the other two writers, presented for approval storyboards they had prepared based on the Thackray/Wilk treatment. The animator's creation featured a "Love Fairy," "Winnie-the-Witch," and "Little Boy Pirates." And as if this unsolicited rewrite weren't bad enough, the offering of the two writers neglected to use all the Raposo songs. "There was one horrendous sequence I'm still smarting from," says Raposo. "They'd thrown out 'Blue,' the Camel's song, and substituted a song for the Cookie Giant!"

Raposo hit the roof. "I said, 'Get me a reservation to London immediately. I won't work with you people. I will not be involved with you. I'm sorry, good-bye!' And I went over to London and called Dick."

Richard Williams was in a depressed mood. He was exhausted from finishing up the titles for Blake Edwards's *Return of the Pink Panther;* he was late animating a British commercial which utilized the Disney-designed Winnie-the-Pooh; and he had decided to break with his business manager. He was also down because he wasn't getting *The Thief* feature together fast enough.

Finally Osterman phoned and asked Williams to reconsider supervising the production of *Raggedy Ann & Andy*—this time on a full-time basis.

Williams hesitated again, so Osterman said, "Joe's coming over. Speak to Joe."

"When you have a good idea," Joe Raposo believes, "you simply have to blast through to it. I feel very personally about the film, having contributed the final draft of the screenplay, written the music and the lyrics and having gone over and begged Williams to come and direct this thing."

"Raposo I liked," said Williams, who used to jam along with Raposo's *Sesame Street* music on TV. "I'd met him once before and we got drunk. So immediately we got drunk again.

"He said, 'Come to New York and talk to these people.' Then he jazzed me up about the possibilities."

The possibilities included the fact that it certainly wouldn't hurt Williams to test his directorial wings on an animated feature that someone like

Bobbs-Merrill/ITT was bankrolling. It was a picture that couldn't help making a noise and enhancing Williams's reputation as animation's Golden Boy. And there would be some extra income that could go into *The Thief*.

Williams began to figure in his mind just how he might handle this production. He thought he would supervise the film, but that was all. He would get Abe Levitow, with whom he had worked so well on *A Christmas Carol,* to direct the picture.

Williams got more excited. Here was a chance to work with American animation pros he had always wanted to hire, and now he could hand-pick a whole team of them. When he heard that Gruelle used to tell the stories to his daughter, he thought, "Gee, all we have to do is find the original Gruelle drawings and move them around to Joe's music. I mean, how can you fail?"

And the music! That was the clincher for Williams. He realized, listening to the track of the *Raggedy Ann* score, that "Raposo is a visual composer. He can't write anything that doesn't fit visually. It's the damnedest thing. He's got a whopper talent for animation!

"So," Williams concluded, "the track will hold the picture. We almost can't miss, because of the soundtrack!"

Raposo, with Williams, flew back to New York.

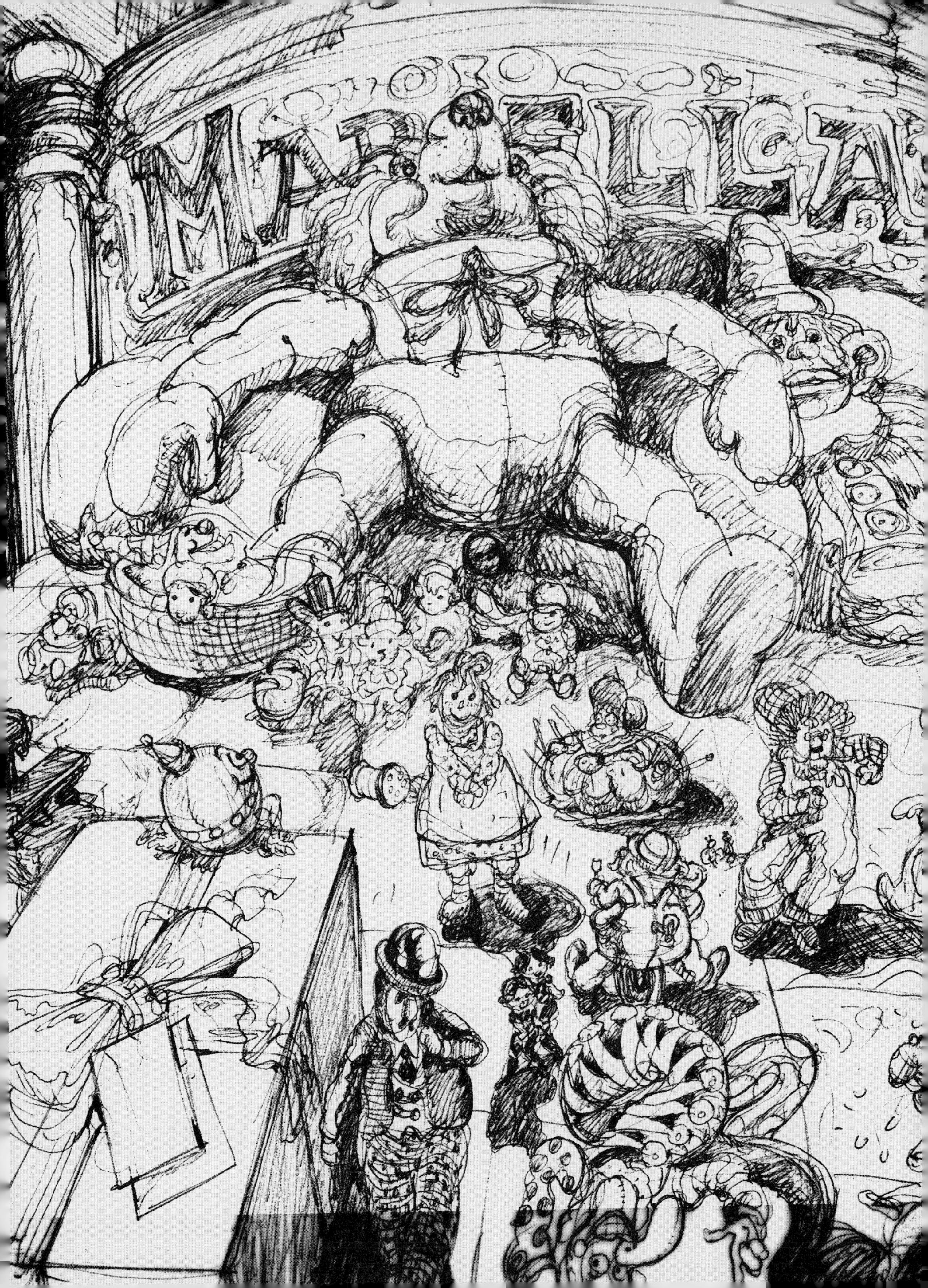

CHAPTER VI
Designing the Production

Corny draws like Daumier. Corny is a genius. I know he's hard to pin down, but so is Dick. I mean everybody is a little flaky in that business. Let's face it—it's like the Mad Tea Party.

—Pat Thackray

You'd have thought it was the Second Coming. Pat Thackray ran across the room and jumped up like a child onto Richard Williams and kissed him. There were happy greetings from the producers, handshaking and all. Raposo had brought back the man who would do the film the way it ought to be done.

"When I got here," Williams said later, "it all sounded marvelous. I got the same lawyer as Joe, who'd made Joe rich. Joe was campaigning for me like crazy."

But a wrench was thrown into Williams's plan to only supervise the production when Abe Levitow, the West Coast artist he had hoped would come to New York and direct the film, "refused to play ball." Levitow, Williams later learned, was dying of cancer.

"At that point," Williams says, "I decided I would direct the feature myself."

Williams rightly interpreted the demand for a film of Disney quality as meaning a fully animated feature with high-quality production values, not a steal of the Disney house-style. It has always been a part of Williams's artistic philosophy to combine "the warm wonderful world" of Disney with the experimental technique of the independent animators and to "go forward with no preconception or limitation of 'style' in any area."

There was never any thought in Williams's mind that he would Disney-fy *Raggedy Ann & Andy*. His graphic versatility allows him to adapt his style to the needs of the particular story he is working on at the moment, as he did in *A Christmas Carol,* a film that contained brilliant animation worthy of Disney but visually resembled nineteenth-century engravings of London and particularly John Leech's illustrations from the first edition of Dickens's book.

Designer Corny Cole's lavishly drawn suggestions for the playroom setting.

Williams spent a week researching the original Raggedy Ann illustrations by Johnny Gruelle. He saw that Gruelle drew naturally and realistically and decided to approach the film's visuals from that direction, allowing a style to come out of the Gruelle drawings. "I decided to get Corny Cole to design it," recalls Williams. "Corny is unique and perfect for this."

Cornelius Cole had worked with Williams for two short periods in London on *The Thief and the Cobbler,* and both artists were eager to work with each other again. Cole is one of the most extraordinary graphic talents in animated films. Working with a ball-point pen because it is fast and because he feels his work is "very documentary, a kind of writing," Cole spins out enchantingly detailed line drawings that bring to mind the sketches of Daumier and Tenniel, and particularly Heinrich Kley's pre–World War I pen drawings of anthropomorphic beasts.

Williams feels that Corny's work "enriches a picture. It's inspirational and shows the possibilities." Cole is also amazingly prolific. For one word of dialogue on a storyboard, he may do four or five sketches. His continuity drawings spill out sometimes at the rate of ninety-five detailed sketches a day.

Sitting half-eagerly, half-guardedly for an interview, without paper or pencil in reach, Cole looks lost. Black-rimmed glasses perch on a generous nose, stringy black hair fights conformity and an advancing skull-line, old sneakers tap nervously on the floor. He resembles a shy forty-six-year-old adolescent who can't wait to go play (that is, draw).

Corny Cole lives in the California beach community of Pacific Palisades with his wife Dawn, their four children, five cats, three dogs, and a turtle. He describes himself as "a very studied artist, almost overtrained. I've had a lot of discipline, a lot of training, probably more than many people."

In addition to working in the animation industry, Cole has exhibited his art in many galleries, where he prefers to be known as "Cornelius Cole," although he insists on "Corny" for his screen credits because "people remember it better."

A recent show Cornelius Cole had in Malibu consisted of a series of seven thousand small pad-sized drawings in ball-point about "the power and fall of Nixon." In the same show he exhibited forty-four feet of stream-of-consciousness, autobiographical drawings on a roll of brown paper. "I was going to make it five blocks long," says Cole, "but I had to cut it for the show."

Corny Cole was born in Santa Monica, served in the Korean War, and attended the Chouinard Art Institute on the GI Bill at night while working days as a caricaturist at conventions. He was an inbetweener at the Disney studio for $28 a week, but lasted there only six months. "I was a lousy inbetweener," he admits. "Got four sties in my eyes. I hated the place! I still hate it."

These drawings of Raggedy Ann and Andy by Richard Williams were based on the original Johnny Gruelle sketches.

ANN

RAGGEDY ANN & ANDY
© COPYRIGHT 1975
THE BOBBS-MERRILL CO. INC.

LATER VERSION

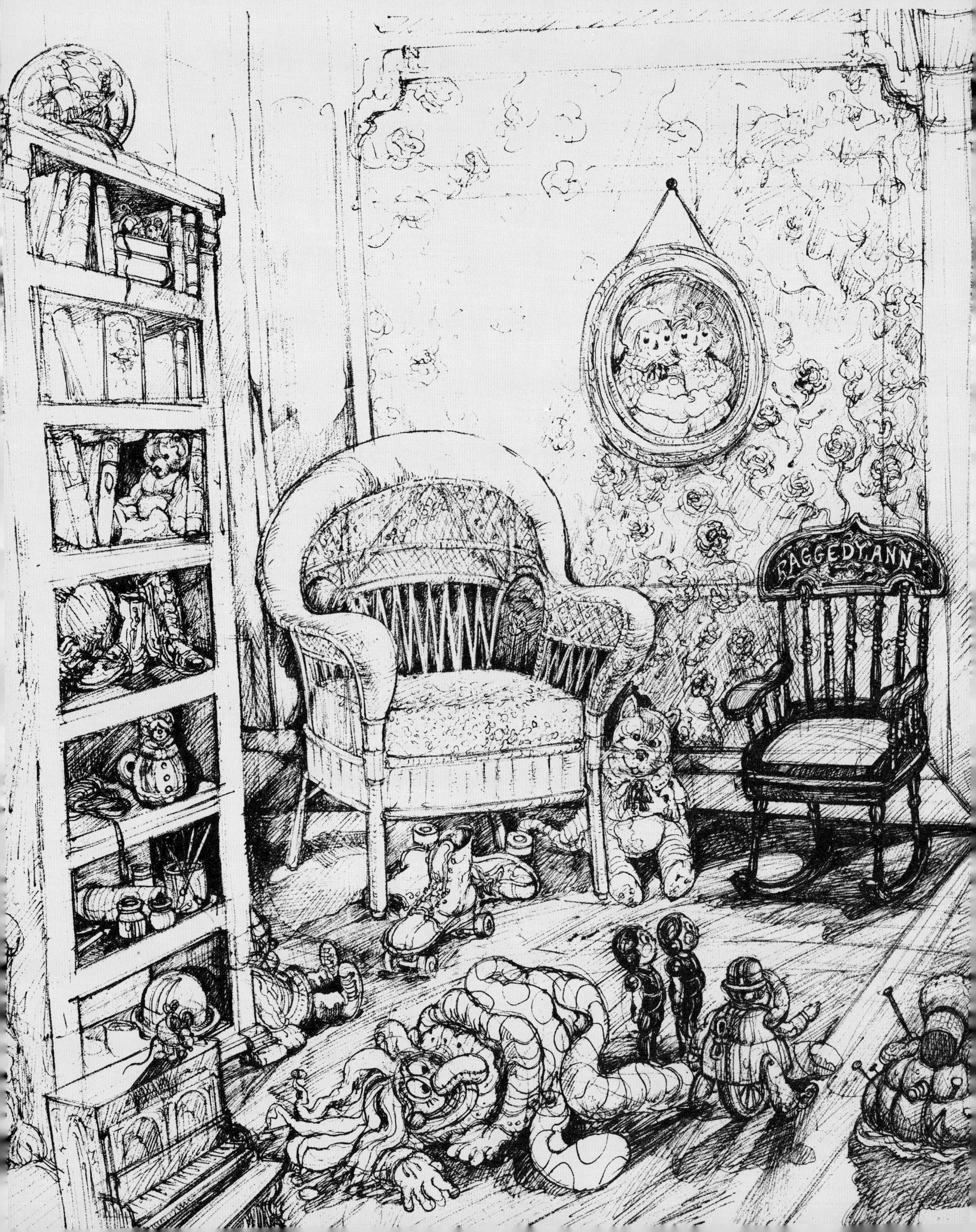
RAGGEDY ANN

A Corny Cole suggestion sketch for the playroom sequence.

Corny Cole.

(*Below and opposite*) Early Cole idea sketches of the Camel, the Captain, and Raggedy Ann.

It was the beginning of years of trying to conform his free drawing style to the house-style of whatever animation factory he worked at. The discipline and rigid style consistency that cel animation requires of its artists was particularly difficult for Cole to get used to. And in fact he never has done so.

He bounced from one studio to another: he spent six years at Warners animating, ending up in story and layouts, then moved on to UPA for three years. He dropped out of the business in 1963 during an "animation depression" and edited a surfing magazine. Two years later he was working for Hanna-Barbera Studios, then went over to Depatie-Freleng for a couple of years. As an art director at MGM he worked on the cartoon feature *The Phantom Tollbooth* (1969), but he disagreed with the director and left. It was at MGM, however, that Richard Williams "discovered" Corny Cole.

Williams was on a quick tour of the MGM cartoon studio when he saw Cole's storyboards of the climactic battle sequence from *Tollbooth*. "I got the biggest professional scare of my life. His work was tremendous!" Williams ran to the film's director, and, excited about this "amazing new talent, this genius," he demanded, "Who is he? I want to meet him. If you don't want him, I do!"

Williams got in touch with Cole and twice brought him over to work at Williams's studio in London.

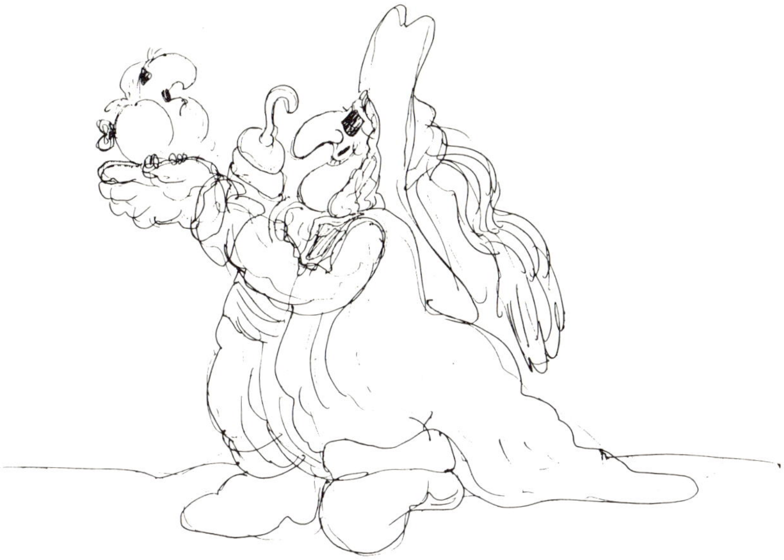

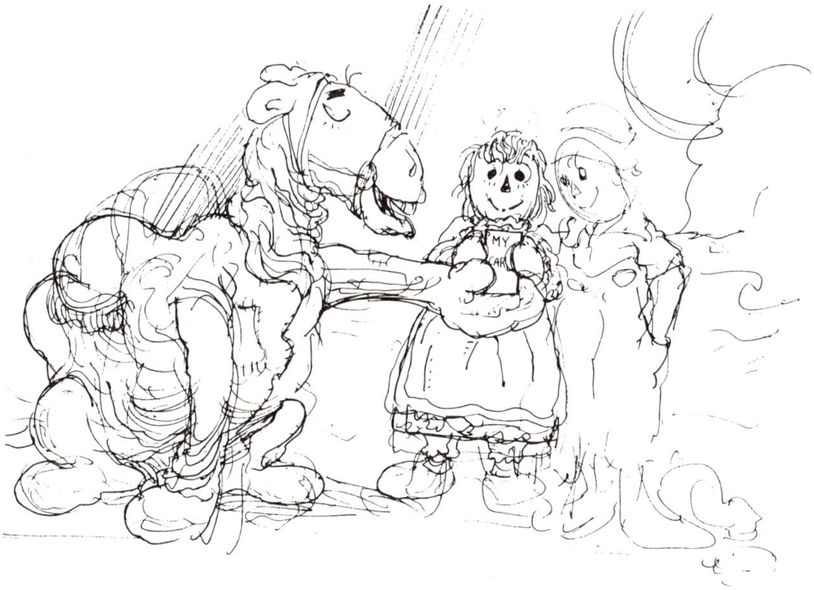
MY

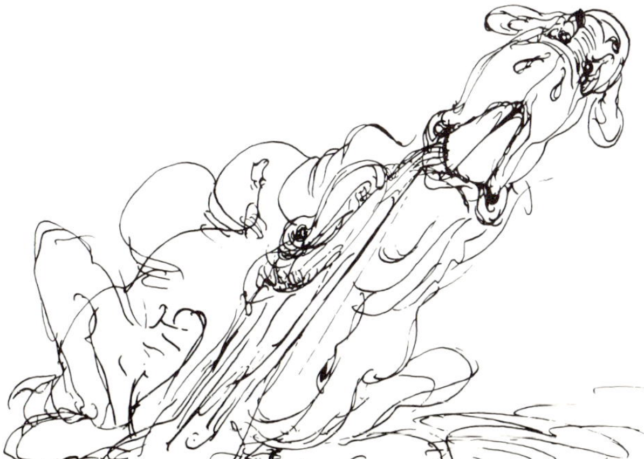

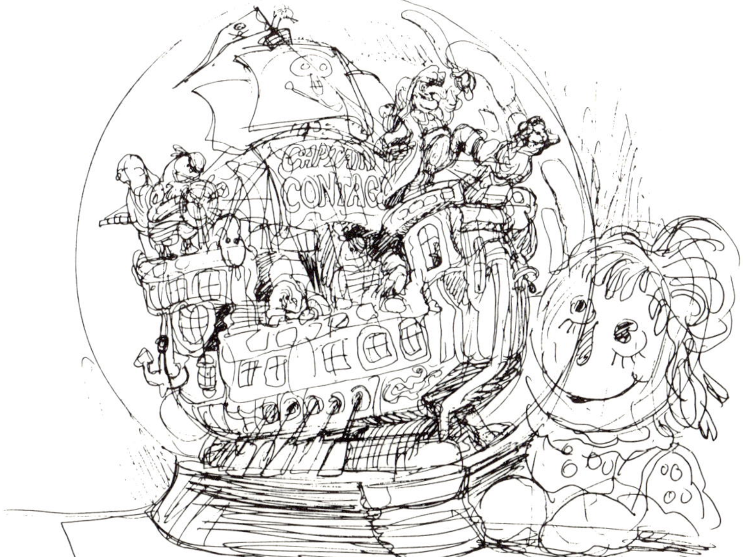

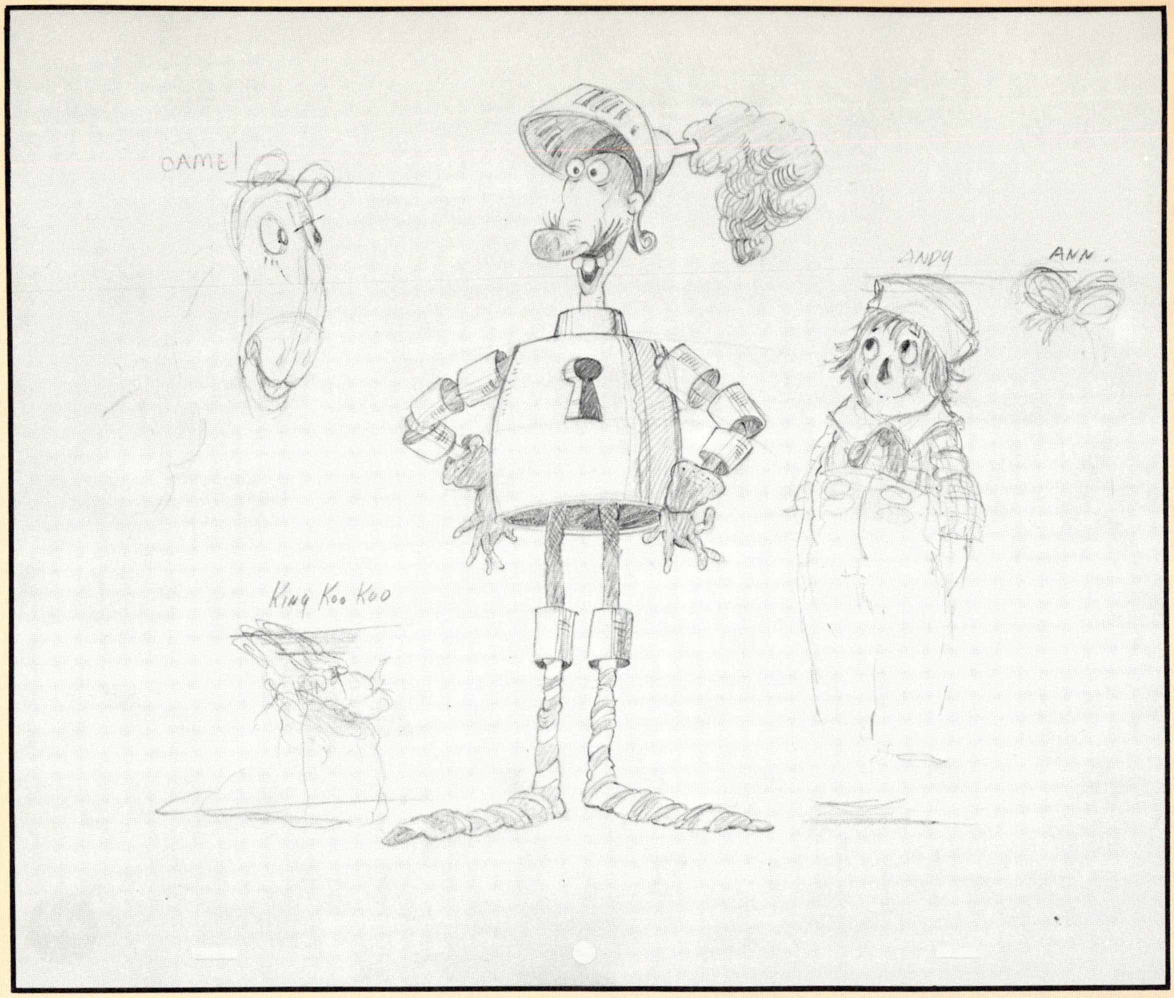
CAMEL
ANDY
ANN
King Koo Koo

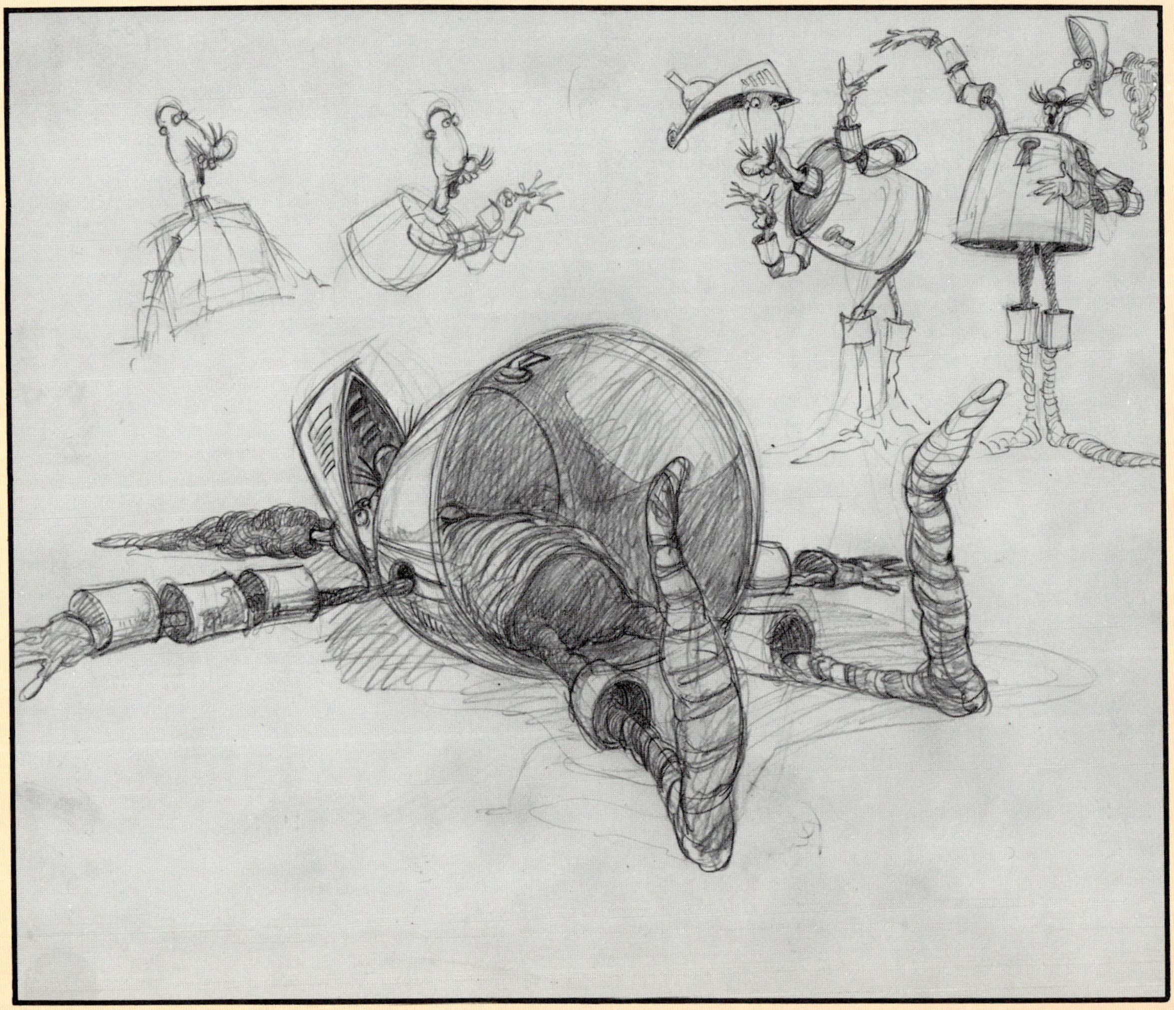

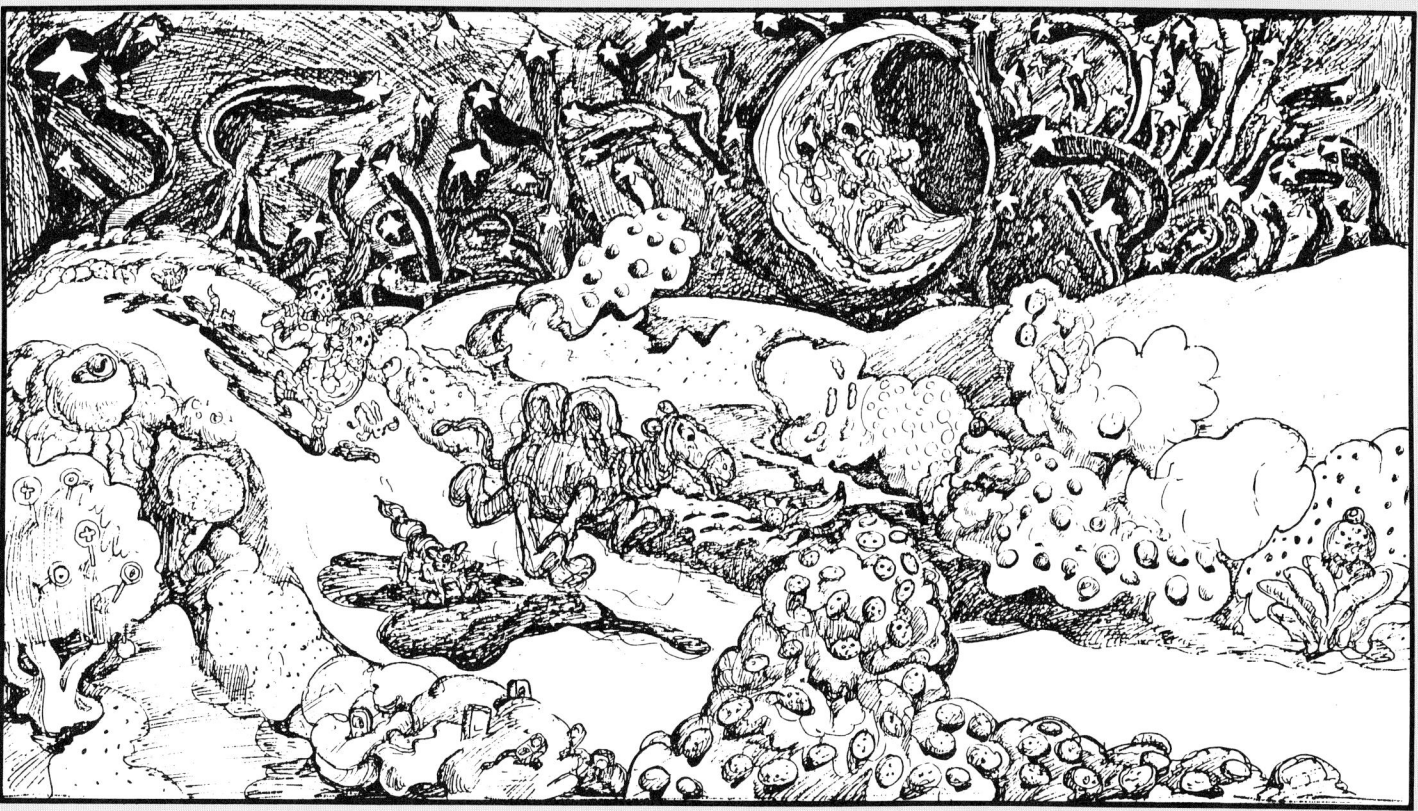

Suggestions for the Camel in the Deep Deep Woods sequence.

(*Opposite*) Corny Cole's original character design for the Loonie Knight.

In January 1975, Corny Cole was finishing up a short educational film job when Dick Williams phoned from New York and offered him the job of designing the characters, layouts, storyboard, color-keying—in fact, the entire graphic style—of *Raggedy Ann & Andy*. Cole accepted and flew to New York the next day. He explains, "I knew if Dick Williams was going to be involved it was going to be a good project."

In New York, Cole attended three days of meetings and worked closely with Pat Thackray; he sketched dolls in the toy section of the Museum of the City of New York while Williams cut out Gruelle drawings for "reference sheets." Cole returned to Los Angeles and worked for three weeks on a color presentation that would be shown to Bobbs-Merrill/ITT at the end of February. This important meeting would serve to introduce Richard Williams as the director of the film and to demonstrate his approach to the material and the style of the final product.

Looking at Corny Cole's preliminary sketches of the characters and settings, one is overwhelmed by the enormous charm, the sheer delightfulness of them. They brim with cheeriness, buoyancy, and invention. An animator couldn't help being inspired by such heady raw material.

Corny says he based his drawings on the first four Gruelle books. He feels that "the early books were good, then he got slicker, more patterned, more formularized." The Greedy was the first of the new characters he designed for the film; his conception of the creature was "spiderlike" with "all kinds of hands," rather different from the way animator Emery Hawkins developed him in the final film version.

Although Corny praised Emery as "the Rembrandt of animation" when the pencil-test footage of the Greedy began to come in that fall, and while Cole feels that the "flavor of the animation is beautiful" in the entire film, he is ultimately not satisfied with the results.

The old bugaboo Corny has fought all his career has reared its ugly head once more: "It's that you can't do it all. The animation has to be such that everyone can take it and follow and retain as much as possible. When you get this involved with a storyboard, you have definite visual ideas that you see and feel, and yet they're very hard to explain to everyone when they're this loose or abstract. It's a frustration that all designers or graphic artists have in animation.

"To me," Cole continues, "this film is an animator's film. It's not a graphic designer's film. The design is a secondary thing.

"Now, *Yellow Submarine* is a designer's film. I think it's the best animated film done since the early Disney because it is inventive and imaginative, and because of the music. I don't like anything to do with Disney.

"It's been frustrating for Richard *and* me. There's a conflict when you work together on something this critical and this tight and the deadlines are pressuring. You're nervous and strained. On a thing this big, working here

Corny Cole's early concept sketches of Babette (*opposite*) and the Greedy.

VIOLET
NOTE
ITS GOING
TO BE A
VERMILLION
BEARD
JX

Cole's color suggestions for the Captain.

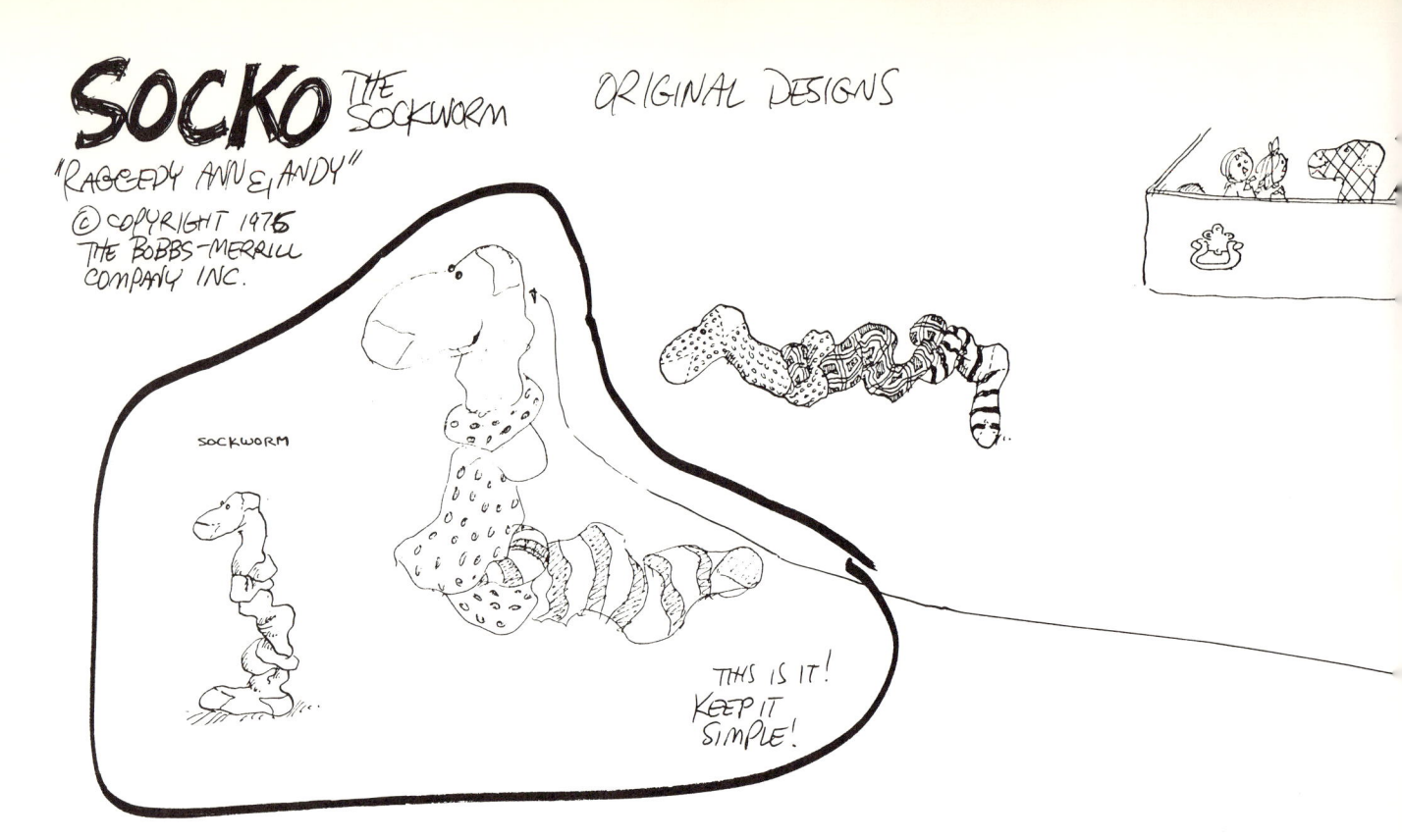

SOCKO THE SOCKWORM
"RAGGEDY ANN & ANDY"
© COPYRIGHT 1975
THE BOBBS-MERRILL COMPANY INC.

ORIGINAL DESIGNS

SOCKWORM

THIS IS IT!
KEEP IT SIMPLE!

Richard Williams's note on this early model sheet of the Sockworm by Corny Cole refers to a conflict that arose between the director and the designer about the overabundance of detail in the characters.

and in New York and not seeing the color until it's back is very frustrating."

"Corny accepts no limitations—period—for time or money," says Richard Williams. "The better he likes a job, the more identified he becomes with it. He fastens on a bit of business, some curlicue. He was five months late with some storyboards. He actually laid out only one-half of the picture. Gerry Potterton did a third of the storyboards and layouts."

Despite Williams's plan that the key animators be responsible for most of the laying out and staging of their individual sequences, it was a serious mistake on the part of both Williams and Cole to presume that one man—Cole—could style the entire feature, lay it out, do the storyboards, color-coordinate it, and design the characters. One need only look at the credits for Disney's *Snow White* to see that there were two men responsible for character design and ten artists involved in art direction. In the more recent *101 Dalmatians*, the feature that introduced Xeroxing cel techniques to feature cartoons and signaled a major modification of the Disney style, we find that though there was one art director/production designer, under him were eleven people in layout and two in layout styling.

Clashes between the director and the designer were frequent; once Cole hollered at Williams, "I'm after Rembrandt, Titian and Turner!" which Williams countered with: "Well, we haven't got *them* on this picture. You'll have to work with *us*!"

Cole was offended by some of Williams's artistic decisions. "Like in the song 'Blue,'" Williams admits, "those stars are almost in bad taste, but they're compelling. They make you look. Corny finds a lot of my decisions crass. And I agree they are. But they're commercial, and this should be a

CORNY —
NOTE: THESE SPOTS ARE AN ANIMATORS NIGHTMARE AND WILL ADD LITTLE · EXCEPT SHIMMER + BOIL — THIS IS THE BEST SOLUTION.

commercial, compelling film that's going to entertain anybody who is going to see it. What I love to do is take a thing and go very far with it. If you're going to charm somebody, go all the way with charm. If you're going to scare them, go all the way in scaring them."

By the summer of 1976 Corny's contract was up, and at Williams's insistence he was hired as a freelance animator on the film. His animation drawings, some involving the ship at sea, were as detailed as his atmosphere sketches. Williams picked "an enormous fight" with him by telling Cole he "didn't know how to animate." The argument was staged by Williams to prepare Cole for "the relief team of assistants and the inevitable changes they would make in his drawings."

Soon after, however, Cole submitted a scene of Raggedy Ann, Raggedy Andy, the Camel, and Babette on the Pirate ship that was so perfect in staging and animation that when Williams saw it on the pencil test reel he thought it had been animated by Hal Ambro, the Babette specialist. Williams "ate crow" and phoned Cole to apologize.

Corny admits he's "not very tactful. And I'm awfully stubborn sometimes and very, very self-critical." Despite personal and professional clashes, Williams declares, "Corny is worth it." To one staff member who early on in the production wanted to fire the "mad artist," Williams said, "If we have to, we're going to jump through hoops to work with Corny."

For, after all, both Williams and Cole were working toward the same goal: perfection. "There have been emotional problems," sums up Corny Cole, "but looking at the overall thing, I've enjoyed the project."

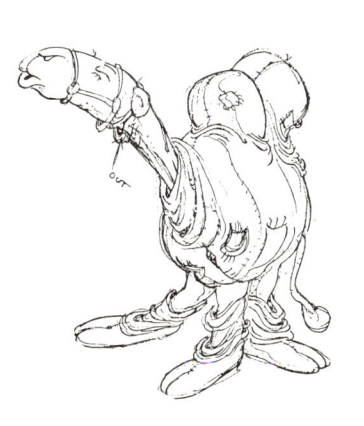

WOULD YOU TRUST YOUR PICTURE WITH THESE MEN? → PRODUCER

RAGGEDY ANN

CHAPTER VII

Auditioning for Bobbs-Merrill/ITT

I feel I have learned to go the distance.

—*Richard Williams*

A meeting was scheduled for February 20, 1975, in a screening room at 1600 Broadway: producers Horner and Osterman were to introduce Richard Williams, their choice to direct *Raggedy Ann & Andy*, to top executives from Bobbs-Merrill/ITT.

It was to be an important event, as Williams well knew, and he had prepared for it for a month. He had assigned Corny Cole to prepare character designs and atmosphere sketches to give a demonstration of the visual style of the film; he had arranged to screen some of his award-winning titles and commercials as examples of his own high-quality production values. Finally, to demonstrate how the Gruelle drawings would be animated, Williams had decided to hire New York animator Tissa David to animate forty feet—approximately 25 seconds—of film.

When David was contacted at the end of January, she agreed to animate the test, but only if she was given a scratch track—that is, a rough version—of music to animate to.

Williams's choice of Tissa David for this crucial pencil test is a good example of his talent for perfectly choosing animators, those so-called actors with a pencil, for the right roles. Williams had never worked with David, in fact had met her only once, but he knew she had been Grim Natwick's assistant for twelve years, and he had seen examples of her work, mostly in John Hubley's films. He was particularly impressed by one scene in Hubley's *Cockaboody* (1973), a film about children's fantasies, for which David was the sole animator. Williams, analyzing her abilities in that film, thought: "A. She's got perfect taste. B. It was beautifully timed and sort of mature. C. It was tremendously warm. And artful. And female."

Williams's choice worked out beautifully, not only for the test film but for the full production of *Raggedy Ann & Andy*. It was Tissa David who would

(*Opposite*) Richard Williams's caricature of himself (*left*), Joe Raposo and Richard Horner.

key the whole production's approach to the two main characters, Ann and Andy; she would "break the back," as Dick put it, of the problem of finding the true personalities for the stars of the film, especially Raggedy Ann herself.

A soundtrack of Joe Raposo singing to his own piano accompaniment was hastily recorded, timed, written onto exposure sheets and given to David. A week later, she delivered her three hundred or so drawings to camera, five days before the Bobbs-Merrill meeting.

The day of the audition arrived. There was a positive, hopeful ambience to the meeting. Williams, his survival instincts to the fore, kicked things off with a short speech ("I've only been on this a short time"); then the reel of his lavishly animated titles and commercials was screened. "Finally," said an ITT executive, "we have found someone on a level with Raposo."

Thus began a series of meetings. Williams began "setting up systems," planning the production in earnest. The first problem was to find a studio in which to make the film—a facility, a "barn." Williams suggested that Horner and Osterman set up their own studio, "an independent entity like you would use for a live-action film," in California.

The producers laughed nervously. "We'd have to have our sanity certified if we went into something we didn't understand," said Lester Osterman.

"It's easy," countered Williams. "I'll show you how it works."

Why in California? they wanted to know.

"From my investigation," answered Williams, "there is no feature cartoon studio in New York, and very few individuals familiar with feature cartoon production or even high-quality animated TV specials. Most 'studios' are very small groups handling production of TV spots—a very different ball game from feature production.

"If we link to any other studio, they will only have to expand and set up roughly what we could set up, and their fee will deprive the production of money needed for the job."

In addition, Williams wanted ten top animators, and most of his choices were on the Coast. "We need Art Babbitt," he said. "We need Emery Hawkins, Charlie Downs, Irv Spence, Hal Ambro, John Kimball, Peel, Chiniquy, Natwick . . ." He spun off a roll of names, mentioning only one New York animator, Tissa David, in the list.

The producers blinked. They had never heard of these people.

Then the showman in Williams took over, and he "put the scare in them" about quality. "We are competing with Disney in his own backyard," he said. "But we are trying to do it with one-half the money and one-half the time that they require to do a feature."

It was true; initially *Raggedy Ann & Andy* was scheduled for completion in little more than a year. This would be adequate for a limited-animation feature such as the *Peanuts* series, where minimal design and movement were all-important and no attempt was made to flesh out character or animation. But for a feature intended to match Disney at his greatest, a high budget and careful planning were necessary. The figure named was little more than Walt Disney spent on his first feature, *Snow White,* almost forty years ago. Today the cost of a Disney animated feature is moving toward seven million dollars, and the film takes three or four years to complete.

"Do you know," Williams asked ominously at one meeting, "that the ground is littered with the corpses of producers who tried to take Disney on his own turf?" He then ticked off the names of several animated feature disasters, including *Gay Purr-ee* (1962), *Magoo's Arabian Nights* (1959), *Shinbone Alley* (1970), and *The Phantom Tollbooth* (1969).

Someone mentioned the success of Ralph Bakshi and his features, i.e., *Fritz the Cat* (1972) and *Heavy Traffic* (1973). Williams replied, "Have you seen any of them? There's one playing right now called *Coonskin,* and I invite you to go see it and then tell me if that's the kind of thing you want. I'm not talking about content but production values. If you want Bakshi, you better hire him and forget about me."

Williams tried to reassure the now uncomfortable executives. "I can do it!" he beamed. "I can make this a feature film that will at least qualify to stand beside Disney's work.

"I can honestly say that my understanding and feel for the ingredients in the *Raggedy Ann* picture assure me that the bases are loaded for a sure-fire success. This project has always had that mysterious something to it—which I understand to be the correct ingredients, the right mix of balanced elements. We have to get the right people, first of all, then carefully ration our special-effects production scenes and keep complication to a bare minimum—and calculate that the simple excellence of our top artists will hold an audience in their seats."

Williams, with Raposo in agreement, suggested that the soundtrack and perhaps some "finishing up" be done in New York, but again he strongly recommended setting up a studio in Hollywood.

Soon after, Bobbs-Merrill/ITT and the producers decided to set up an independent animation studio of their own—in New York City. Hollywood would be used as a mail depot for sending and receiving the West Coast animators' scenes, but New York would be the base of the production and all the other major processes—inbetweening, assisting, Xeroxing, painting, camera, editing, and so on. The reason given for the choice was that New York was closer than California and therefore offered the opportunity for greater "artistic and quality control" of the production, as well as offering opportunities for employment to New York artists and craftsmen.

Williams worried about how to get the equipment and how to train the personnel he would need in New York. Nevertheless, he accepted the decision. "I can do it," he said once again. He reiterated his plan to use a

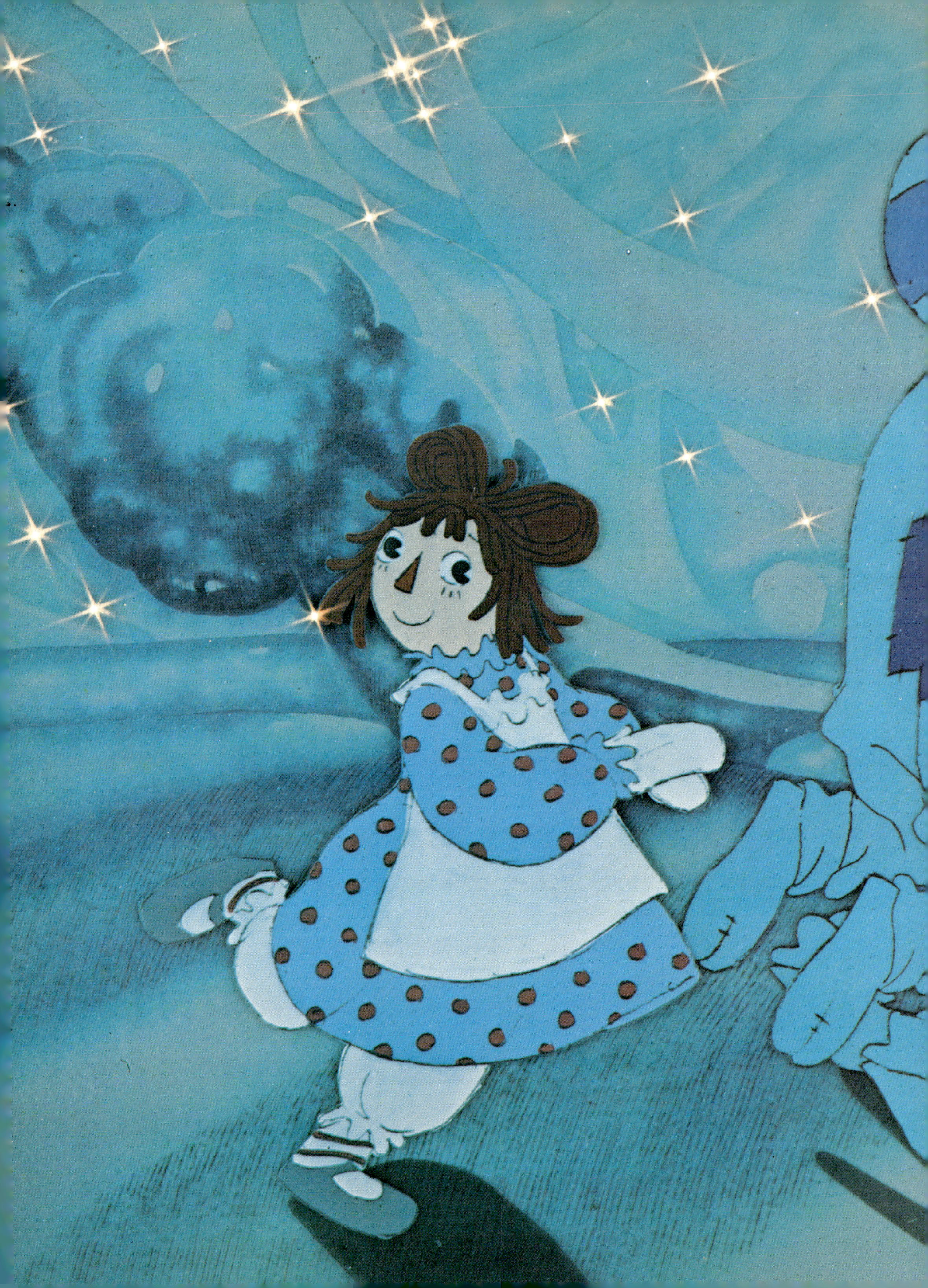

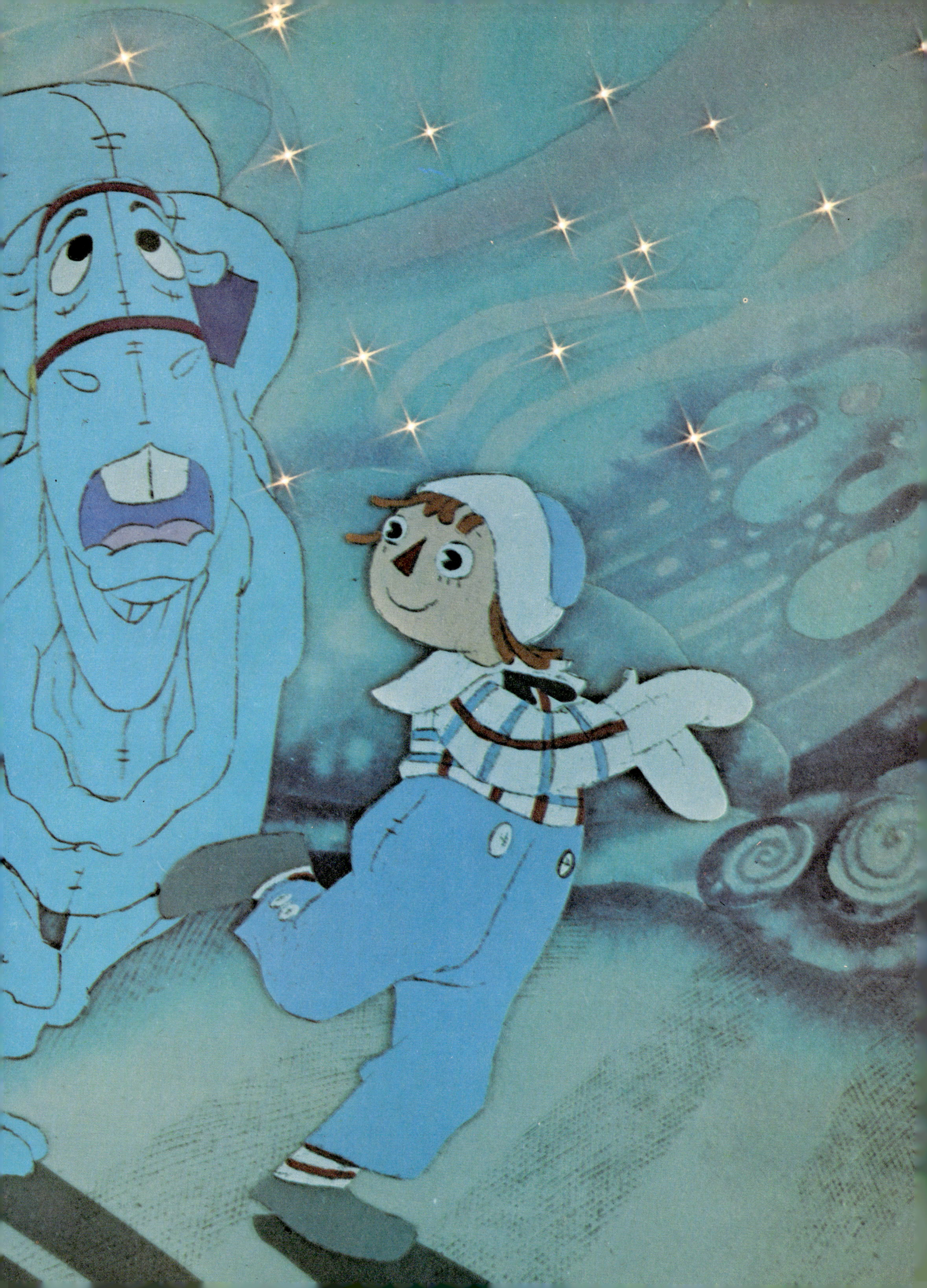

"commando team" of West Coast animation pros to make decisions fast and to "correct our mistakes immediately when we make them." He also suggested they hire an experienced production manager and recommended a friend for the job.

It was agreed that Williams would divide his time on the production three ways: approximately two weeks in Los Angeles, two weeks in New York, and then about ten days in London to attend to his own studio business, then back again—the length of his stay in each place ultimately to be determined by the problems he would encounter.

His plan was to launch the film March 1, 1975, with Corny Cole working for three months on planning and drawing the storyboard. Then three months would be devoted to recording the music and voice tracks while the script was being perfected as they went along. In June the elite crew of animators would begin experimental animation, setting up the characterizations of the main characters; their work would serve as character models for the full crew of animators who would start in February 1976.

By the end of September 1975, Williams continued, a Leica reel (story sketches and pencil tests in synchronization with the soundtrack) of the entire film would have been shot in color. "One of the functions of the Leica reel," explained Williams, "is to expose the dead or fatty areas."

Williams's full crew would ram the animation and work at good speed through the winter. Most of the animators would leave at the end of May; the elite crew would continue ramming till the "last shoot" was in to the labs at the end of August. A finished print would be delivered to Bobbs-Merrill/ITT on September 11, 1976, in plenty of time for a Christmas opening.

Williams's grand plan for the production passed Bobbs-Merrill's inspection, but an ITT executive predicted, "Murphy's Law will get you, and you will finish slower than you expect. You'll see—you'll need three more months than you've figured on."

Unfortunately the prediction came true.

Williams gave Murphy's Law as "Anything that can possibly go wrong will go wrong, and at the worst possible time." Whatever it is, it operated at the beginning and the end of the production. There were difficulties setting up the New York studio, tardiness in getting contracts to animators, lateness with storyboards and layouts and in finding adequate working space, and problems with building equipment, from desk shelves to Xerox and camera machinery. There were staff changes, and there were difficulties in trying to train newcomers in the various animation crafts.

During March and April, Williams was in London, then returned to New York in May to work with Joe Raposo, polishing the final version of the script for the recording sessions, for which Raposo was creating the orchestrations.

When these two superenergetic superegos meshed their talents, it was instantaneous combustion.

Williams on Raposo: "I've met my match with Joe. He's a total master of his technique. He can do anything. He can write stuff in a flash if he needs to but he agonizes over stuff. He can't work if it's not right, and he's very analytical. We would start at eight and end up at three or four in the morning, and he always said I went to sleep first."

Raposo on Williams: "Dick and I are cut from the same cloth. We come from the same school of having paid our dues. He's done the grubby little advertising art, and I've done the grubby little commercial type of thing.

"But I'll tell you something. I will say unequivocally that Richard Williams is a genius and I am a genius. Now, that and fifty cents will get you on the IRT!"

PART THREE:

COMING TO LIFE

RAGGEDY ANN AND ANDY
WILL STAR IN MOVIE

New York (AP)—One of the offerings of Americana planned for the Bicentennial is a movie, for release in the fall of 1976, starring Raggedy Ann and Andy.

The film, which will be animated, is already in the works, according to an announcement made here. It also is said, by its director, Richard Williams, to bear no relation to the animated cartoons seen on TV on Saturday mornings. Williams said it is meant to stack up well in comparison with the best of the Disney feature-length animated films.

AP NEWSFEATURES
June 4, 1975

Joe Raposo conducting.

CHAPTER VIII
Recording the Soundtrack

> It's a wonderful track. It's a top Broadway soundtrack for an animated feature.
>
> —*Richard Williams*

Just in from London and plagued with jet lag, but with his incredible energy welling up and radiating in almost visible waves, Richard Williams rushed down the halls of Media Sound, Inc., a recording studio on West 57th Street in New York. It was May 1, 1975, the first of five days that Joe Raposo had set up to audition actors and actresses for the voices of the *Raggedy* cast of characters.

Williams was afraid he might be late on this important day, but there were other reasons for his being on edge. He realized what a major element the voice is in defining a unique and memorable cartoon personality. (Try to conjure up Mickey Mouse and Donald Duck, for instance, without their distinctive squeaks and squawks.) He was aware of how a good soundtrack can inspire and spur on animators, giving them an aural springboard from which they can leap past graphic clichés into truly inspired moving cartoons.

Most worrisome to Williams were vocal problems unique to this production: how *do* you go about giving a voice to a gigantic taffy pit or to a beanbag? How does a frustrated two-inch-high king with a Napoleon complex sound? Or a slightly nuts, blue cloth camel?

And how do you choose voices for such legendary characters as Raggedy Ann and Andy? Generations of children have read the stories, cuddled the dolls, and created voices for them in their minds. How does one tread on these personal versions of the Raggedys without destroying the bond between the characters and their audience?

Williams quickly scanned the dozen or so actors waiting patiently to be called for their turn before the microphone. When he reached the *Raggedy Ann* staff waiting for him in the "demo room," he realized he had seen what he took to be a good-luck omen. "I think I'm going crazy," he said to Joe Raposo. "I just saw someone out in the hall who *looks* like a camel!"

Actor Fred Stuthman, the voice of the Camel with the Wrinkled Knees.

(*Opposite*) Fred Stuthman demonstrates how the Camel might trip the light fantastic.

The graying, lanky actor Williams was referring to was not just another pretty camel-face. Fred Stuthman had parlayed his long, sad visage and six-foot-four frame into a consistently busy career as a character actor on Broadway, in television, movies, and repertory theater, and his deep but flexible voice had been heard for eighteen years as an actor-announcer on three radio networks. Stuthman had played a lot of parts and attended a lot of auditions, but this one was different: "I knew the role was going to be a camel, and I didn't quite know what to do," he recalls. "But I figured I'd have to do some corny, off-beat voice."

When his turn came, Stuthman entered a soundproofed studio just big enough to contain a tiny glassed-in booth for the staff, as well as a spinet, an accompanist and a stand-up mike for the actors. He was asked to read some Camel copy from the script and to sing a song.

"With a clue that it's a camel, I wavered between 'Road to Mandalay' and 'Hindustan.' I finally wound up with 'Road,' doing it in a nasal quasi-Mel Blanc voice. [Mel Blanc is the voice of Bugs Bunny, Porky Pig, and many other Warner Brothers cartoon characters.]

"After I had sung the song once, someone—Dick or Joe—said, 'Can you do it country-western?' So I went into 'Road to Mandalay' Nashville-style, very broad. Apparently it clicked right away, and the laughter, the hoots were so loud in the booth that they overloaded the circuit on the talk-back from the microphone and they couldn't use it from then on. For the rest of the auditions that day they could only yell through the glass." Stuthman got the job.

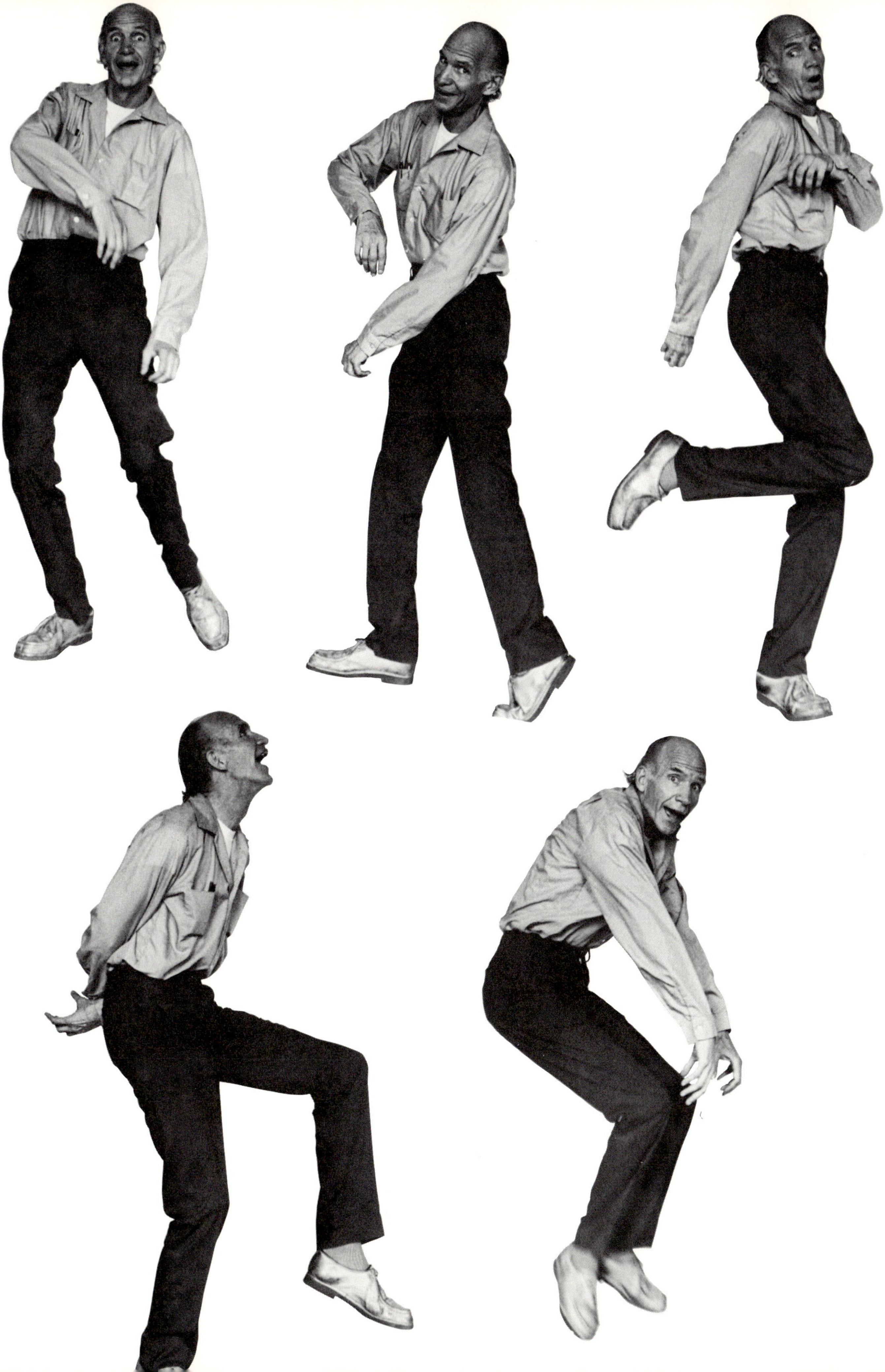

Mark Baker, starring in Leonard Bernstein's *Candide* on Broadway that season, auditioned the same day and proved to have the boyish, spunky voice Raposo and Williams felt was needed for Raggedy Andy. Apparently the good omen was working, for on that same audition day the voice that eventually was used for Raggedy Ann herself was found. Twenty-five-year-old Didi Conn, a vivacious child-woman with the voice of a sexy frog, had acted successfully in the lucrative, extremely competitive New York TV commercial market. In 1974 she moved to Hollywood for, in her words, "fame, fortune, and more pulp in my orange juice." After a slow start, Didi proceeded to do commercials there and has been featured in two series, *Keep on Truckin'* (which she ruefully says "kept on truckin' . . .") and *The Practice*.

In April 1975 she was in New York visiting her parents. "I called all the agents," she recalls, "figuring maybe I could do a commercial and pay for the trip. So I went to this audition looking like a schloomp, thinking it was a voice-over commercial." Didi Conn's Brooklyn accent can be emphasized, diminished, or obliterated, depending on the story she is telling and the effect she is trying to reach, but her charm and warmth are unvarying.

"They asked me to sing. I sang 'Where Is Love?' and they loved it. The greatest compliment I got when I finished was 'Didi, can you take the professionalism out of your voice?' "

Joe Raposo envisioned Raggedy Ann's voice as "eccentric, but not kooky" and possessing a "young quality, yet very old. I wanted to feel that she was as young as a doll for whom a child could have a feeling could be; but the doll would, having been passed on from year to year, also have the quality of age to it, a quiet surety of personal wisdom."

Didi Conn says, "They noticed I had this gravelly thing in my voice and suggested I do more of that." So Didi sang the song again, this time in a very low register, and it came out as a cross between a growl and a purr. "That's what they liked. I guess my voice goes up and down. Dick had a signal for me to keep it down."

Casting director Howard Feuer had suggested several stars' voices for the leading roles, including Tammy Grimes as Ann and Jack Gilford as the Camel, but Richard Horner insisted non-star voices be used.

"It is my feeling," explained Horner, "that none of these animated films that advertise a star's voice pay off. I don't think people pay to see an animated picture because it has a star's voice. I think that's a reason to gloss over other ills.

"Secondly, since New York is the theatrical capital of the country, we have a great number of very talented actors here. We felt we wanted people who could *act* these characters vocally, rather than just people who did cartoon voices."

Mark Baker, the voice of Raggedy Andy.

Didi Conn, the voice of Raggedy Ann.

Didi Conn jokes with animator Chrystal Russell.

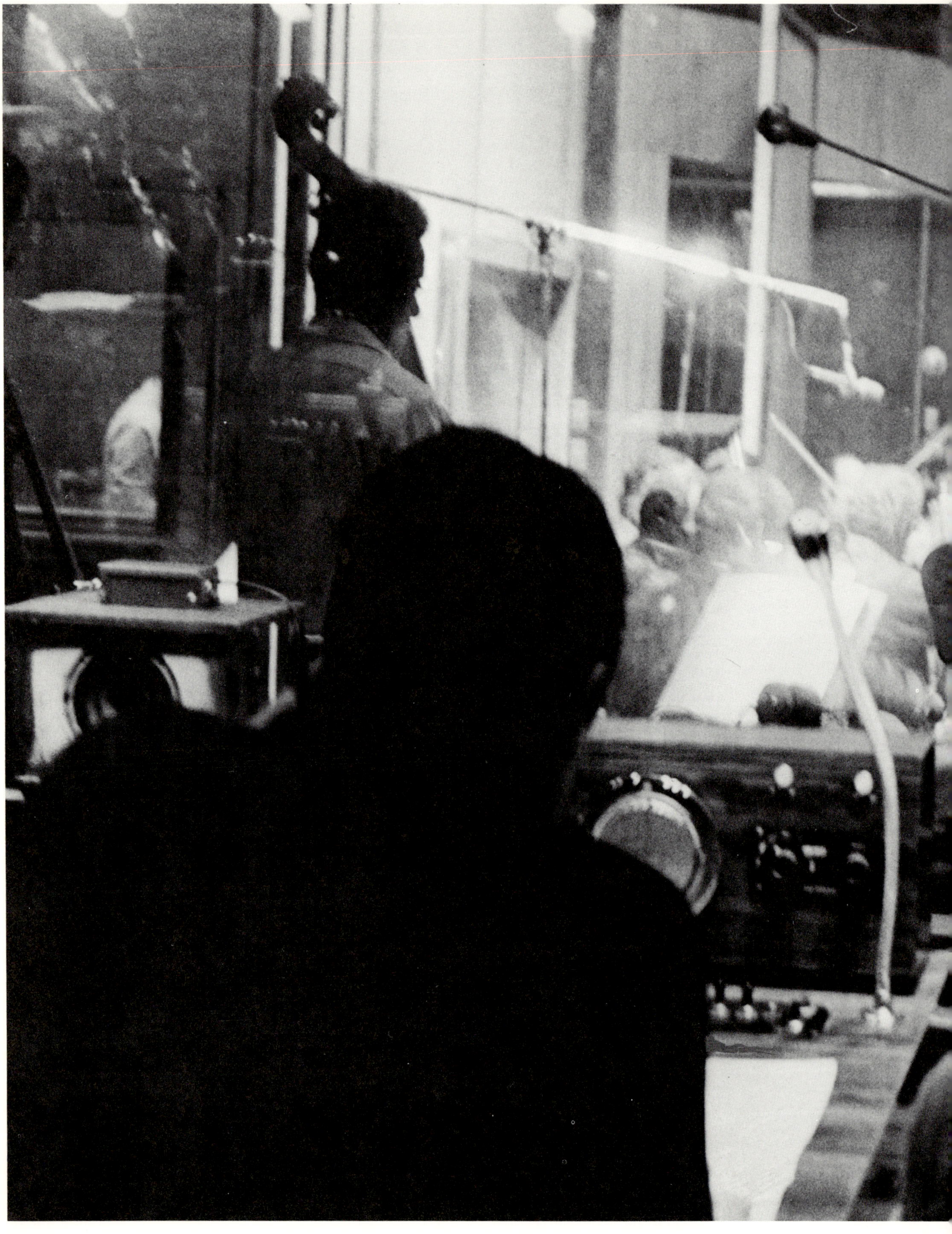

A view of the orchestra from the recording studio control booth.

Another factor was cost; Horner noted that it wasn't worth the expense to fly over, say, Peter Sellers for a day's work at his star salary, when comparable vocal talent was available at considerably less strain on the budget.

Aesthetically it was a good decision, as recognizable star-voices in animated cartoons tend to distract the audience's attention, and the characters cease to be original personalities and become easy caricatures of the vocal stars and their familiar personalities. We were always aware, for instance, in Walt Disney's *The Jungle Book* (1967) that Baloo the bear was really Phil Harris, the tiger Shere Khan was George Sanders, and King Louis of the Apes was Louis Prima. The audience began to look for Harris-isms and Sanders- and Prima-like qualities in the animation, and, unfortunately, generally found them.

"I think it was a terrific decision of Dick Horner's," says Williams. "We got so many good Broadway people of the same high level that they worked together as a team. So we had mainly a week for the voices, and no one wanted to leave at the end. It became a rep company, which is totally different from the way I've worked before with animated voices."

Over a hundred actors auditioned for the sixteen parts, and from this group Williams and Raposo formed their "rep company." The cast includes Allan Sues and Marty Brill as the Loonie Knight and Loonie King; Hetty Gaelan and George S. Irving as Susie Pincushion and the Captain; Mason Adams, Ardyth Kaiser, Paul Dooley, and Allen Swift as Grandpa, Topsy Turvy, the Gazooks, and Maxi Fix-It; Joe Silver, Niki Flacks, and Arnold Stang as the Greedy, Babette, and the Parrot; Broadway lyricist Sheldon Harnick as the Sockworm and Barney Beanbag; and Margery Gray and Lynn Stuart as the Twin Penny Dolls.

A sixty-piece orchestra under Joe Raposo's direction prerecorded the music, and the cast recorded May 29 and 30 and for four days in July at Media Sound's Studio A. Didi Conn remembers: "The first day the whole cast was there, and we all sat around and read the whole script. Everyone but Joe Silver; he was doing a TV series, *Fay*, so he came in one day and did his work as the Greedy alone. We recorded without him, using Joe Raposo's voice as a temporary substitute till they could cut Joe in later."

Dick Williams says laughingly, "We did the music and the voices in two weeks, the whole caboodle. We just banged the stuff out." There were sometimes as many as twenty-four takes for one line of dialogue, but the overall spirit of the sessions was relaxed.

Fred Stuthman recalls, "The whole thing was described to us before we did anything, so we had a very good pictorial idea of what the scene was like. As a matter of fact, Dick encouraged ad-libbing. I remember a scene on the Pirate ship. We are being upended and suspended from the yardarm, so we're screaming and yelling. I just threw in an ad-lib—'Just look at mah pore knees!'—because my character was a cloth doll specifically referred to as The Camel with the Wrinkled Knees, and obviously the knees would sag in the wrong direction. I don't know whether they kept it in or not." They did.

"If we didn't feel comfortable with something," says Didi Conn, "we could change it. A lot of writing was being done on the spot, and it was just a wonderful experience. And I had a cold that week and had laryngitis. I was upset that my voice wasn't what it should be in the song 'Home,' but it sounds like there's a lot of emotion, which there was, and because of the laryngitis there was a little bit of hoarseness. And Dick loved it.

"There was so much love and encouragement from everybody. We all did the Loonie voices, then we sang 'Hail to the King.' Dick Williams and Joe Raposo did some of the Pirate voices. I happen to respond to directors who encourage me. Dick would sit there and give me instructions like 'Keep it low.' Then after a take he'd say, 'Bravo! That was good!' Nothing was passed over."

Fred Stuthman remembers the sessions as "a wonderful group of people having fun. It's not like a play where you run, if you're lucky, some months. With a thing like this it's all over and done with all too soon. I was really quite sad when the thing wound up."

The final recording session involved only Mark Baker and Didi Conn singing 'Candy Hearts and Paper Flowers.' Sentimentality kept clouding their concentration, and they blew take after take of the song. Finally Raposo, who was feeling as melancholy as his two stars, decided to come out of the glass booth and into the studio to conduct them. Didi recalls, "He was there and really getting into it. At the end Mark and I have to sing in harmony, and I was holding one of Joe's hands and Mark held the other hand, and Joe started crying. And when I sang the line, 'Times get bad but I don't worry, 'cause I know you'll see me through,' I just looked over at Joe, and it was so touching. It was one of these rare experiences where things connect.

"I knew the project would be fantastic, because there was such love and compassion and ease in the people who were putting it together that it had to go through the whole production.

"I've never had the experience before of working on a project where everybody liked each other. There was never *any* friction—ever!"

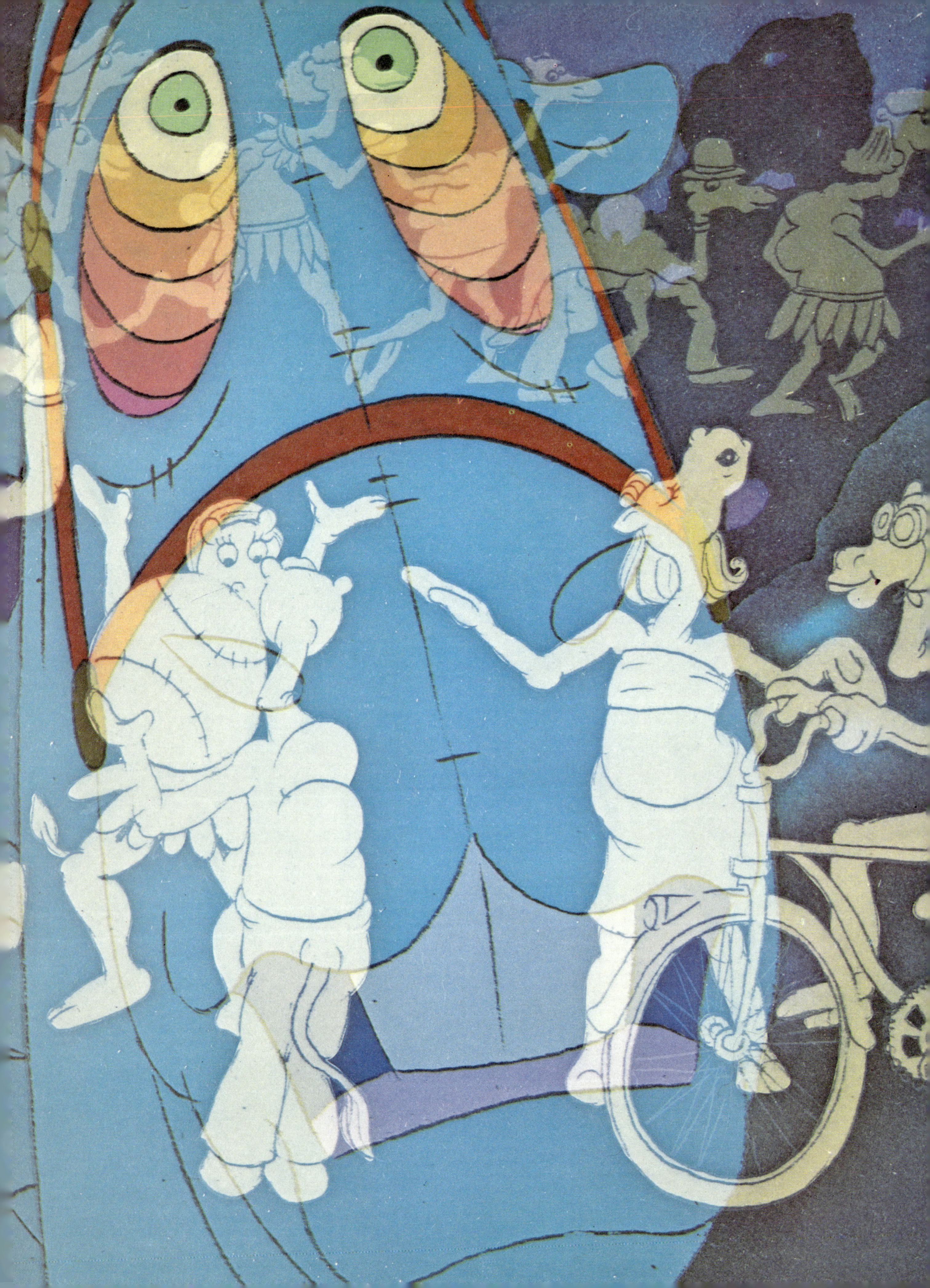

CHAPTER IX
Animation

NOTE FROM RICHARD TO ALL ANIMATORS

The dolls are all dolls. They animate like dolls, not like little anthropomorphic Disney creatures. Barney Beanbag is unable to smile, but Maxi Fix-It, who is able to smile, has a little tin moustache which moves up when he does.

While we can keep the characters reasonably plastic, we should always try to keep in mind the material the dolls are made of. Ann and Andy and the Camel work like rag dolls. Maxi Fix-It works like a tin toy. The Captain is a wooden creature. The Beanbag slumps around like an old sack, slowly and dragging. The Sockworm is an old sock with nothing inside. The Topsy Turvy Doll is weighted with peas or beans, whatever, and slumps around accordingly.

Ann and Andy should blink with difficulty. We should try to avoid all animation clichés, and try to keep as much as possible to the ingredients the dolls are made of and the limitations they have with their movements.

Okay?

Dick
June 17, 1976

Summit Meeting in New York

During the first week in June 1975, a summit meeting of the first five indispensable directing animators hired by Richard Williams was held in New York. The May recording sessions had produced enough dialogue and songs to get this "commando team" started on the animation of key scenes in the film.

These brief conferences were intended to establish the personalities of the cartoon characters and the style of full animation Williams was demanding. The work produced by this highly skilled group would serve as models for the other animators who would soon be hired on both coasts.

Art Babbitt, John Kimball and Fred Hellmich were flown in from California (Hellmich soon left the production for other commitments); Emery Hawkins arrived by train from Taos, New Mexico; and Tissa David, the only New Yorker of the five, took the subway. Fortunately, a vivid audio record of most of the meetings exists, because more than twenty hours of the private conferences were recorded by Tissa on cassette tapes.

Listening to them is a rare opportunity to vicariously participate in the creative process itself and to experience the fertile, imaginative collaboration that the formidable feature required from everyone. The tapes reveal a relaxed openness on the part of director Williams and designer Corny Cole and an obvious trust of and respect for the ideas and talents of the chosen craftsmen and -women. Their enthusiasm added a great deal to the speed with which they were able to build on the basis of the characters' personalities and tighten the script for the final recording sessions in July.

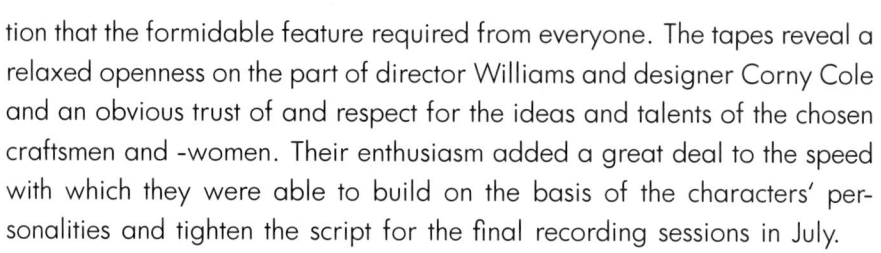

Art Babbitt was assigned a character on which a lot of hopes for stardom and audience appeal were pinned—the Camel with the Wrinkled Knees. The Camel is basically a sad creature perpetually searching for a home and, presumably, love. In order to leaven the rather pathetic persona of the beast, Corny had drawn, in the story sketches that covered the walls of two rooms, a series of "incidental" woodland creatures who would be "observers—not participating animals." Supposedly the Camel could work off these animals, which were adapted from the Gruelle books and were very cute and appealing.

Babbitt, however, immediately had reservations about these linking animals. "You want to avoid looking like a copy of Disney," he warned Corny bluntly. And indeed the similarities between these forest creatures and the woodland animals in Disney's *Snow White* and *Sleeping Beauty* were obvious. It was wisely decided to eliminate the extra animals and to develop a greater interplay between the Camel and the "two kids," as Babbitt called Raggedy Ann and Andy.

Babbitt was also concerned about a puzzling aspect of the Camel's personality. The poor beast is apparently a victim of hallucinations: he perceives Eastmancolor mirages of ghost camels. Babbitt wondered whether the Camel retreats from reality in his camel-mirages, or whether he is actually a con man who plays on Ann and Andy's sympathies (and the audience's) for kicks.

WILLIAMS: It's fishy. He sings for five minutes about wanting to find a home and friends, and then he goes and sees his vision *again*.
COLE: It's a mirage. He's crazy!
WILLIAMS: When Ann and Andy help the Camel up, it's like helping an old tramp up. Annie is like a nurse.
BABBITT: The Camel could say three Thank yous. One to Ann, one to Andy, and one to no one. You see, he's really nuts. It's like that old story: A guy tries to behave normally in an insane asylum. So the doctor says, "If we release you, what is the first thing you'd do?" The guy says, "I'd go get a slingshot and bust all the windows in this place." The doctor decides he needs more time: "We better keep you in."

Months later the doc asks him again. Same thing happens: "I'd get a slingshot and bust all your windows." Finally, the doctor needs the bed space, so he asks the guy again. "Now think hard. If we released you right now, what is the first thing you'd do? Take your time answering."

"Well," the guy says, "I'd get me a—new automobile."

"Good, good," says the doctor. "Perfectly normal. Then what?" "Then I'd get me a girlfriend." "Good, very normal. Then what?" "Then I'd take her for a ride in the car." "Good, good. Then what?" "Then I'd take her out of the car and into the woods." "Yes? Yes?" "Then I'd rip her panties off, take the elastic out of them, make a slingshot and break all your windows!" So the Camel is not normal. He's the same nut all the way through.

The Camel's song "Blue" is long and in dire need of a "hook"—some clue to make it an entertaining number that presents the Camel in all his lovability and craziness.

BABBITT: I had hoped the Camel would do a dance unhindered. Just music. Here the words and song are almost on top of each other.
COLE: What if the music plays without dialogue? But this is country-western, and that doesn't play without dialogue.
WILLIAMS: It's a long song. We should get into it fast and out of it fast. But then he doesn't do anything after that. We should bring him into the rest of the picture.
BABBITT: I'm trying to think what he could be doing that would make him more interesting than just mouthing the words.
WILLIAMS: It's a problem. It's like a Muppets song. All close-ups.
COLE: The Camel's body could do the movement. I like what you said about walking into the distance and turning and looking back. Like hippos do.
WILLIAMS: Space.
COLE: That could be part of the dance. Up over a hill, then he shakes his body. Not much cutting, a three-, four-field pan.
WILLIAMS: Just take it and go, Art.
BABBITT: I'll have to. I was hoping there would be something more tangible. It's not in the song.

Discussion continues about various personality aspects, such as the Camel's recalcitrant attitude toward events—his passive but grumpy nature—which Fred Stuthman brings out in the vocal track.

A portion of the tapes where the mystery of what to do with the long song started to get solved shows the excitement in the room as one idea began to spin off another:

In these preliminary story sketches by Corny Cole, a small rabbit (later eliminated from the final film) lands on the Camel's snout during his song "Blue."

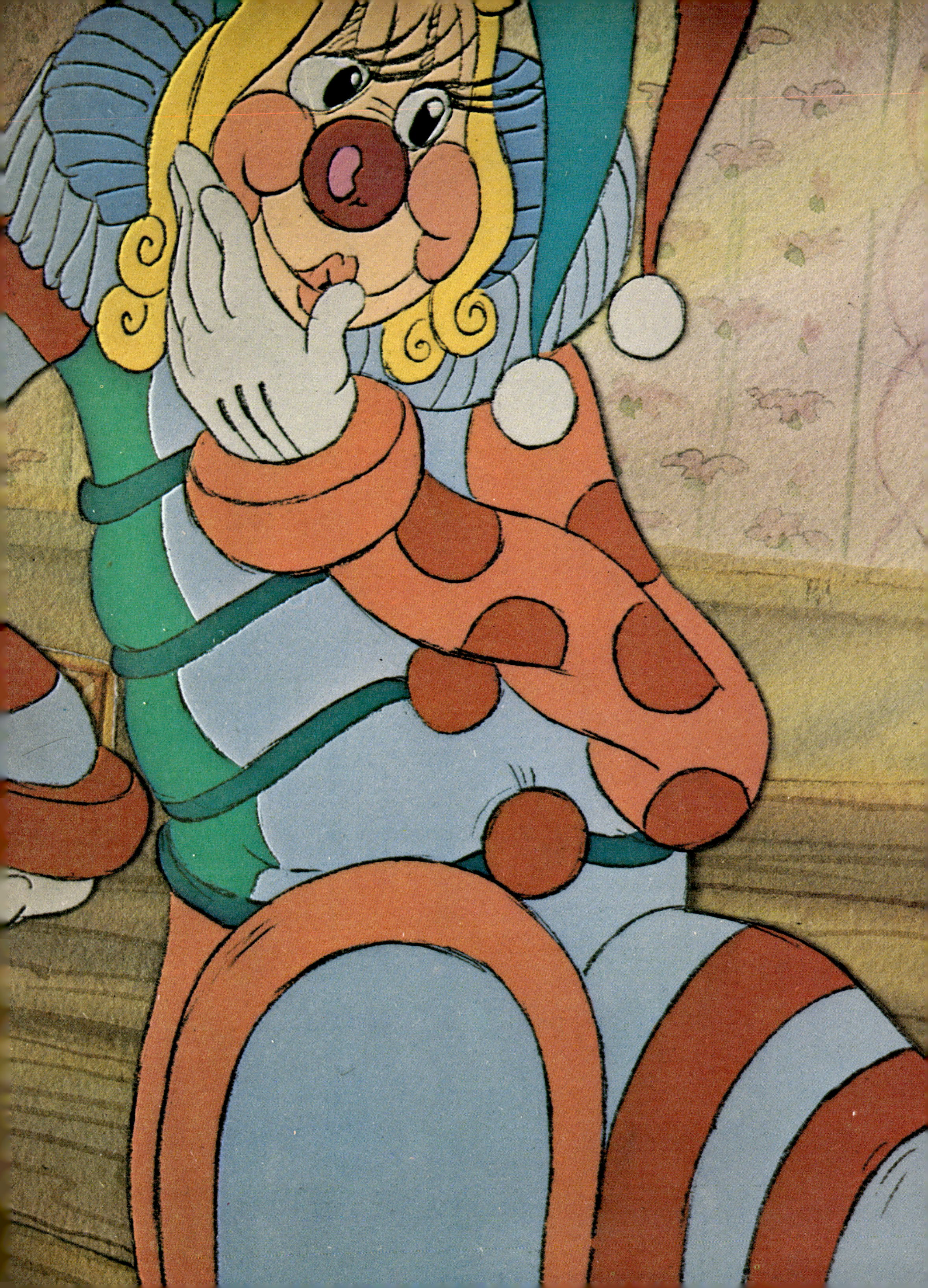

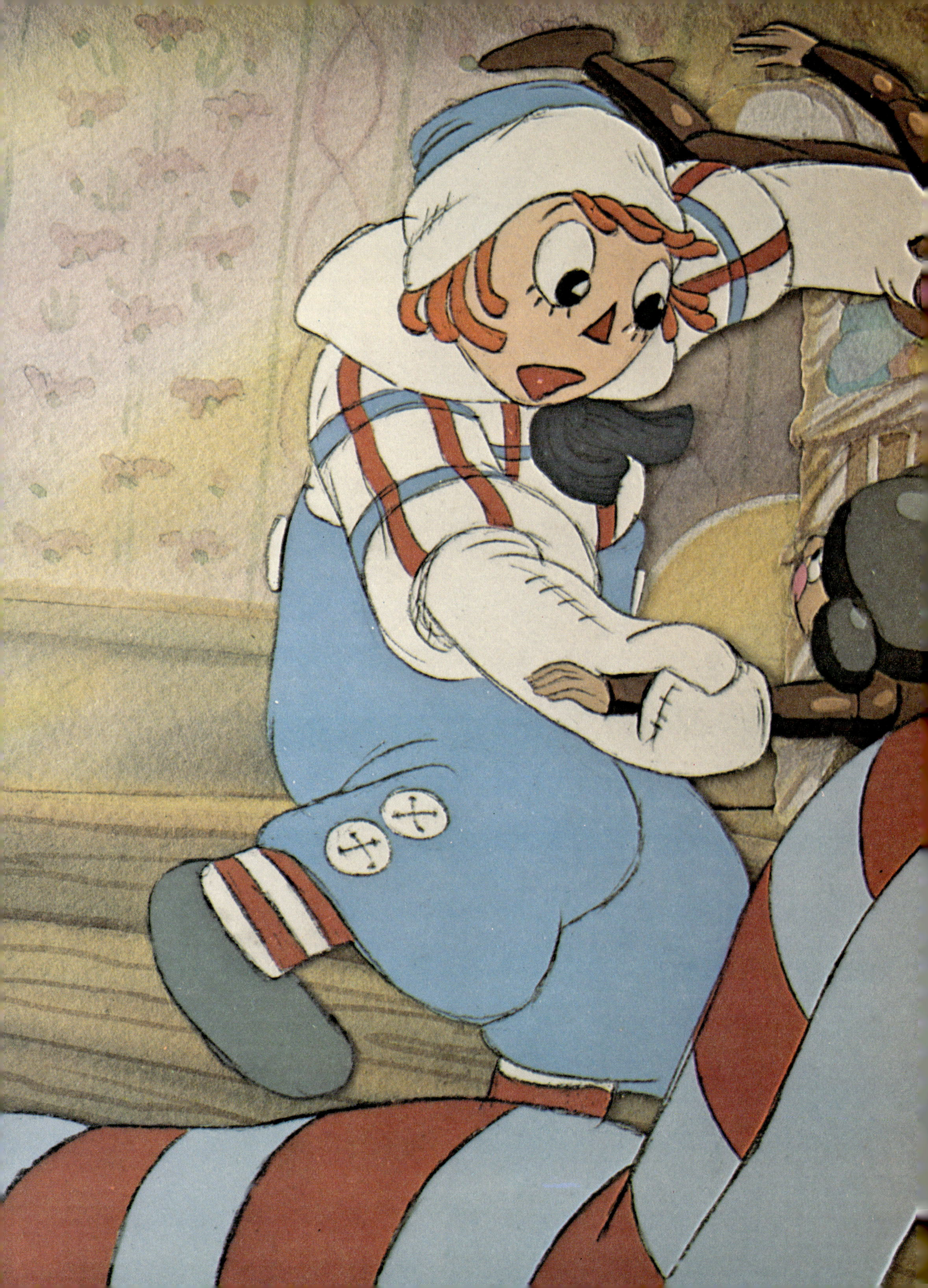

BABBITT: Let's go through the action Corny has set for the words. I have some reservations. It's gonna be a matter of inventing.
WILLIAMS: Isn't that good in a way?
BABBITT: Yeah. It slows you up, but . . . follow up on your idea that it might be two guys in a camel suit. He might be doing something here, and then his back end comes around and joins him.
WILLIAMS: And it's Laurel and Hardy with Laurel in the back.
BABBITT: That's the kick-off. But it could as well be Chaplin in the back.
COLE: It should be broad but subtle—like Disney's.
BABBITT: The front end stops, and the back runs into it.
WILLIAMS: Then the front end stretches out. Yes!
COLE: Pushes into the back end.
BABBITT: The front end is doing something. Back end comes around and joins him. The front end starts and the end catches up. Like real animals—the front foot begins to move, and then the hind leg. In this case the front part might take two or three steps before the back begins.
COLE: Like Dopey in *Snow White*.
WILLIAMS: Yes, the hitch step.
BABBITT: Also, the hind feet in some cases could get into a locked step like when two dancers walk offstage together. . . . Play the song and have Corny pick out what he visualized.
COLE: *(Drawing)* Here. Is this what you're thinking? The back one is rarin' to go. This one is not, just standin' there.
WILLIAMS: There is a danger, though. It still has to be one person looking for a friend.

Note that Williams is concerned that the basic storyline and the personality of the Camel might get lost in all the proposed choreography. Babbitt agrees that "the behavior is like two people, but it's actually one character."

Emery Hawkins was assigned the Greedy. During his conferences the soundtrack was utilized not only to help find bits of business for the Greedy, but also to visualize just what exactly the Greedy is.

HAWKINS: I think it's a beautiful track, everything in it.
COLE: You want the five Greedy versions [we drew] on the board?
HAWKINS: Yes, [photo]stat all that stuff.
WILLIAMS: Nobody has ever used animation for transmogrification, metamorphosis like this.
COLE: That's what this Greedy is. Art and Tissa's Ann and Andy and the Camel is an acting thing. This is a metamorphosis.

HAWKINS: The thing that makes me feel so good is these sweeps, because they go up. Getting dimension.
COLE: As he goes up, these things drop and go in the ice cream.
WILLIAMS: It's the Michelin man. A caterpillar, sort of.
COLE: I see him as an ice-cream man, but I love him grabbing this and swallowing that and the plate disappearing.

The soundtrack intro to the Greedy is played for the umpteenth time, as the music always stimulates the artists' imaginations.

WILLIAMS: There's dialogue over that.
COLE: Right, the dialogue stops—here.
HAWKINS: That [part of the music] just seems to call for a real—revelation! *That's* his forming.

(Replaying trombone intro to vamp)

WILLIAMS: The feeling of an undertow. Like a wave.
COLE: Like a whale.
HAWKINS: If he created a wave, then pan to Ann and Andy, and he rises in relation to that wave.
COLE: *(Shows drawing)* I've got him doing stuff like that.
WILLIAMS: Oh yeah. That's great! Then oooooooz-ing! Right up to the heavens, then [*raspberry*]. Spring sideways. Ooze up. All his little hands like a spinning wheel.
COLE: You know those frosty freezes. How they make them swirl on top?
WILLIAMS: That's it. Then go down flat. That's ninety feet—a minute right there. That'll hold you for a while.
HAWKINS: I'd rather have [the whole track] to start off with. It's better to have the mixed track.
COLE: Boy, that's a juicy number! It's either an animator's dream or an animator's nightmare.

Emery Hawkins, as we shall see, made his sequence a dream of a nightmare.

Tissa David's conferences were concerned with getting the personalities of Raggedy Ann and Andy just right—a formidable task. "You've got the sticky area of the picture," warned Williams at the first conference.

The first thing David insisted upon was "a very clear line of what's going on [in the scene]. All the little details are mine, but I want a very clear idea of the road I'm supposed to walk."

WILLIAMS: They are trembling with fear in the woods. Then we go to the flower dialogue and then Andy sings. Conversation follows, a

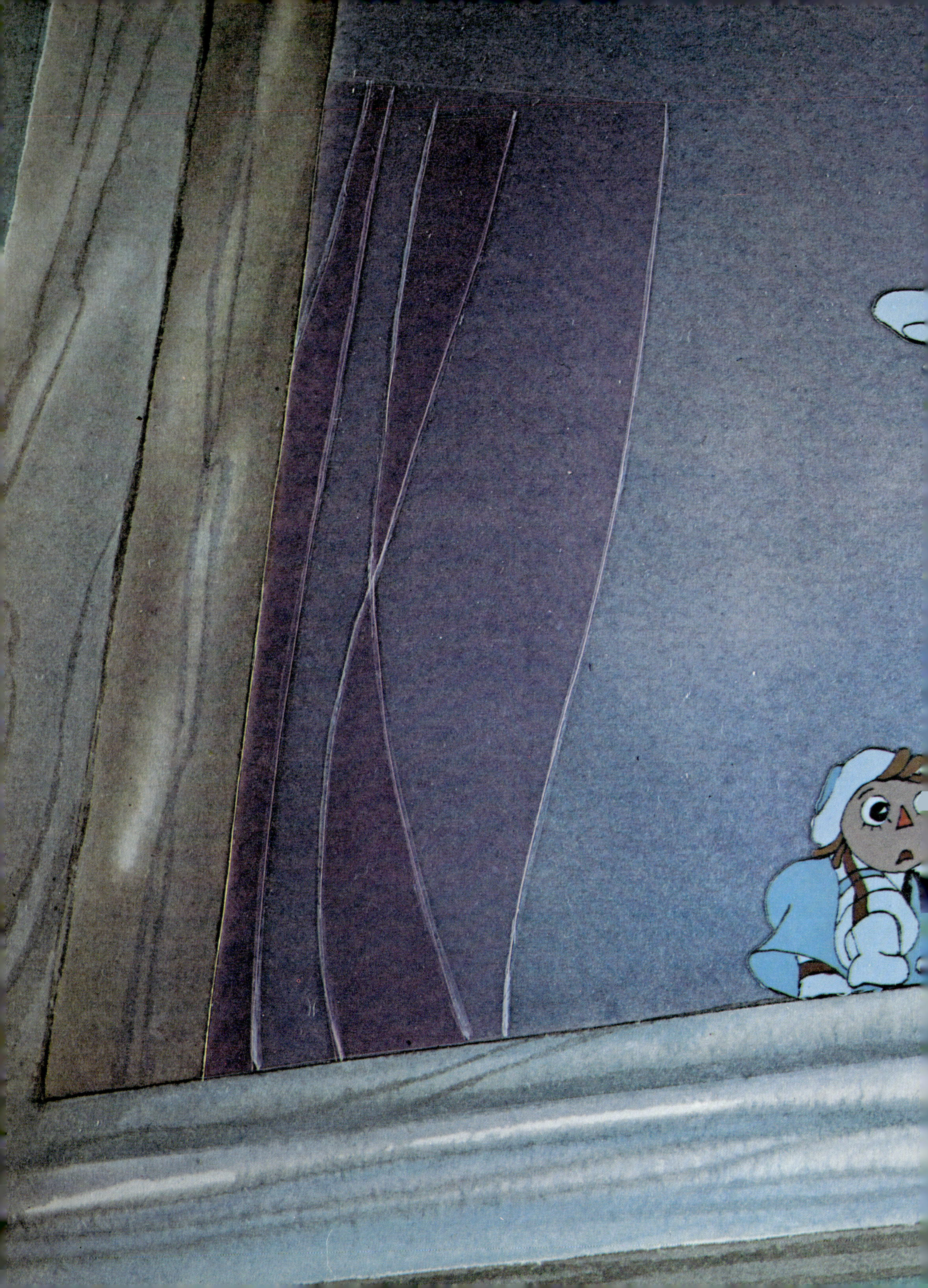

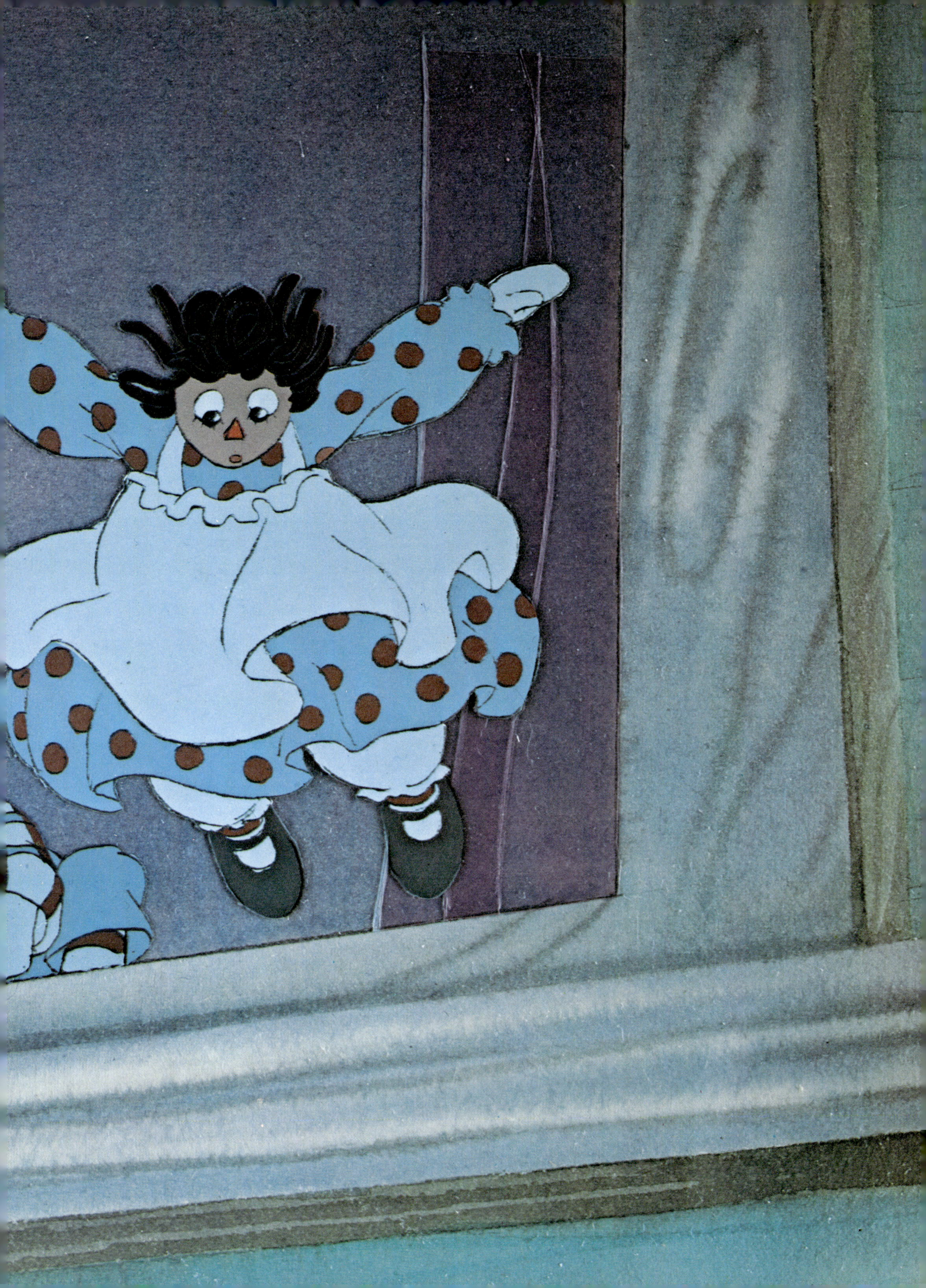

sort of recitative, then Ann sings, then the duet. They start trembling—when they go into the song they use the tremble. Medium close-up, then long shots of their environment. I don't know . . . these are only suggestions, because your test film was so good. . . . They should fall over tree trunks, constantly helping each other. That's a Johnny Gruelle thing: one always has arms around the other.

COLE: Do you have the books? That's a crucial area. This area [in the woods] is real nice, this intimacy here. Mood thing.

WILLIAMS: The problem is to have real charm without its being Disney.

DAVID: Don't worry. I can't animate Disney charm. I will do my own.

WILLIAMS: I want to avoid Chuck Jones or Disney abstractions: where you'll have two characters walking along, then up jumps a caterpillar onto the lens, or a swan goes up to the sky and we pan up to that.

DAVID: Is it possible to have no animals in this section?

COLE: I don't see anyone but Ann and Andy and real flowers and trees.

WILLIAMS: It's the mutual holding each other up. That's the key. It's like going into Central Park at night. In the moonlight you get shadows which I've never seen anybody do—traveling—that's force.

COLE: Here are some thumbnail sketches. The intimacy of him helping her. "Frightened" to me means very small. I think John Hubley does this very well. He gets intimacy from a whole room's scale.

DAVID: I like the feeling of this [sketch]. I'm thinking of the acting. They are not just wandering around. They are going somewhere. . . . You know I will have all those [drawings] around me, then I will come up with something totally different.

Tissa was planning a holiday to her hometown in Hungary for eight weeks, so she would have to lay out her interpretation of the song "Candy Hearts" for the Leica reel before leaving. She could then begin animation immediately upon her return.

She participated in several conferences with Cole and Williams and Raposo after the other animators returned to the Coast, and at one of these meetings on July 15, she tried to decipher who Raggedy Andy is (she was always secure in her ideas about Ann):

DAVID: She picks flowers. I want her to give him a whole bouquet. Now you see, you wouldn't ever think Andy would carry that paper flower with him. This means he's very gentle. I have a sweet nephew, very gentle like that. Then they have a conversation. They can stop for a minute so he can explain. Because he really

WILLIAMS:	cares, Andy really tries to make her understand—when somebody gives you something . . .
WILLIAMS:	It really counts.
DAVID:	. . . it really counts. Then they sing. I thought here, if you don't mind, I would like to do her picking up a flower, falling on her face, and Andy helping her up.
WILLIAMS:	Terrific! The more falling down, the better.
DAVID:	If I can hit another fall without overdoing it. That's why I'm not doing shivering.
WILLIAMS:	No. That's bad acting, cartoon shivering [to show fear]. Don't do it.
DAVID:	I will be so nervous. I will be calling you several times from Hungary. I'm not worrying about the deadline or going away. I just have to get started.

January 9, 1976
FROM: Richard Williams
TO: Art, Emery, Tissa, Hal, Spencer, Corny, Charlie, Irv, Grim, Retta, Paulette, Louie, Mike Sporn, Jim Logan, Dan, Helen, Carl, Mike Sisson, and anybody we forgot.

Everybody agrees that Tissa's handling of Ann and Andy, especially Ann, is the most effective so far. They are the most doll-like; they look like stuffed dolls when animated, and yet are full of personality.

She has not blinked the eyes yet, and feels they shouldn't. We do have some scenes in the picture where the rest of us have been blinking the eyes occasionally, but from now on let's not blink the eyes and see where we get to. It possibly will add to their non-Disney charm to keep them starry-eyed, naive dolls.

She also does not use tongues—only changing mouth shapes, which she tends to place low down on the face (reference her model sheets). Her mouths are also working beautifully, so let's also follow that one and see how far we get.

They *never* have teeth, either. If the Muppets can do it, so can we.

As Art is leading with the Camel, everybody should follow in that department and stick with him. Art *is* using teeth and tongue on the Camel, but somehow it works perfectly for the Camel—so that's the rule for him. And he also has eyelids and blinks.

Of course follow Emery for the Greedy—those that dare. Hopefully Emery will keep the Greedy to himself.

We'll find "rules" for the other characters as we go.

DICK

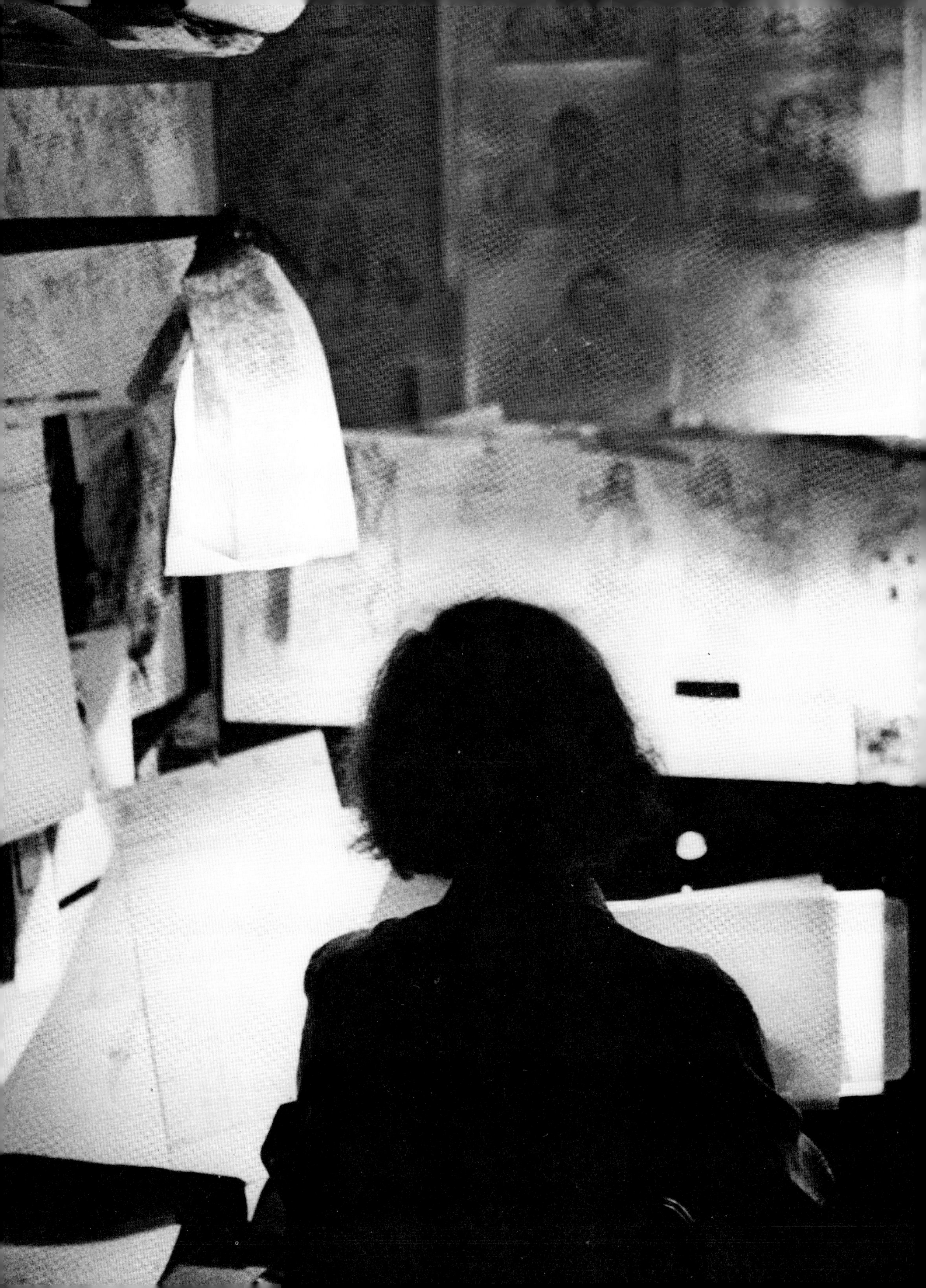

Tissa David–
The Loneliness of the
Long-Distance Animator

She knows perfectly well why she does something. She's an artist, that woman.
—*Richard Williams*

Sometimes my characters succeed to imitate me.
—*Tissa David*

"I am a loner. I always was. It's a disciplined life in a way. But I think anyone who does any kind of creative work has to have discipline," says Tissa David, in the small apartment on New York's upper East Side where she lives and works.

The apartment in an old brownstone contains bookshelves filled from floor to ceiling with art books and European recordings; the walls boast colorful dishes from David's native Hungary and paintings by old friends.

"Every time someone says that my Raggedy Ann is the best of the animators', I say, 'Yes, because I *love* her!' It's true. I think you do have to love her. Not as a little cartoon character but as Raggedy Ann. It's like a little thing that is alive. I think that's very important."

In the smaller back room, normally the bedroom, the first woman in the world to be recognized within the industry as a master of personality animation holds forth on her art. The room appears to be in some kind of organized chaos, and David is surrounded by an explosion of paper. Hundreds of drawings are piled on several small shelves and an improvised table over her bed (she is sleeping on a couch in the living room for the duration). Model charts of the Johnny Gruelle illustrations of Raggedy Ann and blow-ups of drawings from the film are taped to the walls, scene folders overflowing with animation sketches are lying on whatever space is left, and everywhere there are caricatures of herself and her co-workers—tacked to the walls, taped to each other, and pinned on the drapes that keep this room perpetually in subdued light.

Tissa David at her animation drawing board.

"Animation is *the* most creative art of all, because you are creating life. You are making a drawing come alive. You can't be more creative than that!"

Tissa David animates while she converses, her drawing table illuminated only by the light shining from underneath it. This special type of table, which all animators use, holds a metal disk containing pegbars and an opal glass insert. Under the glass is a light bulb that enables the animator to see through several sheets of paper at one time and thus gauge the consistency of spacing, size, and appearance between one drawing and the next. Tissa gingerly takes three drawings off her animation disk. The drawings are on paper that has holes punched in it to assure correct alignment when fitted over the registration pegs on the disk's pegbars. These pegs and holes are standard for the entire animation process, from animators' drawings through cel painting to camera; they assure correct positioning of the drawings throughout the production.

Tissa adds the three drawings, in their proper order, to sixty-six other drawings that comprise the complete action of the small scene she is working on. She then performs a ritual that has been part of animation since its earliest days: it's called flipping, or as Tissa David says in her charming Hungarian accent, "fleeping." She holds the set of drawings firmly at the top of the page with her left hand, allowing the bulk to rest on her left forearm. With the thumb of her right hand she gracefully riffles through the group of drawings so that they fall at an even rate and give the illusion of movement. A perfect "fleep"!

To check the smoothness of the character's movements, Tissa David flips the sequential drawings as she sketches.

ANN & ANDY   TISSA'S WORK SHEET #1

© COPYRIGHT 1975
THE BOBS-MERRILL
COMPANY INC.

NOTE TO ALL:
THESE PROPORTIONS
ARE GREAT—
DICK

Work Sheet #1, made from Tissa David's rough animation drawings.

(Opposite) Tissa David Work Sheets #2 and #3.

Raggedy Ann, during the flipping, appears to say something as she slips off a large chair onto the floor—*ker-plop!* "This is the first scene in the film after her opening close-up where she is really moving," Tissa comments. "She just flops off that chair. But this is really personality animation. You have to know a character before you can do a scene like that."

It was not the first scene Tissa had worked on in the film. Cannily, Richard Williams gave her the long sequence where Ann and Andy escape into the Deep Deep Woods to animate first; it contains over six minutes of dialogue, singing ("Candy Hearts and Paper Flowers") and dancing. Williams figured rightly that by the time Tissa got through that, she would really know who those two characters were, physically and emotionally.

It was in this sequence that Tissa set the personalities of the film's two stars. Her drawings were used as a guide to the rest of the production team, as we can see in Work Sheets Number 1, 2 and 3 from June 1975. On them Williams has made the notations, "Excellent proportions" and "Not a clean-up guide—but this is *it* for feel and other respects." In early 1976 a definitive work sheet called "The Ann and Andy Model Sheet" made the rounds of the studio; as we can see, it was based on Tissa's early work but contains "rules" to guide the assistants. ("At that stage you can kiss good-bye any further creative development," says Dick Williams, "because they are now a set blueprint.")

RAGGEDY ANN & ANDY
© Copyright 1976
The Bobbs-Merrill Co.

TISSA'S ACTION ROUGHS — March 1976
THE CHARACTER OF ANN and ANDY —
NOT A CLEAN-UP GUIDE — BUT THIS IS IT FOR FEEL AND OTHER RESPECTS —
— Dick

KEY REFERENCE — SHEET #2

ANN & ANDY — Tissa's Work Sheet #3
© Copyright 1976
The Bobbs-Merrill Publishing Company Inc.

NOTE: EXCELLENT PROPORTIONS ON ANN & ANDY
DICK

THE ANN & ANDY MODEL SHEET

"RAGGEDY ANN & ANDY" © COPYRIGHT 1976 THE BOBBS-MERRILL CO. INC

THIS

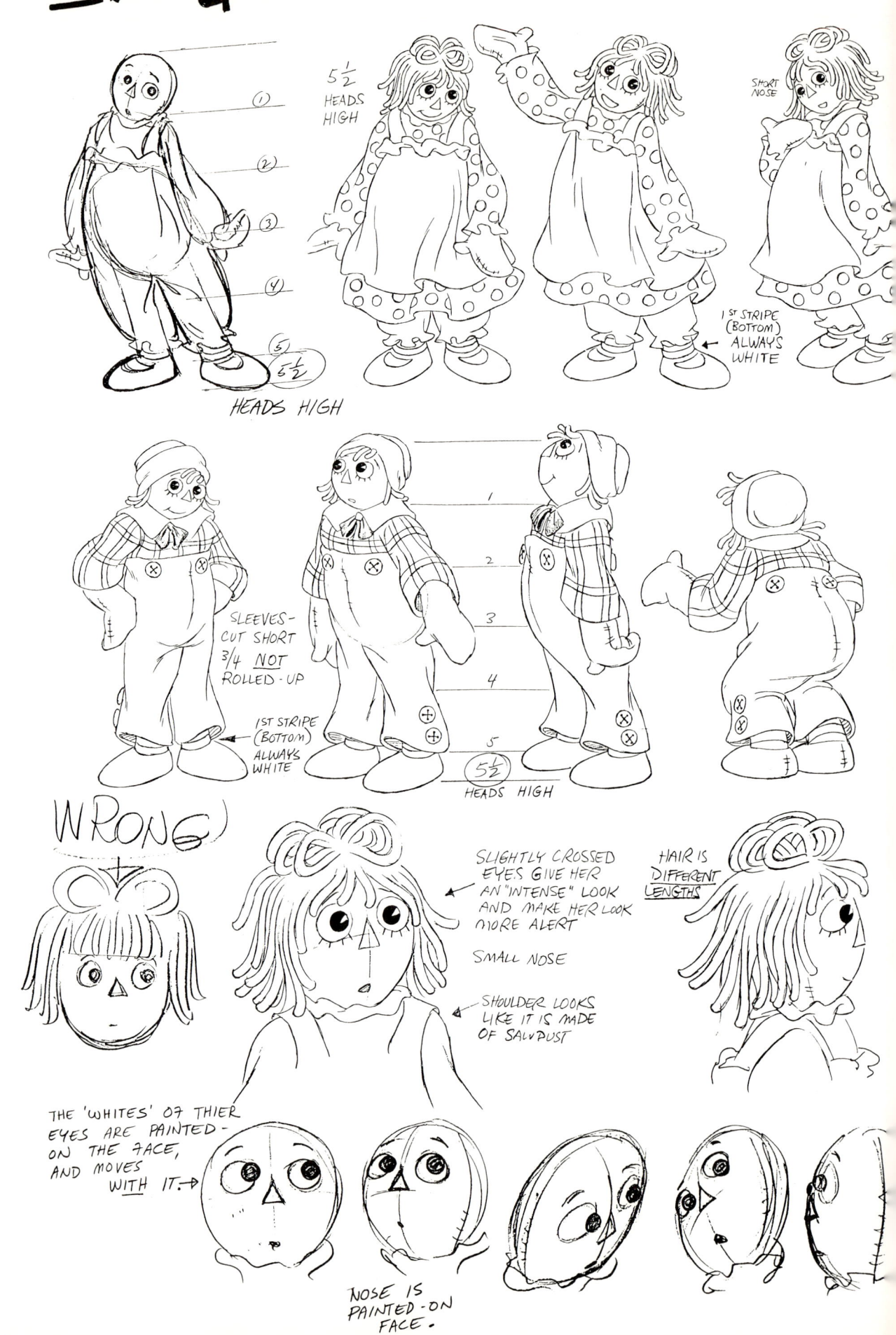

5½ HEADS HIGH

SHORT NOSE

1ST STRIPE (BOTTOM) ALWAYS WHITE

5½ HEADS HIGH

SLEEVES - CUT SHORT 3/4 NOT ROLLED-UP

1ST STRIPE (BOTTOM) ALWAYS WHITE

5½ HEADS HIGH

WRONG

SLIGHTLY CROSSED EYES GIVE HER AN "INTENSE" LOOK AND MAKE HER LOOK MORE ALERT

SMALL NOSE

SHOULDER LOOKS LIKE IT IS MADE OF SAWDUST

HAIR IS DIFFERENT LENGTHS

THE 'WHITES' OF THIER EYES ARE PAINTED-ON THE FACE, AND MOVES WITH IT.

NOSE IS PAINTED-ON FACE.

The June 1976 model sheet that defined for the assistants and inbetweeners the ultimate look of the film's two stars. Drawn by Richard Williams.

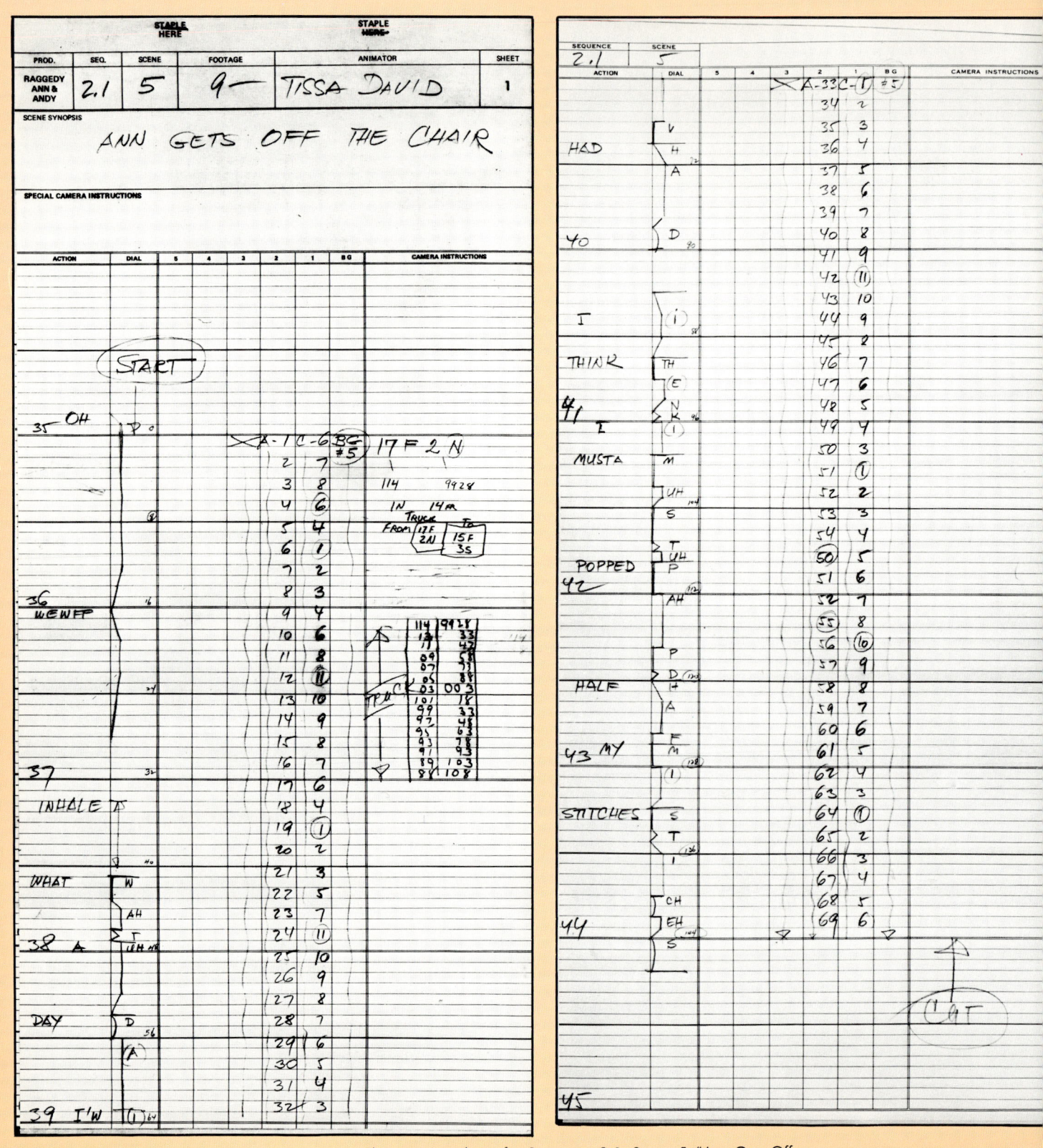

The exposure sheets for Sequence 2.1, Scene 5: "Ann Gets Off the Chair." On the facing page, twelve animation drawings by Tissa David from 2.1, 5.

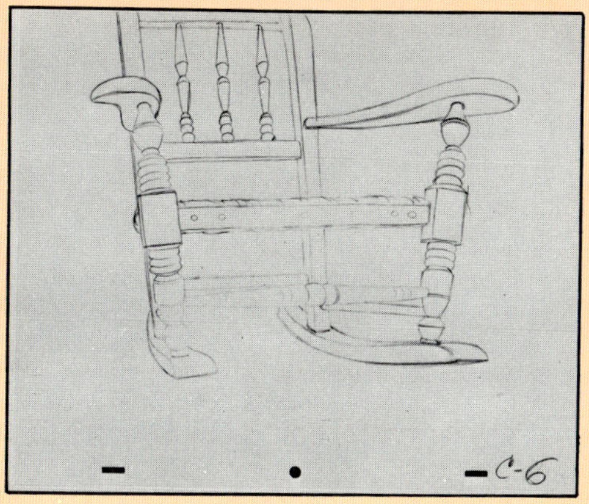
C-6
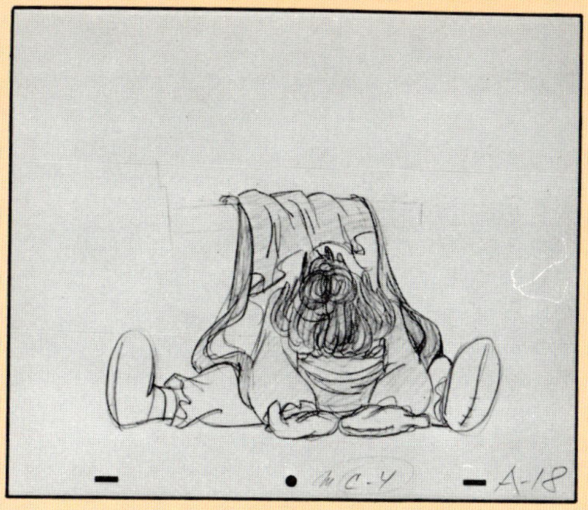
A-18
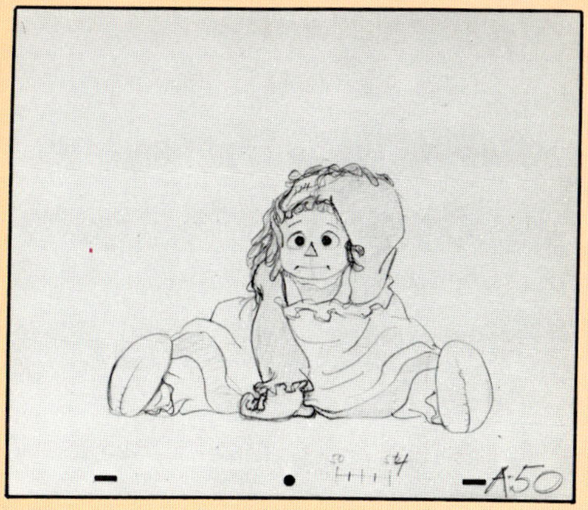
A-50
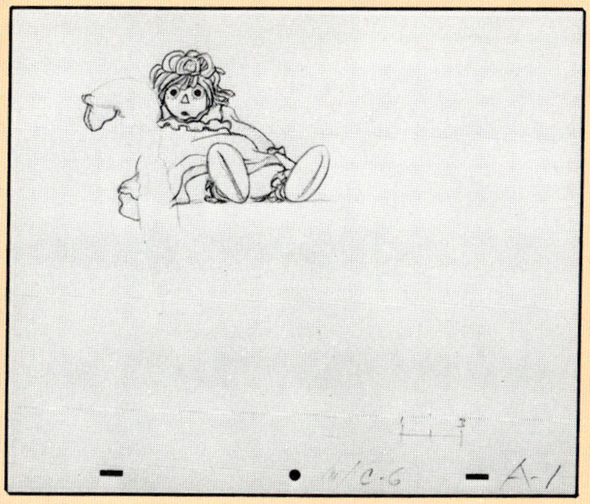
A-1
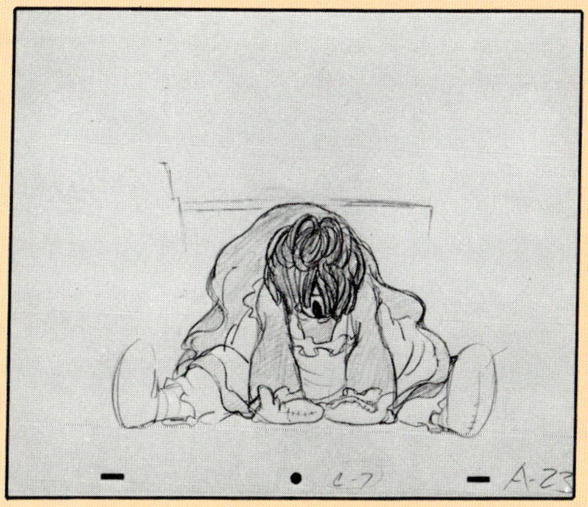
A-23
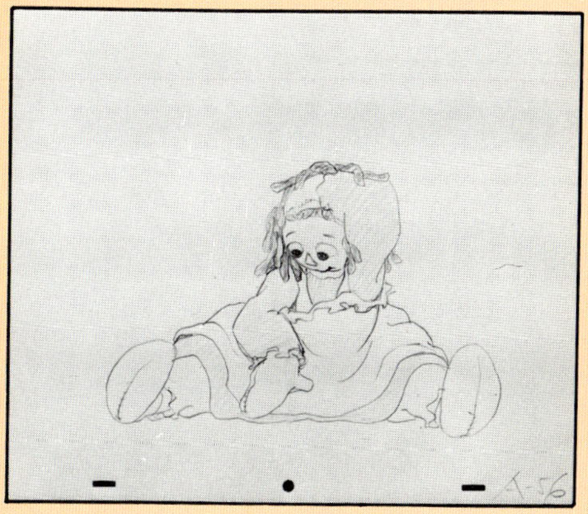
A-56
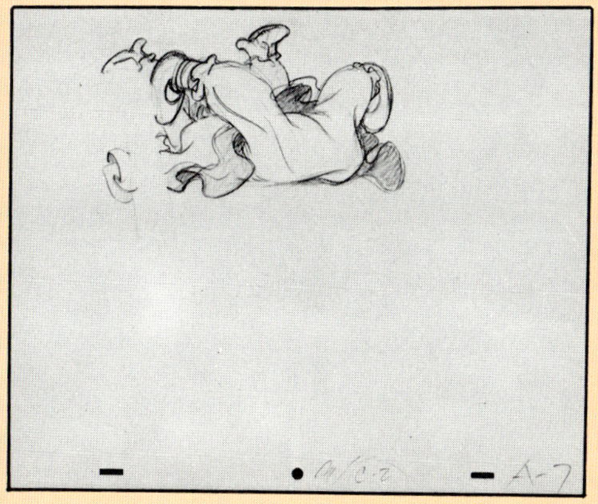
A-7
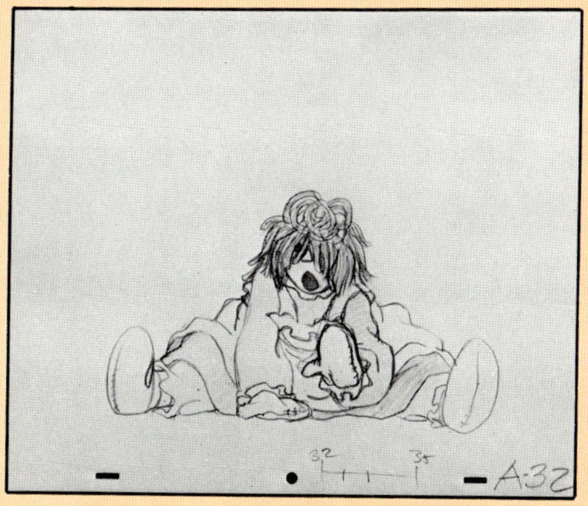
A-32
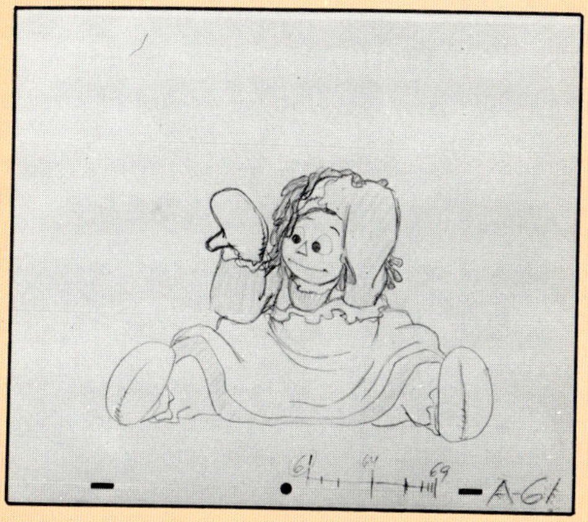
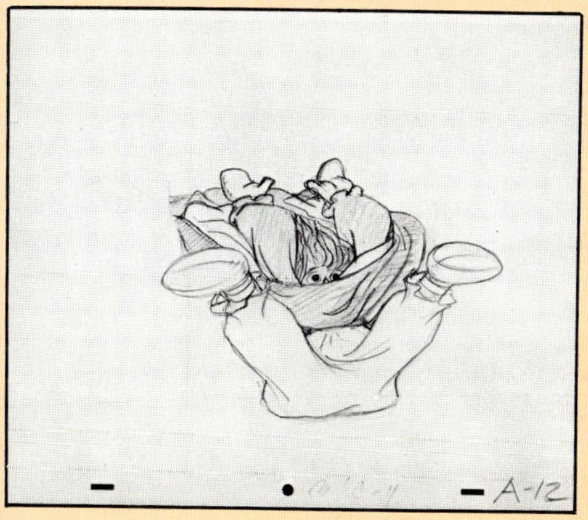
A-12
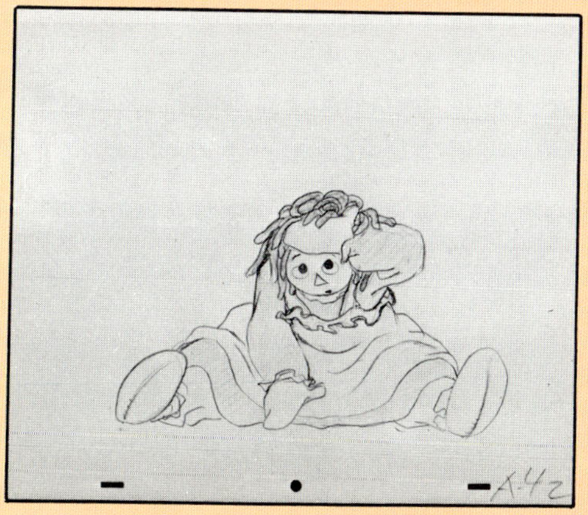
A-42
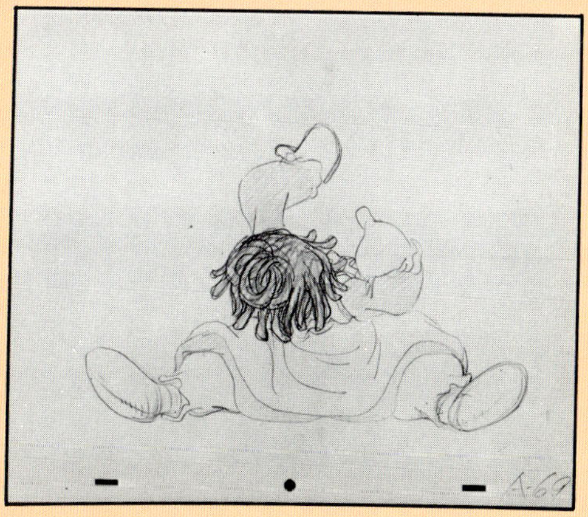

The drawings on Work Sheets Number 1 to 3 are in their roughest state because they were put down on paper immediately, as Tissa felt them. The emotions in these roughs are pure and clearly legible; the strong poses of the characters are a form of shorthand communicating these emotions to the audience. We can plainly discern Ann and Andy's fear, Ann's tentativeness, her trustfulness, Andy's bravado, the tender concern they feel toward each other, and their gay abandon as they attempt to dance their fear away. The drawing at the bottom of Work Sheet Number 3 of Andy holding up a slumped-over Ann is remarkable in its demonstration, through just a few simple lines, of the feeling of weight and strain.

As drawings, these roughs can be compared in their vitality and directness with the sketches in Japanese art known as abbreviated drawing, or ryaku-ga.

Photographed and projected onto the movie screen, Tissa's drawings reveal a superb sense of timing and a droll wit. (Observe Ann's reaction in the film to the cloud shadows overtaking her, or the unexpected sharpness in her reaction to the noise of the approaching Camel.) More difficult to describe or explain is the feeling of warmth that Tissa's animation conveys, an almost tactile sensation that must, of course, be seen to be appreciated.

An animator is very much like a Method actor in search of a character. Both utilize observation, intuition and remembered emotion in attempting to define a personality. Tissa David has made Raggedy Ann, her "little Annie," very personal and real. "I think one does oneself in every character," she says. "I even do it with Andy. I'm sure I project a lot of myself into Raggedy Ann, although she is very gentle, which I am not. Maybe I would like to be. She is very trustful—she trusts everything. That's very much me.

"She's afraid in the dark forest, and so am I, only even more so. She is brave because she is scared to death.

"Being bright or dumb doesn't come into question here, because she is like a little animal that goes purely by her emotion, intuition, instinct. She is wise, that's for sure. She is seventy years old, don't forget, so she's a wise little girl."

The vocal track was a vital help to Tissa in developing Ann's character: "Whatever I do in animation, I listen to the voice over and over and over from morning to night. Ann's voice tells me who she is. Not only the tone of the voice, but also the way she delivers lines. I like very much this voice [of Didi Conn]. Now, if there had been another voice, Annie would have been a different personality."

The voice track was recorded onto magnetic tape and later transferred to magnetic film. The magnetic film was then locked into a synchronizer and measured in frames; this process, done by film editor Max Seligman, is known as "reading" the soundtrack. The information was then written on exposure sheets, which represent every frame of film in the complete production and are used to synchronize the picture and soundtracks. By referring to X-sheets, animators are able to perfectly match their animation to the voice, music and sound effects.

Let's look at one of Tissa David's X-sheets and the drawings that match it. This is an exposure sheet for Sequence 2.1, Scene 5. Scene synopsis: "Ann Gets Off the Chair" (the scene Tissa just flipped).

Notice that the footage box is marked "9 feet." In 35-millimeter film, 16 frames of film equals one foot, so there will be a total of 144 frames in this scene. This does not mean that Tissa will make 144 drawings. Each one of those horizontal lines on the X-sheet represents one frame. You will notice she has filled in the consecutive numbers in Column Two, leaving spaces between them. This indicates that each drawing will be photographed twice ("shot on 2's"). Also notice on X-sheet Number Two that some of the numbers are repeated, so that by reusing certain drawings and shooting on twos, Tissa's action drawings of Ann falling off the chair come to a total of 69 drawings. "Naturally, it is a million times more beautiful on 'ones' [one frame per drawing]," she says, "but when you have a picture that runs over an hour and a year to do it in, then you can't. Still, I have quite a few scenes that have to be on ones."

Flashed onto the screen at 24 frames per second, these 144 frames will last six seconds; the running time for the entire feature is 86 minutes.

"BG" on the X-sheet means "background," and the background painting will be put in place first as the layers of the picture are assembled. Column One represents the level for drawings of a rocking chair moving back and forth (see Drawing C-6). Column Two is the animation of Raggedy Ann, at first seated in the rocker (see Drawing A-1).

Bear in mind that the chair and Ann, by the time they reach final camera, have been Xeroxed onto transparent celluloid and painted in various colors on the back so that they can be animated in front of opaque backgrounds that do not have to be redrawn each time.

Columns Three, Four, and Five are for extra cel levels, if needed; Tissa is not using them for this scene. "Dial" means "dialogue," and here the soundtrack reader has indicated that the actual dialogue begins 41 frames into the scene, and he has spelled out in frames the exact length of each word and of the pauses between the words. For example, "What a day . . ." takes 22 frames to say, with six frames going to "What," seven to "a," and nine to "day." Raggedy Ann's legs and dress cover her mouth as she slides off the chair, so the first time you actually see her mouth moving in lip-sync with dialogue is drawing A-23, the "ah" of the word "what."

"I start out with Frame Number One and go straight ahead," Tissa explains. "I can't animate in key drawings. I have the whole sequence posed

(*Above*) A caricature by Tissa David of herself as Raggedy Ann hangs in her studio amid model charts and typed scene-breakdowns.

(*Right*) The final color version of Raggedy Ann after she falls off the chair.

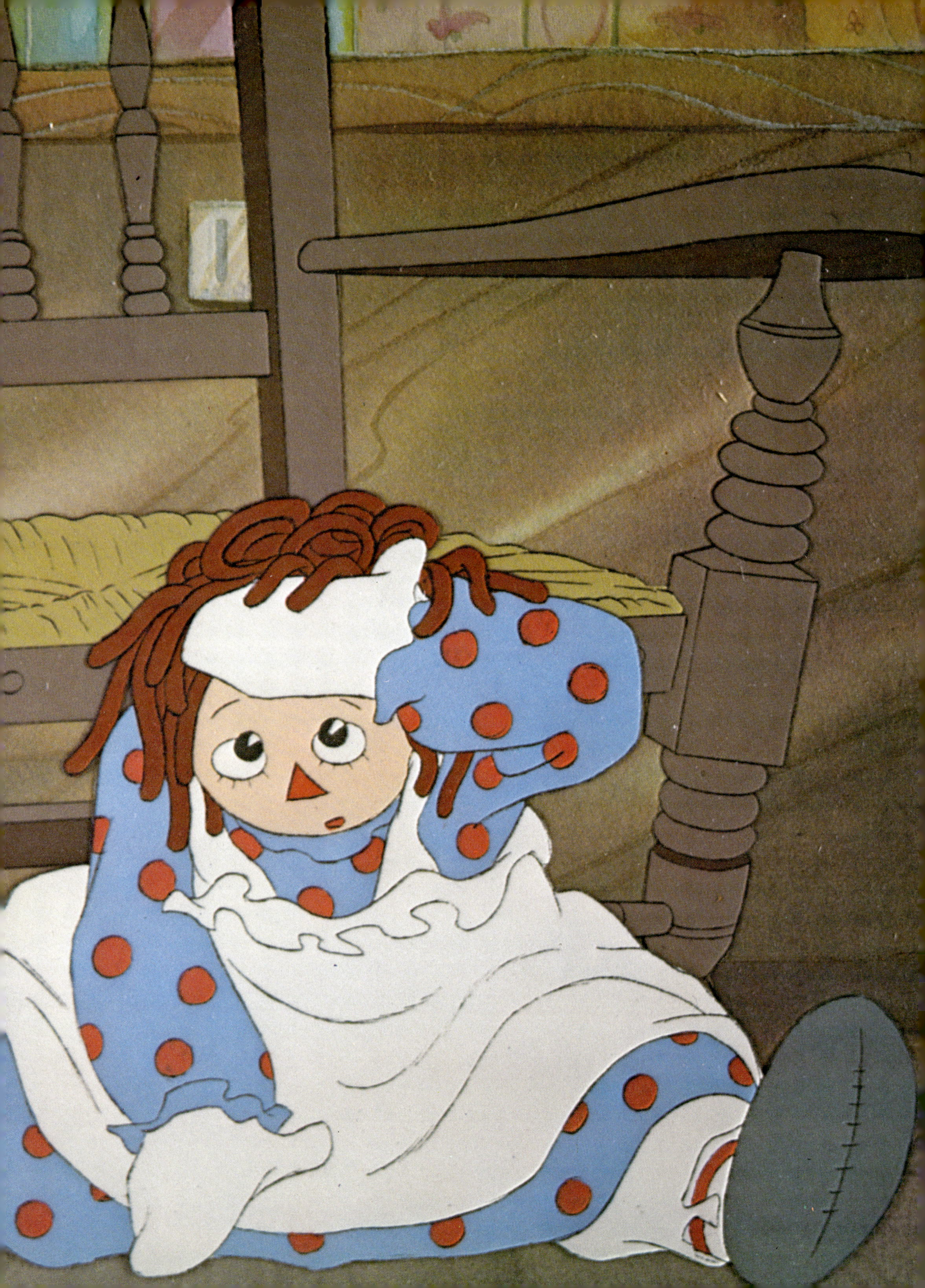

out so I know the general direction I go toward. As I go along, it changes. I work rough first, in black pencil. I put it down so black it takes me a terrible time to erase if something is wrong!

"The hardest part was animating the chair. I spent a week on that lousy chair! Because this chair has three key angles. Now, when it moves forward and back, those angles should move in perspective. This is the small doll's chair from the live-action, and I had several photos of it from different angles. If you see the scene, you'll see that the chair moves very little. It isn't erratic timing [see Column One]; it goes faster down and slower back."

In this scene Tissa uses a mannerism for Ann that she developed while animating the big "Candy Hearts" sequence—Ann pulling her hair downward or pushing it back—and the gesture has been repeated in several other scenes. "It now becomes a part of her," Tissa comments. "Now *here* [A-12], she went down *plop!* The hair is in her face [A-18]. Now she starts to talk to us [A-23]. She has to push that hair out in order to see us [A-42, A-50]. The gesture developed naturally."

Tissa stops for a moment and points out something else in Drawings A-42 and A-50: "It's a very important thing, and you will see that when you watch the film. I *always* have the character on the screen make a little eye contact with the viewer. For example, here. If she was talking to Grandpa off-screen, it somehow for me doesn't make any contact.

"Have you read *The Little Prince* by Antoine de Saint-Exupéry? The fox says to the Little Prince, 'You only know a person if you make a contact with that person.' And my characters always have those little seconds toward the audience. A director pointed out to me that I do that, and he said that it's magic. I don't know whether it is, but I think it's so important."

The other two columns on the X-sheet are the Action Column, which Williams says is for "planning notations and girls' phone numbers," and the Camera Instructions Column. Tissa explains, "Every camera move is called a 'truck.' The reason for this truck is that Annie is sitting way up there [on the chair]. Then she slides down and the camera follows her. I close in on her very slightly. She also is animated in progressive perspective, because she falls forward. And the final pose [A-69] is a very tight shot. She sort of fills out the screen."

Tissa feels that she and Chrystal Russell, the young animator in California, are the best of the animators working on "little Annie": "Chrystal is really very, very good. See, this proves a point. The only thing that Disney never understood is that to animate girls, one must *be* a girl! I do believe that. It isn't true the other way around; I can successfully animate a boy. But a man can never successfully animate a girl.

"The big advantage of Chrystal and me is that we were little girls. I think there is something very deep in women in general. Men—and this is not a judgment or criticism; it's a fact——men are generally more close to the surface. Women are much more mysterious.

"I think animation, this creation of life, is very feminine."

Tissa David was born "fifty-some" years ago in Kolozsvar, Transylvania. She grew up in Szeged, a small university town about two hundred kilometers from Budapest. Her father, Dr. Louis David, was a professor at the University of Szeged; his wife Szaniszla bore him ten children, of whom Tissa is the second eldest.

"When I was young," she recalls, "the people of the University called me 'Házi-sárkány'—the 'House Dragon'! I remember I was always very strong. I was always a leader in school and a rebel. I was never led."

In school plays she was cast always as the comedienne: "I know I am probably a frustrated actress. It was very easy for me to make a clown of myself in plays, but still I don't like the spotlight. But by animating, I am in the spotlight."

Tissa was a teenager when she saw Walt Disney's *Snow White* in 1938, and although she was "absolutely bewildered by it," she felt that "this is what I want to do. I always enjoyed animated cartoons. They opened up a world." An uncle brought her a small ad from a newspaper calling for artists to work in an animated film studio in Budapest. Tissa, who was at this time attending the Academie des Beaux Arts in that city, applied at Magyar Film Iroda and got the job: "There was no animation in Hungary before this guy started a short. I went in and had to make a test. I had to draw one cartoon character from different angles in the same pose, like a statue. So I did. I remember he said, 'I'm not a prophet, but you might be doing pretty well in this business.' "

She worked on the film from September 1943 to December 1944. The war was on and Budapest was occupied by Germany. "We had three bombardments every single day for a whole year. Eleven in the morning were the Americans, who came and bombed strategic points. Nine o'clock at night were the Russians, who were light bombers and just dropped fire-bombs on the town. And the English came around four o'clock in the morning."

Through it all Tissa kept on animating. "They never hit the studio," she says, "but they hit everything around it." On her resume she would give as her reason for leaving: "The Siege of Budapest."

After the war, she teamed up with a young man and free-lanced, animating theatrical commercials; soon she became co-owner of a studio that had been successful before the war and was starting up again—Studio Mackassy and Trsi. She recalls, "It was quite a successful thing for five years." In 1949 the State took over all small, private businesses, and in March 1950 Tissa and a friend illegally left the country for France. Broke in

Paris, living in "total misery," Tissa finally found work as a housemaid to a countess and then, "climbing up the social ladder," became a cleaning woman. In 1951 a friend sent her to see Jean Image, a Hungarian animation producer in Paris. He hired her to do most of the animation and all the layouts, track readings, and editing of a feature-length cartoon, *Bonjour, Paris* (1953). She was paid about $100 a month.

Seven months of unemployment followed her stint with Jean Image, and then she worked a year assisting animators on American commercials at La Comète Studio: "The French work this way—you have a deadline to meet in December, and in March we are still working on the film. I enjoyed it."

In 1955 her visa came through, and she arrived in the United States. United Productions of America (UPA) was all the rage at that time in animation, with its design-oriented cartoons—Mr. Magoo, Gerald McBoing Boing, et al.—and Tissa applied for work at their New York office. Some months went by before they called her in to test as an assistant to Grim Natwick.

Natwick, who designed and animated the first Betty Boop films for Max Fleischer and animated most of Snow White's scenes for Walt Disney, came bounding out to interview the frightened Tissa and boomed, "Do you know what animation is?"

Understanding very little English and speaking even less, she shyly answered, "Animation is—animation."

"You can't argue with that," chuckled Natwick, and thus began a "very close" personal and professional relationship that lasted twelve years.

After UPA closed in 1958, Grim and Tissa free-lanced as a team; "I learned absolutely everything from Grim," she says today. "I think he is the greatest animator and the greatest teacher. He just pours out knowledge." It was a happy coincidence that she was working with the man who was a major contributor to the film that inspired her to become an animator, *Snow White*. "We'd pick up a job. Grim would animate half, I'd do half, then I'd clean up the whole thing so it looked like one."

In 1967 Grim retired to California to paint. Tissa remained in New York and experienced some bad times again—there was no work. The industry was going through one of its periodic depressions, and animation studios were closing right and left.

When things picked up, what little work was there was not available to Tissa. "Nobody," she explains evenly, "would hire me as an animator. Nobody even considered the possibility that I, a girl, wanted to animate. Unheard of! Absolutely ridiculous! They'd say, 'Oh sure, we'll call you.' Because there were no women animators, nobody even considered it possible that a woman *could* animate. In America, animation was a jealously guarded men's field. So girls should be assistants, inkers, painters—not animators.

"But it's also women's own fault, because they don't stay with it long enough. You can only have one love if you want to be an animator: animation. You can't devote yourself to it part-time. Ten years go by before you can even call yourself an apprentice animator.

"It is such long, hard work; you have to keep doing, doing, doing to learn. You have to learn so hard that few women have the patience, the endurance, the interest. For some stupid reason girls here like to get married, have babies, and forget the world. I grew up in another world. I was brought up to think that getting married was only one thing in life—not the only thing. Women can find work in animation if they have enough will to follow through and really do it. Even today, I'm always saying that if I keep busy long enough I will become a good animator."

Tissa hung in there, working as an assistant to other animators whenever a job came along. She and Grim had animated some TV spots for John Hubley in the early sixties, and it was Hubley who finally gave Tissa her chance as a solo animator. She animated on several of his films—with other animators, on *Of Demons and Men* (1970), *People People People* (1975), and *Everybody Rides the Carousel* (1975); and alone on *Eggs* (1970) and a series of Children's Television Workshop segments, *Cool Pool Fool, True Blue Sue, Truth Ruth*. It was her work in Hubley's *Cockaboody* (1973) that caught Dick Williams's eye.

Now with *Raggedy Ann & Andy*, Tissa David has proven herself to be a master animator, as worthy of that title as Art Babbitt, Emery Hawkins, or her teacher Grim Natwick. It is a unique position that is deeply satisfying to her. "I do consider myself," she says slowly, "somebody who walked the road for the first time."

But the most exciting thing to Tissa David—artist, immigrant, refugee, student, housekeeper, assistant, and master animator—is "just to exist. To be. And I always felt that, even when I was totally miserable and hungry. I thought life is the most exciting thing there is.

"In Paris, when I was walking the streets at night to pick up the cigarette butts for my next day's smoking, I still believed that life is the most exciting thing I could think of."

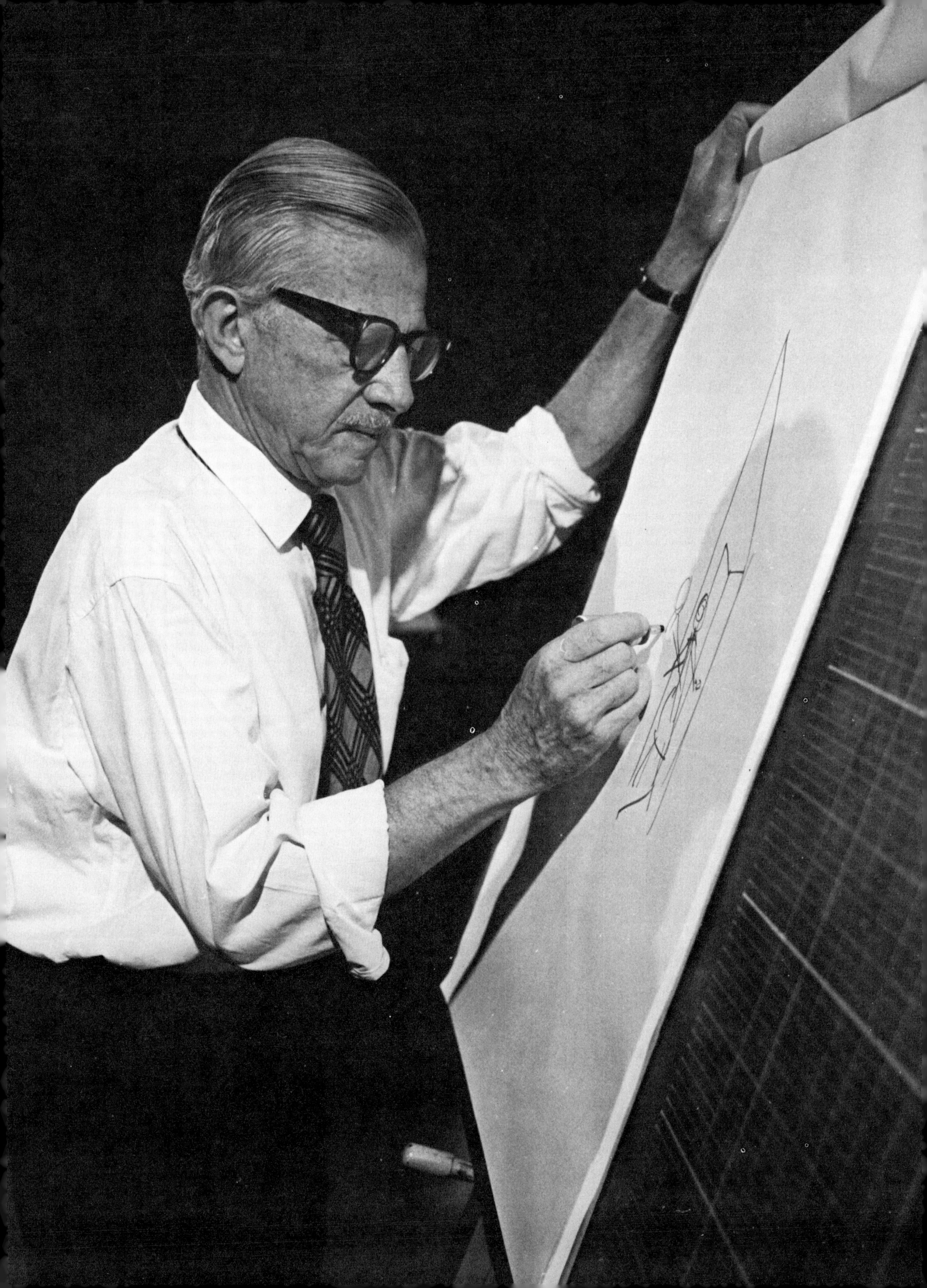

Art Babbitt– The Animator As Legend

I have tremendous respect for the craft itself—what the craft could be, not for what it is. Because even the very best of Disney is just the beginning . . .
—*Art Babbitt*

Art Babbitt should have calling cards printed: ART BABBITT—LEGEND IN HIS OWN TIME. Not that he would ever describe himself as a legendary figure; still, he is quite aware of the several awesome reputations he has acquired during his half-century in the animation industry.

First and foremost is the legend of Art Babbitt the master craftsman. Babbitt was one of the four animators on Walt Disney's *Three Little Pigs* (1933), the great breakthrough in personality animation. Babbitt animated the drunken mouse in the Academy Award-winning short, *The Country Cousin* (1936). Harvard art professor Robert D. Field, author of the 1942 *The Art of Walt Disney*, called *The Country Cousin* a "tour de force. For mastery of animation, apart from technical ingenuity, a point was reached that has never been surpassed." (Field autographed Babbitt's copy of his book, "To Art—the greatest animator of them all.")

Babbitt took a weak character named Goofy whose only distinction was his voice and developed him into a specific character with subtleties and personality traits all his own. An example of Babbitt's intellectual approach to animation and his attention to detail can be seen in this excerpt from the lengthy "Character Analysis of the Goof," which he wrote for the Disney animators in June 1934: "He is loose-jointed and gangly, but not rubbery. He can move fast if he has to, but would rather avoid any overexertion, so he takes what seems the easiest way. He is a philosopher of the barbershop variety. . . . His brain being rather vapory, it is difficult for him to concentrate on any one subject. . . . He is a good-natured dumbbell what thinks he is pretty smart. . . . Never think of the Goof as a sausage with rubber hose attachments. . . . The looseness in his arms and legs should be achieved through a succession of breaks in the joints. . . ."

From animating silly pigs, Goofs, and drunken mice to conjuring up the magnificently evil Queen in *Snow White* (before she turned into a hag) is quite a jump, one that only an animator with Babbitt's versatility could achieve. In *Pinocchio* (1940) he again demonstrated his virtuosity by bringing to life the charming old toymaker Geppetto. And in *Fantasia* (1940), in the balletic "Dance of the Chinese Mushrooms" from the *Nutcracker Suite* sequence, Babbitt's sense of timing and his affinity for dance created a little masterpiece in less than one minute of screen time—as nearly perfect as a Degas pastel. His use of perspective as a secondary action while the constantly moving mushrooms bow and change position was years ahead of its time, and the exquisite sequence remains perhaps the most universally admired in the entire controversial film. (Babbitt likes to tell the story about a teacher friend who wrote that after she had taken her pupils to see *Fantasia* they asked if those guys who made the film were on drugs. Babbitt wrote back, "Yes! I personally was addicted to Pepto-Bismol and Feen-A-Mint.")

After Disney's, Babbitt was one of the bright lights of UPA. In *Rooty Toot Toot* (1952), for example, he animated the dancing Defense Attorney and the heroine Frankie; the film won an Oscar for director John Hubley. During the fifties and sixties Babbitt won more than eighty awards for TV commercials he animated and directed, and from 1966 to 1975 he was director of the commercial department at Hanna-Barbera. Before tackling the *Raggedy Ann* assignment, he contributed sensitive animation of a mime and a pair of abstract dancers to Hubley's TV special based on Erik Erikson's writings, *Everybody Rides the Carousel*.

In 1974 his peers in the International Animation Film Society (ASIFA Hollywood) awarded Babbitt their highest honor, the Winsor McCay trophy, as an expression of admiration for his craftsmanship. "An award for longevity," muttered Babbitt with typical mock gruffness.

These are just a few examples of Babbitt the craftsman. But there is another side to the man. If Babbitt were introduced at a party to a Disney loyalist who had not yet forgiven him for the leading role he played in the famous and bitter 1941 strike at that studio, the party would be over. For here we run head on into the legend of Art Babbitt the firebrand, as he describes himself.

Ask him about the strike and the memories come back hot and angry: "We wanted union recognition, and the money issue was a minor one. Once you're recognized as a union, you're able to come in and bargain, representing a body of people as opposed to one person. See, Walt Disney wanted to be the benevolent uncle. If good was to be done, he was the guy that was going to do it. At the strike Disney drove through the line of pickets like he was having a hell of a good time. That's when I said, 'You ought to be ashamed of yourself, Walt Disney!' He started coming for me, and all the pickets closed in on him, and he thought better of it.

"This sounds like sour grapes now," he says, frowning. "Mind you, I want to give full credit to the genius of Disney the entrepreneur, a very forceful guy who was willing to risk everything for quality, who surrounded himself with the best people, who was a hell of an editor. He was not a creator, he was not an artist, but he could pick out what was good. He had the innate bad taste of the American public. He was audience-wise. If it hadn't been for him, I don't think the medium would have made the advances it did. But as far as his politics were concerned, they were medieval! He was a caveman, an America Firster, as was his brother. I was investigated till hell-wouldn't-have-it by the FBI and the Office of Naval Intelligence. My Marine Corps enlistment was canceled, and I had to fight to be taken into the Marine Corps as a buck private."

Disney unwisely fired Babbitt ("four times"), citing his union activities as a reason, a direct contravention of the Wagner Labor Relations Act. As a result the Screen Cartoonists' Guild voted to strike. While he was in the Marine Corps for three years, Babbitt's case was being tried in three cities and finally by the U.S. Supreme Court. The results were totally in his favor, and when Master Sergeant Babbitt finished his Corps duty he went back to Disney's "to prove a point." He insisted that everything be the same as it had been before he left, including wall-to-wall carpeting in his office, a Moviola and the same rate of pay. He was assigned to a film that was never intended for production; he and Disney would pass each other every day but never again spoke to each other. After a year Babbitt left.

A more pleasant legend concerns Babbitt the Hollywood playboy, a womanizer *par excellence*. Ward Kimball, one of Babbitt's peers at Disney, recalled, "I guess I sort of looked up to him as an early 1930s swinger because he was the model bachelor at the studio and he did everything Hollywood style. Where all the rest of us were renting apartments and living in little rooms, he had a beautiful home on Tuxedo Terrace.

"He wasn't the key animator, but you'd think he was president of the company. His car was usually bigger than Walt's, which took a lot of nerve. . . . Babbitt can be best described this way: he was the first guy in the studio who owned and could afford a Capehart Automatic Record Player. They played the old 78s, and that meant he could be making out on the couch for a whole half-hour without having to get up to change his Bach sonatas or whatever." The first of Babbitt's three wives was Marge Belcher, a dancer who modeled for Snow White; she later found fame as half of the dance team of Marge and Gower Champion.

Today, happily married to actress Barbara Perry, Babbitt the former swinger has gladly swung into the calm domesticity of a happy home life and the joys of being doted upon by a beautiful wife and three lovely daughters.

The final legendary view of Art Babbitt is that of the great teacher. In a magazine article, Dick Williams once wrote about the lecture-demonstration

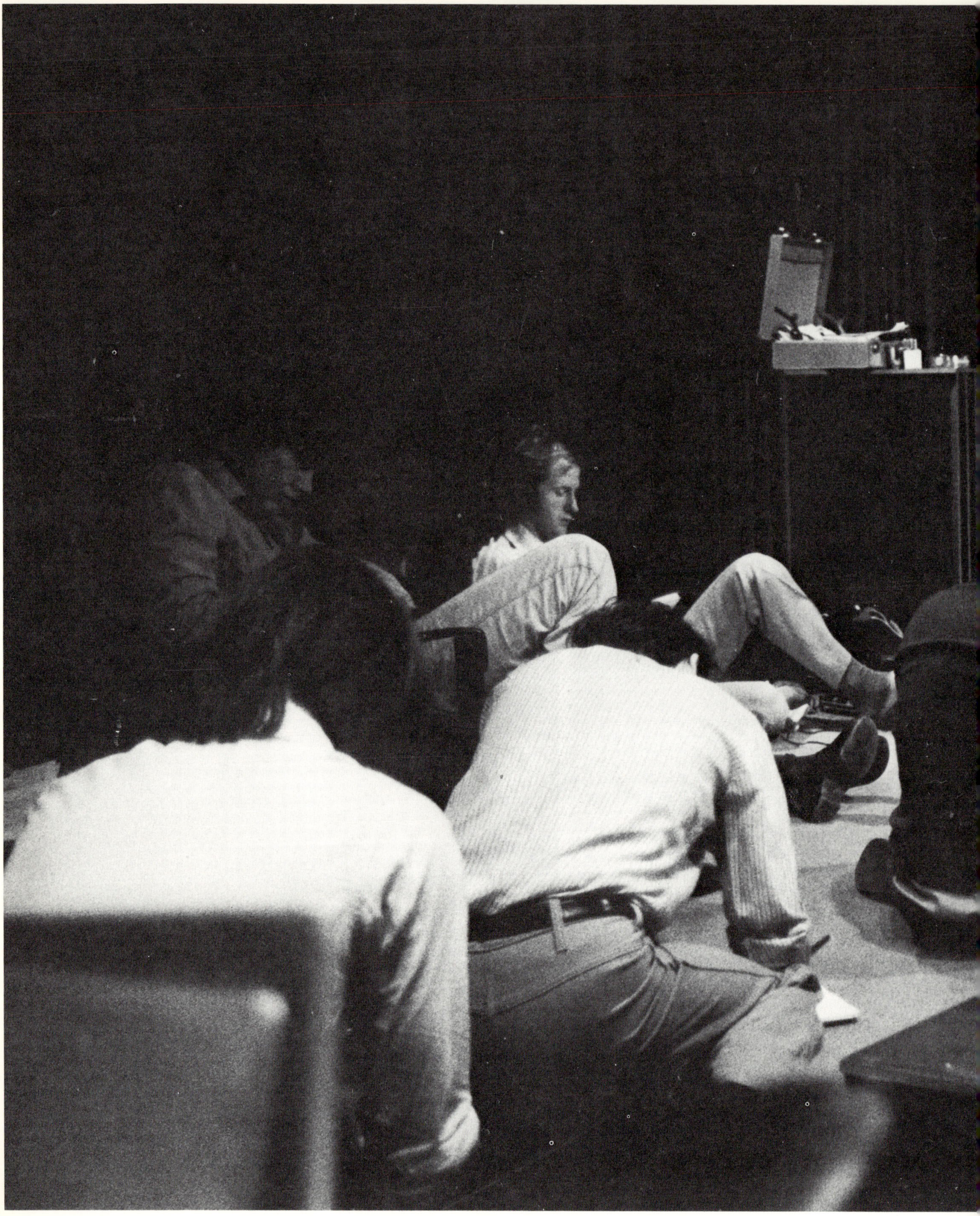

Art Babbitt teaching an animation class at Richard Williams's London studio.

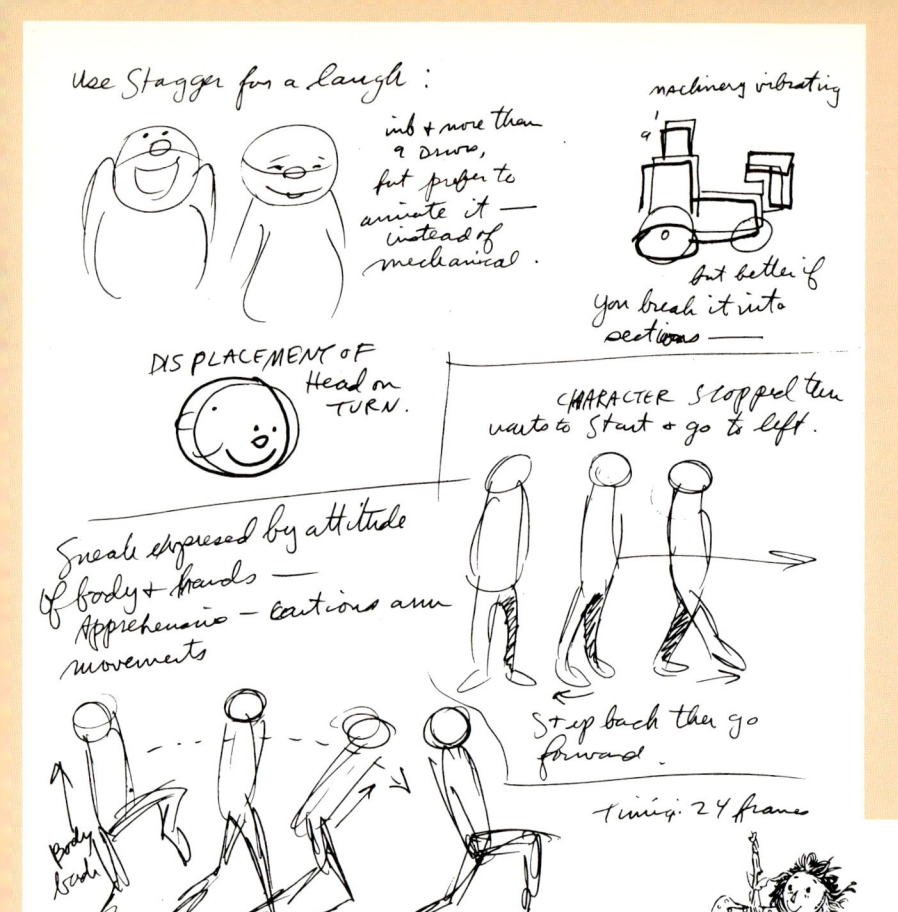

(Above) An example from the author's notebook of the detail covered in the accelerated five-day course.

(Right) A form-letter invitation to attend Babbitt's animation seminar for the *Raggedy* crew in New York City.

LESTER OSTERMAN PRODUCTIONS
RAGGEDY ANN & ANDY

January 12, 1976

Mr. John Canemaker
New York, New York

Dear John:

This is to formally invite you to Art Babbitt's glorified animation assistants' seminar lasting five days starting 9:00 A.M. Monday, January 26th and ending Friday, January 30th.

Lectures will be from 9:00 A.M. till approximately 12:00 noon.

Place is Precision Screening Room on the 14th floor of The Film Center Building, 630 9th Avenue (between 44th and 45th Streets).

Please be on time in fairness to Art who can't stand sloppiness. The purpose of the seminar is to rekindle the almost lost art of versatile and fine assistant work. To do this Art will really be giving a course on animation, as by his definition, a real assistant is an artist just **about** to animate. Mornings for one week is ridiculously inadequate time but we hope to achieve a great deal nevertheless, because of Art's unique teaching ability and the high quality of the "students".

Bring a notebook.

Looking forward to seeing you then.

Richard Horner   Dick Williams   Michael Sisson

RAGGEDY ANN NEW YORK

PS - We may not be able to hire everyone we have invited for two reasons:

1. We may be overbooked in other parts of the country.

2. Our Director is moving around so much he has a full plate directing the present, somewhat scattered crew of animators - and flow of production has not yet settled into a predictable pattern. We do, however, hope you will be with us one way or another, sooner or later.

EAST 19 WEST 44th STREET, Room 702, NEW YORK CITY, NEW YORK 10036 212 869 8156
WEST 5631 HOLLYWOOD BLVD. Room 101, HOLLYWOOD, CALIF. 90028 213 462 0967

seminars Babbitt conducted at Williams's London studio: "He has an astonishing lucidity, a surgeon's mind. . . . Most animators are completely incoherent; they are unable to tell you what they are doing. But Art doesn't have any difficulty in showing you how a thing works. . . . He's tough as nails; yet his patience was beautiful."

In the steep hills way above Hollywood Boulevard are expensive Spanish-style homes hidden by a profusion of plants, tropical trees and flowers. In one of these homes, the Legend lives and sometimes toils at his drawing board.

Relaxing in the large carpeted living room, the Legend (his wife calls him by his nickname, "Bones") talked about *Raggedy Ann & Andy* and the challenge it represented to his reputation as a craftsman. "I found it an extremely difficult assignment," he admitted. "I hadn't devoted myself to animation in a good many years. I'd been concentrating on direction and fixing other animators' stuff. But to sit down and handle an assignment by myself was a new experience. I suffered badly from stage fright, was very insecure, so I had to find myself again."

And find himself he did. From the moment that Camel with the Wrinkled Knees comes galumphing on the screen following the zany camel-mirage he thinks will lead him home, we the audience know we are in the hands of a great entertainer. Every star comedian and eccentric dancer's turn is brought to mind—he is Eddie Foy, Jr., Ray Bolger, with a bit of Charlotte Greenwood thrown in for good measure.

Babbitt presents us with a completely new screen personality, but one we seem to feel we have always known, like Dopey or Dumbo. When the patched-up humpback goes into his musical number "Blue," he looks as if two uncoordinated dancers are inside his hide. Every stop is pulled to entertain us while advancing our knowledge of his personality. Babbitt actually makes us feel sympathetic toward different *parts* of this creature's anatomy. It is no accident that our sympathies and funnybones are manipulated so effortlessly and so often. The Legend has calculated it all, down to the *n*th eyelash flutter or Charleston kick.

"In my analysis of the character," he says, "the Camel is really three identities. There's a back end, which is pretty dumb, and there's a front end, which is a little bit smarter, not always more physically facile than the back end, but a little resentful of the back end's capabilities. Then there's the head. So there're really three separate elements that make up the Camel."

In animating the character, Babbitt found he had to do the back end as one entity on one sheet of paper, then the front end on another sheet, and then the head on a third. Each part had its own timing—two parts sometimes waiting, for instance, for a third part to catch up or slow down—and all three sections had to be combined onto one sheet of paper so that they would look like one drawing.

Three different parts of the Camel's anatomy—head and front and rear legs—were animated on three sheets of animation paper.

All the Camel parts retraced on one paper.

Art Babbitt as the Camel. Caricature by Dan Haskett.

Fred Stuthman, the voice of the Camel, was brought in one day in New York while Babbitt was there in order to dance a gangly impression of how the Camel might move. This was filmed for possible use as a reference for Babbitt; while it gave him "a slight hint of the phlegmatic structure of the Camel," Babbitt followed none of that live-action exactly. "I looked at it, got my impression, put it away, never looked at it again. And that's the way to use live-action, really. As an inspiration or acknowledgment that this is all wrong and you're not going to use it."

As for what was in the mind of the Camel, Art had that all figured out, too. "I got to thinking about this guy's character," he said. "What he's trying to do is make the kids feel sorry for him. He's really not as distressed as he appears to be. The kids [Ann and Andy] are pretty dumb because they're falling for this baloney that he's feeding them."

The CAMEL — ART'S WORK SHEET

RAGGEDY ANN & ANDY
© COPYRIGHT 1976
THE BOBBS-MERRILL CO. INC.

This Camel work sheet, made from Babbitt's animation, was used as a guide for other animators of Camel scenes.

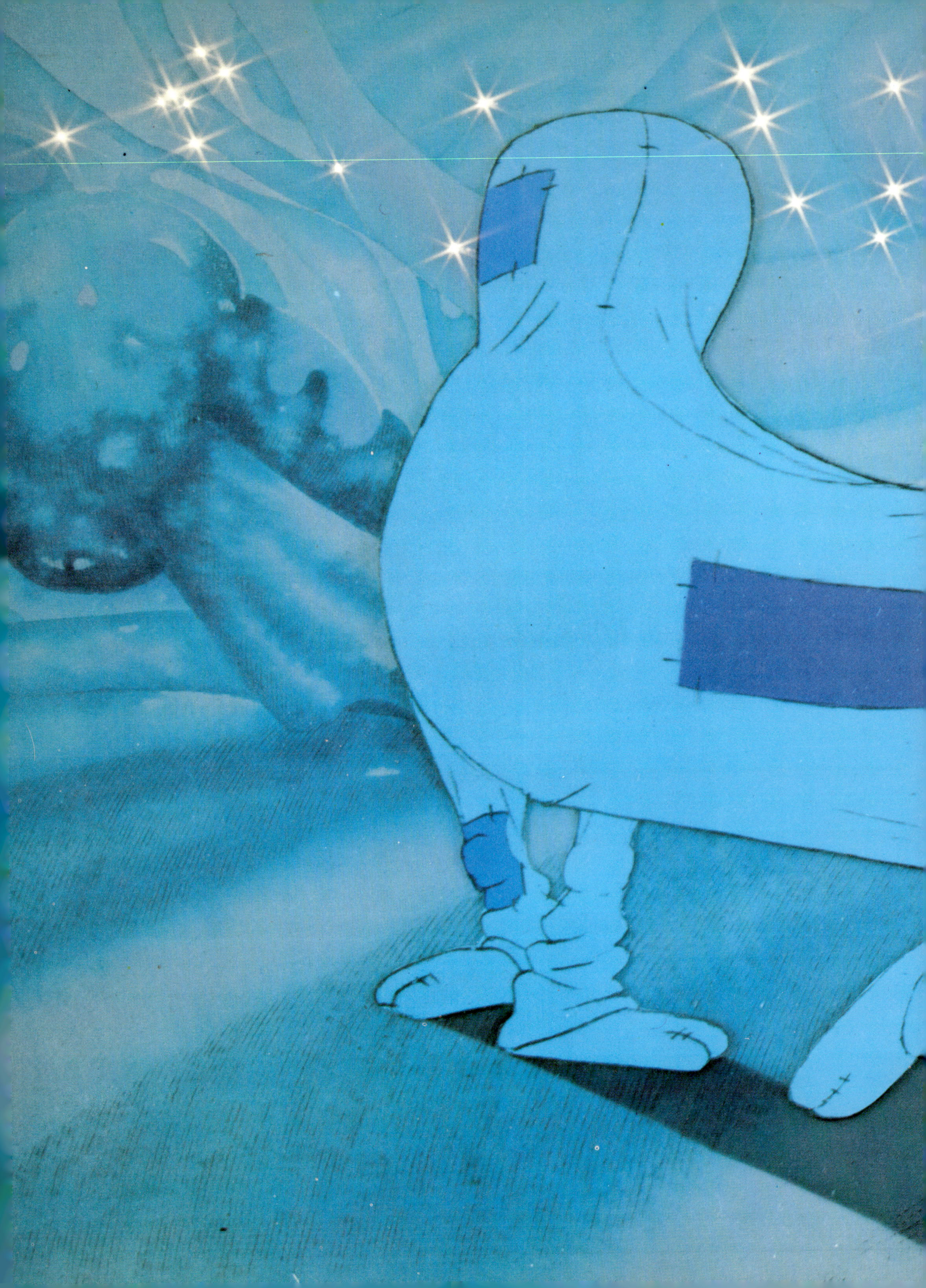

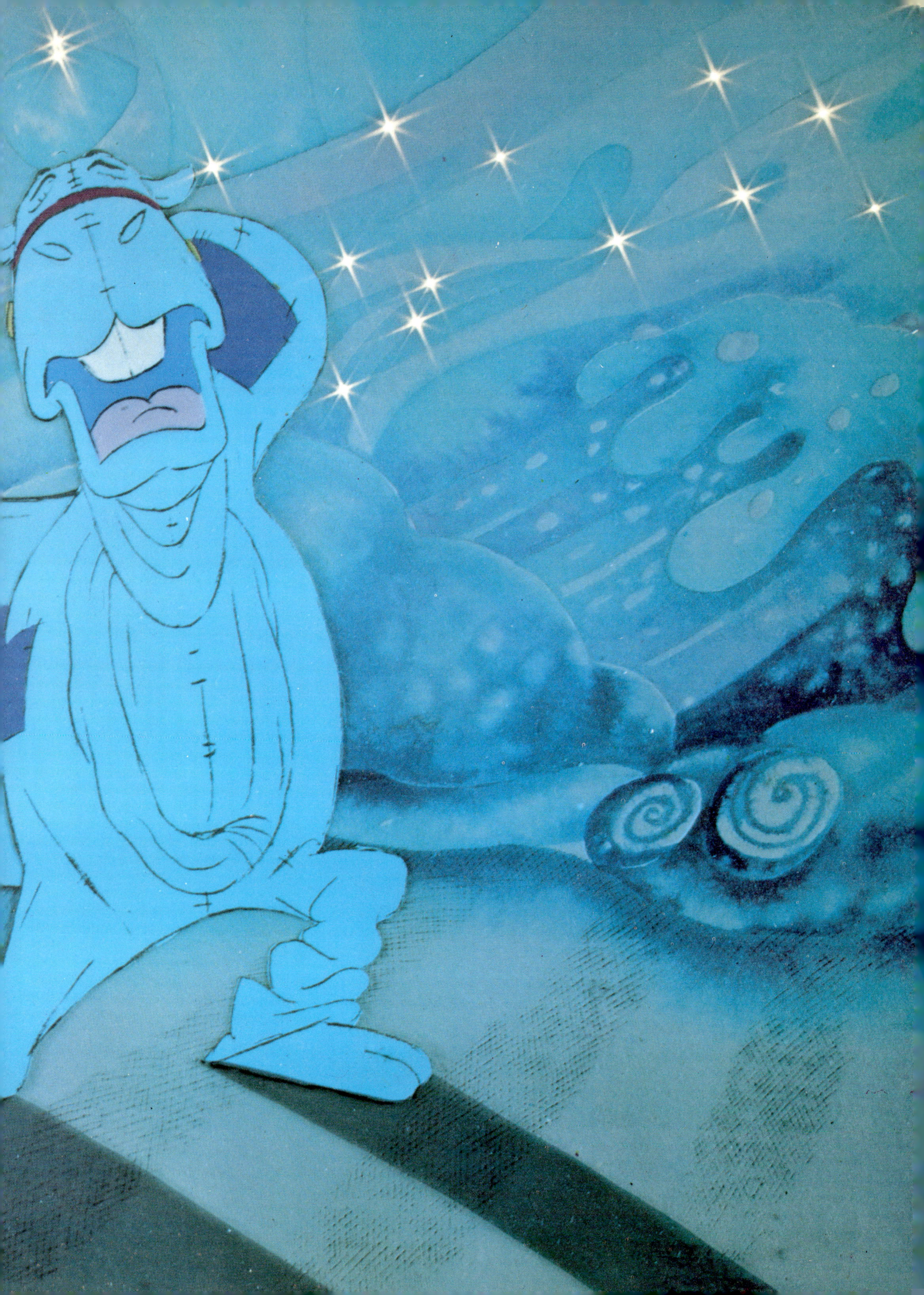

*When you're wrinkled and cold
And your fortune has all been told
And you're nobody's "I love you,"
How can you be happy?
How can you be smiling?
How can you be anything but lowdown saggy and ba-loo?* *

"The mirage he sees is interesting in that when he sees it, he sees [John] Kimball's animation, which with all due respect is sort of primitive compared to some of the other animation. Whether it's deliberate or not, I don't know. But it's the way a *camel* would see a mirage; it's not the way a human would see it. It's a camel's version and perfectly fitting."

Babbitt looks fit and is full of energy; he resembles, in a way, Geppetto the toymaker in *Pinocchio*. But because of a traffic accident in London two years ago it is sometimes actually painful for him to animate, and he must spend several hours each day in traction. "My vertebrae are all screwed up, and to maintain the use of my right arm [his drawing arm] I have to do a set of exercises. The ulcers come up every time I'm aggravated, and if the work is not going well that brings on more ulcers."

Babbitt has fought many battles in his sixty-nine years, but his greatest fights and victories have taken place on that special artist's battlefield—the drawing board. He has won in the eyes of his peers, but to himself he could always have done better. "I have no illusions, because every time I look at the work I've done I cringe. Because I see what *could* have been."

What could have been for Arthur Babbitt, the eldest in a family of eight from Sioux City, Iowa, was a career as a psychiatrist if things had been different. As a teenager, he ran away to New York, slept on empty church benches, ate day-old bread and overripe bananas, and did odd jobs to try to save money for tuition for Columbia pre-med. It was an utterly hopeless dream.

His father, always a loser in business, became paralyzed. Art always sent money home and later moved his family to New York. He hustled for ad illustration jobs and fell into animation while doing theatrical commercials. Fascinated by this new art form, Babbitt worked hard, pushing his way into Paul Terry's studio; then, in 1932, he pushed himself into Disney's and the beginning of his several legends.

Now, after a long, hard-driving career in which he has never compromised his high standards, Babbitt wants to extend his art even further. "I don't want to be artsy-craftsy. I don't want to be abstract or intellectual. I just want to entertain," he says.

"Very simply, I want to be, pardon the lack of modesty, a Charlie Chaplin of animation. That's it. If I get that far it will be a tremendous achievement. I would like to tackle Molière, Boccaccio and Racine—things of that stature.

*© copyright 1976, Jonico Music Inc., The Bobbs-Merrill Company, Inc.

There's so much material that hasn't been touched, and it doesn't have to be over anybody's head. How many times can you keep doing Jack and the Beanstalk? It's time to go on to something fresh. Mentally, at least, I'm prepared for it."

After finishing *Raggedy Ann & Andy,* Babbitt plans to go to London and work on Dick Williams's *The Thief and the Cobbler* "mostly in an advisory capacity." While there he will be devoting a great deal of time to a gigantic animation technique book that will distill the experience and knowledge acquired in his more than twenty-one years as a teacher and his fifty years as an animator. Williams wants him to call it *The Animator's Bible,* and it should be one of the greatest source books on the art ever written—a proper legacy from this complex man and artist.

"You have to aim high," he says of an animator's integrity. "If you want to be satisfied with Saturday morning shows, that's another story," he adds with distaste. "It's a way of getting by. You earn your bread and butter; you don't get ulcers or strokes or heart attacks. But there's no gratification there. It would be wonderful if I could leave a legacy—and I know this is *very* presumptuous—leave technique, mechanics, and an *inspiration* for the future of what to strive for!

"Then I feel I will have accomplished something. A goal which *I* can't reach, but one I'm sure somebody in the future can."

Art Babbitt and Richard Williams in London.

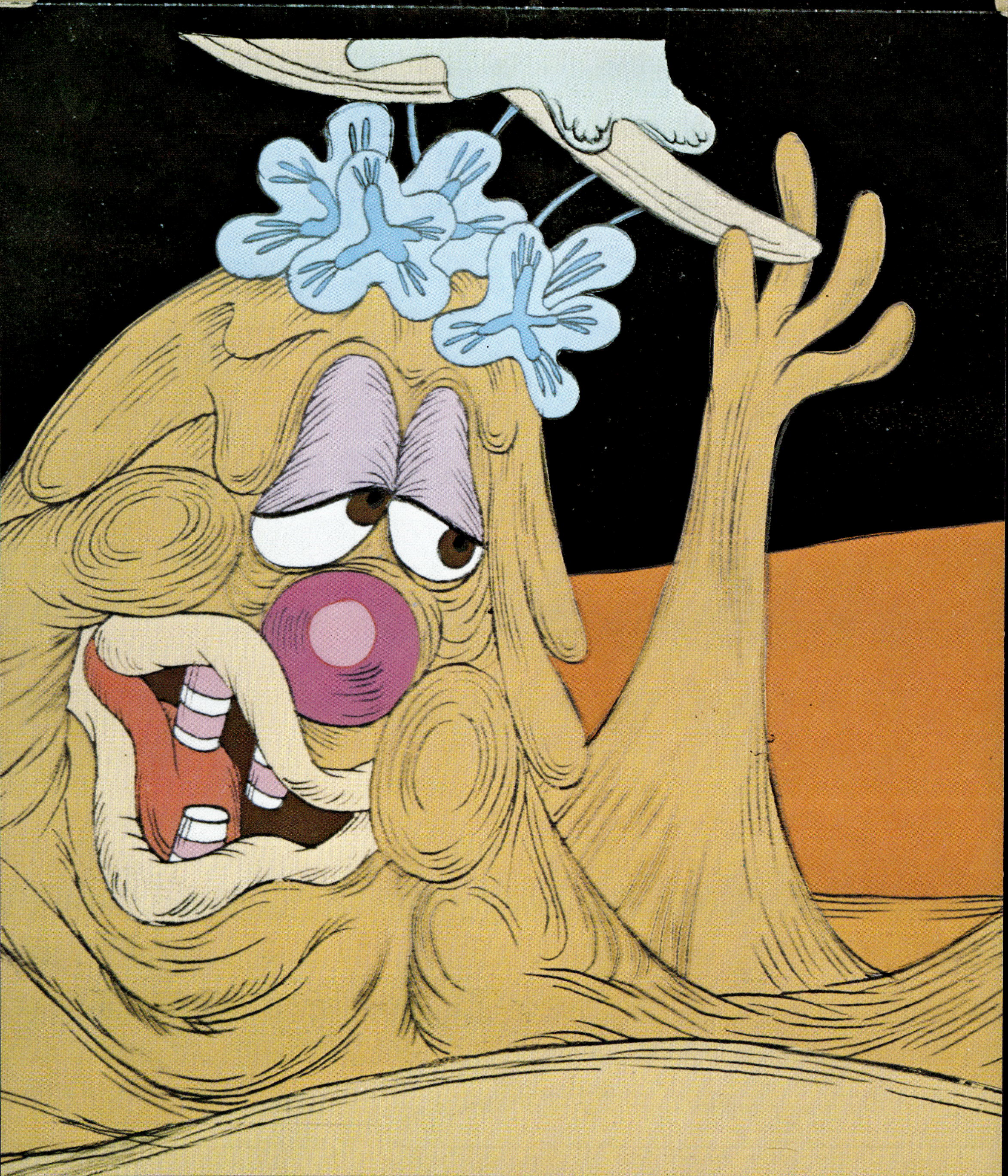

Emery Hawkins— The Restless Cowpoke

Emery Hawkins is the only animator I know who can go completely insane in his animation and make it seem rational.
—*Grim Natwick*

The only limitation in animation is the person doing it. You can do anything—and why shouldn't you do it?
—*Emery Hawkins*

"*Fabulous, adj.* 1. Passing the limits of belief; incredible; astounding. 2. Of, like, or recorded in fable; fictitious; mythical."
  If the English language in general and adjectives in particular were not so debased, it might not be so difficult to describe Emery Hawkins's accomplishment in *Raggedy Ann & Andy*. The word defined above could then give a slight indication of the quality of Hawkins's animation of the Greedy, the Taffy-Pit monster fated to eat eternally, never to find satisfaction until it happens upon a "sweet heart."
  Perhaps it would serve to hear Art Babbitt's opinion of Hawkins's work in the film: "It's masterful. I have never seen anything to top it in any animated cartoon, anywhere, anytime! It's original; it's a tour de force! I sent him a fan letter, the first one I've ever sent in my life to anyone, including Mary Pickford." High praise, indeed, from the Legend.
  At the biweekly screenings that began the summer of 1976 at the plush Rizzoli screening room in New York, whenever Emery's latest pencil tests were shown to the *Raggedy* crew, spontaneous applause always followed them—a reaction very unusual for the not easily impressed sharp-eyed professionals whose sole reason for viewing the now-familiar reel is to look for mistakes.
  Of course one must see the Greedy on the movie screen to get the full effect. The still drawings from the sequence, beautiful as they are both in Emery's rough form and in the clean-ups by Dan Haskett, must be seen in motion, as they were made to be seen, in order to be appreciated. And one viewing will not do, for the incredible detail and subtle visual witticisms are

(*Opposite*) The Greedy tips a banana-split hat. Notice the pegbar, which holds the animation cels in correct alignment for filming.

193

Emery Hawkins.

so plentiful that one can watch the footage half a dozen times and still get caught up in following a single action and miss three or four other equally glorious moments.

Hawkins's sequence begins so disarmingly that we expect nothing and therefore are at first startled and then overwhelmed by the Greedy, as are Raggedy Ann, Andy and the Camel. Floating in an empty paper cup on hypnotic waves of whipped cream and cherry-banana taffy, Ann, Andy and the Camel taste the "real delicious" mixture and marvel at a gigantic cherry as they float by.

The cherry inverts with earthquake tremors, forming a tidal wave of taffy that knocks our heroes out of their cup and toward a gaping hole. (Drawings Number 89 and 105).

Now the monster starts to form (Drawings Number 114, 122, 134), oozing peppermint candy canes, crème de menthe chocolate sundaes, lollipops, and multicolored gum balls. The sugary mass builds itself up into a volcanic mountain, while gravity pulls Ann, Andy and the Camel in the opposite direction.

"What's 'at?—huh—(burp)—excuse me, I was asleep (belch). —Pardon me—(burp)—who are you?"

The deep basso voice of actor Joe Silver is heard (Drawing Number 157) as the Greedy's nose and mouth twist skyward, gasping and belching. Eyes form—rather pretty eyes with long lashes—by Drawing Number 170, as the vocal flatulence continues.

Within fifteen drawings (about half a second of screen time) the Greedy has already undulated his features into new shapes: the eyes protrude a la Picasso (Drawing Number 185), the candy-cane teeth grow (Drawing Number 199), and several hands form to stuff more goodies into the grotesque mouth (Drawing Number 211). All of these transitions take place within approximately twenty-five seconds; Drawings Number 237 to 245 are, in fact, only the belch and "Pardon me" of the above dialogue.

"It doesn't matter what his form is," said animator Hawkins. "He's not a character, he's a place! A crossroads of energy and action. He's not only in a viscous flowing mass, he's part of it! And being part of it, he ought to flow and change the same way.

"The whole thing is changing—his nose, his eyes and his hands. Hands form out of parts of him (Drawings Number 317 and 325), and they may be like a chicken claw one time and a glob of taffy the next. And to me that sets up a tension. It's interesting in itself, you know? And I think it'll fascinate kids."

Kids, of course, but everyone else as well—adults, teenagers, heads, cartoon freaks, artists, students, the butcher, the baker—can appreciate some facet of Emery's sequence, for the glutinous, gooey, grossly gorgeous Greedy hits all the bases—visually and intellectually.

Just trying to follow the stream-of-consciousness images that illustrate the dialogue can boggle one's mind. When the creature introduces himself ("I am—urp!—the Greedy. Welcome to the Taffy Pit!"), he lifts a banana-split hat and twirls a candy cane in the best side-show huckster tradition, part carny barker, part master of ceremonies Joel Grey in *Cabaret*.

"The Taffy Pit is my domain" shows us a brief image of the Greedy as the Prince of Darkness, banana horns pointing majestically from behind a regal (but slippery) head.

"I eat all the time—except when I'm asleep," and the shrinking mouth has just enough time to yawn as several gooey arms stretch and disappear in the goo. The Camel is sure that the monster has had enough to eat "with all this stuff around," but the Greedy reappears unexpectedly from the other side of the screen with a gigantic telescopic eye which, like the "NO!" the Greedy screams, is truly frightening in its sudden ferocity.

Hawkins wanted to "go further than this" in his animation of the Greedy's song, and Williams enthusiastically told him to go ahead. (This is another example of Williams's directing technique—allowing the animators he trusts complete freedom to create. Hawkins says it reminds him of the way the business began in the early days of making cartoons: "One guy would do the front part of a picture, another guy the middle, another the last. It made them participate in the creation of something.")

> *You can give me candy, cotton candy,*
> *Choc'late bar or lollipop!*
> *Fill me up on ice cream,*
> *Dripping fudge sauce,*
> *Butterscotch and nuts that never stop.* [*]

Undulating and rising out of the amorphous taffy comes a rump to be reckoned with: encased in a gigantic girdle that is held together (just barely) by licorice cords (Drawing Number 80), an enormous androgynous belly-dancer grinds into shape.

The Greedy, now a honeyed hermaphrodite, wears a Carmen Miranda fruit-hat and turns slowly, sensually around, sticky fingers gliding over an invisible tabletop. As this cupcake drag queen continues whirling (Drawings Number 102, 113, 143, 147), a magical force draws from the Pit cotton candy, lollipops and chocolate bars, which fly in an orbit around the singing blancmange.

This is the part of the sequence Hawkins likes the least, because it is the only manifestation of the Greedy that does not change. And Hawkins is soon done with it, plunging the creature into the Pit after a sexy shower in dripping fudge sauce. The next surprise comes from squashing a handful of taffy into

---

[*] © copyright 1976, Jonico Music Inc., The Bobbs-Merrill Company, Inc.

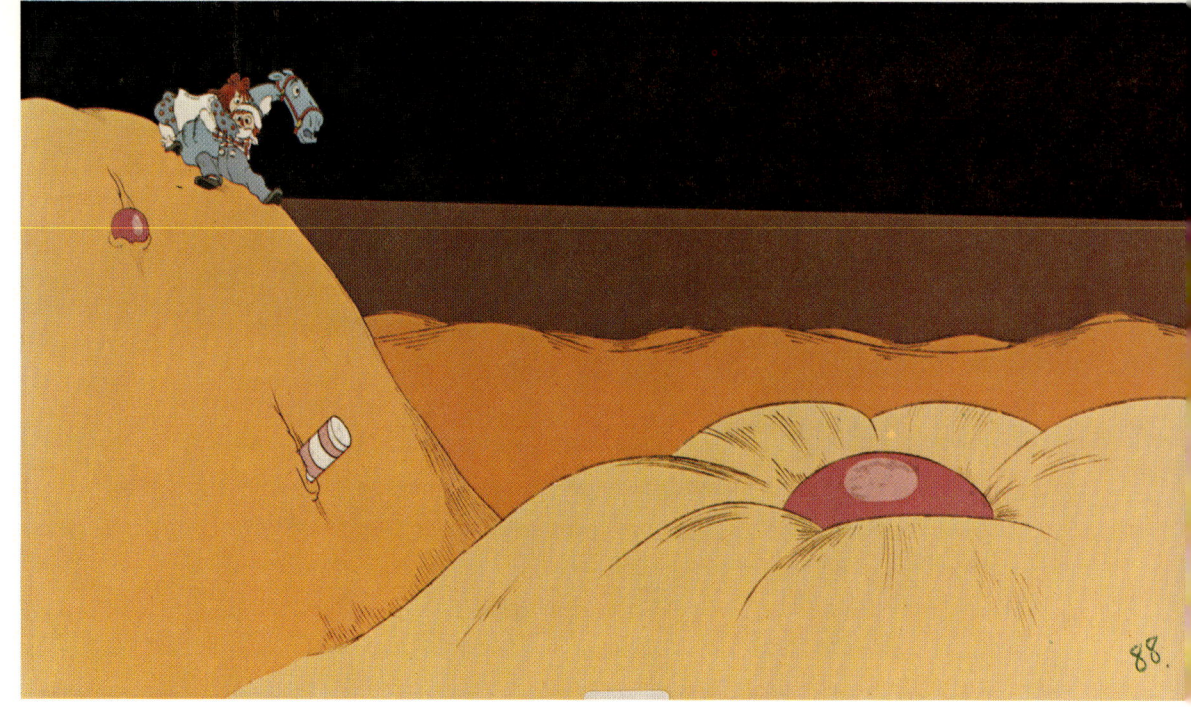

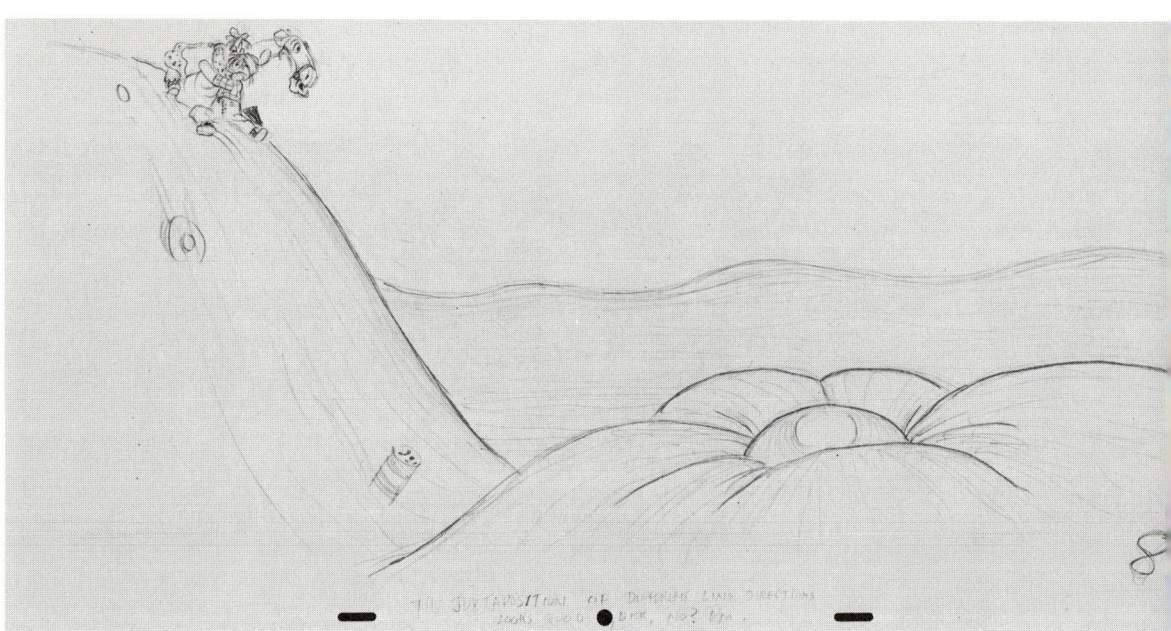

This page and the following two pages: Emery Hawkins's rough animation drawings for the Greedy sequence.

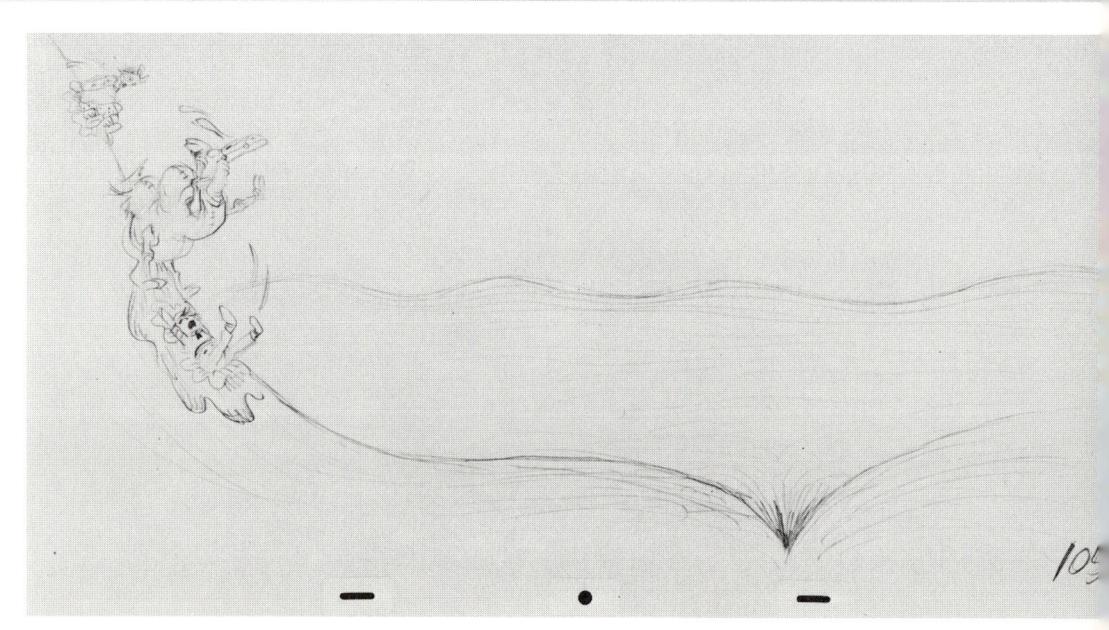

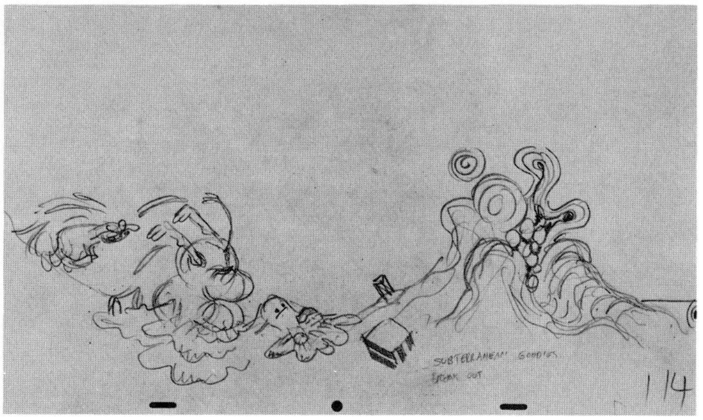
SUBTERRANEAN GOODIES
114

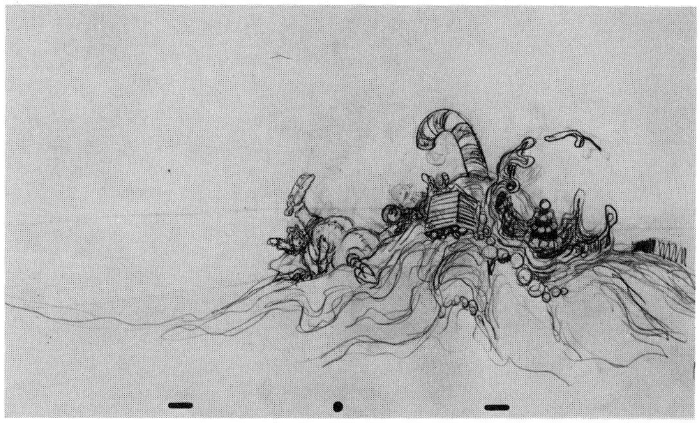

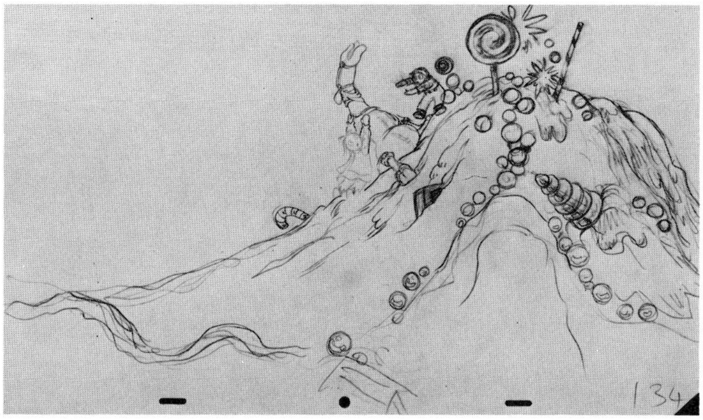
134

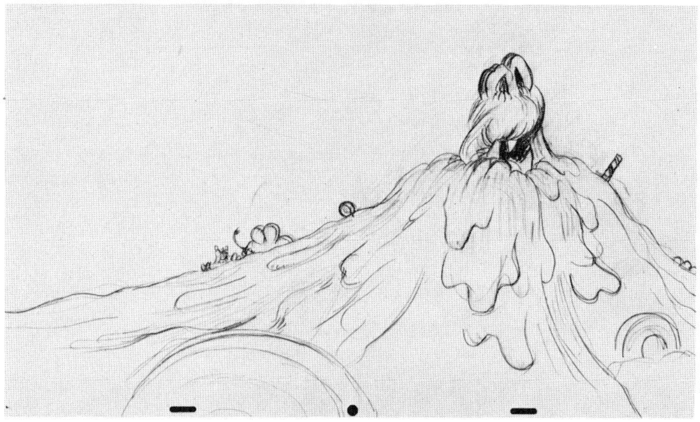

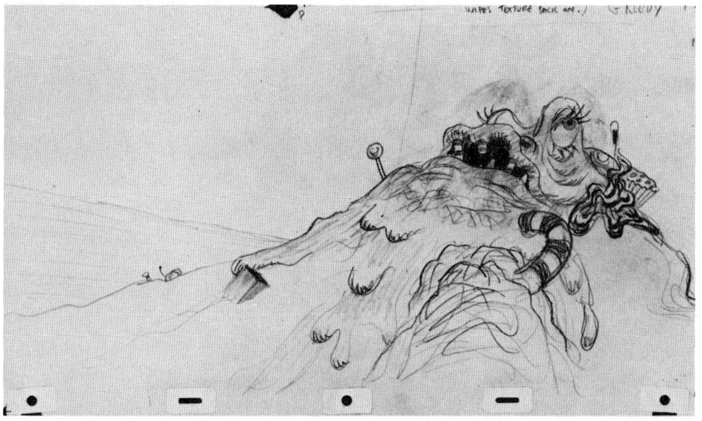

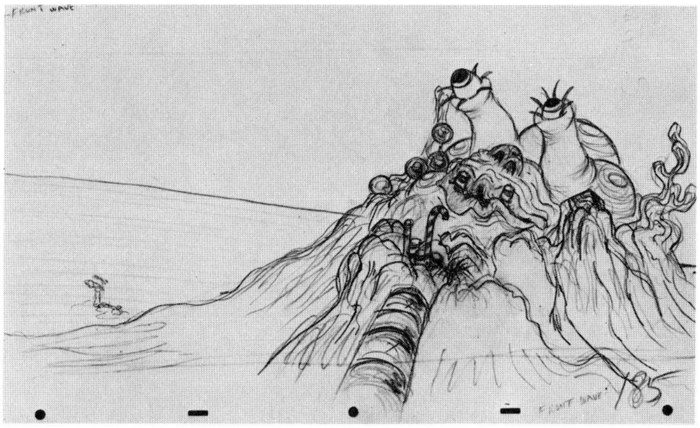
FRONT WAVE
185

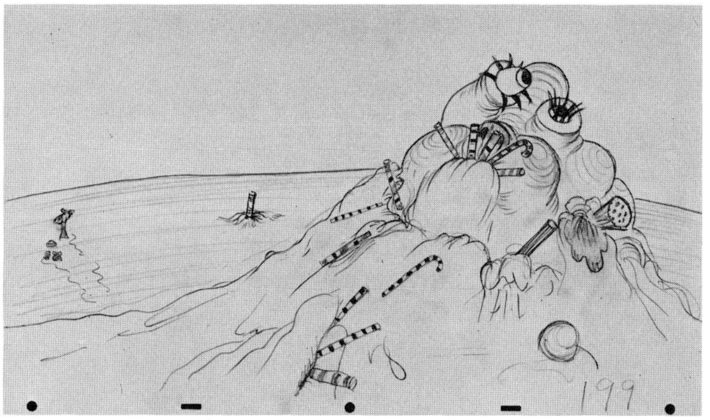
199

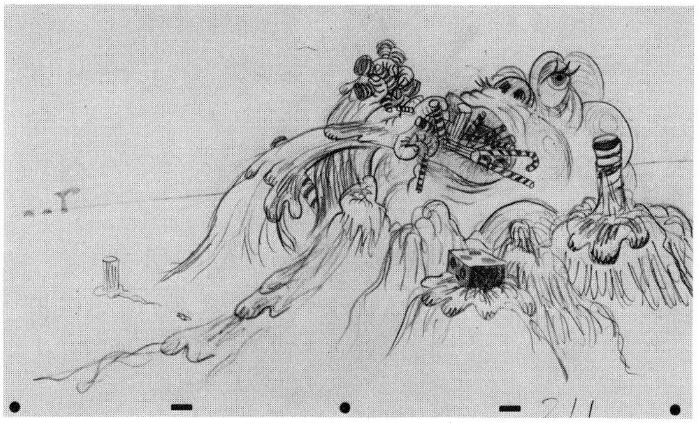
211

237

ONE KIND OF ICE CREAM ON HUMB.

245

EYE LIDS 305 317

317

325

AS GREEDY RISES ROTATING HIS FINGERS SHOULD LOOK LIKE HE'S MOVING THEM OVER A TABLE TOP. DRAWINGS #98 TO 111 SEEM TO LOOK LIKE THAT.

80

102

113

143

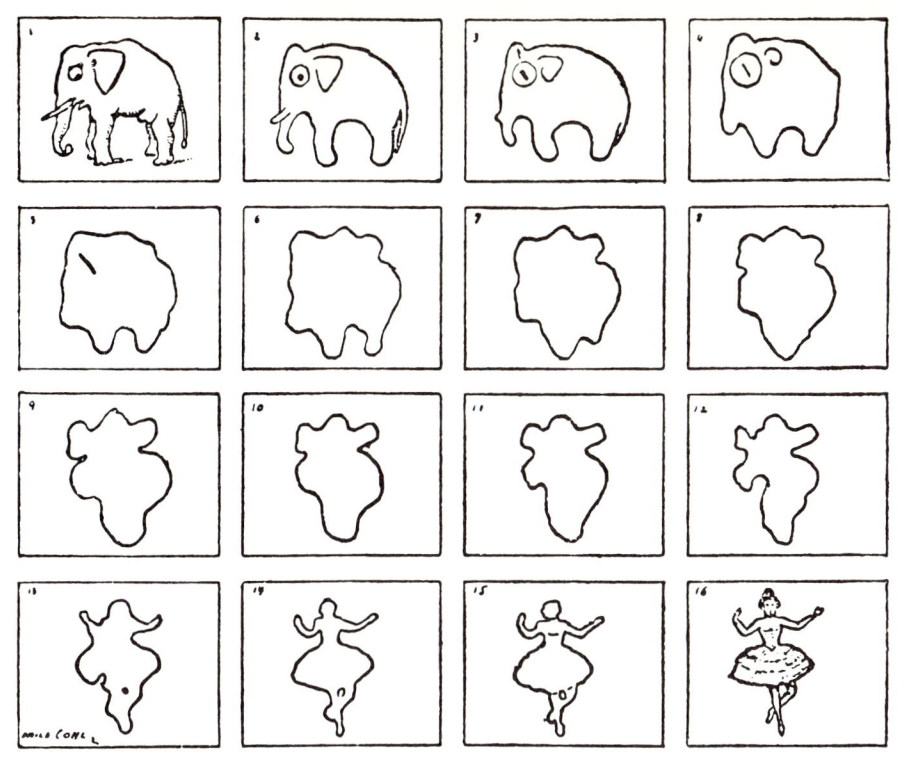

An Emile Cohl metamorphosis from 1908.

several huge bananas in synchronization with the lyrics: *Squash me a banana drowned in jelly tutti-frutti by the score.*

Very excited now, the Greedy grabs onto the "tutti-frutti" line as he bounds into the air with an ice-cream-cone nose.

> *Marzipan and pastry drenched in butter,*
> *Caramel and gingerbread galore;*
> *I can gorge forever, but I'm just an empty shell,*
> *And without a sweet heart*
> *I don't feel so well.* *

During the above, the Greedy flattens himself out into a superhighway with hundreds of candy vehicles speeding into a Panavision horizon.

Things calm down somewhat for dialogue within the song, but the Greedy's desperate emotional state builds gradually ("You must help me find a sweet heart! I cannot go on living like this!") into an explosive beginning for the second half of the number.

> *Oooooooooozing—where's the sugar pop to stop*
> *this misery?*
> *Oooooooooozing—is this endless eating all there*
> *is to be—or not to be?* *

The "oozing" line catapults and stretches the Greedy into the sky for miles. When Dick Williams was an overweight teen, he often took hold of the

---

*© copyright 1976, Jonico Music Inc., The Bobbs-Merrill Company, Inc.

199

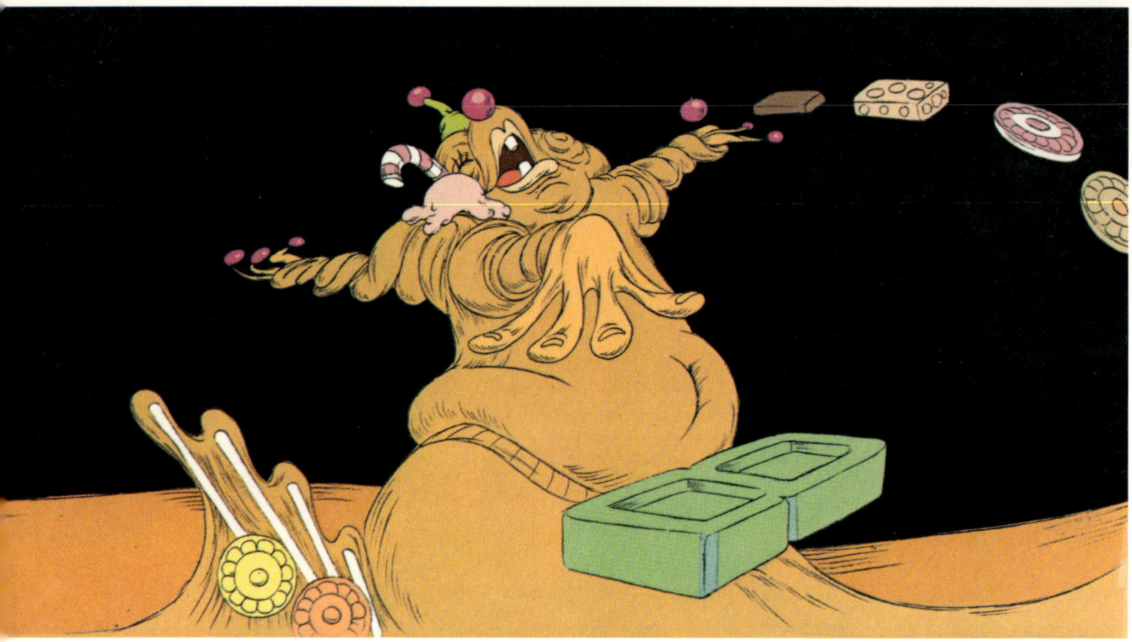

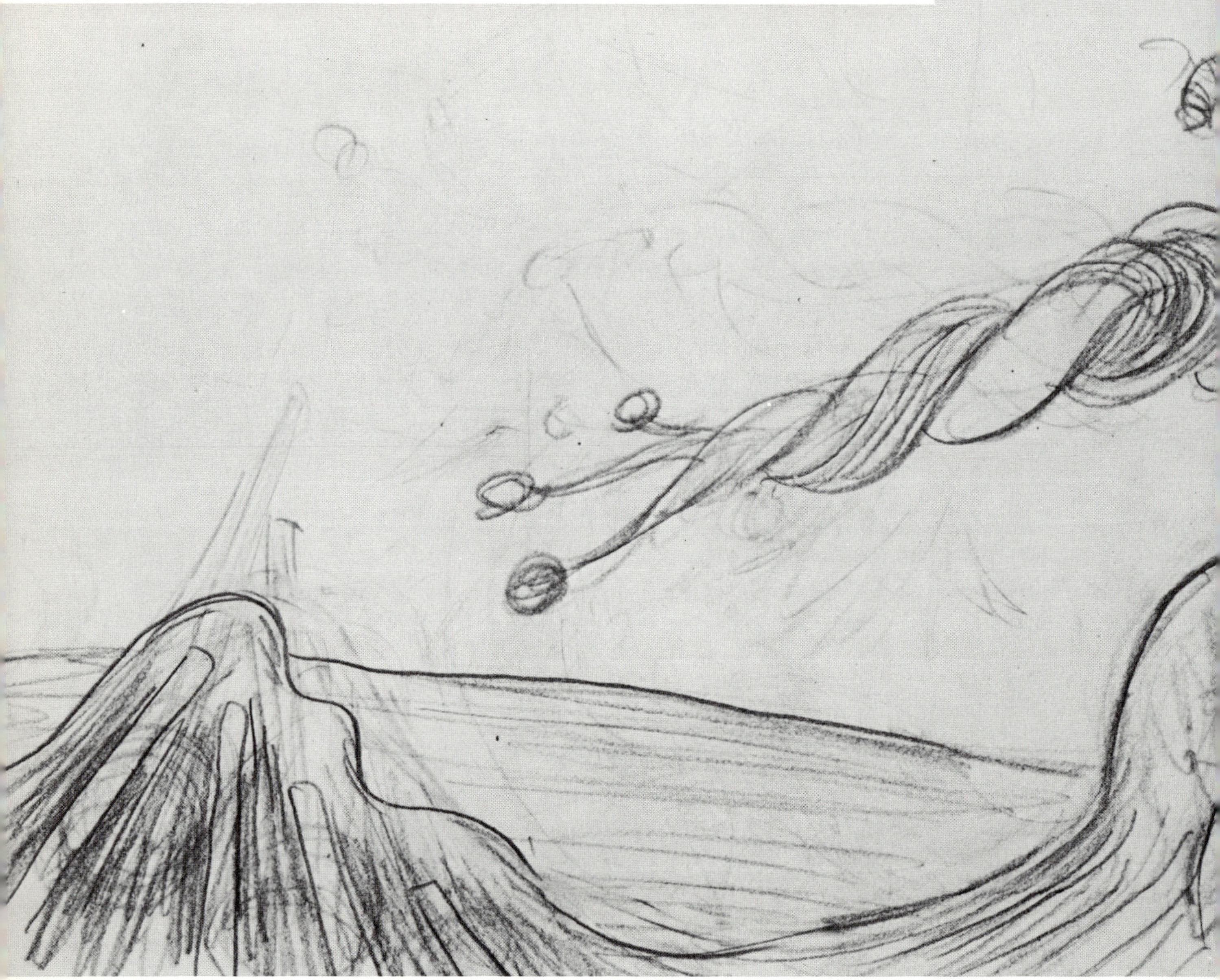

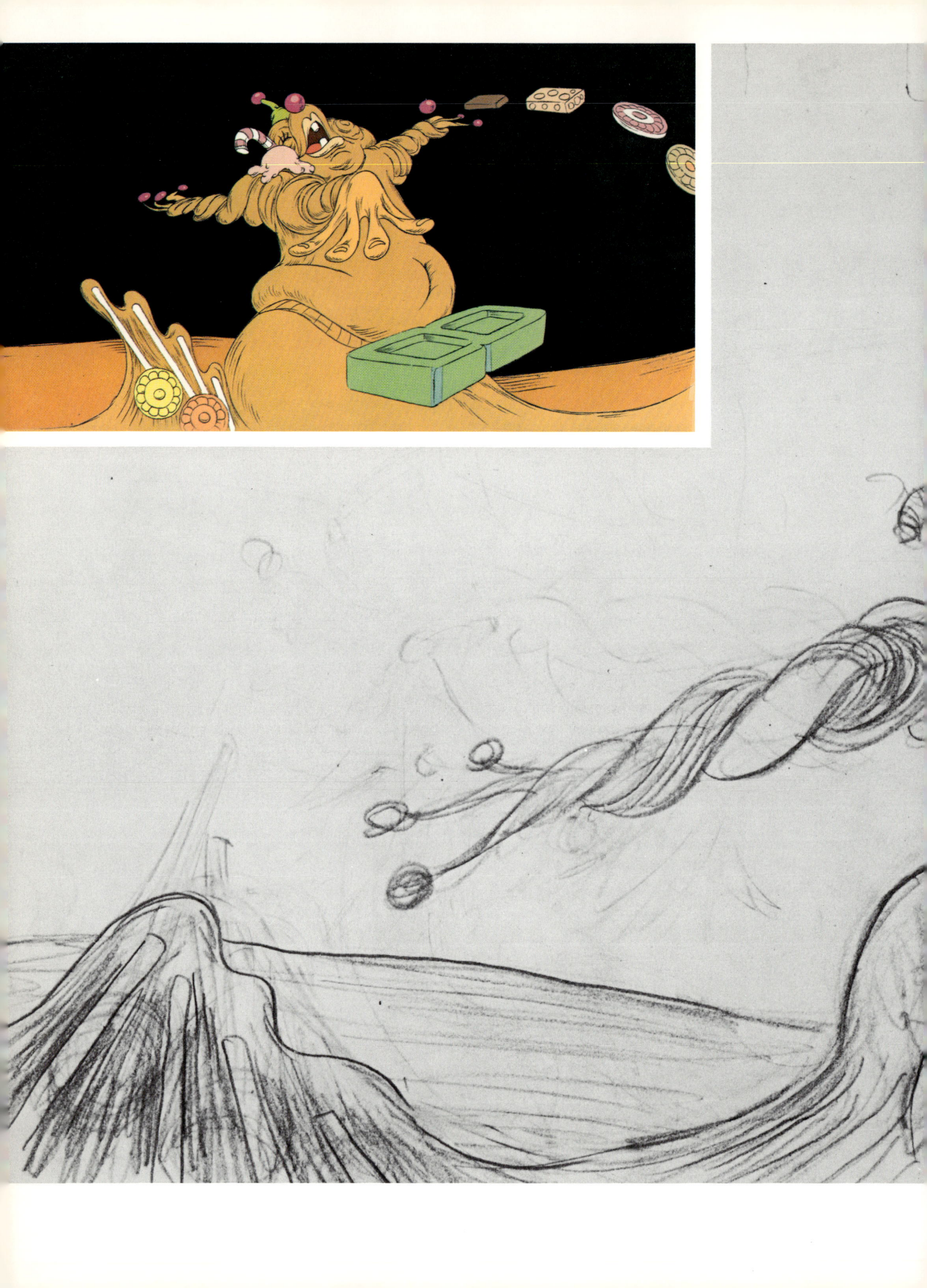

SEQ. 5 - SC - 14

147

excess fat around his ribs, trying to squeeze and tear the hated blubber off his body. That was the feeling Williams suggested Hawkins try to get into the scene. Toward the end of the song the Greedy, now a towering gooey mass, begins to fall from the sky, but is still stretched like a taut rope. In the finale he literally blows his head off, and it bounces like a gigantic ball around the Taffy Pit.

"The thing that has always intrigued me is the actual process of the forms changing," Hawkins said, discussing his particular animation specialty, metamorphosis. "I was always fascinated with the idea of not going directly from one thing to another, but going *by way of* something else, so that you wouldn't know what you were seeing."

Metamorphosis is a technique favored by animation filmmakers as far back as Emile Cohl's matchstick figures in 1908. In fact, it predates motion pictures; in the nineteenth century it was used in "flipper book" advertisements that children cut out of the newspaper, wound a rubber band around and amused themselves and their friends with by flipping the consecutive drawings to life. Countless schoolchildren have doodled idly in the corners of textbook pages, changing dots into lines that undulate and change into fish or dinosaurs or rockets that explode. Emery Hawkins has taken this common technique and made it startlingly uncommon. He has developed a surreal, totally innovative animation that is more ambitious, difficult and successful than anything ever before seen in motion pictures. Disney's literal and tightly logical fantasies do not come close to Hawkins's totally unreal transfigurations—not the Queen's transformation in *Snow White,* not Lampwick becoming a donkey in *Pinocchio,* not even the Pink Elephants' march in *Dumbo.* Marvelous as they are in their own right, these Disney sequences do not present, nor have any animated features until *Raggedy Ann & Andy,* such an unabashedly anarchic, joyously illogical presentation of metamorphosis technique.

Naturally an achievement of this order takes time, and Emery's weekly footage from June 1975 to the next January was the lowest of any of the animators on the film, which of course drove the producers wild. Williams was bombarded with the constant question, "Where is the work?" Williams recalls, "There were bits of it coming in, all brilliant. But it was so short in duration they thought, 'Well, he's off having holidays.'"

It wasn't until the middle of January 1976, in fact, that Hawkins felt he had found the key to the Greedy. It seems he had animated the entire opening scene three times, each time in a different way. "Now that I've done these three scenes I really know how to do this character," he said.

Cartoon director Friz Freleng recalls that once at MGM in the late thirties he and Hawkins were working on a Katzenjammer Kids film. "Emery had to animate a short six-foot scene of a chick carrying a large tomato. Well, by the time he got through, it was up to thirty feet of the most gorgeous animation. He had that little bird going up hills and losing his balance and trying to hold on to the tomato—everything—and *no repeats*. It was so beautiful I cut some other scenes to keep it in the picture!"

Experimentation aside, Hawkins's *Raggedy Ann* animation was by nature a time-consuming task. The big problem was to coordinate the several action levels: generally Hawkins would draw first the little characters in the cup, then the three main waves, and finally the Greedy. "Sometimes I would start with the waves and find the characters taking over. Then I'd do the three in the cup first, so the Greedy could address them. I tried to use all of the large 18 field—so the staging had to be different. You have two things to look at—the action in the cup and the Greedy itself—and it's all something you can look at over and over and find something new. I used the Greedy behind the waves and then in front like Punch and Judy behind and before a curtain."

The work is so complicated that Hawkins never got out of the Taffy Pit. He animated through the entire Greedy song and leading up to the battle in the Taffy Pit, though most of his pre-battle ideas got "the chop" in October 1976 when the production was being frantically pushed through. The Taffy Pit battle itself was handled by two young animators from the Hollywood studio, John Bruno and Art Vitello.

Emery felt, as did all of the directing animators, very protective of his creation, and he sent a set of commandments to Bruno and Vitello to guide them in their Greedy work. Some of his rules included:

Thou shalt not feel that the Greedy has a distinct anatomy. He is a bag of parts—one big bag of opportunities.

Lumps rise and turn into hands. Hands rise and turn into lumps. His dialogue is a flatulent bubble-up.

Generally there are three waves getting darker as they recede. I *try* to make the waves relate to main Greedy action.

It's wide screen, so I've tried to make it look like a three-ring circus, rather than just one ring at a time.

That "three-ring circus" is a marvel of animated invention, but at the time even Hawkins himself had occasional doubts. "You know, it's awful easy to feel like you're nuts when you're doing it," he said laughingly. "In other words, I don't know when I'm being screwy and just missing the boat or when it's entertainment. There's no way of judging until somebody looks at it and reacts."

According to Hawkins, he's had trouble following the rules ever since he started in the business. "I've always been a renegade, to be honest. I've moved about forty-seven different times at different jobs. I'd do little parts and bits of a picture and off I'd go."

Hawkins was born in Jerome, Arizona, a little town on the side of a mountain honeycombed with mine shafts. His father, a cattleman named

C. T. Hawkins, was voted "the all-round cowboy of Arizona" two years running. Emery says his father "won everything, and he's in the record books. Roping, riding, throwing; he could play a fiddle and jig and call a dance all at once!"

After Emery's parents split up, his mother married a cabinetmaker, and Emery, an only child, lived with them in Hollywood. Emery always drew cartoons, and he says, "I always did animation. I did it on notebooks, figured it out on flip books."

At age sixteen he took to the Disney studio a scene of a clown walking which he had animated. He was turned away. "They said, 'We don't want copy work.' They didn't think I had done it." When he was eighteen Hawkins got a job inking cels at Walter Lantz's studio but was fired in a few months, after he changed all the cels because he "didn't like the way they were animated."

Next he went to the Charles Mintz studio and officially became an animator, and in 1932 he joined the Disney studio. He worked a little on story material, but most of the time he was "doing changes in sequences for other animators."

Hawkins was never allowed to work on a feature at Disney—incredibly, *Raggedy Ann & Andy* is his feature film debut. "I found it oppressive at Disney," he says. "I would spend weeks trying to get something the way some other bloke had done it. It was just not fun. I guess I'm too stupid to work with formulas. I just can't resist the temptation to take the formula and change it. Everything I've ever done, I've always changed changes. Change, change, change, change! Try to push a thing, stretch it, go further. Lots of times this didn't go over because they had fixed characters with fixed walks and so many beats. And I was always fighting that."

He left Disney's during the strike, went to Lantz again, returned briefly to Disney in 1944, then moved on to Warners, MGM, and small independent companies.

"I shuttled between studios. I was bobbing. I worked a number of times at all of them. Couldn't stay put. My father was like that."

In the fifties, Hawkins worked at most of the New York TV commercial studios, particularly for Jack Zander and John Hubley. "For years," Hawkins reflects, "I developed a real neurosis with pencils: I couldn't work without a certain kind of pencil, and it always turned out to be a pencil they quit making. Years later it dawned on me that I had been bored and was creating artificial problems. As soon as I got into TV I could draw with a flashlight, because I wasn't bored anymore. The curious thing is that my jobs have been getting longer over the years. I guess I'm slowing down. I'm not bobbing so fast."

Hawkins and his wife have lived in Taos, New Mexico, since 1963; he works there, receiving animation paper, exposure sheets and tape cassettes of soundtracks from New York and Hollywood, and sending his completed animation through the mails.

Hawkins likes to visit New York because it is, after all, a *change*. Visiting the New York *Raggedy* studio one cold January day in 1975, he wore his wide-brimmed cowboy hat, leather boots and string tie. He talked about his art in his slow, twangy voice with articulation and passion.

"I animate every way: backwards, forwards, and then straight ahead. Upside down, in and out, this way, every way. Every scene needs a different kind of thing. I envy animators who only animate one way, because it kind of settles the nerves and makes problems easier.

"I studied [Kimon] Nicolaides's book [*The Natural Way to Draw*] for fourteen solid years. I never got past the second lesson ["The Comprehension of Gesture"] because I got hung up on gesture. I'd sit near a bus stop in my car, draw people waiting for buses and fill the back of my car with roughs. Studying the core and the contour and the mass and the gesture of a figure until I could see it in my sleep. And when I got through I couldn't animate the same as I used to.

"I ended up having to go to extremes. For instance, I'd make the end drawing or the middle drawing and build from there. It destroyed that thing where you make a loose little soft drawing and the next and the next, so you end up with the action. I felt I had to get the guts out of it and get *this* thing first!

"For years I had made a soft light line and then gone over it and made it clean, animating. I got pretty good results, but it was a terrible strain on my nerves. After the Nicolaides book I stopped animating that way and started drawing these rough figures of people, how the figure is shaped and how it bends getting into poses, how the neck and torso work. It started getting fascinating, and I could see it in Daumier's work and other artists'. It's an *alive* thing!

"I think that for a person learning animation the most wonderful thing would be to get acquainted with the human race more."

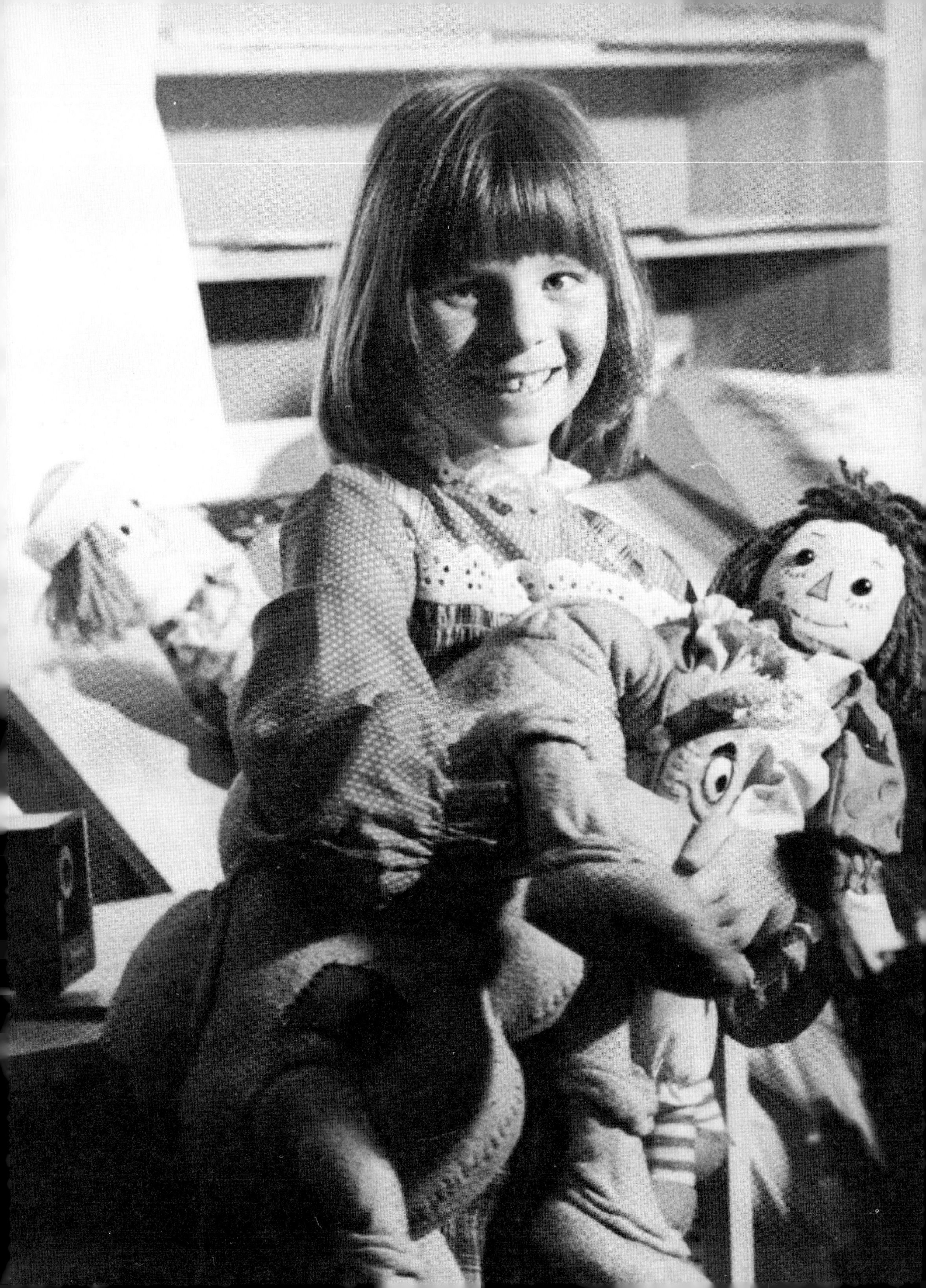

CHAPTER X
Notes at the Halfway Point

Claire did an 18-hour day the last day, which I guess is not allowable if you're not her father.

—*Richard Williams*

Shooting the Live-Action

The brief live-action sequences of *Raggedy Ann & Andy* feature Richard Williams's six-year-old daughter Claire as Marcella; they were filmed the week of October 20, 1975, in Boonton, New Jersey. The location was found by William Mickley, the film's set and costume designer.

Mickley, a member of the United Scenic Artists Local 829 and a busy stylist for television, industrial shows and theater since graduating from Brandeis University in 1971, was recommended for *Raggedy Ann* by Max Seligman, the film's soundtrack reader.

"In late July and early August I had meetings with Dick Williams and Richard Horner," says Mickley, "and we all liked each other. I was hired, and the first decision was whether to build a set in a studio or shoot on location.

"Dick felt that a location would give him the feeling of reality he was after, so I started scouting possible houses in my home state of Jersey—beyond Paterson, where the trees start growing again."

Mickley shot slides of a dozen possible houses he "impulsively" chose because of the visual attributes of their exteriors. Williams decided on a charming octagonal house, a "Victorian oddity" built in the mid-nineteenth century, on Cornelia Street in Boonton.

The house, which belongs to the Reverend and Mrs. Thorne, had "a good feeling," according to Mickley. "Full of funny angles, with walls at forty-five-degree angles to other walls. There was a coziness and a gingerbread quality, but not a hard-sell gingerbread."

For all its perfection, the location itself and the interior of the house had to be worked over. Beginning on October 14, Mickley and a pair of scenic

(*Opposite*) Claire Williams.

207

artists "tore rooms apart," painted and wallpapered one suite (which would be Marcella's playroom), built a ceiling grid for the lights (which made the already tight space even smaller), dug a backyard pool and "enhanced" the autumnal foliage by spraying leaves on the trees red and gold and importing more leaves from nearby neighborhoods.

While these cosmetic procedures were being completed at the location, Linda Locker, the costume stylist, went shopping for dresses with young Claire and her stand-in. The dolls in the playroom were constructed by four people: The Camel doll, the Twin Penny Dolls, the ship and the Captain in the glass globe were built and the Grandpa doll was rebuilt by Frederick Nidah, the professional mask- and prop-maker who made the *Equus* horse heads, the Tin Man in *The Wiz,* and the gorilla mask in the movie *Cabaret;* Richard Williams's mother fashioned Raggedy Ann and Andy, Topsy Turvy, and the Sockworm; Bill Davis in California made Barney Beanbag and Susie Pincushion; and Judy Sutcliff, a ceramicist, fashioned Babette, the French doll.

Mickley bought or custom-made various props, such as the large Victorian dollhouse in which Babette arrives.

Larry Albucher, thirty-seven, an assistant director with extensive live-action credits, including work on *Hello, Dolly; Love Story;* and *Hospital,* was chosen to assist Dick Williams.

"Considering that it was his first time out directing live-action, Dick did brilliantly," says Albucher. "He's like a sponge. He listens, he communicates. He sees everything he shoots, every movement—in Technicolor."

Albucher hand-picked a crew of over thirty-five people, including cameraman Dick Mingalone, who worked four days shooting from early morning until midnight; it was a full movie crew with a script supervisor, wardrobe woman, propman, drivers, lighting and sound men, grips, make-up artist, assistant to the assistant, and so on.

Williams shot quickly, with no more than five or six takes for each set-up. Williams's wife Margaret and his mother were on the set to see that Claire didn't become too exhausted and to keep her well supplied with her favorite orange sherbet. Joe Raposo, another member of the cast making a screen debut, has one line as the schoolbus driver.

The Reverend and Mrs. Thorne were compensated for the use of their home and the inconvenience they suffered during the filming; after the shooting, Bill Mickley spent two weeks restoring the house to its original condition by removing all prop fixtures put in for the film, filling in the pond in the backyard and steaming off the special English wallpaper used in Marcella's playroom.

Albucher feels the shooting went well: "The weather cooperated beautifully; the attitude of the crew was good. Everybody loved working with Williams. The only problem was that the playroom was so tiny—it would have been better shot on a set. But nothing was too difficult for our crew."

For the live-action sequences, a Maxi Fix-It doll was built by Frederick Nidah; Babette the French doll and the Susie Pincushion doll were fashioned by Judy Sutcliff and Bill Davis, respectively.

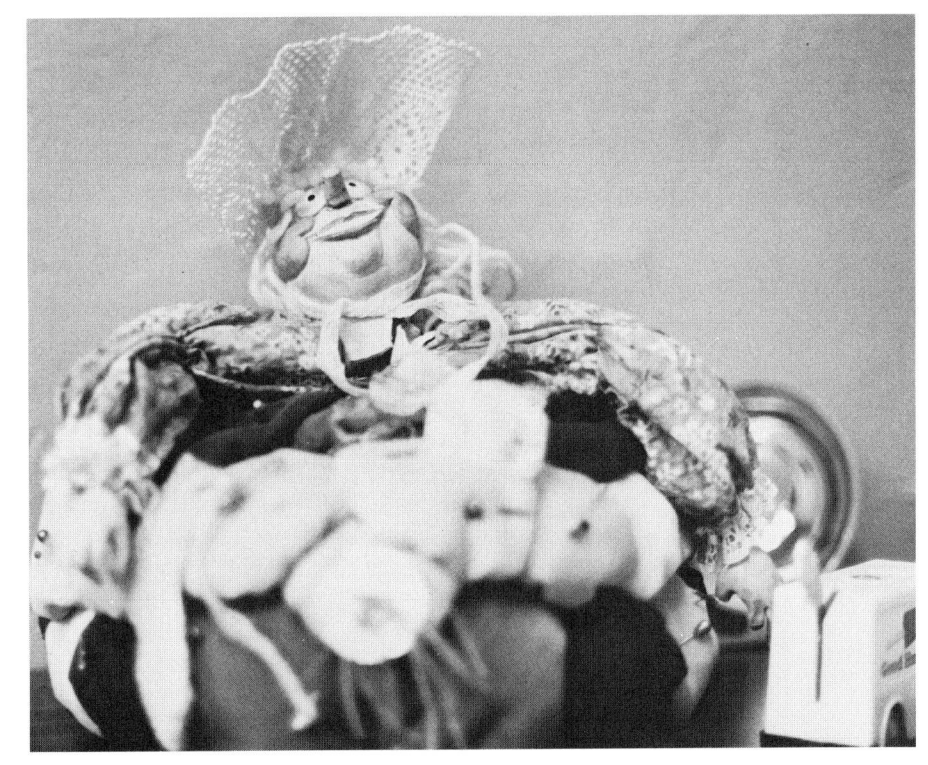

The Leica Reel Race

As predicted, Murphy's Law did indeed take its toll on the production. Williams's proposed completion date for the Leica reel was delayed three months, until mid-December. The entire production, in fact, was getting off the ground like a bowling ball in a taffy pit.

One of several technical problems that needed attention was the requirement that the film be made in Panavision for greater impact and design quality. "There were complaints from people who hadn't worked in it before," Williams recalls. "But then we got the live-action Panavision lens on Al Rezek's camera." It wasn't until September that they acquired the lens.

Williams then insisted that Polaroid filters be placed over the camera lens and on the lights to eliminate any scratches or dirt on the cels. He knew that since at least two sequences were going to be rendered with black backgrounds, cel abrasions would be a major problem. "We had never tried it here in the East," said Al Rezek. "There never was any need for it."

The cels themselves proved a troublesome, time-consuming item. Williams wanted a .004 celluloid that he used in London, a softer, lighter cel that is thinner than the American .003, which tends to darken as the cel levels pile up under the camera; if four cels are photographed in one set-up, there is roughly a twenty percent light loss in the value of the color painted on the back of the bottom cel. Unfortunately, the European .004s tend to buckle when the weather changes or too much paint is applied, and the Xerox process scratches the delicate things excessively. They finally located a Mylar-based cel from the Midwest that proved to be the perfect compromise.

Al Rezek had to design and build the Xerox processor and camera that would outline the original paper drawings directly onto cels. Then Williams went wild over a gray Xerox line he saw used in a Disney feature then in production, *The Rescuers*. "I noticed this beautiful charcoal-gray line, more beautiful than an ugly fat black line. So we phoned around the country and finally found the source of the chemical toner." It turned up in the East, of course.

Story sketches and art work were not arriving fast enough for use in making the Leica reel, so, with the big screening fast approaching, Williams flew in a friend from Canada, producer/director Gerry Potterton. Of Potterton, Williams says, "Gerry is an ideal transition between me and Corny. Gerry thinks extremely simply and clearly, and Corny is rich and ornate and demanding. I'm kind of between the two in my own way of working. Gerry's sense of cutting and construction is first rate."

After the screening of the Leica reel in mid-December, the reactions and consensus were generally positive, and for the Christmas holidays Williams went to London for a brief rest before the big push in the coming year.

In a letter dated December 22, Horner commented on the Leica-reel presentation and made several specific suggestions regarding the production. "If we can keep the quality I see coming and tighten the whole thing up dramatically—eighty-five minutes, say—I think we'll have a winner."

72 "MARCELLA COMES HOME"
LIVE ACTION SUGGESTIONS

Corny Cole's suggestions for the live-action sequence of Marcella coming home.

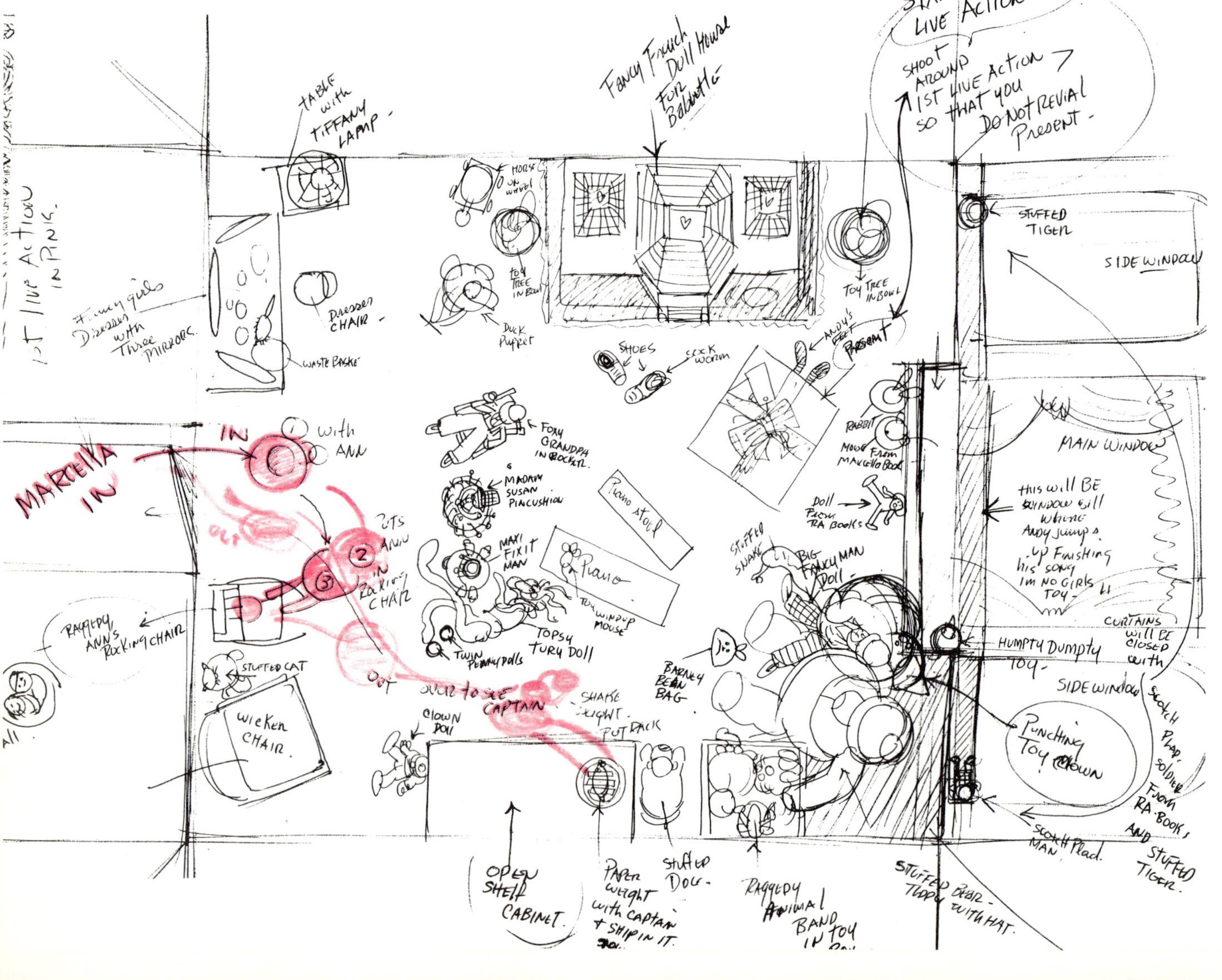

STARTING LIVE ACTION
SHOOT AROUND 1ST LIVE ACTION SO THAT YOU DO NOT REVIAL PRESENT.
Fancy French Doll House For Babette
TABLE with TIFFANY LAMP.
1st live Action in Pink.
Fancy girls Dresser with Three Mirrors.
DRESSER CHAIR.
WASTE BASKET
HORSE ON WHEEL
TOY TREE IN BOWL
DUCK PUPPET
Toy Tree in Bowl
STUFFED TIGER
SIDE WINDOW
ANDY'S BELT
PRESENT
SHOES
SOCK WORM
FOXY GRANDPA IN ROCKER
MADAM SUSAN PINCUSHION
Piano stool
MAXI FIXIT MAN
Piano
TOY WINDUP MOUSE
TOPSY TURY DOLL
TWIN PENNY DOLLS
MARCELLA IN
IN
with ANN
PUTS ANN IN ROCKING CHAIR
OUT
RAGGEDY ANN'S ROCKING CHAIR
STUFFED CAT
WICKER CHAIR.
OVER TO SEE CAPTAIN
SHAKE SLIGHT.
PUT BACK
OUT
CLOWN DOLL
RABBIT
MOUSE FROM MARCELLA BOOK
Doll FROM RA BOOKS
STUFFED SNAKE
BIG FANCY MAN DOLL
BARNEY BEAN BAG
MAIN WINDOW
this will BE WINDOW Will where ANDY JUMPS UP FINISHING his SONG I'M NO GIRLS TOY.
CURTAINS will be closed with
HUMPTY DUMPTY TOY.
SIDE WINDOW
Punching Toy Clown
SCOTCH PLAID SOLDIER FROM RA BOOKS AND STUFFED TIGER.
SCOTCH PLAID MAN.
OPEN SHELF CABINET.
PAPER WEIGHT with CAPTAIN & SHIP IN IT.
STUFFED DOG.
RAGGEDY ANIMAL BAND IN TOY
STUFFED BEAR-TEDDY WITH HAT.

Claire Williams and her father, director Williams.

On January 2, 1976, Dick Williams wrote a vivid account of where the production stood at the halfway point and how the director's mind was working in several areas at once.

I shouldn't worry about the reel running 108 minutes at present. This is because the third is in a state of rough assembly only and I didn't have time to even attempt to tighten up the last three reels . . . 23–28 minutes can come out with a little work.

The large cuts you suggest:

1. *The Greedy*. I quite agree with you that this sequence runs too long, and the place to cut is where you suggest: where Raggedy Ann shows her candy heart up to their escape. . . . The lengthy dialogue should go, but I think it is important we keep as much dramatic action and threat going on, because we need the tension in there to contrast with the long sentimental passages in the movie. . . . Another good reason for tightening this area up is that it is wildly expensive animation. I had already planned to cut this area and arranged with Emery before Christmas to have him come to New York at the end of next week so that he can (a) see the Leica reel working, and (b) collaborate on the cutting of this sequence. . . .

On the facing page (*top*), set designer William Mickley's ideas for Marcella's live-action playroom set. (*Bottom*) A bird's-eye view of the playroom set marked for camera moves and, in red, Marcella's (Claire Williams's) movements.

213

Claire rehearses with her father.

2. *Loonieland*. I quite agree—much too long. . . . I plan to give it the torture of the thousand cuts, but this will take a little time. I agree that your suggestion to cut directly from the rug that rolls them into Loonieland to King Koo Koo's descent will work, but I have some other ideas. This area again was slopped over, and it is not yet made clear that the Knight is motivating and controlling all the nonsense in Ha Ha Hall. . . .

3. *The Gazooks*. The tickling sequence certainly is twice too long. Nobody thought we could even get this strung together in time for the Leica reel, but in [an] all-night frenzy it got thrown in and is obviously in pretty sloppy shape right now. . . . Don't worry about any doubtful areas going into animation. That is another function of the Leica reel, to make sure that doubtful areas do not go into expensive animation work before they are resolved. Even the work that went into preliminary animation last July for developing the characters was all work on scenes that will be in the finished picture.

I notice most of your comments, and other people's, apply to the *unfinished* parts of the Leica reel. The first third is where I have almost completed timing and planning—everyone seems happy about this. It's the old problem of solving a working outline before it's resolved.

Although we should get the Leica reel into shape as quickly as possible, I must go to California after a week in New York, because . . . while one is confident that people like Babbitt can direct their own sequences, I am not confident that the other animators are capable of working without my direction, and I'd better get out there quick to make sure we are not wasting expensive animation time on false starts. . . .

Claire's voice. You say it must be dubbed, and you say unless I come back with her lines O.K. *this time,* [you] don't think we should waste time trying to get clarity from her. I have not done it this time, as I have been trying to get some sleep, spend some unprofessional time with my children, and do master clean-ups of Tissa's animation. I react very strongly against your other suggestion that an adult dub the voice. If there is one thing I have learned in twenty-five years of producing television adverts for children's products, it is that you *never* use an adult voice imitating a child. Maybe you could fool an adult viewer with this, but you certainly cannot fool a child. This is why Disney's always use actual child voices of the actual age and, dare I say, often the director's own children. . . .

The live-action sequence is deliberately devoid of music and other glossy supporting effects, so that it will be *believable* to a child audience. Whatever we do, it must not *look* phoney, fake or dubbed. For example, no one wants to hear Deanna Durbin's voice coming out of Dorothy's mouth in *The Wizard of Oz*. . . . What I would prefer to do is to get Claire to post-sync the muffled or muffed lines at a later date. There is no rush as I see it. If she is still found to be too English, then let's get a clever American child of no older than seven and go over everything. I would prefer an *untrained* voice, and this was my reason for homey and believable effect, never mind mistakes. Nepotism was not my reason for foisting Claire upon the production. [Claire's voice was eventually dubbed by an American child-actress.]

. . . I am really delighted that you feel bullish about the quality of what we are coming up with. . . . If we can keep the quality that is coming and can tighten it up drastically to, say, 85 minutes, I do agree we'll have a winner. This picture always had this feeling about it, and it is obviously increasing all round. . . .

Anyway, thanks a lot for your positive letter, and I am delighted you are pleased with what this cutthroat cottage industry can produce.

I will ring you immediately I get in and present my glorious report.

Best wishes,
Dick Williams

By April, Bobbs-Merrill/ITT had increased the budget and postponed the release of the film to Easter 1977, thus giving Williams and company until December 30, 1976 (an extra three months), to deliver a final color answer print of *Raggedy Ann & Andy*.

PART FOUR:

A CLOSER LOOK

June 22, 1976
TO: ALL ARTISTS
FROM: DICK WILLIAMS

It is *very* important to keep layouts, storyboard blow-ups, and layout sketches *with* the scene in the scene folder! Do not animate the scene and throw away the layouts; they are necessary for a guide for the people right down the line.

    The rule is to keep the scene together. That means all relevant information stays in the scene folder.

                                                                               Thanks,
                                                                               Dick

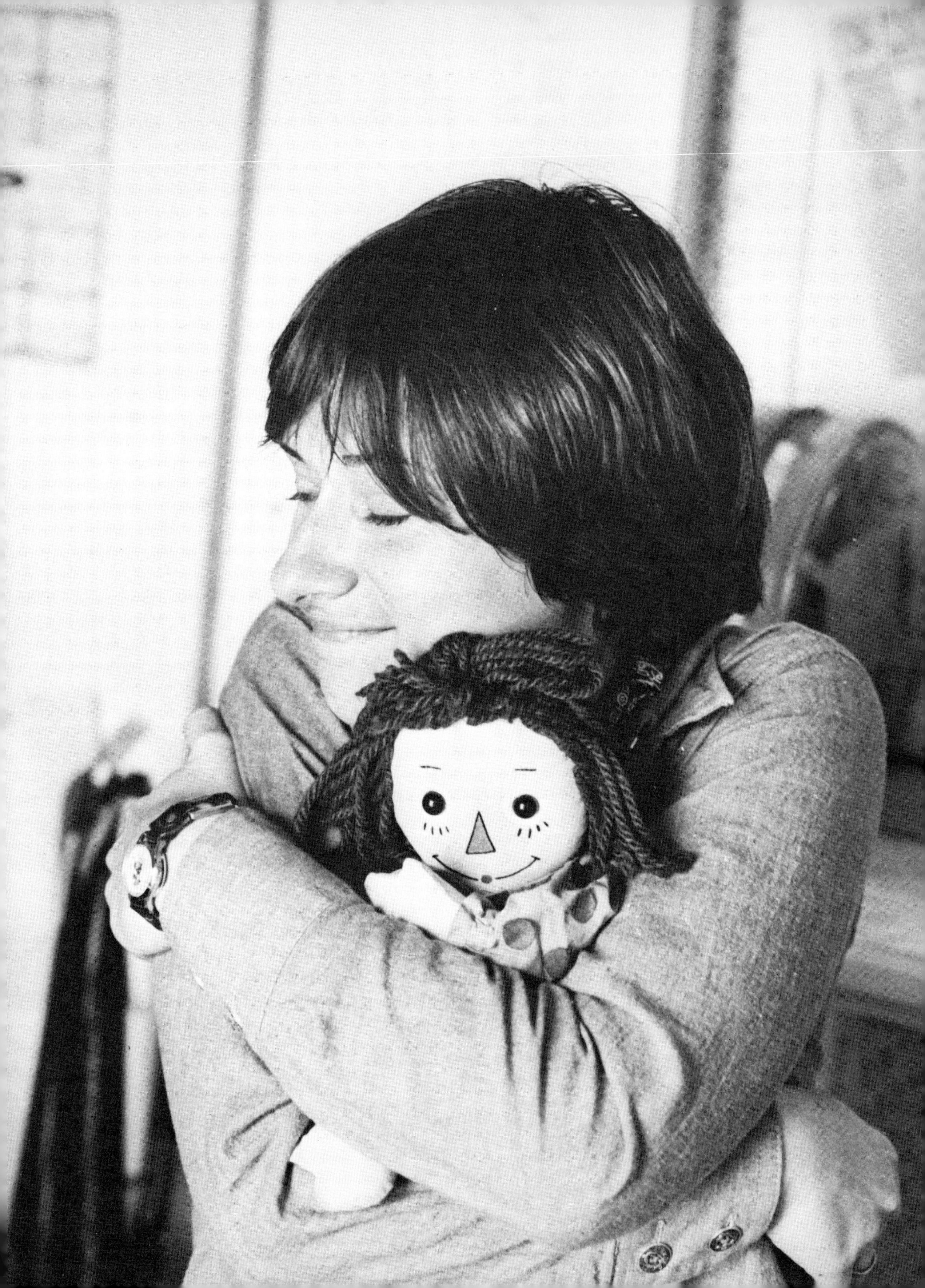

CHAPTER XI
Raggedy Ann West: The Hollywood Studio

Cars are made in Detroit and movies are made in L.A.
—Richard Williams

It is a typically hot, smoggy July morning in Los Angeles. Half a mile from Vine Street on Hollywood Boulevard, near Wilton, the *Raggedy Ann & Andy* studio, West Coast division, is located. But it is not easy to find. A large sign on the garish orange two-story building reads "Quartet Films, Inc." Only a tiny sign taped to the glass of the front door indicates that upstairs is, indeed, "Lester Osterman Productions/Raggedy Ann."

Quartet, a busy TV commercial animation production house, has leased various cubicles and offices throughout the building to *Raggedy Ann's* producers. The carpeting on the stairway and in the entrance hall establishes a hush that pervades the whole place. There is a calm here away from tacky Hollywood Boulevard and the heat; people speak sotto voce, and blue-bladed plastic fans softly flutter the pages of story sketches tacked onto cork boards.

There is no apparent concern among the artists that this is a temporary studio, that it will not exist three months from now. It's more than the infamous "laid back" California attitude; there is a quiet confidence that they will get another job when this one is over. These folks are animation pros; they are veterans at rolling with the unemployment punches.

Sixty-five-year-old Gerry Chiniquy animates with a cigarette dangling from a pair of lips that curl and drop devastating bon mots about certain parties in the New York studio; the digs fall sideways out of the smiling lips in a mock-French accent, and everybody cracks up.

Chiniquy is known in the business as a dance animator, and in his long stint with the old Warner Brothers studio ("Termite Terrace") he specialized in making Bugs Bunny, Daffy Duck and other zanies trip the light fantastically. Chiniquy resembles Gene Kelly (everyone tells him that) and says he gets "99% of all dance animation" because he has "a feel for it."

(*Opposite*) Animator Chrystal Russell.

Animator Gerry Chiniquy. On the facing page, six of Chiniquy's rough animation drawings of King Koo Koo.

Paulette and Charlie Downs. On the overleaf, five of Charlie Downs's roughs of the Captain and one rough background suggestion for the ship's prison.

Chiniquy, who began on *Raggedy* in February 1976, is animating the dancing Twin Penny dolls, who do everything together—dance, sing and talk. "It's a challenge," Chiniquy admits, "this dance thing. I haven't done it in one hell of a time. The feeling is a little bit of rock. The beat is on eights. Donnie and Marie Osmond might do as models."

Chiniquy is also animating mad King Koo Koo, the midget monarch who can increase his size only when he laughs at the misfortunes of others. King Koo Koo is reminiscent of Yosemite Sam, a bombastic despot whom Chiniquy animated at Warners, but Chiniquy points out that while Sam was also small and "a bastard, a no-good," he mostly screamed at the top of Mel Blanc's lungs. Koo Koo "does dialogue."

Across the hall is fifty-year-old Charles E. Downs, who is animating—with an enormous sense of fun—the outrageous lovesick Captain and the Pirate's parrot-servant. Seated at an animation board next to Downs is his wife Paulette, who assists Charlie by cleaning up his rough sketches.

Downs was at Disney's for nine years, starting on *Peter Pan,* and he feels that the Captain is "almost the same as Captain Hook, only fatter." Downs believes that the first scenes he animated on *Raggedy* were too stiff: "Usually you develop, but here there's no time to go back. In the early scenes you'll notice that his mustache is shorter than later, too.

"Distance is the biggest problem on this picture," Downs complains. "The communications aren't good. Three scenes were repeated unnecessarily. I think that on a feature everyone should be in the studio, and there should be *one* studio. You can feed off one another, go over and see how a scene or characters are being handled, make drawings to explain things."

Despite the hassles, Downs thinks that "this is a fantastic picture! The first feature with the possibilities and expectations of a Disney picture. This picture has been fantastically lucky. Dick Williams took care of everything."

DIDN'T

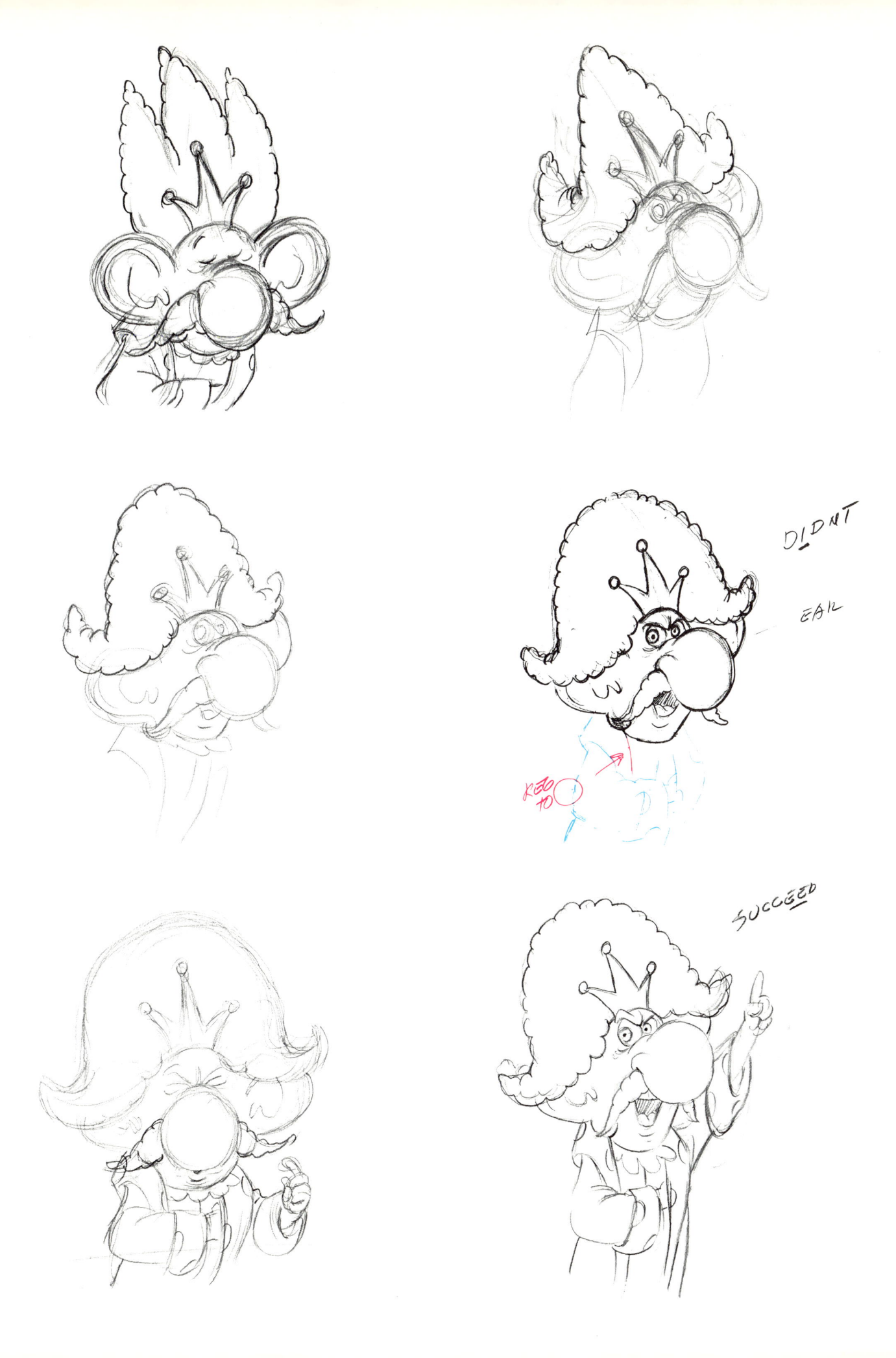

EAR

REO
TO

SUCCEED

119
125 127
123
129
119

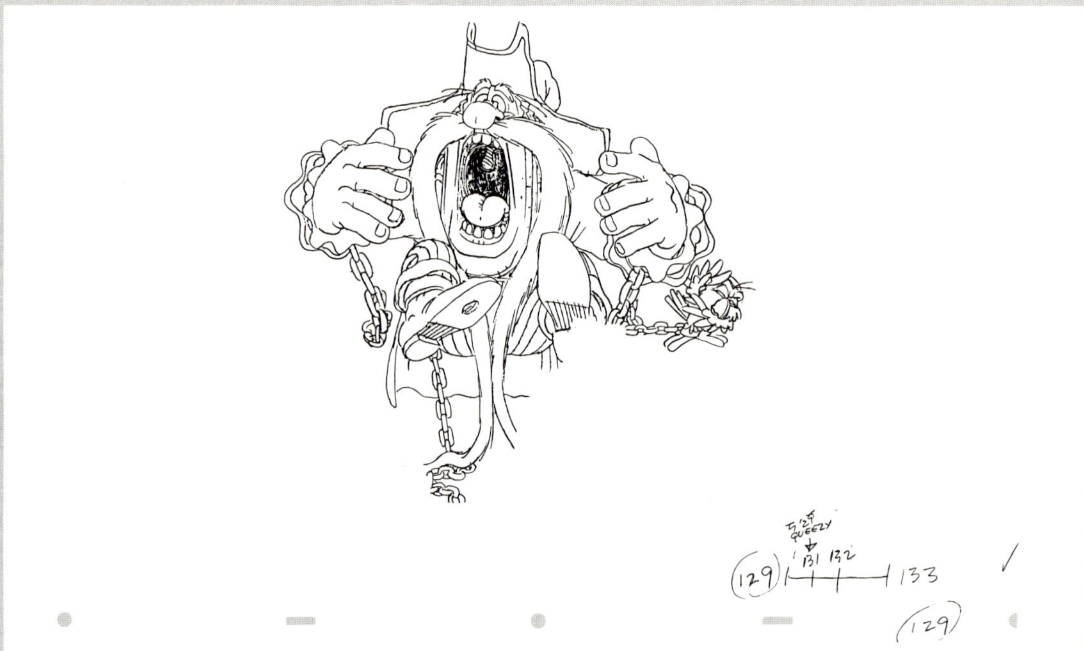

QUEEZY
131 132
129
133
129

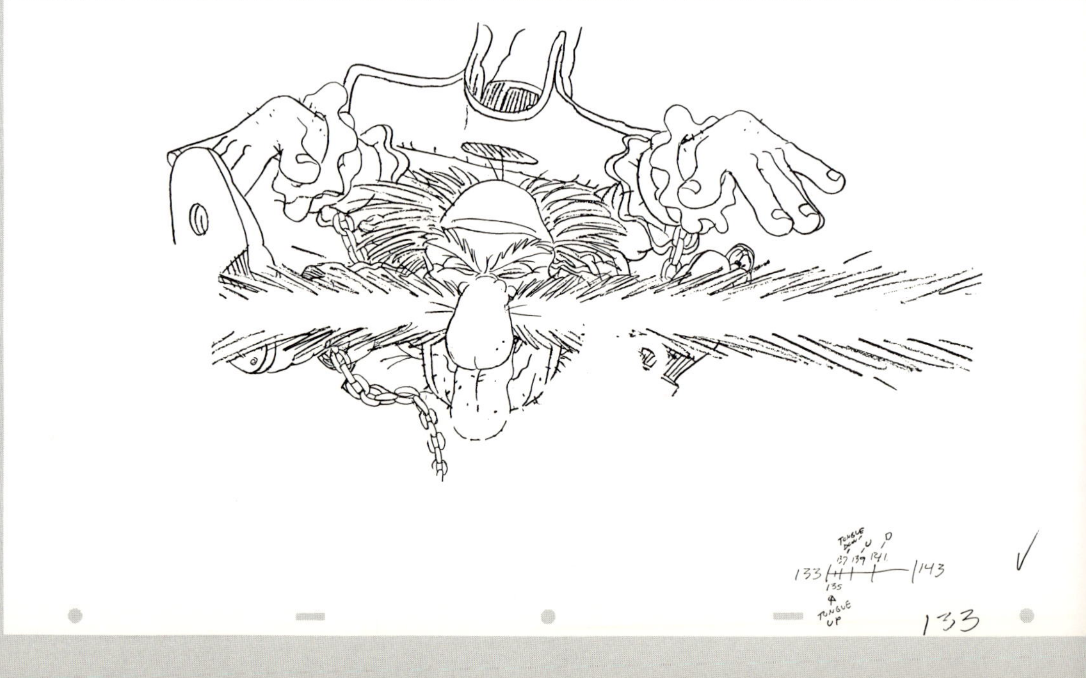

TONGUE
137 139 141
133
143
135
TONGUE UP
133

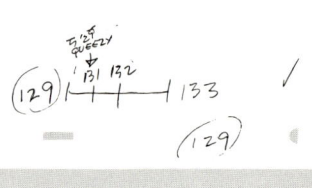

SAW DUST ON FLOOR   SEG 8   PG 39

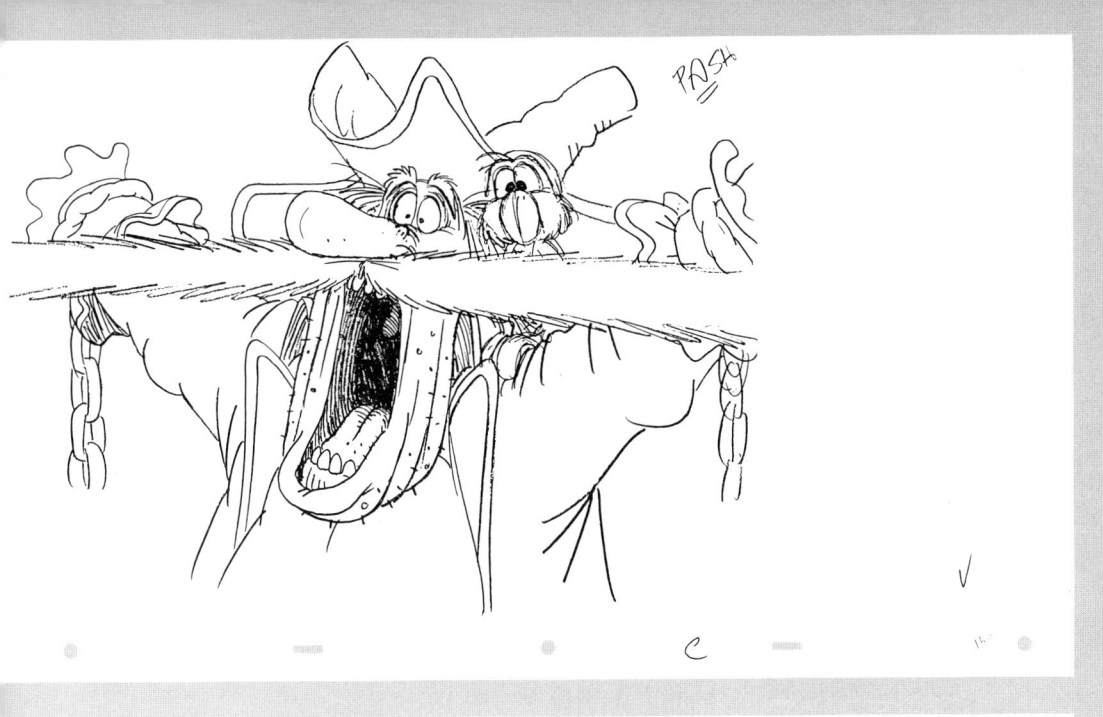

Marlene Robinson, head of assistants and inbetweeners at Raggedy Ann West.

In the room with Mr. and Mrs. Downs is another team of sorts. John Bruno and Art Vitello, who have both worked for Ralph Bakshi, are tackling the Greedy battle where Emery Hawkins left off. Quiet, catlike Bruno animated the wild perspective shot of the dolls reading the note on Marcella's gift box and is responsible for a chorus or two of the "Rag Dolly" number.

Down the hall is a small square room that holds four assistant animators, all carefully cleaning up, retracing and embellishing animators' roughs. One of these patient people is Marlene Robinson, who has been designated head of assistants and inbetweeners at *Raggedy Ann West*.

A long-haired kid in faded jeans comes in from the inbetweener pool for some help from Marlene. He can't seem to get the wriggling strands of Raggedy Ann's hair correctly placed on three drawings. This may not sound like a crucial thing, but when it is blown up on a Panavision screen, any inconsistency—a hair strand that does not move where it should, colors that don't match from frame to frame, shapes and sizes that vary even slightly—will jar the eye, distract the audience, and disturb the entire film.

"See, this strand should go here, and then the others follow, like so! Consistently." Marlene gently shows the kid the error of his ways for ten minutes. On her off-hours she is studying to be a nurse.

Perky, big-eyed Alissa Myersob is in the young inbetweener pool. She is now twenty, "as old as Marlene has worked in the business." Alissa is inbetweening a Charlie Downs Pirate Captain scene, filling in rough drawings between Downs's main action sketches. She giggles as she flips her drawings. "It's a funny scene. His moustache gets hard."

At Boardner's, a cartoonists' hangout on Cherokee Street, Carl Bell, the *Raggedy* West Coast animation coordinator, and his wife Jan, the film's West Coast office manager, relax for an hour away from the office and the July heat.

Carl Bell, animation coordinator of Raggedy Ann West.

"For the last six months," Carl Bell says in his soft voice, "we've had no free time. Working with Dick means there's no such thing as a forty-hour week. But that's the way it has to be done."

"Carl is very loyal," says Jan. "He works eleven, twelve hours on the weekend just to keep ahead of Dick."

Carl Bell met Dick Williams in 1950, when they were students at the Ontario College of Art. He traveled to Disney's on one of Williams's forays and has worked there and for Chuck Jones; he animated on Bob Clampett's *Beany and Cecil* TV series, and was Abe Levitow's production coordinator for six years until Levitow's death.

In June 1975 Bell began to coordinate the *Raggedy Ann* animation that was starting to be mailed to Los Angeles from New York. At first the studio was little more than a glorified messenger service, with Bell working out of his home and delivering scenes and art supplies to Art Babbitt, John Kimball and Corny Cole in their homes, but as more animators were hired in California and the project grew, it became apparent that more space was necessary. Babbitt, who helped found Quartet Films in the 1950s, had arranged to see pencil tests on their studio Moviola. He heard that space was available there and suggested to Horner and Osterman that they grab it.

Carl Bell has no problems fulfilling his obligations to Dick and the film, because first and foremost he loves his work (although he sometimes frets about not being "on the board"—animating). Jan Bell feels that their biggest headache is "people second-guessing Dick. And the lack of organization at the beginning. If it weren't for Dick it would all fall apart. But the biggest obstacles have made it the beautiful thing it is."

Jan and Carl's duties include "assigning scenes, taking care of exposure sheets, storyboards, the soundtrack. Following through on all information related to each scene—including pencils."

225

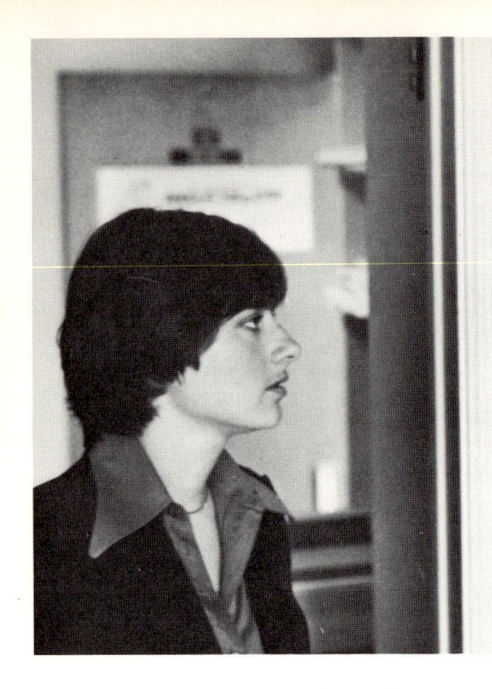

An impromptu conference between Chrystal Russell and Dick Williams.

Back at the studio, one of the most exciting new animators to come along in years is quietly working her magic on Raggedy Ann's opening song, "I Look and What Do I See." Chrystal Russell is one of the few women in the ranks of the top animators.

Born in Pasadena, thirty-year-old Chrystal Russell studied with Art Babbitt in his advanced class in 1973; she was going to be a biological illustrator, she thought, but got "scared of the chemistry" and quit. Filmation, a large TV cartoon factory, then hired her.

Babbitt says, "Chrystal actually does better than most men. When I gave tough assignments she worked at them. She added something to every test, never picked an easy out. She's a find, one of the naturals. There is her love of the medium, her seriousness, which has given her the start that she has. She has all her objectives lined up. This is an unusual talent that should be encouraged."

Chrystal, like Tissa David, became a Raggedy Ann specialist and animated her not only in the opening song but also in many other scenes throughout the film. She thrives on Williams's energetic presence, as do all the animators. "He's always right there, encouraging you—'Go! Go!" Sometimes her responsibilities get a little too heavy, as witness a letter written in September to a friend:

. . . This has been one of those weeks. It's always sort of hard to keep it together when Dick's gone.

Everything in the world dropped on my head last Mon. The girl doing inbetweens on a scene of mine kept having problems, and it turned out some fool had lost all of the ruffs from the scene *and* the background. Then the [background] from another scene came up missing. A boy doing asst. [messed] over one of my scenes, and I had to give it back to him. . . . And somebody told me that I'd missed Paul Simon on TV. . . . That started the week. I came down with the stomach flu on Wednesday and was relieved to escape from the studio. I hope they're all still alive over there. Whew!

Down peaceful, wide, clean Edinburgh Street, between Santa Monica Boulevard and Melrose Avenue, are cozy-looking houses surrounded by generous bushes and large palm trees. In a courtyard splashed with sunlight, Grim Natwick strides purposefully across the yard from the bungalow he lives in to a second small bungalow which he uses as a studio.

Eighty-seven years old, Natwick is tall and handsome, like some ancient tree. A former track athlete from Wisconsin who brought new sensitivity to animation with his early cartoon work, Natwick remains a vigorous man, with a mind that cracks like a brand-new whip.

Grim Natwick has attacked his latest assignment, the Loonies in the King Koo Koo sequence, with all the enthusiasm he put into his first day at the Hearst studio in New York in 1924. "I'm doing a very small part. They threw me a lot of crowd stuff, which is very hard to make interesting. Other fellows have worked on the Loonie crowds, and I felt they were getting very drab. So I've tried to handle the crowd as a background area and throw in an extra character to kind of give the thing a little personal feeling."

He admits he is quite proud of Tissa: "Tissa's a great worker. She could do the work of two or three assistants if she wanted to. Tissa has a great feeling for the characters."

But the pedagogue in Grim overwhelms him and rushes to the fore. "Only thing is—I've told Tissa a few of the holds [drawings held in place for repeated photography] were stopped on what I would term a moving drawing or action pose. A hold is basically a rest, even if it's only eight frames, and it should not have the feeling of action. I mean if you have bent knees and swinging arms you feel as though it's an animation drawing.

"A hold is a drawing about to spring to life. Tissa agreed with me."

(*Above left*) Grim Natwick. (*Above*) Natwick in the courtyard between his living quarters and his studio.

A Natwick animation rough of one of the Loonies.

227

3.1
Sc 20
32

HANDS OUT
OVER RAIL
#34 — 38
PART II
3.1
Sc 20
38

18 F.
SEE SCENE
FOR RAIL TO
Background #20

Hal Ambro, in his early sixties, stops by the studio to pick up and deliver some Babette scenes. Ambro, a gentle Santa Claus look-alike, started at Disney and remained there until 1966. He decided to free-lance because "there's only so much room at the top of the ladder at Disney," and he realized he wasn't going to reach those rarefied heights occupied by a select corps of Disney animators.

"I've had a lot of training in the human area in the Disney films. Humans are most difficult in the sense that you have to elaborate—*exaggerate* is a better word—their actions. But not too much. You don't make a face look like Jell-O, but you can do an action that reflects a stretch in the whole posture.

"I think Dick sees Babette visually as his wife. We looked at some film of this French singer who is no longer alive, Edith Piaf, at the way she talked, in a big-lipped sort of way. He thought we might be able to use some of her gestures, but by that time I'd worked out a whole pattern for Babette's balcony song in the playroom sequence. When she's on board ship she becomes a women's lib type, sort of."

To the question of how one makes a cartoon sexy, Ambro answers: "Without making her more bosomy, which she is in the Pirate ship, you can make her look coy, and it comes off as sexy. With a little child and a different delivery of words it would be coyness, but with an older person you'd have to label it sexy."

Hal Ambro

(*Opposite*). Two animation drawings of Babette and a layout drawing of her balcony by Hal Ambro.

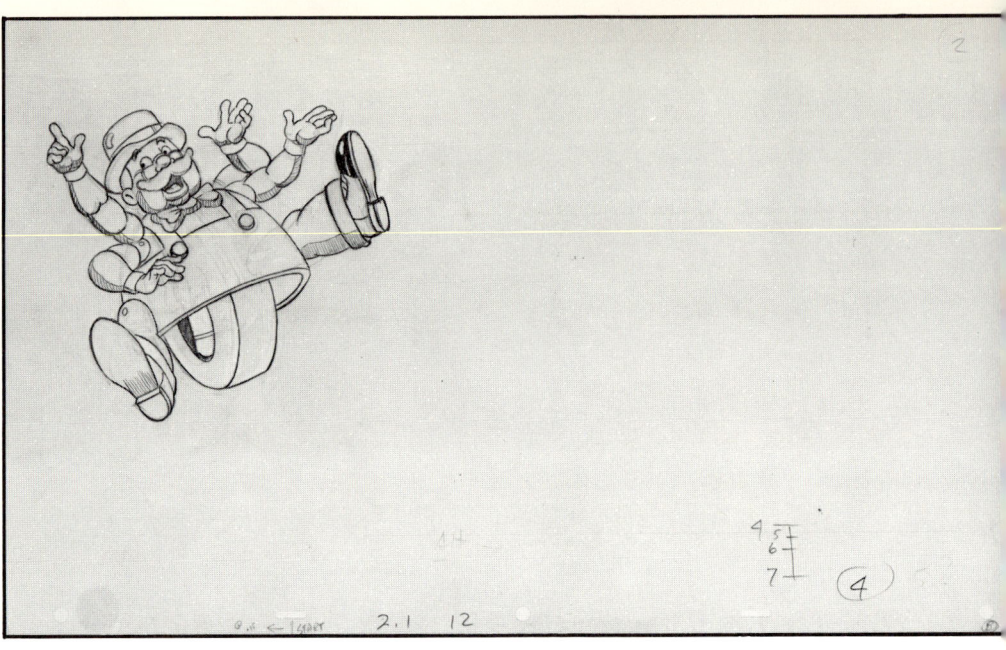

Six animation drawings of Maxi Fix-It by Spencer Peel.

Spencer Peel, also in his early sixties, is animating the majority of the scenes involving the playroom dolls. "Spencer took a long time to get going," says Dick Williams. "Now he's going, and he's the expert on those characters. Nobody can handle Maxi Fix-It and Susie Pincushion like him. Terrific charm!

"But he went in slowly. Some guys go in slow, and that's what's so hard to make a businessman realize: that if an animator is sitting at his drawing-board scratching away or looking out the window, he's working! A carpenter, a good one, will sit and size up how he's going to make a bunch of shelves.

Peel, shy and sensitive, explains that for some scenes he had to devise layouts and animation for ten dolls. At 16 frames per foot of film, Peel was making 160 drawings for every *foot* of those scenes!

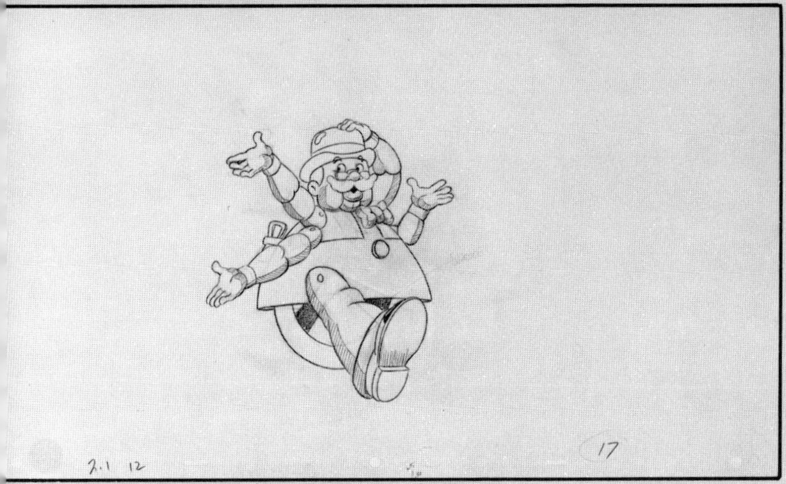
2.1 12
17

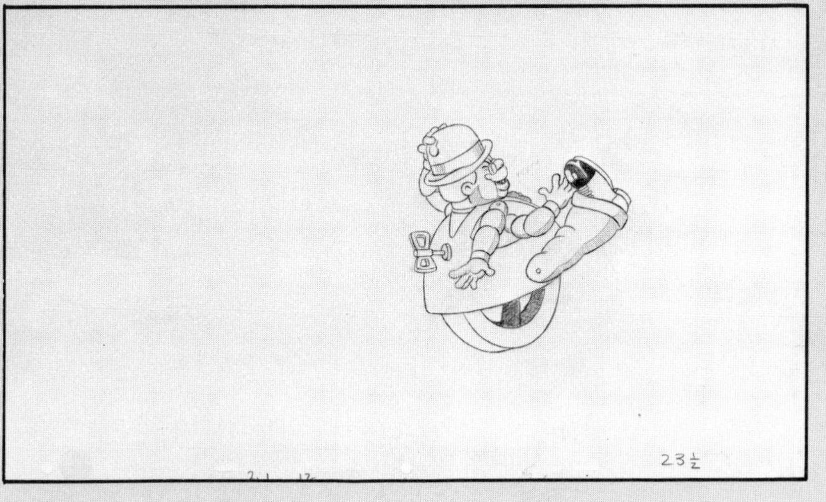
23½

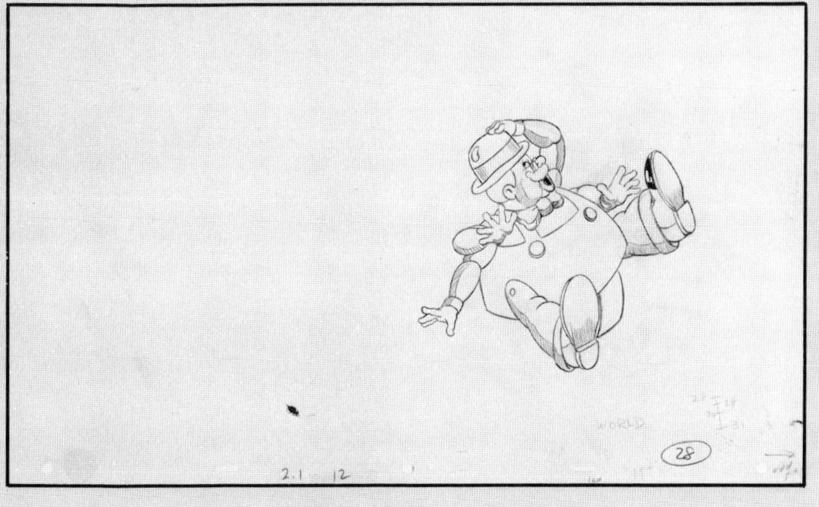
2.1 12
28

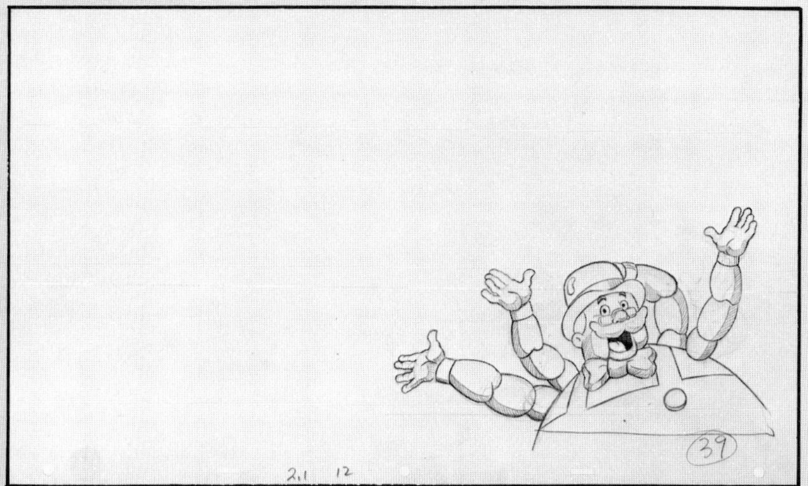
2.1 12
39

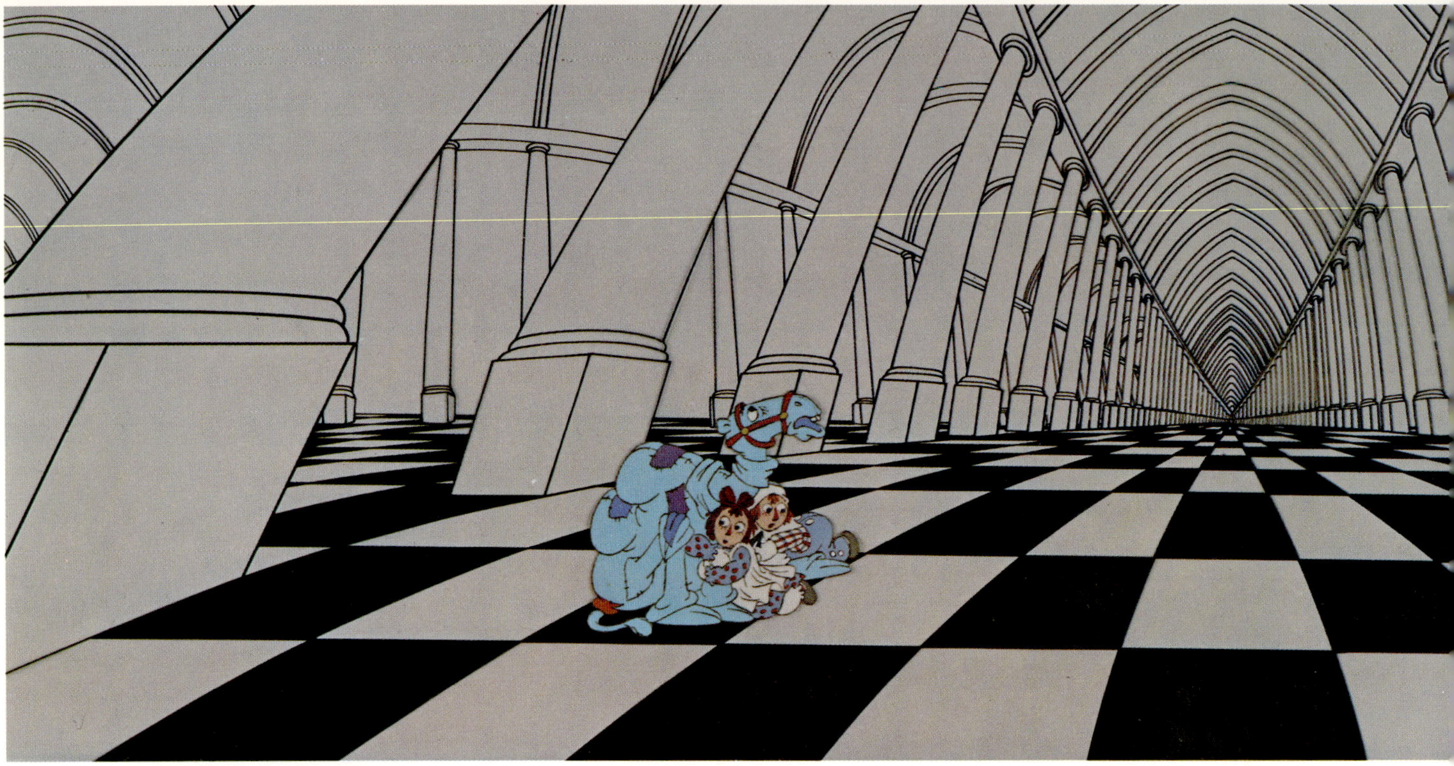

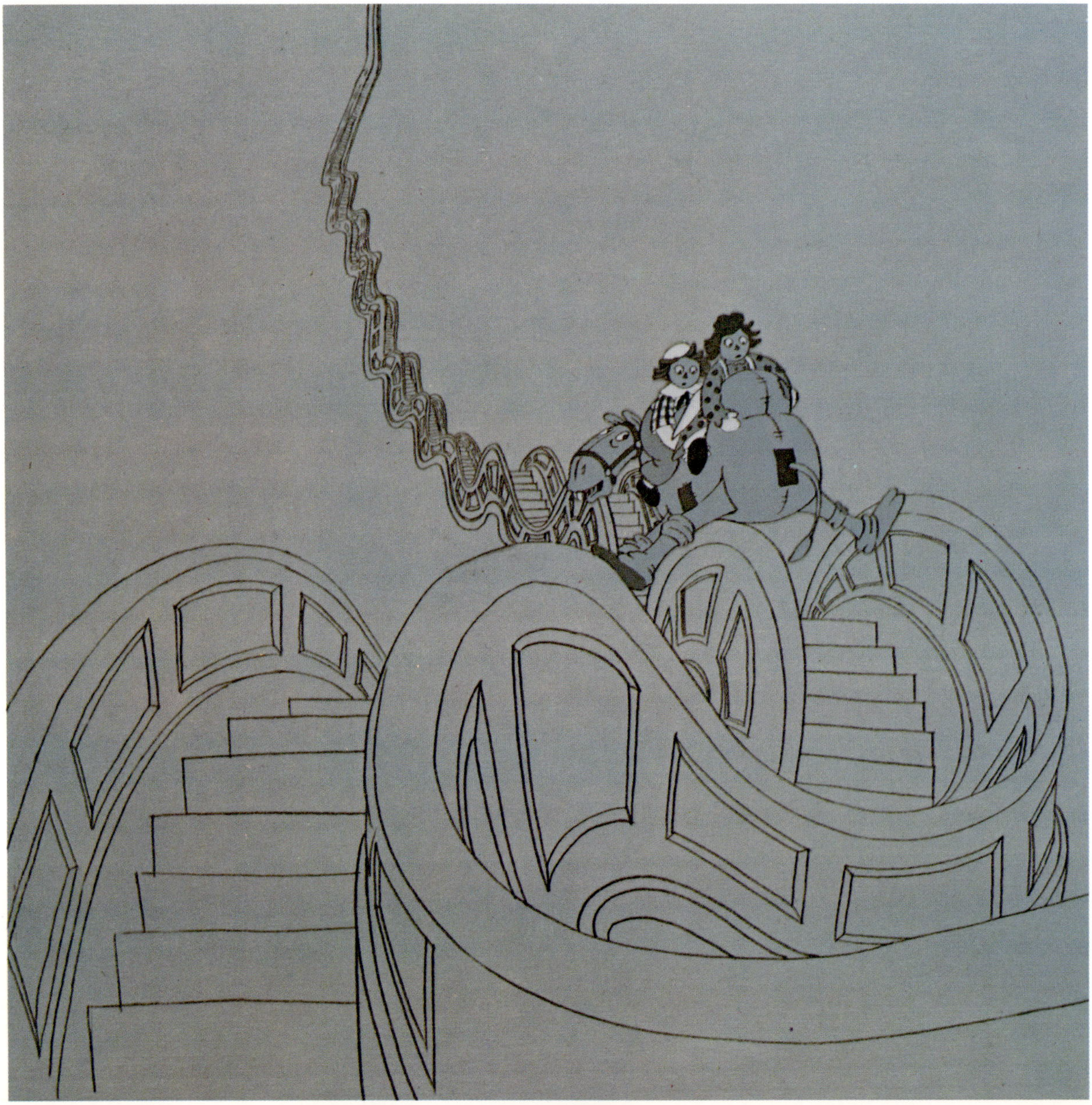

John Kimball, in his mid-thirties, hirsute and cheery, bounces into the studio from his home in Pasadena. Kimball is working on the zany Loonie Knight sequence, the weird Camel mirage, and the spooky, nightmarish Ha Ha Hall.

"They wanted something a little terrifying, sort of like a dream where you're falling from some high place. I stretched horizon lines, pulled them in. I used a lot of M. C. Escher's and Winsor McCay's concepts—optical illusions—where I constantly change the point of reference. The hardest problem was figuring out the speeds of the spiral staircase stuff and the speeds of the Camel, Ann, Andy and the Knight on the staircase in Ha Ha Hall.

"All the people working on the picture have a tremendous pride in what they're doing. They're trying to do the best animation they can under the circumstances. Going to the weekly showings turns you on. There's a kind of competition in a way, but it's healthy—a mutual admiration society."

The work load and the strain of the production are beginning to show on Richard Williams. He still has that eternal-youth bounce and enthusiasm, but in his few quieter moments the fatigue he has been battling catches up with him.

"I find the jet lag coming this way a killer," he says, smiling. "If you talk to my wife, she'll say I'm in bad shape. But I don't feel that. She told me not to stop as soon as this was finished. I'm forty-three; I've got to taper off. She said, 'Go work on *The Thief* for a month or two and run down, and *then* take a holiday, but don't stop all at once.'"

Gerry Potterton, associate director (*left*), talks with animator John Kimball.

On the facing page (*top*), Raggedy Ann, Andy, and the Camel enter Ha Ha Hall. (*Bottom*) The wild staircase ride begins.

LITTLE NEMO IN SLUMBERLAN
COME ON, MAMA SAYS FOR US TO GET OUT OF HERE! WE'LL SLIDE DOWN!
CUT IT OUT! CUT IT OUT PROFESSOR! HIS MOTHER DOES NOT LIKE MUSIC! WE'LL SLIDE DOWN!
FOR MERCYS SAKE STOP THAT NOISE! WHO IS THAT PLAYING THAT HORRIBLE MOUTHORGAN WHY DON'T YOU ALL COME DOWN STAIRS AND GO OUT IN THE YARD!
ARE YOU READY? SAY THE WORD.
WAIT A MINUTE! WAIT A MINUTE!
I AM EDDY RAY!
AH! HERE WE GO! A MILE A MINUTE!
BE CAREFUL!
GO FASTE GO FASTE WHAT'S T DELAY?
GOING FAST ENOUGH TO SUIT ME!
THIS IS THE WAY TO SLIDE A BANISTER! YOU SEE? TAKE IT EASY!
THIS STAIRWAY LOOKS AWFUL BIG TO ME ALL AT ONCE!
I DONT CARE HOW BIG IT IS! I'M COMFORTABLE! SEE?
I NEVER KNEW IT WAS SO LONG. HUH!
OOK LAY OU TA! IS THAY IS A ARP SHAY URVE .CAY! EE BAY AREFUL CAY!
WOW! WHAT WAS THAT! OH! OH!
IT'S A SHARP CURVE! OH! FLIP! WHERE YOU GOING?
I OLD TAY OO YAY OO TA OOK LAY OUTAY IDDEN DEY I DE?
WHAT AILS THIS STAIR WAY ZOWIE!
MAMA! MAMA! SOMETHING IS THE MATTER WITH THIS STAIRWAY!
CAN'T YOU COME AND HELP YOUR LITTLE BOY?
IS THAY IS I MAY INISH FAY!
OH! THERE GOES KIDDO OH! OH!
OW NAY OR FAY A OOD GAY UMP BAY! OH!
I NEVER KNEW THIS STAIRWAY WAS SO LONG!
SURELY THERE IS AN END TO IT SOMEWHERE OH! IF I COULD ONLY STOP!
I'M GETTING DIZZY! WHERE CAN THIS PLACE BE? OH! I'M SO DIZZY!
HELP! OH! OH! HELP ME! HELP ME!
OH! I'M GLAD MAMA DID NOT HEAR ME! HUH!

Six animation roughs by John Kimball for the dizzying staircase scene. (*Opposite*) Winsor McCay's *Little Nemo in Slumberland* comic strip of April 18, 1909 inspired the staircase effects in *Raggedy Ann & Andy*. Strip reprinted with the permission of Nostalgia Press.

The Raggedy Ann studio on Hollywood Boulevard.

(*Above*) Carl Bell speaks on the phone, while Dick Williams confers with Art Babbitt, back to camera.

(*Left*) Editor Lee Kent.

Art Babbitt acts out a storyboard scene for Williams.

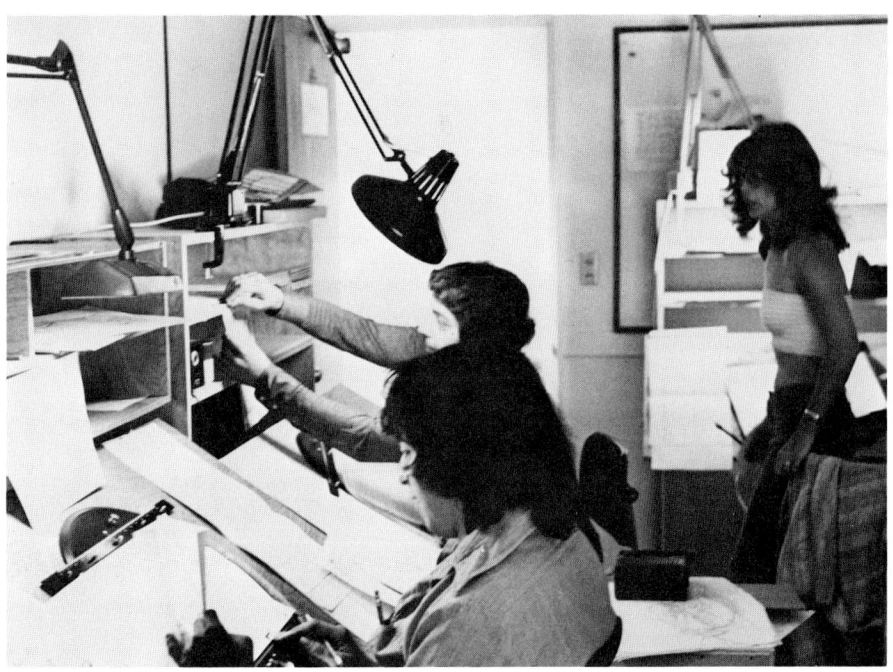

(Above) Art Vitello and, behind him, John Bruno, at work animating. At right is animation assistant Paulette Downs.

(Right) West Coast manager Jan Bell on the phone to New York.

At the Walt Disney studio in Burbank, top animators (*left to right*) Frank Thomas, Eric Larson and Ollie Johnston relax in front of the Animation Building at the corner of "Mickey Mouse Avenue" and "Dopey Drive."

Out in Burbank the Walt Disney Studio sits proudly and securely amid manicured green lawns; its pink and gray buildings gleam in the warm sunshine. At lunch in the glassed-in executive section of the studio cafeteria are Frank Thomas, Ollie Johnston, and Eric Larson.

All three men were part of Walt Disney's favorite phalanx of animators, which he liked to call "the nine old men," after President Franklin D. Roosevelt's term for the nine Justices of the Supreme Court. Today Larson heads up the Disney trainee animators' program, and Johnston and Thomas plan to write a book after they retire next year—on animation, of course, but concentrating on the "philosophy of entertainment and communication."

Thomas, with his bespectacled, amiable face and crooked grin, doesn't look like the fellow Chuck Jones once called the Laurence Olivier of animation. But under his lanky, just-folks exterior beats the heart of perhaps the toughest appraiser of animation acting—his own and others'—around. His standards come direct from Olympus via Walt Disney.

"The reel I saw of *Raggedy Ann*," says Thomas, "reflected the visual delights for which Dick is famous. He has a way of seeing a situation in a whole new light and making it exciting and fresh and unusual.

"But," he continues, "from *my* standpoint . . . I miss an involvement with the characters and the story.

"At Disney's, the traditional way has been to establish personalities that have strong audience identification. Dick has asked them to draw real rag dolls. We would have asked them to draw certain, definite personalities as rag dolls.

"I do envy him and his freedom to put down what he personally feels about a subject. At Disney's we follow the venerable rule, 'If an idea can't be clubbed to death [in story conferences], it must be strong and good and true!' *Of course* we play to the audience; we have to at our prices. And of course it would be fun to break loose and do something entirely different."

"Frank is a genius, and I honor him, but I disagree with him on this point," says Williams. "Besides, he's only seen one reel.

"We *started* with characters with strong identities and personalities. Frank does it through sincerity; Raggedy Ann and Andy are more wide-eyed, naive. Deliberately so. With Ann, Andy, and the Camel in the Taffy Pit, Frank and Ollie would have concentrated on terror when faced with this mountain of pudding—there'd be awed looks at each other. What we did I feel is *also* involving: Ann, Andy, and the Camel have no idea what they're faced with. Like children in an adult world. It's the difference between Chaplin and Keaton; Chaplin is sentimental and Keaton is visual. Gerry Potterton did a film with Keaton and says he treated himself, his body, like a rag doll.

"The test is the audience. For twenty years I've gone with my gut feelings and trusted those of others, like my directing animators. I've found that when I've put in things I like and taken a risk, those are the things the audience loves. And here's the kicker: Walt Disney himself put things on the screen *he* wanted to see and hoped the audience would like, too.

"I think we have *great* character development. Wide-eyed wonder is a valid thing. The discipline Frank follows is wonderful. Chuck's Roadrunner discipline is also wonderful, though different, and mine is different.

"I think we *are* doing it, but differently," Williams concludes. "Take a look at the whole picture. Ten minutes isn't enough."

October 1976—Vol. 7, No. 9
The Peg-Board—Official publication of Local 839
Motion Picture Screen Cartoonists I.A.T.S.E., AFL-CIO
Editor: Jim Carmichael
The Business Representative's Report—A Monthly Summary of Our Union's Affairs

We are now rapidly phasing into our annual situation: all the studios are fulfilling their contracts, completing network commitments and entering final phases of production. Unfortunately, this state of affairs also applies to those shops that have been engaged on theatrical features. These studios have been of inestimable help in keeping a large number of our members employed for an extended period, but this situation is now coming to an end. . . .

Raggedy Ann West is finished as far as the Hollywood operation is concerned. A few animators are still at the boards, but the assistant and inbetween phases will be completed in New York. For this purpose and to assure artistic consistency, this company has taken eleven of our members to Gotham, all expenses paid.

—Lou Appet

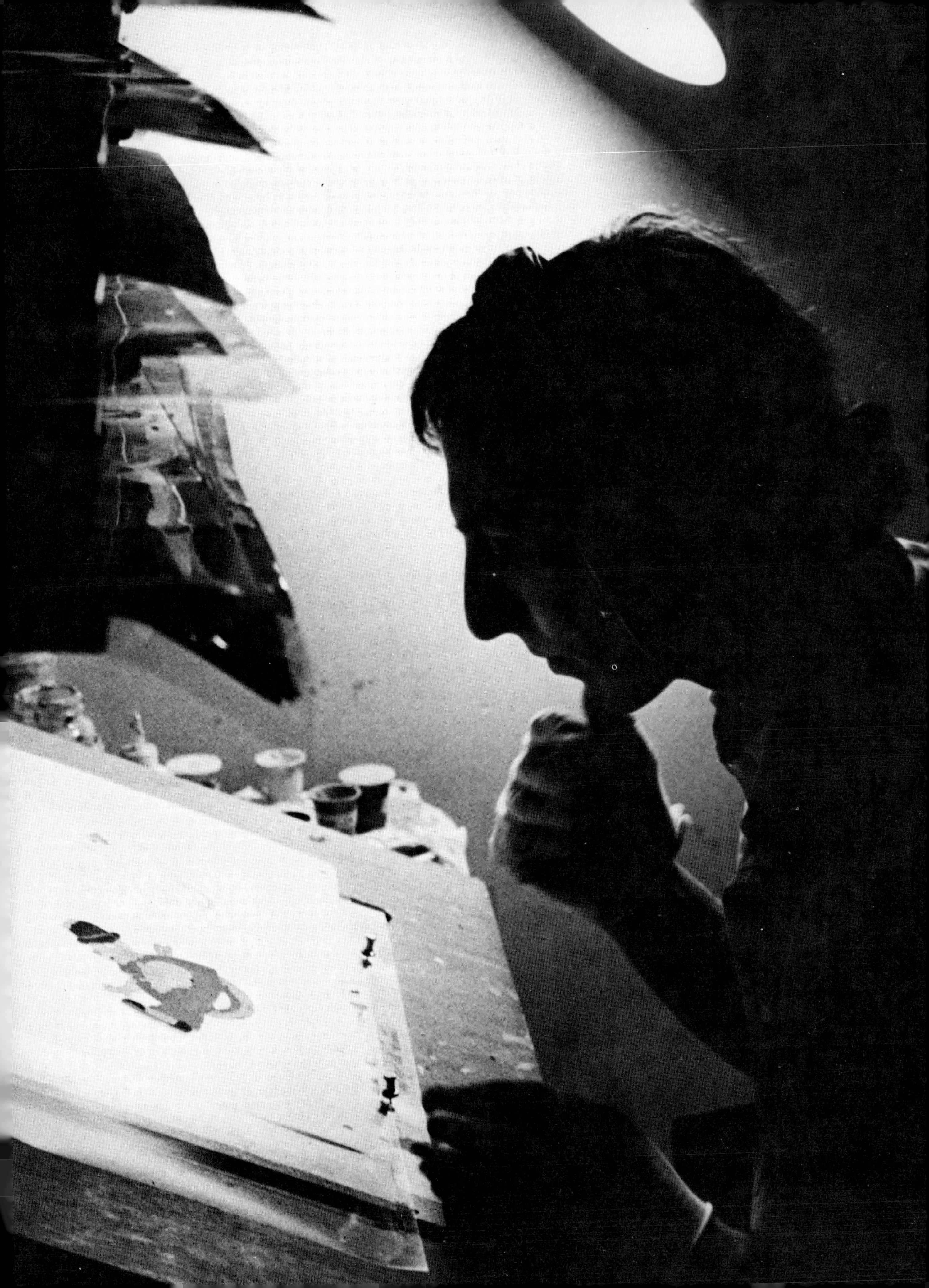

CHAPTER XII

Raggedy Ann East: The New York City Studio

I've managed to survive so far. It was a little overwhelming—lots of loose ends—and this is where it all comes together.
—Ida Greenberg, Head of Ink and Paint

The kids who came on in New York, this is the first time they've gotten real experience. . . . They're getting valuable knowledge working with the greatest animators in the world.
—Michael Sporn, Supervisor of Inbetweeners and Assistants in New York

New York City is cold and wet and altogether uninviting this first week in October. From out of murky skies comes a contingent of sunny survivors from the L.A. *Raggedy Ann* studio. Marlene Robinson, Chrystal Russell, John Bruno, editor Lee Kent, and a handful of inbetweeners and assistants have been reassigned to the Big Apple to help finishing-up processes at *Raggedy Ann East,* the production's base of operations.

The *Raggedy Ann* studio is housed in the Berkley Building, which straddles 44th and 45th streets. This area is the heart of New York film and other media activity. Go-fers loaded down with cans of exposed film rush on foot and on bicycles to nearby labs, and magazine production assistants with layouts dash to stat offices with the latest product publicity. TV ad campaigns are hacked out in offices on Madison Avenue one block over from Fifth.

Howard Beckerman, an independent animator for twenty-five years and a producer for ten, shares a small studio on the third floor with a commercial artist. "Animated film grew up in this area," he says. "Originally it was publishers; then in the twenties J.R. Bray, Paul Terry and Max Fleischer had studios on Broadway, and the area later became known as Mickey Mouse Alley. In the thirties Ted Eshbaugh did color cartoons of Cubby the Bear on West 45th Street. In the late forties the Fleischer company also moved to West 45th after their Florida studio flop. It then became Famous Studio, doing Popeye and Little Lulu.

(*Opposite*) Phil Schwartz opaques while he listens to music over radio earphones.

241

Fred Berner (*left*), assistant director, confers with Cosmo Anzilotti, associate director.

(*Right*) Doug Crane, who animated the complex Pirate ship in the playroom sequence.

"Dozens of TV commercial cartoon studios opened in this area in the fifties and many closed in the sixties; right now business is slow." Beckerman counts off who is "not too busy" and what studios are laying off. Then he brightens. "It's a good year for the *Raggedy* people. They've got a steady job."

The *Raggedy Ann* production has now grown to occupy a number of large spaces on four floors, each process separated from the others by hastily built walls. The heat is definitely on to get this film finished by December 30 for an Easter release. Rumors that 20th Century-Fox is distributing and that there may be a premiere at Radio City Music Hall circulate down to the lower echelons.

Everyone seems to be running scared; there's no time for idle chitchat in this animation factory. The name of the game is footage—keep those heads down and pencils up!

Get it out but keep the quality is the nearly impossible motto. Miraculously they are doing it. The latest rushes look great. Judicious cuts are being made in "fatty" scenes. Bobbs-Merrill/ITT is happy, the producers are happy (though still worried), even the never satisfied Richard Williams seems pleased. "We're doing it," he beams.

Williams shares a large office space with his associate director, Cosmo Anzilotti. Cosmo, who is thirty-eight, got into the business right out of high school, and he still has a kid's eagerness about the art of animation. He was with Terrytoons for a dozen years: "It's generally felt that Terrytoons didn't measure up to a lot of other studios. You can't really compare it to *Raggedy Ann*. Terrytoon animation was charming but very soft. It lacked the Warner Brothers feel of snappiness or the personality of Disney. As we look at the old cartoons again, we appreciate another quality—this very corny thing. Not only nostalgia but the style—that soft, rubbery type of thing."

On *Raggedy Ann* Cosmo "hooks up loose ends and makes creative decisions" when Williams is out of town. "I wish we could have him here every day," says Anzilotti. "I'm glad he's working on the production. I don't think it would be this good if he weren't on it. It might have been like Saturday morning, you know?"

Anzilotti demonstrates the constant push for quality by showing around a group of cels, all finished and painted. It's the close-up of Babette's fan, which she flips open during her song, revealing a lacework Eiffel Tower.

"Dick saw the tests, and on one cel—one frame—a color 'popped off.' One of the painters forgot to paint a certain color on the fan. Now another studio would say to let it go through, but Dick hates that kind of thing, so it's going back to the paint department and then will be reshot.

"In the meantime we looked at the background behind the fan, and now we feel we should add a couple of characters for a better design and for audience appeal and involvement. So the film takes another step up, and we gain in quality."

Up on the tenth floor they've clustered some New York animators. Doug Crane, in his early forties, is making the Captain's ornate ship roll and twist on the sea, a tour de force of technical animation. Williams raves that Crane is "a terrific find. He can do all the stuff nobody'd dare to do. Anything that would scare a normal animator, you give to Doug. He gets it on the nose every time!"

To Crane it's simplicity itself. "The ship is just a shoe box that turns. I make a box construction first in a number of poses and to that add the water. Then add depth to that." This "simple" job took Crane eleven weeks to complete.

Concentration is the key. "I put myself *past* the paper on the drawing board," he claims. "It's like you open a window to another world, and at the end of the day I've got to climb out of there."

Next door George Bakes, forty-six, is listening to a tape of the Gazooks monster, which he is animating. "Booooooooooring!" says the Gazooks, Lord of the Deep.

"That's six feet long, that word," Bakes says laughingly. Bakes once worked with the late Bill Tytla, a great Disney animator and close friend of Art Babbitt. "No matter how complicated the character was drawn," says

George Bakes flips his animation of the Gazooks.

243

Richard Williams with Michael Sporn, the supervisor of New York assistants and inbetweeners.

(*Right*) Young inbetweeners Mary Szilagyi and Carol Millican in the "taffy pit room."

Assistants and Inbetweeners

Bakes, "Bill had this simple conception of force. The Gazooks is a blubbery mass, an inner tube, like a waterbed in reverse—with the water outside. A character like that can flatten out very easily unless you put a bit of form here. Too many lines don't strengthen the pose, and shading hides a bad drawing. Mine are the simplest around here. I refuse to work that hard."

Across the room from Bakes, Jack Schnerk, who worked on *Fantasia* and *Bambi*, at Warners and UPA, and on tons of commercials in New York, toils over an animated cuckoo clock that moves across a wall as the eye follows, changing the whole room's perspective. "This is the most ambitious feature ever attempted," says the weary Schnerk.

Thirty-year-old Michael Sporn is the highly organized Supervisor of the New York Inbetweener and Assistant Pool. He hands out scenes to thirty-two young and not-so-young craftsmen and -women and makes sure their work is up to snuff. Sporn works a twelve-hour day and likes to come in on Saturday: even on Labor Day he labored.

Sporn worked closely with the gifted John Hubley for a couple of years, and he tries to "get on jobs I can love." *Raggedy Ann* has been for him "a love-hate relationship, because you're working on the sugary story; but at the same time because of Dick Williams it will probably be the best animated feature to come along since the early forties and Disney's. We can all see the problems, the holes in the story, but we can also see the fantastic animation that's being done. I'm able to learn something by watching Dick and Cosmo Anzilotti and Tissa work. To paraphrase Dick, you almost learn by osmosis."

Sporn is obviously emotionally involved with his work. He admits, "I sit and complain, but I really love it. I love every second of it. And working seven to seven isn't working. It's my life!"

Sporn hired most of the young people on the production, the ones who are getting their first professional animation experience. "I knew a lot of the people before I hired them," Sporn says. "I'd seen their personal films. I knew they deserved a chance but wouldn't get one at the TV commercial houses in New York. There are about six or seven assistants in New York who

Assistant animator Gian-Franco Celestri corrects a drawing by inbetweener Amanda Wilson.

constantly get all the work for the same studios. There's no room to train a new person. I don't appreciate this, though I understand it."

According to Sporn, another reason for hiring younger assistants and inbetweeners is that many of the older New York assistants could not be trained to do the delicate line work needed for this film. Sporn feels that "the young can be molded into whatever you want. But when the film is over, all these people are going to be on the street, though some of them are better than some assistants and animators in New York right now. There won't be jobs for them when they leave *Raggedy Ann;* there's a dearth of work in this city."

Gian-Franco Celestri, in his late twenties, is one of the younger assistants Sporn is trying to boost up the animation ladder. In his office on the eighth floor, Celestri explained the function of an assistant animator. "He takes what the animator has drawn, the hastily sketched roughs that capture an action or a mood in a scene, and, keeping the animation as is, makes the characters conform to the model sheets. Everybody draws a little differently, so it's a problem keeping a film's look consistent throughout. That's why we have model charts made up of the correct proportions, clothing and props of all the characters, so we can refer to them and correct the drawings that are 'off' the character."

As Celestri lightly pencils over the original animation drawings on a clean paper, it becomes apparent that he does not merely trace the animator's original drawing—he corrects, embellishes, adds detail and makes dozens of quick decisions per sketch. "Are the Camel's eyes positioned too high on his head? Is the snout in need of elongating? The nostrils should be more almond-shaped." And so on until each sketch is cleaned up, while still retaining some of the vigor and spirit of the original.

Two other assistants in their twenties have emerged as stars of the New York Assistant Pool; Dan Haskett and Eric Goldberg display a dazzling draftsmanship and a sensitive attentiveness to dramatic action that should enable them to become two of the new generation's finest animators—given the breaks.

A caricature by Dick Williams of Grim Natwick and Tissa David as Raggedy Ann and Raggedy Andy.

Tissa's self-caricature bemoans the many other "priority" scenes that kept her from swift completion of the big "Candy Hearts" song.

Haskett cleans up Emery Hawkins's enormously complex Greedy. He talks about being young, gifted and black in the animation business: "The industry doesn't seem to have been open to *anybody* in the past few years, any young people at all, black or white. When I was pounding the pavements nobody would ever come right out and say it, but there've been times when there was no good reason not to hire me except for racial bias. I think one reason there are not more black folks in it is that the business itself is clandestine. You have to sniff it out somehow. If you don't know about the union, you're up the creek."

Eric Goldberg, twenty-one, is like a shy mouse with the soul and gifts of an ancient animator. He lived more than half his life in Cherry Hill, New Jersey, running around flipping little notepads filled with animated characters. No one paid him much attention. In 1975 he won the Grand Prize in the Kodak Super-8 filmmaking contest, and they flew him out to USC in Hollywood to teach him how to make—prize-winning Super-8 films. No one paid him much attention on the Coast, either.

Animation studios, including Disney, wouldn't hire him. "California really left a bad taste in my mouth. They seemed to have too much sand on the brain and surf in the ear. In New York it seems people are concerned a little bit more with working harder. I got the impression in Hollywood that guys like me were a dime a dozen. They weren't very encouraging at all."

Goldberg came back to New York, and all of a sudden *Raggedy Ann* paid some attention to him. "I got here and it's been like a miracle, you know? It would have taken me four years at Disney's to accomplish what I accomplish here." The gifted Goldberg began as an inbetweener and four months later became Tissa David's favorite assistant. "Eric is the only one who can clean up my Annies," she says.

In his mid-fifties, Jim Logan is one of the best assistant animators in the business; the clean, strong lines he is giving to animator John Kimball's Loonie Knight are beautiful to look at in themselves. He is the second vice president of the National Cartoonists Society, he boasts proudly, and claims he would not do assistant work "if I didn't get a bang out of good animation."

But Logan also admits he "might have gone down a different road" and become an animator if in the 1950s a certain director hadn't taken his confidence away. "What he did was psychological warfare," Logan recalls. "He would have some guy make up huge charts—that's all he did all day long. If you made a mistake you had to go and write in the box what mistake you made for that day. At the end of two months the mistakes were added up, and whoever was making the most mistakes would be let go. I wasn't fit for opaquing when I finished there."

Dick Williams, realizing Logan's hidden potential, has been handing over to him larger and longer hunks of unfinished animation, and Logan

246

attacks them the way a hungry man goes after a steak. The assignments have restored his confidence. His talent has always been there; it manifests itself in the humorous and devastating caricatures he draws daily to relax.

In his cubicle on the same floor as the animators Sheldon Cohen, a young Canadian, described his responsibilities as an inbetweener. "It requires great concentration. I place a drawing on my light board and the third in sequence on top of that. Then I take a clean sheet of paper and draw what will be the second drawing in the series of three, directly in the middle of the other two drawings. And so on through hundreds of others.

"Constantly flipping the three drawings as you draw is the only way to see what kind of movement the animator intended. It's a technique I had to learn. See, the ears of the Camel are up in this position in the bottom drawing, and on the third they are down. Now I must place them right in the middle on the second drawing. It's difficult, but I am learning about animation this way, and when inbetweening is done well, it can become a sort of art form. Still, it does get tedious at times."

Like Logan and Goldberg, Cohen occasionally resorts to caricature to relieve the ennui. This provides the assistants and the inbetweeners with a healthy release from the often boring, repetitive tasks they must do every day. The caricatures may also represent a search for personal identity in the impersonal work of a cartoon factory—an attempt to "humanize the work environment" and a confirmation of the "informal work group," as Richard Balzar put it in his *Life Inside and Outside an American Factory*.

The issue that preoccupies many of these apprentice cartoonists is this: Where is the art in mindlessly tracing somebody else's spontaneous drawings until all the life is gone from them and nothing remains but an impersonal, inert sketch? Where is the creativity in obsessively crouching over light boards, tracing and flipping, flipping and tracing, all day, every week? Why can't the work of the animators—the pencil tests—be released to the public in its original form so that all the talent that is now funneled into sterile tracings can be released for more imaginative work?

Unfortunately, the public has not been trained to accept an animated feature in any form except the glossily packaged style Disney pioneered almost forty years ago. The experimental, personal animated cartoon exists, but its textures, forms and techniques have certainly not been absorbed into the mainstream of public consciousness.

Dick Williams's direction of *Raggedy Ann & Andy* attempts to individualize some artists' work within the large-scale animated film by giving certain animators some freedom in presenting their sequences. Within the set style of the entire picture, the differences in approach are easily discerned once one knows that Emery Hawkins developed the Greedy, Art Babbitt

Richard Williams as King Koo Koo in a caricature by Dan Haskett.

Eric Goldberg's self-caricature.

Art Babbitt in a neck brace. Caricature by Dick Williams.

247

An Eric Goldberg caricature of birthday-boy Dan Haskett and inbetweener Lester T. Pegues, Jr.

(*Below*) Dick Williams's caricature of himself and Tissa David.

Emery Hawkins's self-caricature as the Greedy.

(Above) A caricature of some New York inbetweeners and assistants by Eric Goldberg features himself as the Captain, Jim Logan as Grandpa, Dan Haskett and Judy Levitow as Raggedy Andy and Raggedy Ann, Lester Pegues as the Greedy, Mike Sporn as the Camel, and Lester Scarborough as the Sockworm.

Jim Logan's caricature of Dick Williams flipping a watchful Tissa David's drawings.

worked on the Camel's song, and Tissa David controlled the "Candy Hearts"/Deep Deep Woods sequence. The animation is, of course, packaged in the traditional way, traced onto cels by many hands and so on.

Williams's views on the traditional packaging of animation are firm: he believes "one gets tired looking at drawings after an hour or so. Graphic things, like pencil tests and rough drawings, are okay for a short film. But if you want believability in a fantasy, full-color cel technique is the way to do it." His position—basically the same as Disney's—makes considerable sense, but there should be room for more variety in presentation, more daring and experimentation. Perhaps someday there will be.

The work of all the assistants and inbetweeners on *Raggedy Ann* is not only arduous; it is time-consuming. Mike Sporn talked about how long it took to complete one short scene:

"There's a fifty-four-foot scene of the taffy [36 seconds of screen time], the first scene of rising taffy. It took Dan Haskett almost two months to clean it up. It took four people four months to inbetween a forty-four-foot scene. And the scene where the Loonie Knight, Ann, Andy, and the Camel are thrown from the bannister to the tile floor, and two tiers of curtains go by—it's six feet of film, four seconds on the screen, and it took two weeks to inbetween!"

Xeroxing

The animation drawings, having been cleaned up and inbetweened, are tied into bundles and brought to the Xerox room on the seventh floor. This department is run by two young men, Bill Kuhanek and Cosmo Pepe.

Pepe, an Italian from Hoboken, demonstrated the complex process of transferring the cleaned-up drawings onto sheets of transparent celluloid inside one of two wooden darkrooms containing equipment designed and built by cameraman Al Rezek. "The image is shot onto these plates," he began. "The big ones are worth around $120 apiece. The drawing is set up, face down; then the transfuser that charges the plate is pulled out. It takes ten seconds to charge it; then the plate is put into this toner or developer. The image is there, but you can't see it till these toner beads tumble over it. They go over the plate, and the image comes out.

"The inside man sets the plate in a box, where the outside man takes it, wipes it clean. A plastic cel is placed on top of the plate, and the image is then transferred to the cel. This has over 13,000 volts going through it, so afterwards it picks up a lot of dust because of the static electricity.

"Once that's done, the cel is put into a fusing box—which we also made—which has a chemical inside it. The plate is cleaned off and returned to the box. Once the chemical dries, the image is almost baked on the cel. Two checkers examine the cels before they leave this department to make

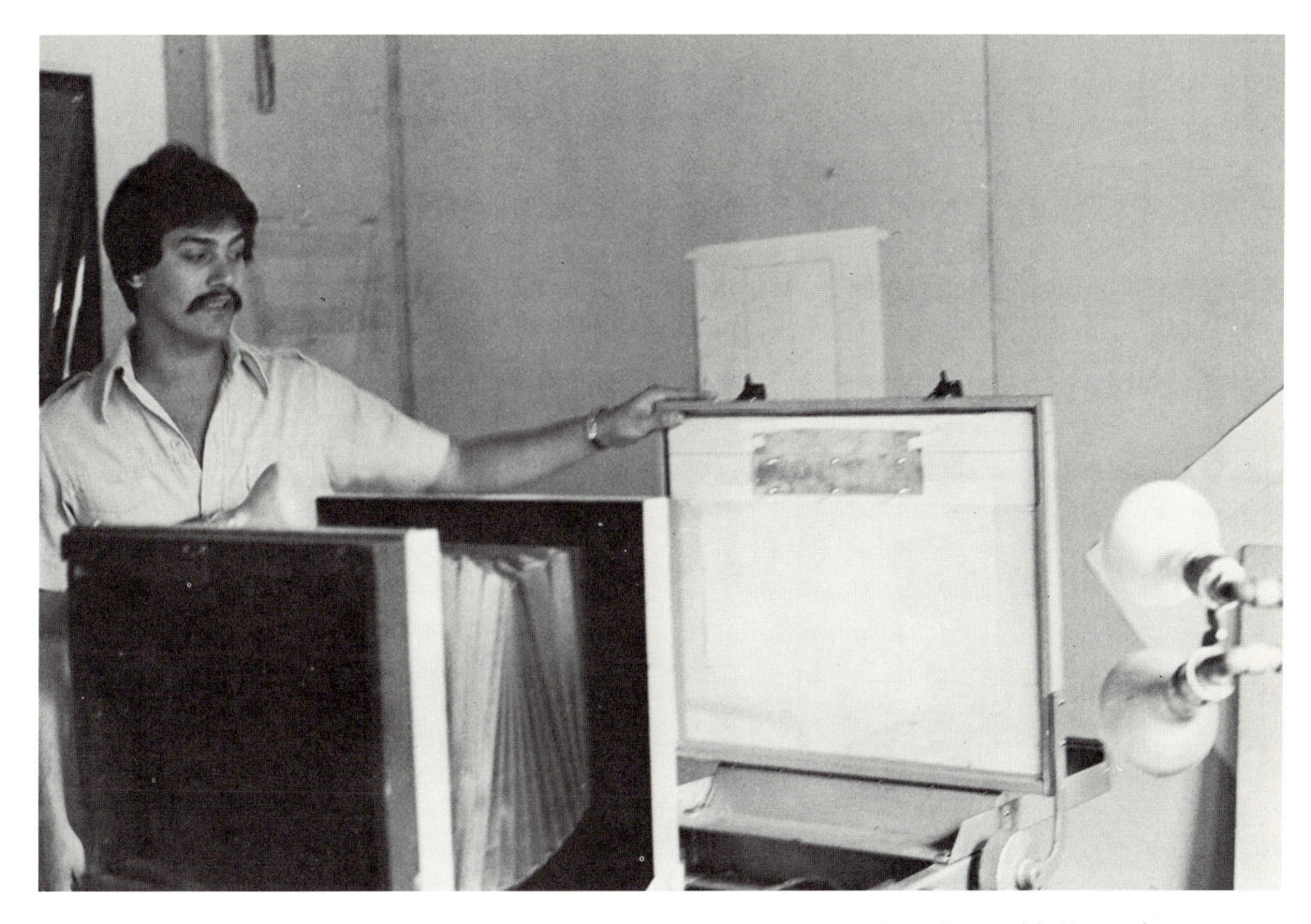

Cosmo Pepe and the Xerox enlargement camera.

sure there are no scratches on them. Fine scratches are filtered out by the Polaroid filters on the camera, but deep scratches are brought back to us."

Cosmo Pepe steps into the next room, where he demonstrates the Xerox enlarger, a vertical camera that saves time by reducing, enlarging, or repeating images that are too small, too large, or too numerous to be animated. "We can go up to a four-foot cel," he says proudly. This set-up was also built and is owned by Rezek.

Pepe anticipates no problem completing the over 500,000 cels on schedule. "Not on our end, no. If we had to, we could put on another shift at night. If one of us is out, one of the checkers or the darkroom men could take over. All of us know this department inside and out."

The only problem the Xerox people have had was the gray toner Williams saw at Disney's and insisted on having. "We went through a lot of tests to get the toner the right density that Dick wanted. He had his own reasons. Now we have people coming to us asking how we developed it. No, we're not telling. It's supposed to be top secret."

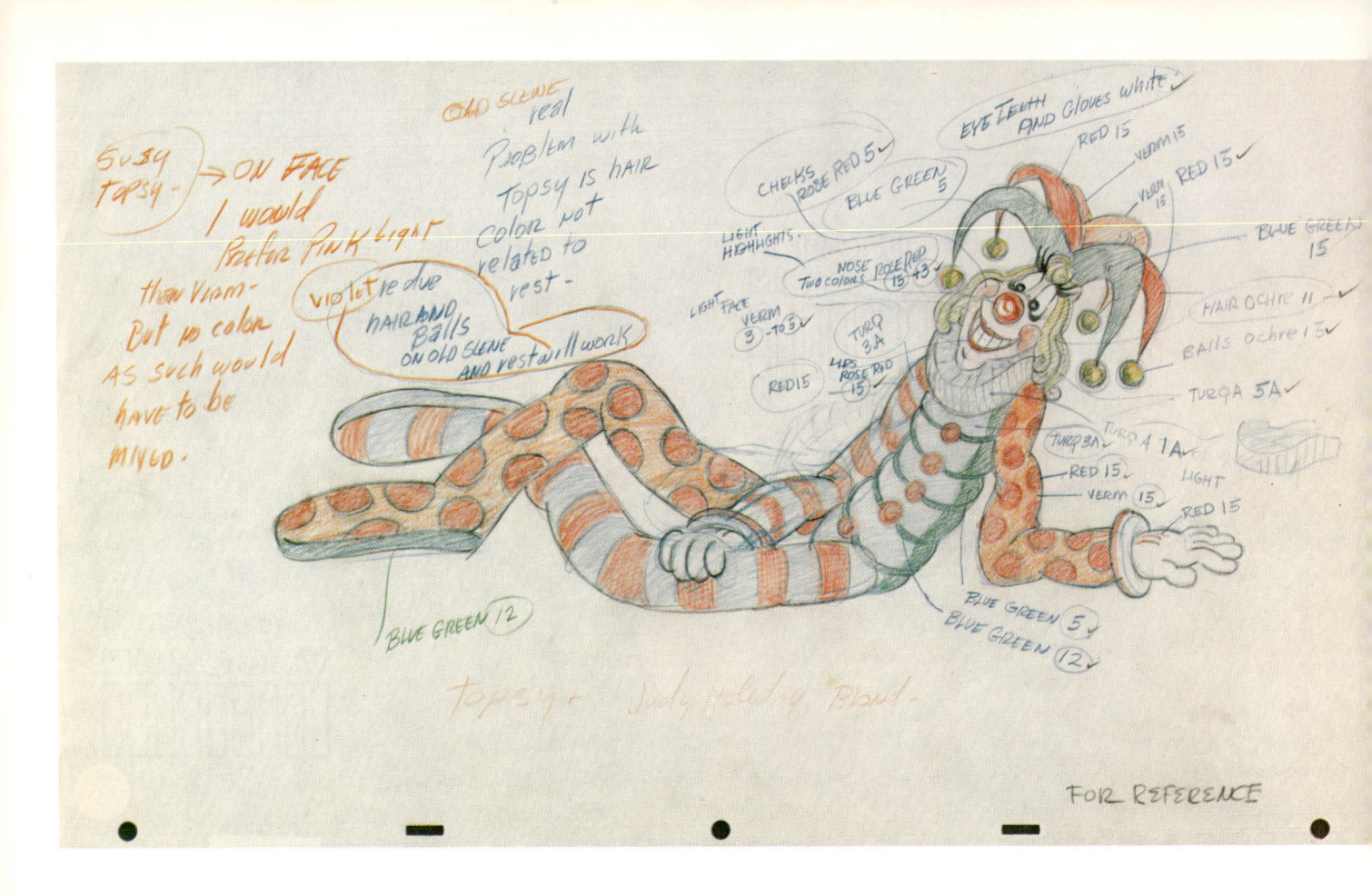

Colored-pencil suggestions about colors for the Topsy doll appear on this reference sheet. (*Below*) A final color model of Topsy painted on a cel, with numbers indicating the location of various colors on the character's anatomy and costume.

A color model of the Captain showing (top) the smooth surface the cel presents to the camera, and (below) how a cel of the Captain looks to the opaquer who applies the colors heavily to the reverse side.

Checking and Opaquing

Down on the sixth floor is the ink and paint department, a misnomer because no inking is done here, since the cels have instead been Xeroxed.

This department includes a subdepartment of Xerox planners and checkers.

Xerox planners inspect the animation drawings before they are Xeroxed onto cels to make sure the mechanics—the staging of the scenes and the consistency of the drawings—are correct. In cases where there are more than four levels, the planners may combine the levels onto one sheet of paper, provided there are no variations in the timing of the various levels.

Before the animation is shot for pencil test, and after the cels have been painted, the checkers scrutinize the exposure sheets and the individual drawings against their backgrounds. They make sure everything is in order—color, positioning within the field, speeds of background pans and camera moves—before it goes to camera.

The painters (called opaquers) are specialists in applying opaque paint to animation cels. The paint is applied to the reverse side of the cel from the Xeroxed side; thus the opaquer can paint up to the Xerox line and not over it, and the heavily applied paint presents to the camera a smooth surface that hides any inconsistencies in texture.

The technique used by opaquers to apply the paint is unusual: they must allow the thick paint to gather in a blob at the tip of the brush; when placed on the cel surface, the paint must be pushed around rather than stroked, to avoid streaks on the front of the cel.

Ray Jenkins, a young black with dreams of directing an animated feature someday, is the *Raggedy Ann* paint dispenser. It was his idea to dole out the separate colors in small plastic containers inserted into empty egg cartons. "The painters usually don't need more than twelve colors at a time for a scene," he says, "so this works out." Ray says the selection of fifty colors comes premixed from the Cartoon Colour Company in California.

Organizing and assigning work to more than forty-five men and women in this department is a five-foot-three dynamo named Ida Greenberg, who began her career in 1939 at the Fleischer studio. With her pretty blue eyes and clear skin, she looks like everybody's sweet Aunt Ida who shops every other day at Bloomingdale's in the housewares section. But talk to this woman for five minutes and you get the message that, disarming though the eyes and the soft voice with the New York accent may be, Ida Greenberg is a pro. And tough too. Dick Williams admiringly calls her "the Rock."

She has to be strong and resilient, super-organized and inventive, because she has been on the job little more than a year, having inherited the department in 1975. Because of her expertise the footage rose dramatically.

"What I did," she explained, "was organize it into three groups of painters, three separate rooms. And I put one person in charge of each group, and that person hands out the work.

"If it's a large scene, they divide it up into sets of ten or fifteen cels to give to an individual painter. In this first room Evelyn Rezek is in charge of the group concentrating on Ann, Andy, and the Camel. Also the parts that hook up with the mirage. The middle room is supervised by Steve Hartman. I've been giving him scenes that take place in the playroom. Evelyn Spencer in the third room is concentrating on the King Koo Koo scenes, and the Greedy is broken up among different people.

"I give them scenes and they look through the material to color-key certain things that might look confusing to a painter in animation." (Color-keying is the assigning of specific colors to all of the characters in a film. Charts called "color models" are made of the characters before opaquing, with numbers written on the parts of their costume or anatomy that vary from each other in color. The numbers correspond to the numbers assigned to the paint; e.g., Gray-32, Flesh-14, Ochre-16, Red-13, and so on.)

"For instance," said Ida, "I'm wearing a skirt and blouse, and maybe in moving around it would be difficult for an inexperienced person to decide where this top part ends and the bottom part begins. Like Susie Pincushion—she's so enormous, and she's got so many things on her as she turns in different colors, that you have to carry through the colors. And Topsy-

Ida Greenberg (*right*), head of the *Raggedy Ann & Andy* ink and paint department, discusses color models with her associate, Nancy Lane.

255

Suzy Pincushion

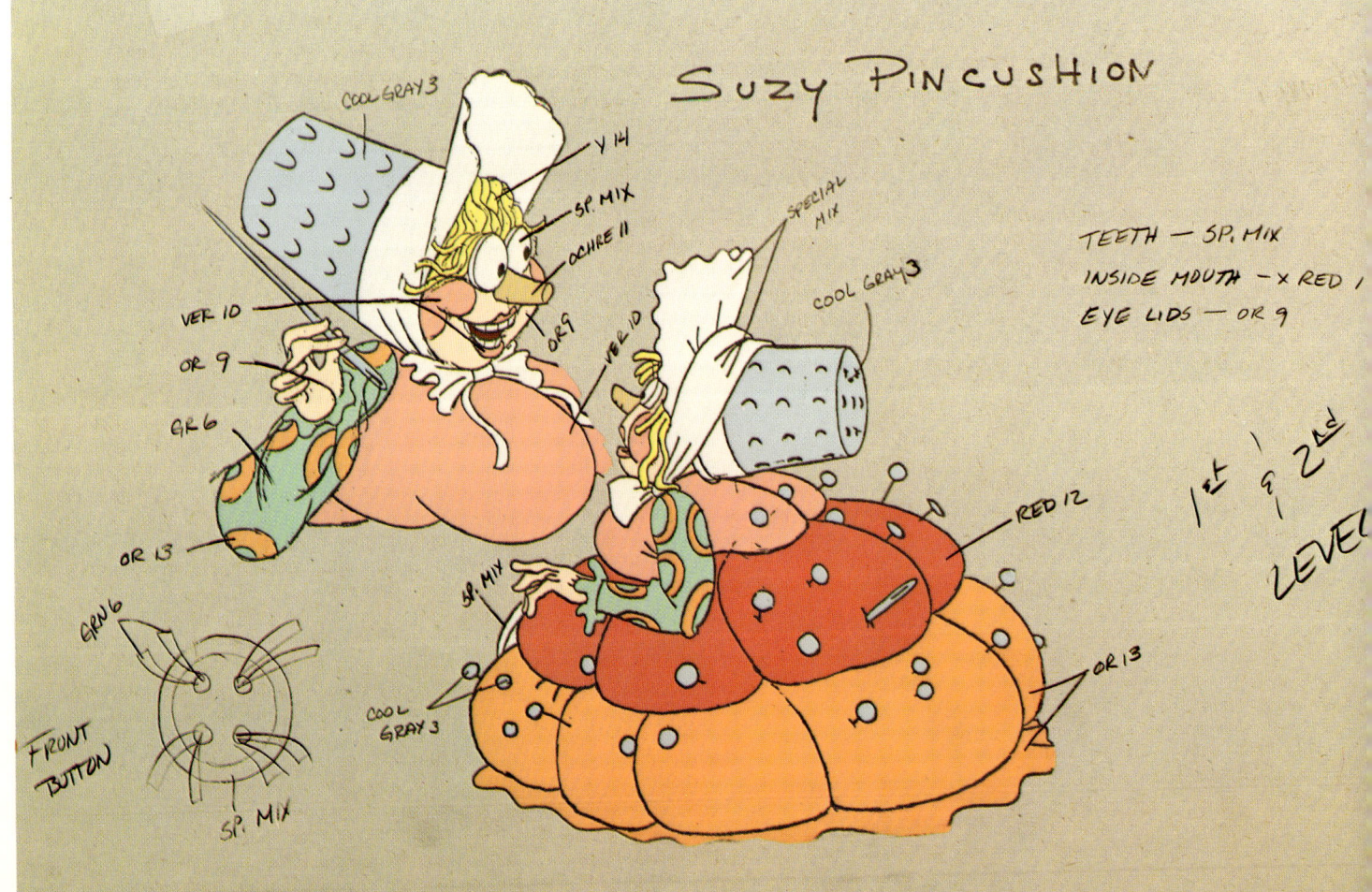

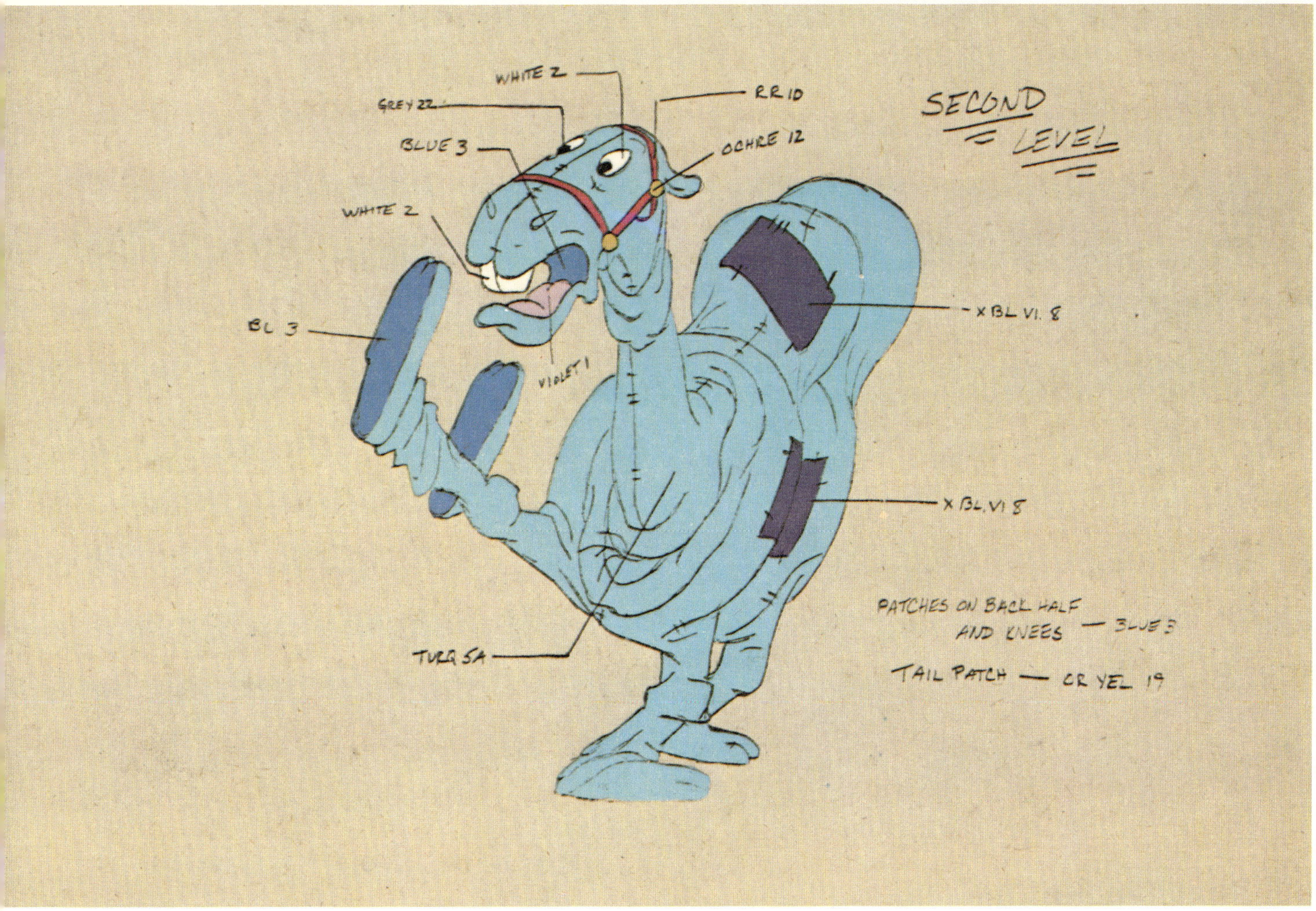
SECOND LEVEL
WHITE 2
GREY 22
RR 10
BLUE 3
OCHRE 12
WHITE 2
BL 3
VIOLET 1
XBL VI. 8
XBL.VI 8
TURQ 5A
PATCHES ON BACK HALF AND KNEES — BLUE 3
TAIL PATCH — CR YEL 19

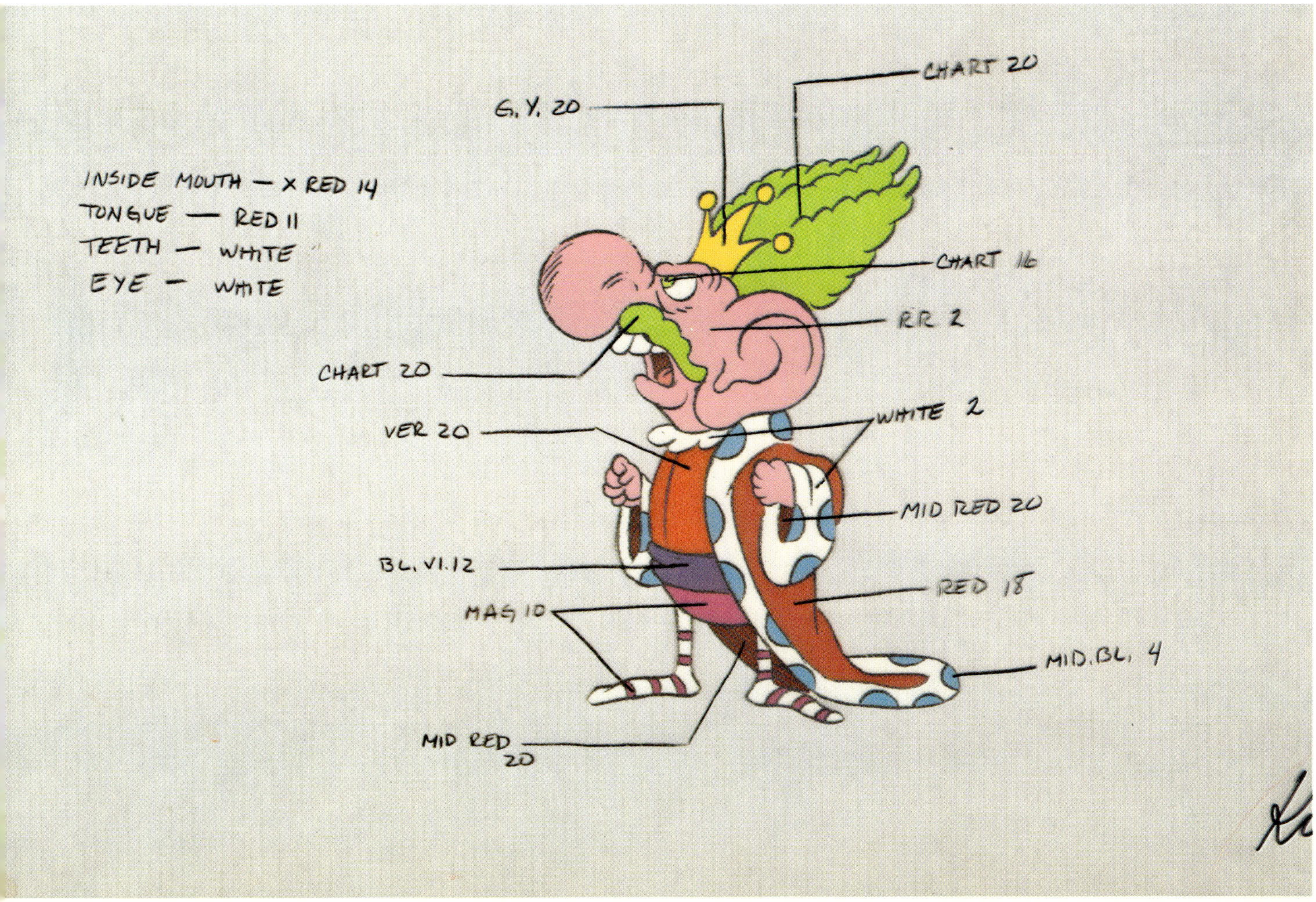
CHART 20
G.Y. 20
INSIDE MOUTH — X RED 14
TONGUE — RED 11
TEETH — WHITE
EYE — WHITE
CHART 16
RR 2
CHART 20
VER 20
WHITE 2
MID RED 20
BL. VI. 12
RED 18
MAG 10
MID. BL. 4
MID RED 20

Turvy—gee, she must have twenty colors. We color-key to make sure the right color is put on by the painter."

The painting of the Greedy presented Ida with a big problem: "Those big masses of taffy took an awful long time to paint, and it was 'wall-to-wall' painting. So I thought it would be wiser to use colored Pantone paper that would match up with the color selected." On this particular day Elizabeth Olivier, a Haitian, was carefully securing the paper to the cels, then reversing them over her lightboard, tracing in pencil the shape of the taffy on the back of the paper, and cutting the paper gingerly with a sharp scalpel, and finally attaching the paper to the cel, color facing out.

Ida finds that the major difficulty in her department—maintaining a speedy flow of work—stems from the design of the characters. "There's too much detail to concentrate on checking through. One of the characteristics of designers is that they look at something as a still drawing—it's going to be a masterpiece! They don't realize that all that detail is not workable when it goes into production."

"Inking and painting is tedious and almost completely lacking in creative opportunity," according to a 1941 "occupational brief" called *Motion Picture Cartooning* prepared for western colleges by a California personnel service. Under a subheading, "What Jobs for Women?" the brochure states that "Practically all women employed today in the animation industry are in the inking and painting department of the cartoon studio. In most studios there is a very slight chance for promotion from this department. There are only a handful of women working on animation and story sketches. Walt Disney points out, in this instance, that future opportunities for women are more promising since the cartoon is moving toward the aesthetic type of presentation which requires delicate, feminine handling."

The stereotyping of male-female roles within the cartoon industry has gone on since the beginning, and as recently as fifteen years ago a Disney book on animation described their ink and paint department as "a cool feminine oasis a short distance from the Animation Building." The inhabitants of the latter building were described as "predominantly masculine."

Times have changed somewhat: there are women animators and female assistant animators, inbetweeners and supervisors, and men *do* work in the paint departments in today's animation industry. At *Raggedy Ann* a certain number of painters were tested for drawing ability, and some were promoted upstairs to the inbetweener pool.

Nancy Massie is a *Raggedy Ann* checker who in 1938 at the age of eighteen was an inker at the Disney studio. "I was young and needed the work, and I thought this Disney plant was so beautiful and modern," says Nancy. "It even had air-conditioning."

She remembers that Disney's had something called "the speed-up system": "There were people who did nothing but time the inkers—you had five

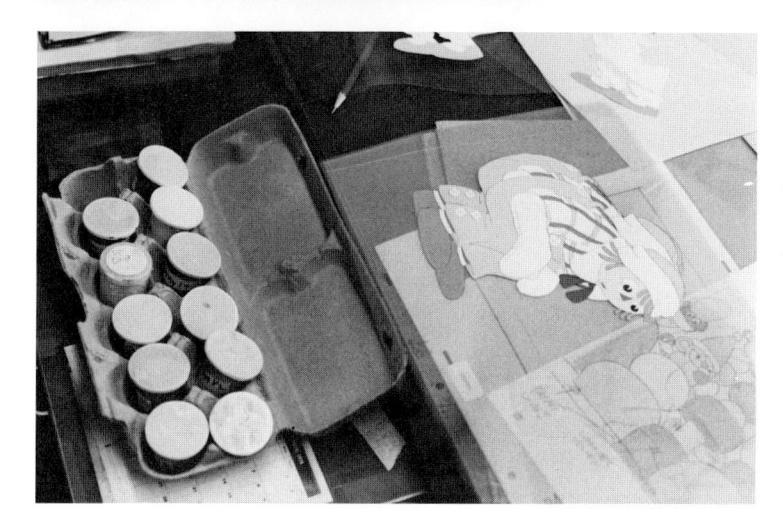

Small plastic containers of paint lie in an egg carton on an opaquer's desk next to completed cels of Raggedy Andy.

An opaquer painting Raggedy Ann and Andy.

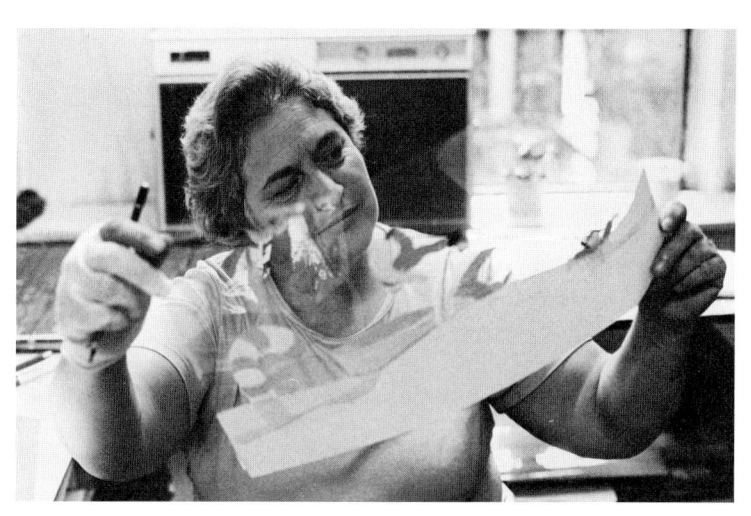

Opaquer Camille Marinelli inspecting a cel of the Greedy.

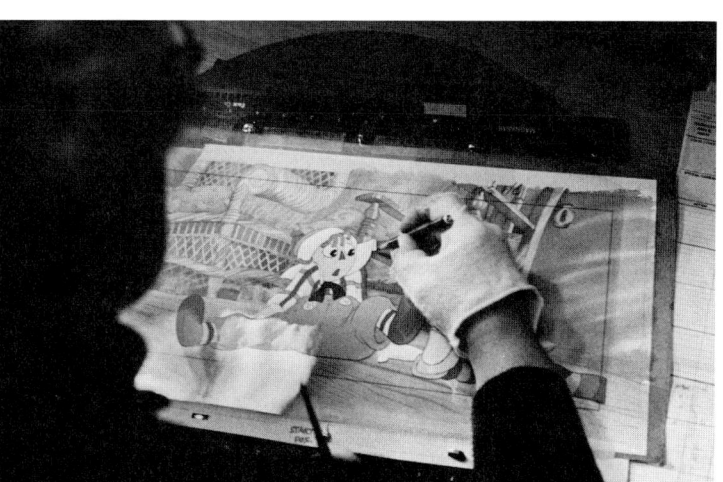

A checker examining a completed Raggedy Andy cel against his background to make sure this scene is ready for camera.

5/12 G-99

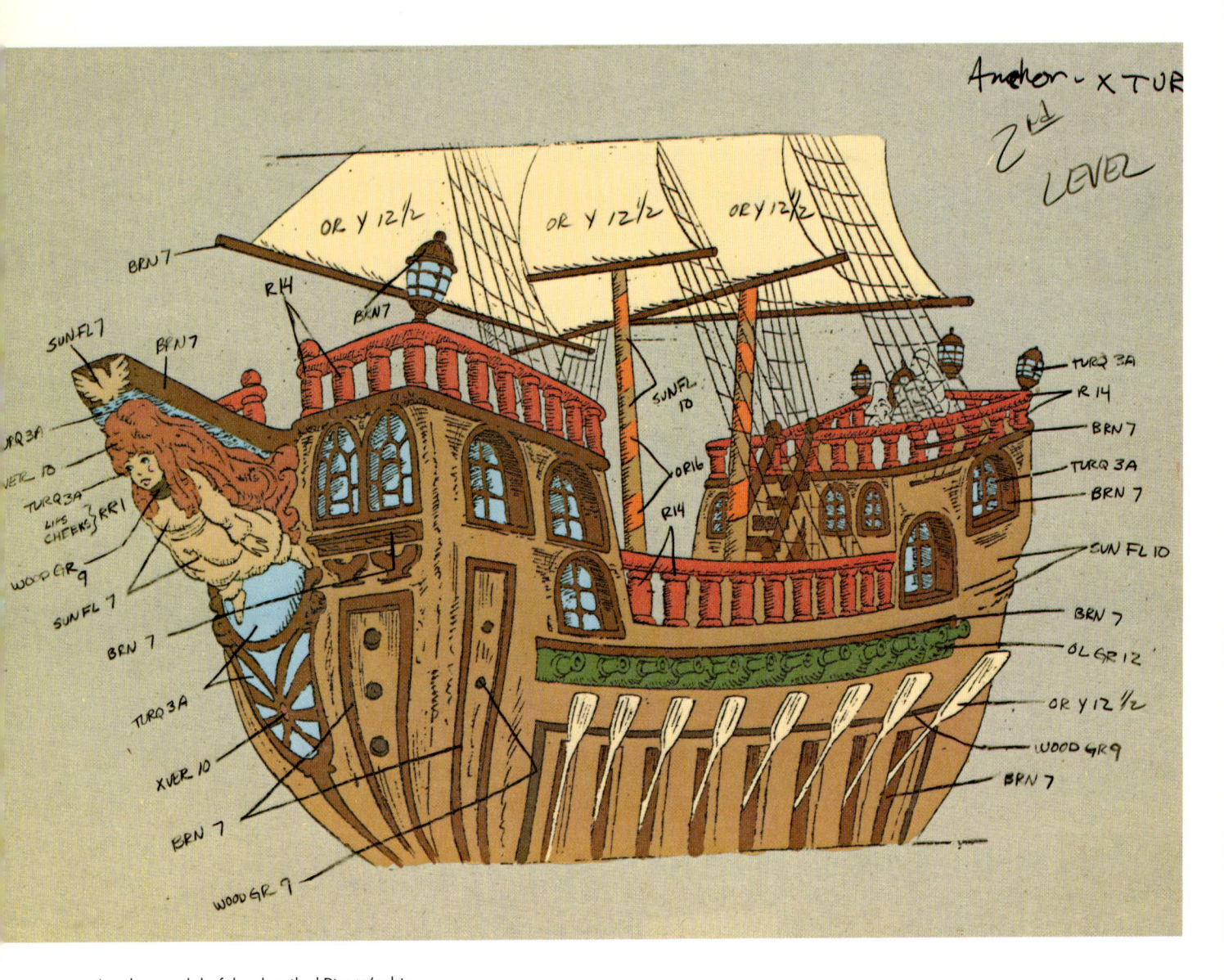

A color model of the detailed Pirate's ship.

(*Left*) A Greedy cel attached to—and ready to be cut out of—orange-yellow Pantone paper.

minutes to ink a Mickey Mouse cel and a little longer for certain characters in *Fantasia*. And charts were made of where you stood above and below the average.

"One of the girls told us tricks to keep our speed up, like 'Don't lift your head when you pick the paper and cels off the shelves in front of you.' It became a mechanical process of grabbing a paper drawing with your left hand and placing it on your board as your right hand grabbed a cel and put that down, while your left hand took the tissue paper that protected the cels and threw it over your shoulder. Then your right hand would take the crow-quill pen that was stuck in an inkwell, and you'd ink the cel *fast*. They had people who would come along and pick up the tissue papers on the floor behind you and fill your inkwells. It was a six-day week, eight hours a day, with a 15-minute break in the afternoon, and lunch too, of course." She was paid $16 a week. In 1976 Nancy was earning about $335 with overtime as a checker.

"Oh, we got the pictures out—*Fantasia*, *Bambi*. I got to be second fastest. I was ambitious. I could ink 25 cels an hour." (That comes to almost one every two minutes!) "The kids working on *Raggedy Ann* painting don't know how to work. They're amateurs, most of them."

Ida Greenberg agrees. "The experienced New York painters are mostly free-lancers. They make more money free-lancing, and when the job is done they can get unemployment and rest up between jobs. They don't want to work on a long project like *Raggedy Ann* for $165 a week. That's the situation in New York."

Ida related a story about a young man who painted cels during the summer at *Raggedy Ann*. "He kept asking me for time off to go to some film courses he was taking!" she says, her blue eyes flashing at his nerve. Then she drops the last straw. "One day he asked for an hour off to go to his *hair stylist!*"

Ida had no choice but to hire and train a large contingent of young art students in the techniques of cel painting. "I guess they were just anxious to get into the field. Two-thirds of my time was spent interviewing young people looking for jobs. I guess they're so desperate for work they'll do this."

Work in New York is "not even seasonal," says Nancy Massie. "It's just precarious!" Klara Haden, a checker who came from Hungary in the fifties, says, "Very bad business in New York. This work is dull, but you have to live."

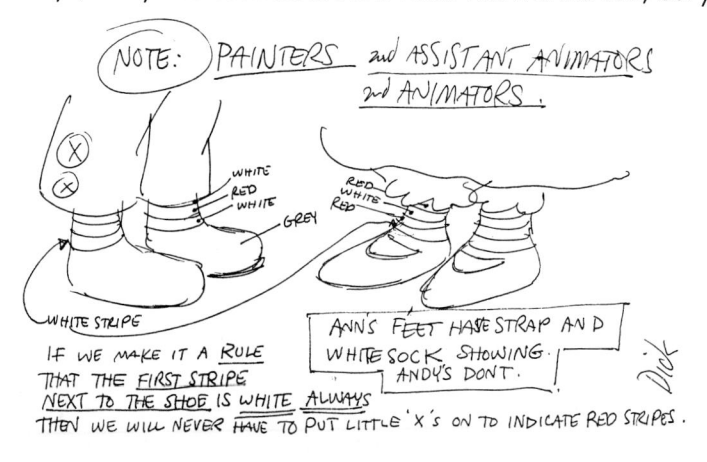

A batch of freshly painted cels of Raggedy Ann, Raggedy Andy and the Camel drying reverse side up on an opaquer's table.

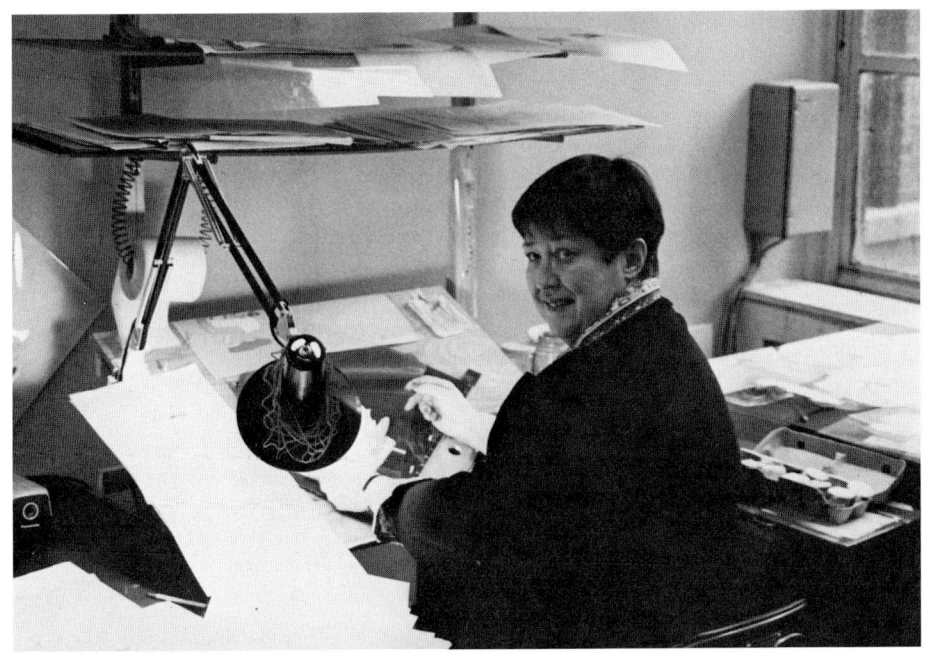

Checker Nancy Massie.

Checker Klara Haden.

NEEDS O.L.X   SEQ. 4.1   Sc 14

SEQ 4.1   BG.1

A black-and-white penciled layout drawing of a background for the "Blue" song, and the completed full-color background.

Backgrounds

"Backgrounds should complement and help stage the animation. They should set a mood, not take over the characters."

Sue Butterworth, blond and aloof, talked in her quiet British accent as she dipped a water-soaked brush into Luma watercolors splattered on a large tin palette. She dabbed a bit of Indian yellow, added to it some moss rose and a touch of turquoise, and painted the new mixture onto a French paper called Arches Cold Pressed which was stretched and taped onto her drawing board.

The moment her brush touched the pre-dampened paper, the paint blurred and spread in a liquid dance of muted color. This background from the playroom sequence was just one of almost a thousand that Sue is responsible for in the film.

Three of the sequences use black as a backdrop, so this saves Sue and her assistant, Michel Guerin, a bit of work, but it's still a big assignment.

"This little department is moving out!" she suddenly crows triumphantly.

Sue works facing a sunny plant-filled window and doesn't seem the least bit overburdened by her task. "How much time it takes to do a background depends on what the background is," she says with a shrug. "I can do two of these playroom backgrounds a day now. I first did them last year, and now I want to redo and reshoot some of them, so it's like I know the formula now."

The walls of her small room, which she shares with Guerin and a girl painting character color models, are lined with examples of her exquisitely painted backgrounds. There are blue, moody scenes from the Deep Deep Woods, sun-splashed playroom shots, and views of the rococo Captain's ship. Some of the panorama (pan) backgrounds are ten feet long, so in order to control the work on these monsters, Sue divides them up into, say, four parts and cleverly disguises the seams by cutting along the grain of the floorboards, the outline of a large chair and so on.

"I've always painted, but I got into this whole animation thing by mistake," she says. She was born the daughter of a telephone engineer in London, and after getting an art degree in fiberglass sculpture she took a boat to Montreal, intending to teach art to children. On the boat she met a cartoon director's wife who told her that if she needed a job in Montreal her husband could help her.

It turned out that she did; she left the teaching position because she didn't like "the restrictions" imposed on her by the school, and called the director, Jack Stokes, for work. She began as an opaquer at $60 a week at Gerry Potterton's studio; later she became a checker and found the experience invaluable for what she did on *Raggedy Ann & Andy*.

"One day the background woman left, and they said, 'You're doing backgrounds.' I said, 'What's a background?' So they very kindly put up with me for three weeks while I did the most atrocious drawings you've ever seen in your life!"

(*Opposite*) A ten-foot layout drawing by Corny Cole of a panorama (pan) background used in a scene in the playroom. Note the strong handling of perspective and the use of distortion in the vertical (N-S) movement. Such boldness gives excitement and sweep to a scene.

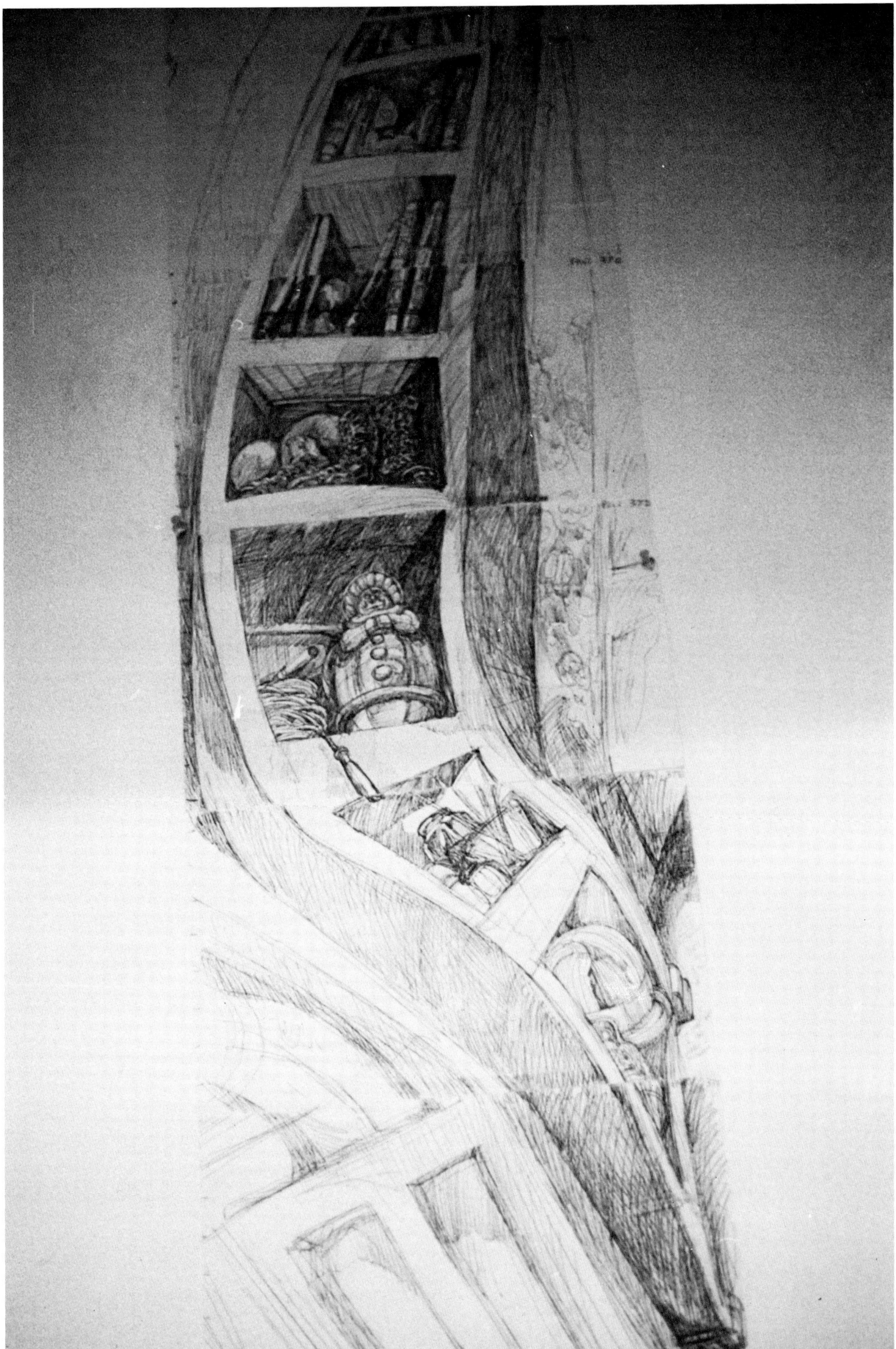

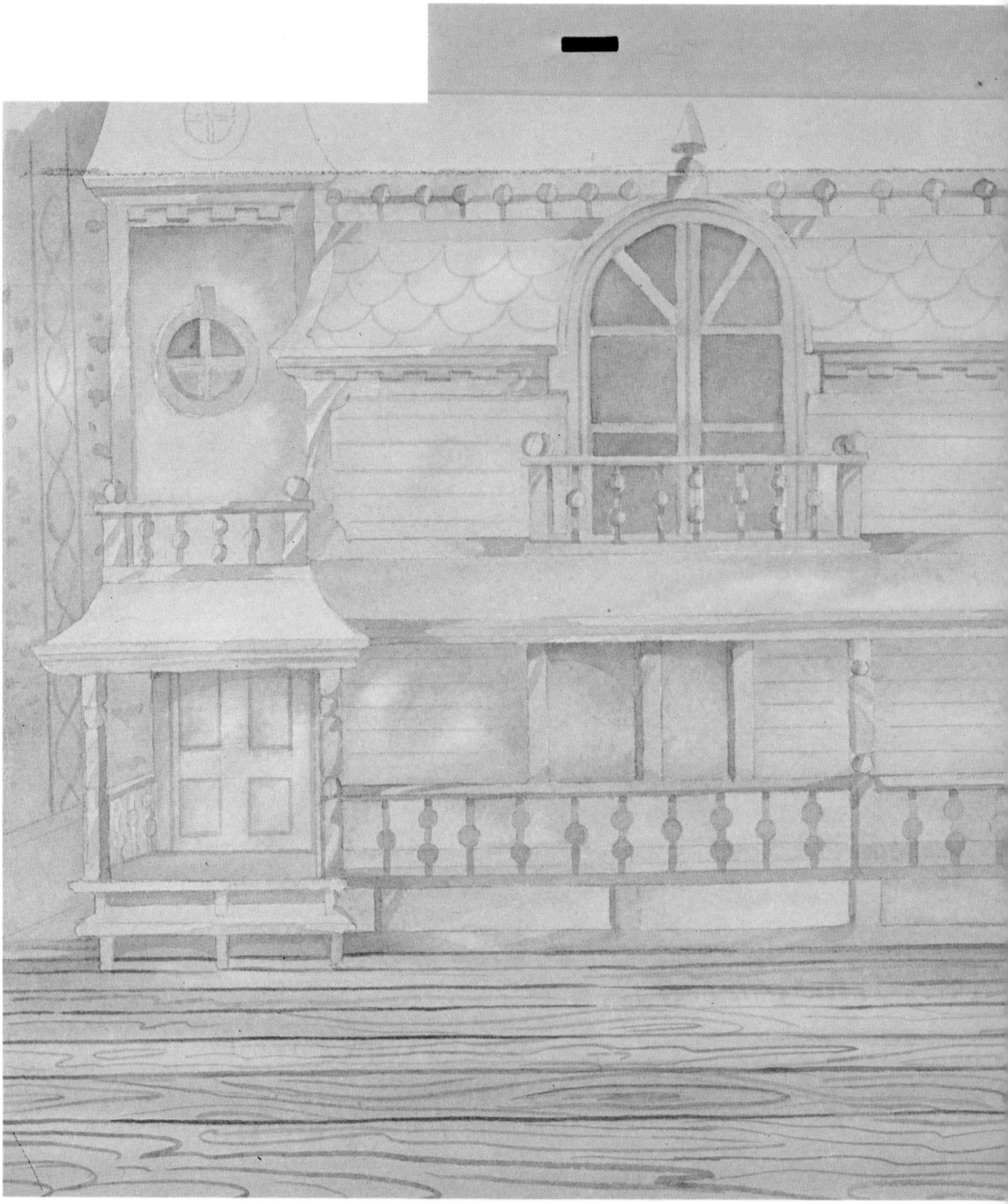

NB cross check with LIVE

1 B|G 4.

Williams saw her work at Potterton's. In March of 1974 she was working in Paris as a social worker "because I couldn't get another kind of work." One day a telegram came from Dick saying he wanted her to work on *Raggedy Ann*.

"He had seen my stuff in *The Selfish Giant* and *The Happy Prince*," says Sue, and what convinced her to take the job "was a two-hundred-pound debt I had and the fact that I'd never been to the States. And even though I'm not an animation buff, I'd heard that Richard Williams was one of the best, and he convinced me it was going to be a quality film."

She enjoys the actual "sitting down and doing a background," but she doesn't enjoy the "running around" involved. "There are several different sequences in this film in different styles. The playroom is different from the Deep Deep Woods, which is different from King Koo Koo. And the main problem is one day you may be working on one thing, and the next day—or even the same—you may be working in a different style.

"You may have done Scene Number 42 months ago, so for Scene Number 43 you have to find Number 42. You may have to run up to camera, or it may be in the paint rooms, and then you have to cross-check it to make sure there's no color difference. That's hard. If you work in sequence, it's fifty times easier."

Sue is drawing tiny lines on a cel over a background to darken the whole thing. "I have no idea what I'll be doing after this. If somebody offers me a job I'll go where the job is. I like traveling."

(*Facing page, top*) Sue Butterworth, artist in charge of all *Raggedy Ann & Andy* backgrounds, with her associate Michel Guerin (*back to camera*).

(*Bottom*) A Grandpa cel rests on a pencil tracing of its background. The tracing onto watercolor paper was made directly from a layout drawing. The next step in the background process is to render the drawing with colored inks.

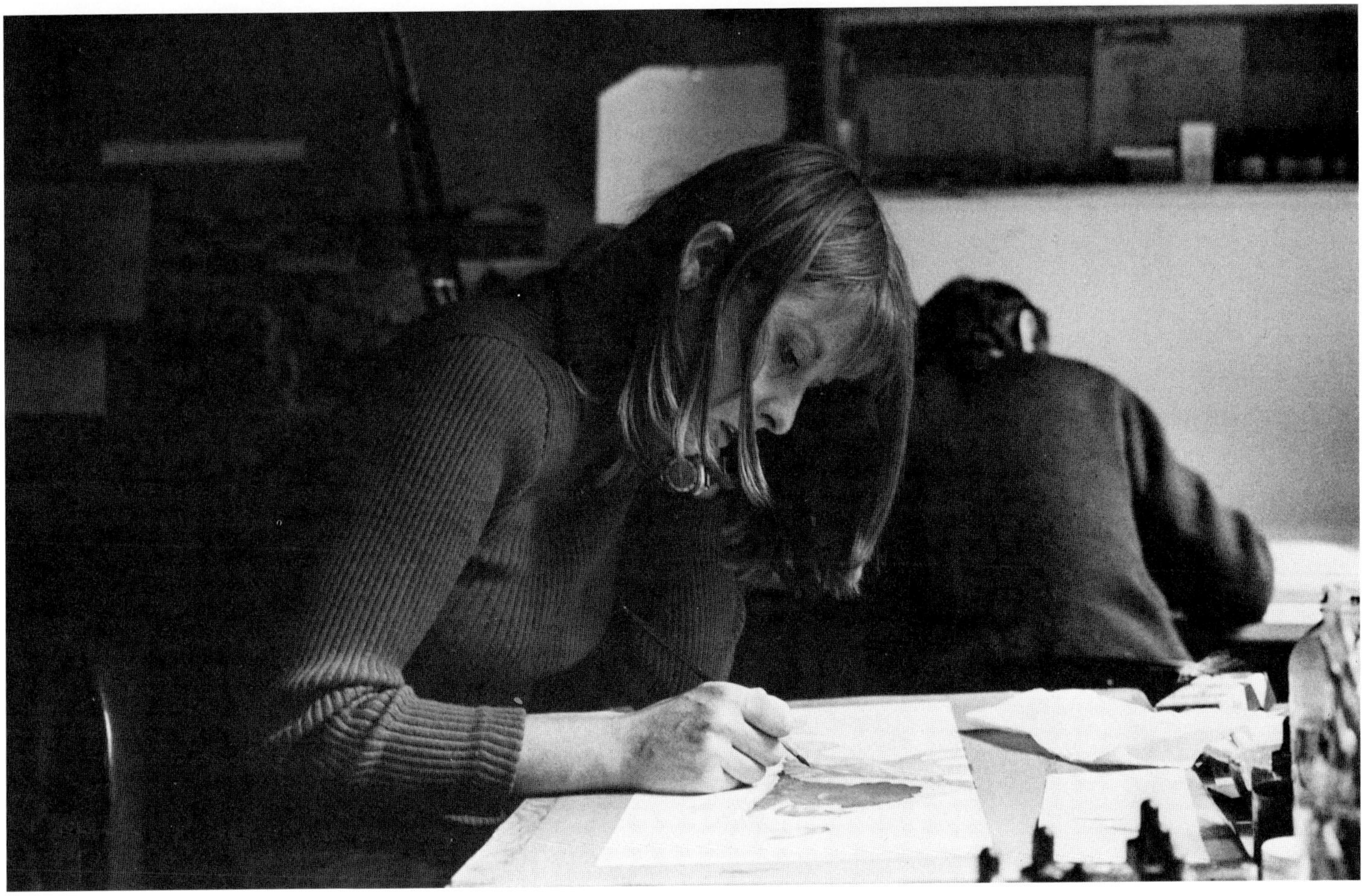

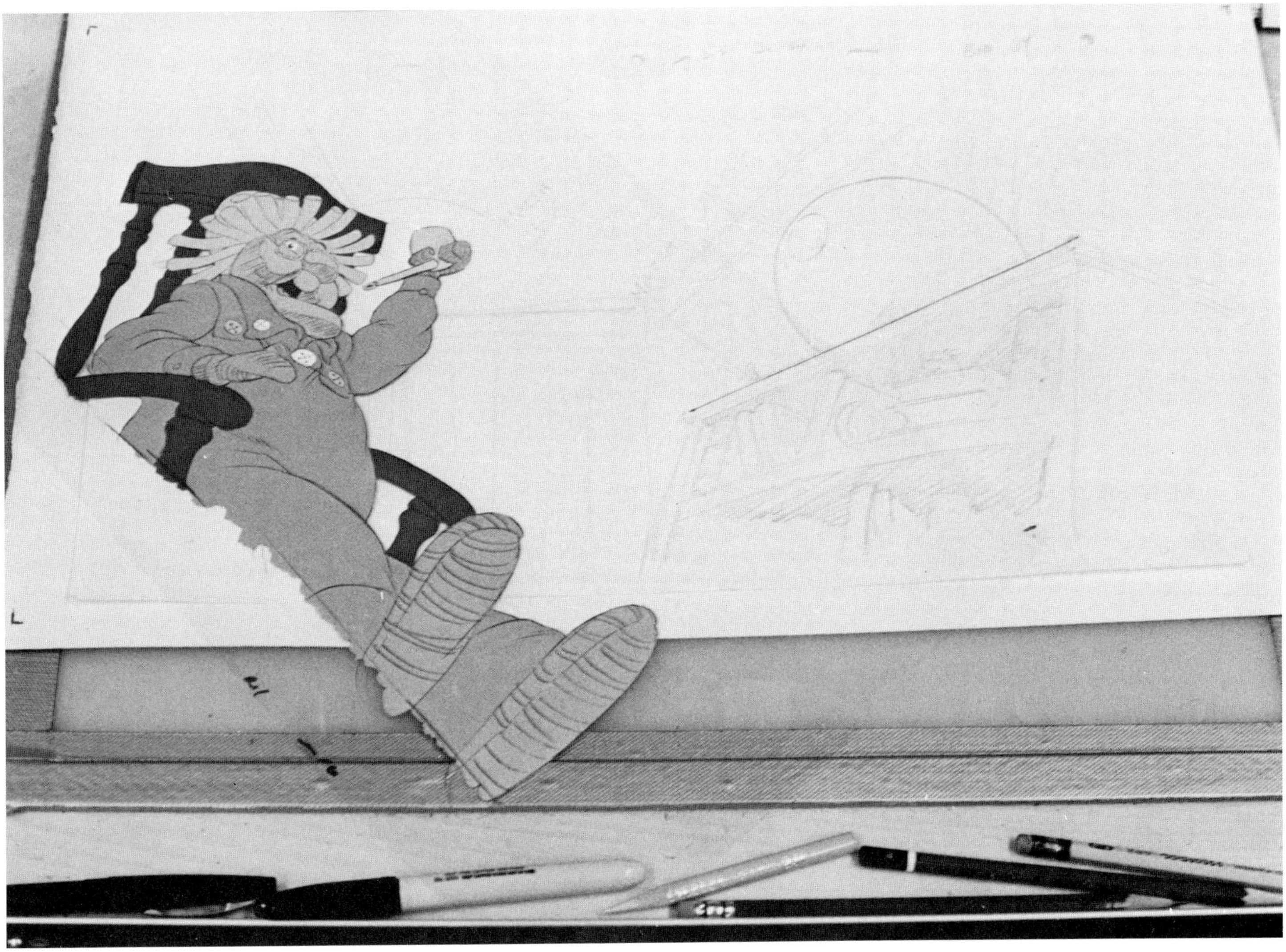

(*Facing page*) Three test backgrounds of the playroom and Deep Deep Woods sequences.

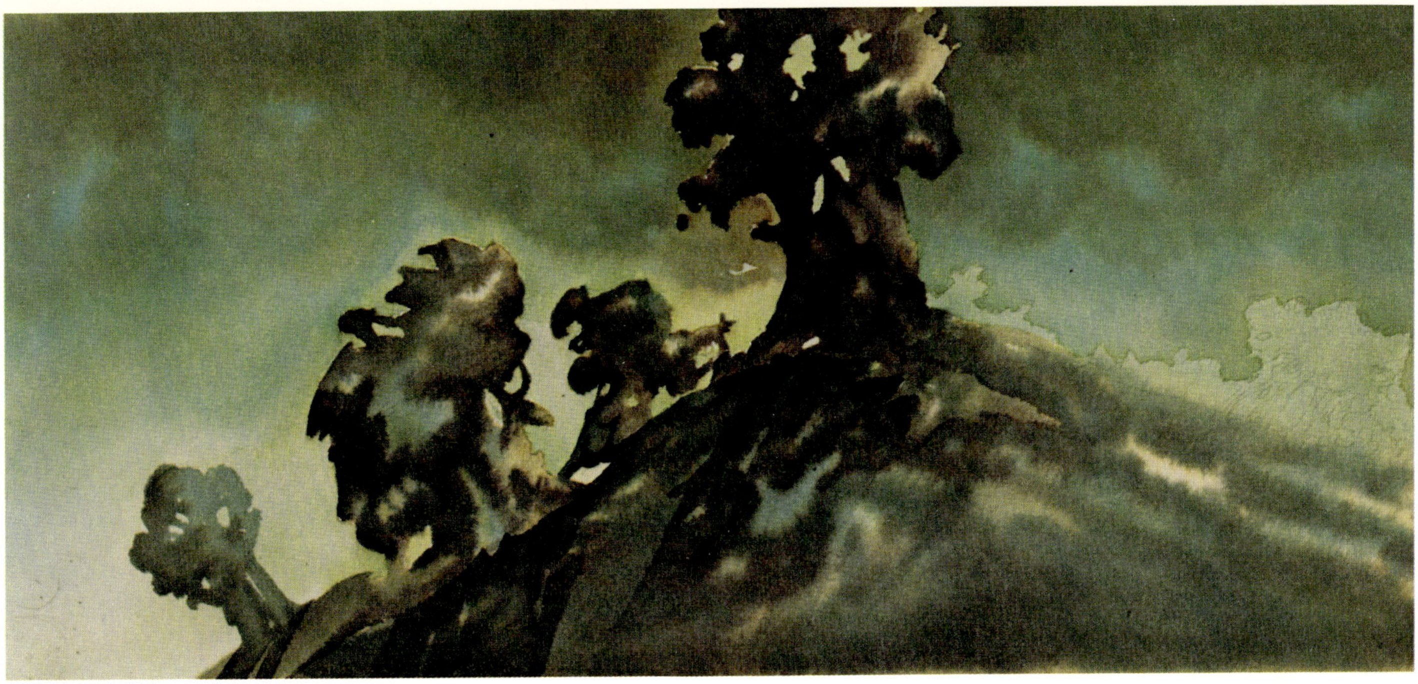

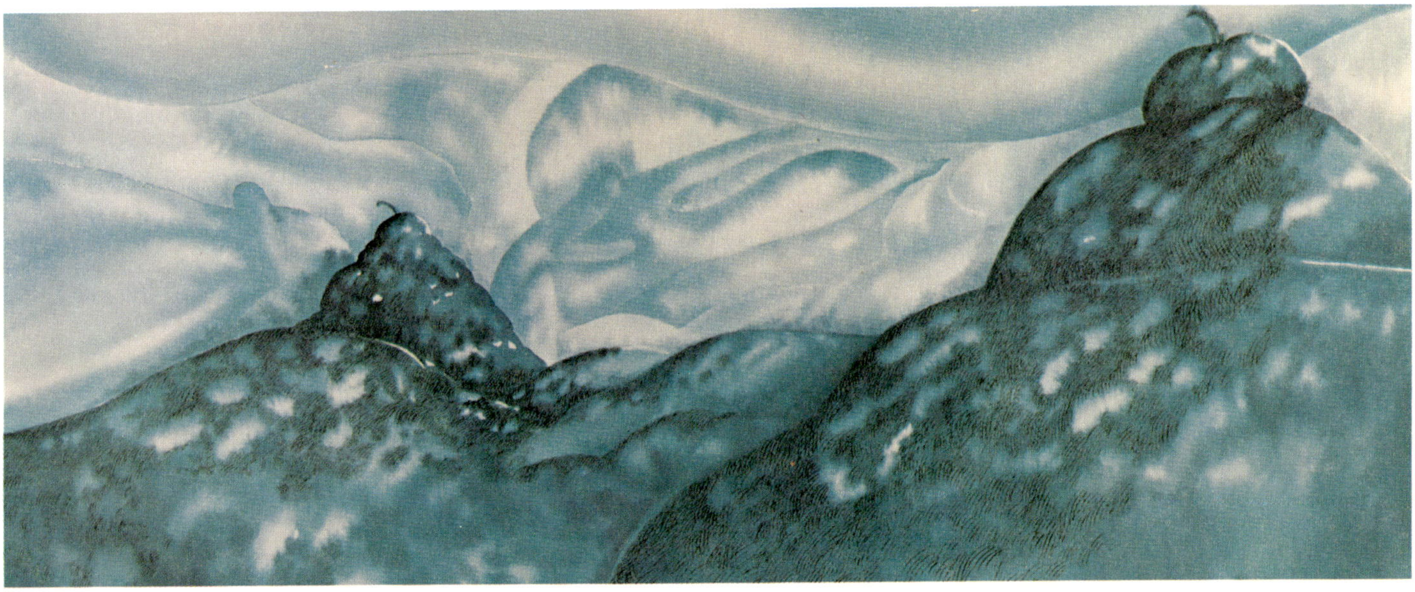

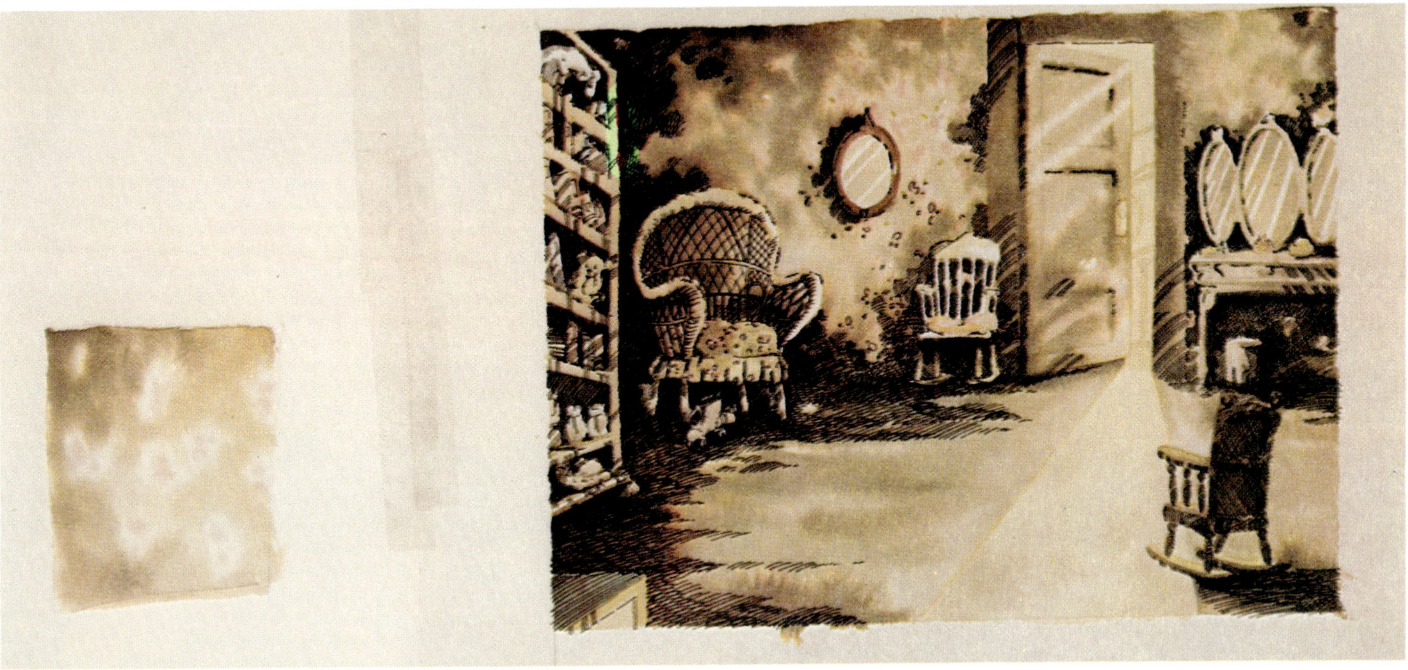

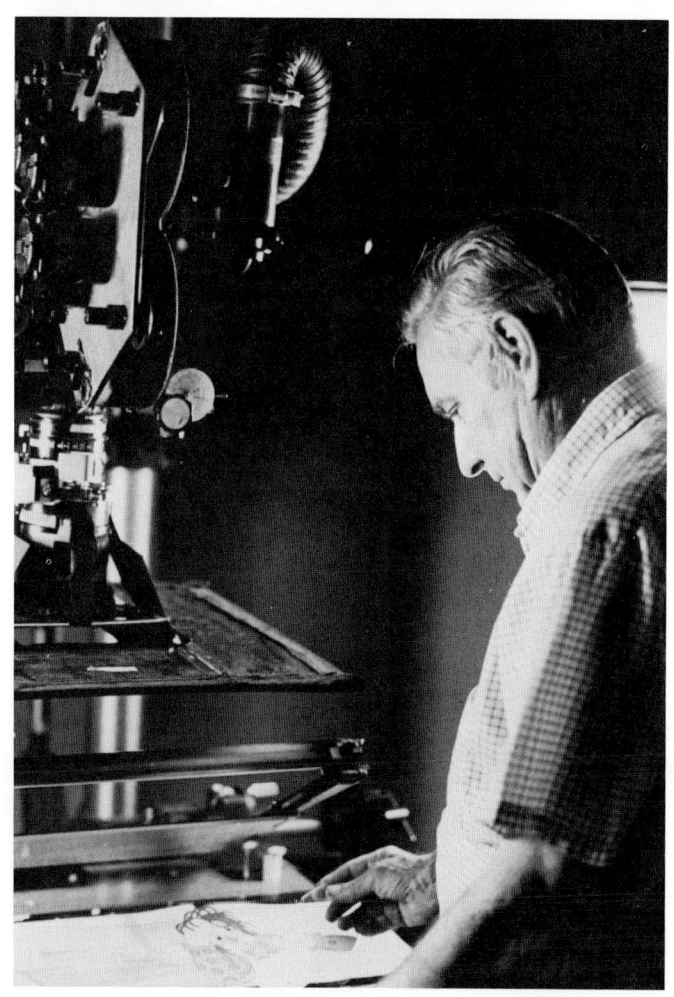

Cameraman Al Rezek at work.

Camera and Sound Effects

The approved drawings, having been Xeroxed and painted on the back of the cels, are returned to the checkers, who inspect them once more against their proper backgrounds for correctness. Then the cels and backgrounds are bundled up to final camera on the tenth floor.

The giant camera burps twice and two frames of color film whirl through its mechanical guts. Al Rezek, sixty-three, lifts the glass platen that holds flat the cel and background of Raggedy Ann in the playroom.

"On some commercials I've worked sixteen hours shooting," says Rezek as he removes a cel of Raggedy Ann and replaces it with another. "The pressure on making a long film is not as great. But we average right now ten hours a day shooting. It's going to increase tremendously."

Rezek replaces the platen, and all cel buckles and shadows disappear. He checks an exposure sheet for the correct frames required for this set-up.

Click. Whirl. Click. Whirl. Another one-twelfth of a second in the 86-minute feature is captured.

"We're using two cameras. There are four of us. When this production is in full force, we'll be using two cameras, two shifts on each camera, day and night."

Platen up, remove a cel. Put down another cel, platen down. Click. Whirl. Click. Whirl.

And so it goes every day for Rezek and his small crew. Of all the monotonous, enervating jobs involved in making an animated cartoon, filming the thing frame by frame has got to be the most exhausting. Yet here is a man who has spent almost forty years doing it. He's made a career out of it and is thought by many to be the best on the East Coast. How has he stood the tedium all these years?

"Sometimes I wonder," he admits. "It gets you after a while. At this point I'm not doing too much of the actual shooting. It takes my time just to keep things in order and organized. I'm also involved as a consultant on the film in Xerox planning."

Disney's multiplane camera added a tremendous illusion of depth to his animated features, but it was a huge contraption, almost eighteen feet high, and required at least ten operators. Al Rezek shot some scenes in *Raggedy Ann & Andy* in multiplane (e.g., parts of the "Candy Hearts" song in the woods), but *his* device rises less than three feet off the animation stand under the camera.

For the special star effect in the Camel's song sequence, Rezek devised a "star grid"—a black card with clear spaces representing stars, through which bright lights below the animation stand could shine. Underneath the card there were two sets of lines moving across each other in opposite directions, and their "strobe" effect on the underlighting created a flicker like that of stars in a night sky.

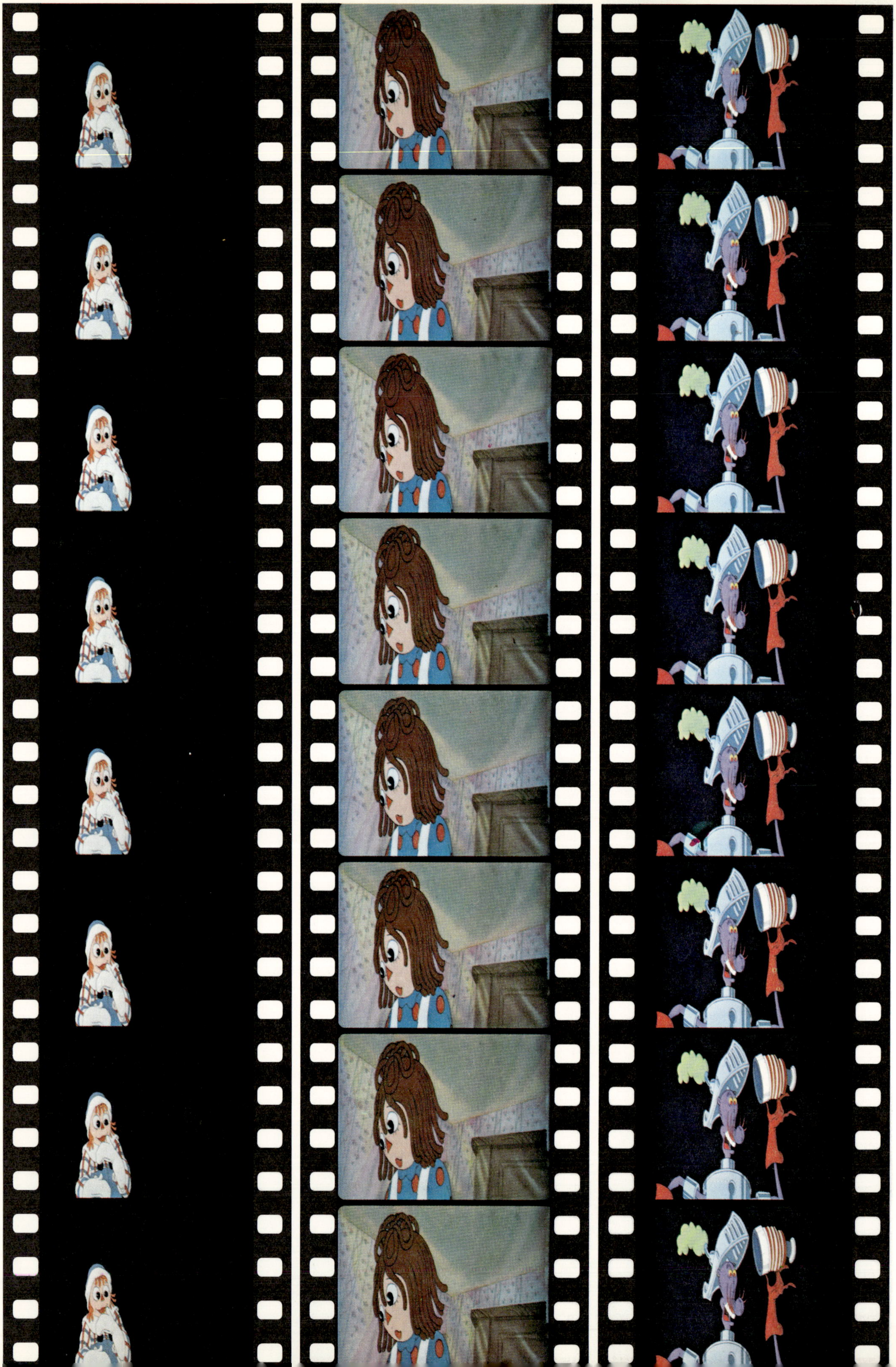

Five strips of 35-mm film from *Raggedy Ann & Andy* show the "squeezed" image the art work acquires when photographed through a Panavision lens. A similar lens on the movie projector "un-squeezes" the distorted image for the theatre's wide screen.

This flickering star effect was double-exposed over the background painting of trees and hills (masked by a black matte during the first run through the camera, just as the characters on cel were doubly opaqued on the back, so that no light could shine through them). This process was enormously time consuming, as it sometimes required four separate camera runs of the same film footage. Had the shadows cast by the characters in some scenes not been created by cutting out translucent paper and pasting it under the characters on the cel, they would have required another run through the camera to attain the right degree of vaporousness.

"Dick Williams is a perfectionist, and I'm a perfectionist," Rezek states. "He's trying to maintain that same quality level, which makes me feel good. I appreciate that."

Click. Whirl. Click. Whirl.

Jim Petrie, a grown man of thirty-six years, dips pieces of paper toweling into water, wads them up and throws them at shaving cream he has smeared onto the glass of a soundbooth. Petrie is not an inbetweener who has finally gone mad from an overdose of retracing, but a highly skilled and imaginative technician who is responsible for creating some of the hundreds of sound effects used in *Raggedy Ann & Andy*.

The effect he is trying for right now is the sound of a soggy pie being splattered in someone's face. "Somehow," Petrie says, "a real pie doesn't sound right when it splats. So I add a heightened quality to it by putting the microphone real close to this shaving cream and later adding an oral sound to the whole thing."

Petrie lets out with a raspberry of the kind that will be mixed in later. Very effective.

But Petrie is only warming up. He and his assistant, Cheryl Wise, bounce around his studio laughing as they show how they get the right effects out of the simplest objects.

The cloth feet of the Camel needed soft "clop" effects, so Petrie put on boxing gloves and punched different wood surfaces. He made the various Pirate-ship creaks by bending an old shoe close to the mike. "Close-mike technique is another world, another dimension," Petrie exclaims. He created water by using a recording of the natural sound and embellishing it orally, as he also did with wind. For the "Taffy Valley," as he calls the Greedy, "I did various mouth pops, mouth sounds, raspberries, with the mike on my throat." The Loonie King's expansions were balloon stretches, and the King's deflations were "balloons' air going out."

"So far there've been no problems. We are moving along. One reel of the film required fifty different effects. I make a tape of the sound; then the editor, Harry, gets an okay from the director, and he says, 'We need ten pops, or bangs, or whatever.' So I transfer the one effect ten times onto tape.

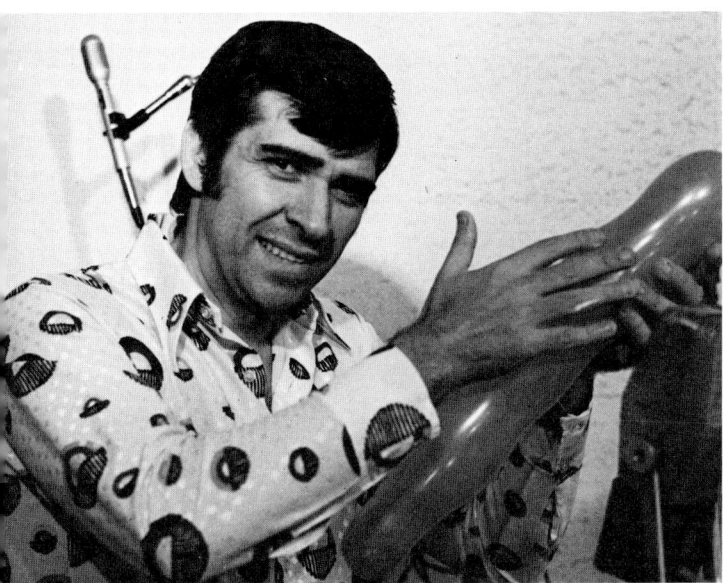

Harry cuts it in on the effects track, and at the final sound mix it is all blended in with the voices and the music.

"Yes, you have to be musical and creative, have imagination for this job. The talent for it is within you. Let me show you how I once did a roller-coaster ride effect...."

Sound-effects man Jim Petrie.

* * * * *

The original animator's drawings (the "ruffs") are by this time battered from all the flipping and handling by the animator, his assistant, the inbetweeners, and even the paint department. Eventually they will be discarded, having served their purpose; their vitality remains on the paper, but it has been transferred and transformed—given to the cause. A few of the animators, aware of the strange beauty of their rough drawings, will ask for them to be returned to them. On occasion they will take them out of a closet or an attic and admire them as one admires a Pontormo sketch of a dancing figure or Daumier's studies for "Don Quixote," except that the animator can do more than admire: he can, with the merest flip of a thumb, bring his drawings to vivid life once more.

Friday
October 22, 1976

MEMO: TO ALL PERSONNEL
FROM: RICHARD HORNER

Since the meeting Thursday morning, I am sure that you are all aware that the firm deadline for delivery of the film is December 31st. We will have to make every possible effort to increase the production flow.

In order to help Dick Williams accomplish this, Gerry Potterton, Associate Director, will have the responsibility of expediting all phases of the production. Marlene Robinson will be responsible for overall supervision of the reorganized clean-up groups supervised by Michael Sporn, John Bruno, Chrystal Russell, Art Vitello and Tom Roth.

We are in the stages of final production and every minute counts. We will expect everyone at work promptly at 9:00 each morning, and the lunch hour will be 1:00 to 2:00 and will be held to one hour, with the exception of an extra 20 minutes on Friday for banking.

Richard Horner

The Berkley Building in New York, home base of *Raggedy Ann & Andy*.

DIRECTIVE #1: RAGGEDY ANN HEADQUARTERS
27 OCTOBER '76
CODE NAME: CLEAN UP

THESE STEPS ARE BEING INTRODUCED IN ORDER TO SAVE TIME IN DRAWING AND INK AND PAINT. THEY WILL BE FOLLOWED ! ! !

---

(1) ELIMINATE INBETWEENING WITH BLUE PENCIL WHENEVER YOU CAN USE BLACK. IT ELIMINATES A STEP. MOST IMPORTANT WHEN INBETWEENING (ON ONES). IF YOU CANNOT DO THIS YET—LEARN ! ! ! NOW!

---

(2) LINE QUALITY IS NOT AS IMPORTANT AS FORM—JUST DO THE DRAWING.

---

(3) DO NOT INBETWEEN THE CROSSHATCHING—IT ONLY NEEDS TO BE READ AS A SHADED AREA.

---

(4) ASSISTANTS! ! ON ALL OF YOUR DRAWINGS ADD FIELD SIZES IN BLUE PENCIL! ! ! !

---

(5) INBETWEENERS: DRAW ONLY ABOUT 1/4 INCH PAST FIELD SIZE. CONTINUE TO CHECK ON THIS!—IT SAVES A LOT OF TIME.

---

(6) ANN:
    A. HAIR DETAIL CAN BE ELIMINATED EXCEPT ON CLOSE-UPS.
    B. TRY TO DRAW FEWER DOTS.

---

(7) SUSIE:
    A. ELIMINATE PINS EXCEPT ON CLOSE-UPS.

---

(8) GREEDY:
    A. ELIMINATE DRAWING DETAIL IN CANDY SQUARES AND BALLS.
    B. SIMPLIFY ELABORATE DESSERTS.
    C. DO NOT CROSSHATCH OR SHADE DARK AREAS. EXAMP: APPLES, DARK CHOCOLATE, ETC.
                       DO IT! . . . . . .

****IF YOU HAVE ANY QUESTIONS ASK YOUR SUPERVISOR.

You are invited to a

Christmas Party

December 11, 7:00 P.M.

BRING BOTTLE

EPILOGUE
From Rags to Riches

Next winter in your favorite theater America's most beloved storybook dolls will become America's most beloved movie stars.
—*Variety* ad, March 3, 1976

In the final week of December 1976 at the New York *Raggedy* studio, the camera department was shooting in double shifts on both cameras, and the Xerox department had three shifts. The California contingent, for the most part, had returned home. Most of the animators and assistant animators were finished with their tasks and were let go.

The paint department, now the biggest threat to the deadline because of the slow, careful nature of the process, was on day and evening shifts. To speed things along, bundles of Xeroxed cels were shipped for painting to two independent companies in Hollywood and to one in New York. The soundtrack was being mixed reel by reel from the work print of the film. Many of the scenes were still in black-and-white pencil test.

Toward the end of the production, a great deal of responsibility for pushing it to the finish line was taken off Williams's overburdened shoulders and shared with Gerry Potterton, a veteran of TV animation and commercials and Williams's old friend. Williams's pride was stung by this move, but having no choice in the matter, he reluctantly accepted the producers' decision. Potterton used his experience to accelerate the work pace of the project considerably by eliminating some scenes and some details within scenes.

Potterton's help enabled Williams to concentrate on working closely with his animators and assistants, and Williams personally finished animating several scenes with Babette; most of Andy's song, "No Girl's Toy"; and the film's titles. He was tired but "happy about the quality of the film. It's still holding."

On December 8, 1976, a two-page ad in *Variety* estimated that seventy million people watched Raggedy Ann and Andy dance the "Rag Dolly," choreographed by Peter Gennaro, for "a full two minutes" during the Macy's Thanksgiving Day Parade on network television. The dance and the ad were

"RAGGEDY ANN" — Sequence 12

58A: I'M HOME

58B: OH THIS IS WONDERFUL!

58C: OH YOU 2 ARE JUST THE BEST — OH I THINK IT'S JUST THE BEST

58D: OH YOU ALL ARE JUST THE BEST

59A: YOU'RE

59B: THE BEST.

90A: TIMES GET BAD BUT I DON'T WORRY —

90B: CAUSE I KNOW YOU'LL SEE ME THRO' —

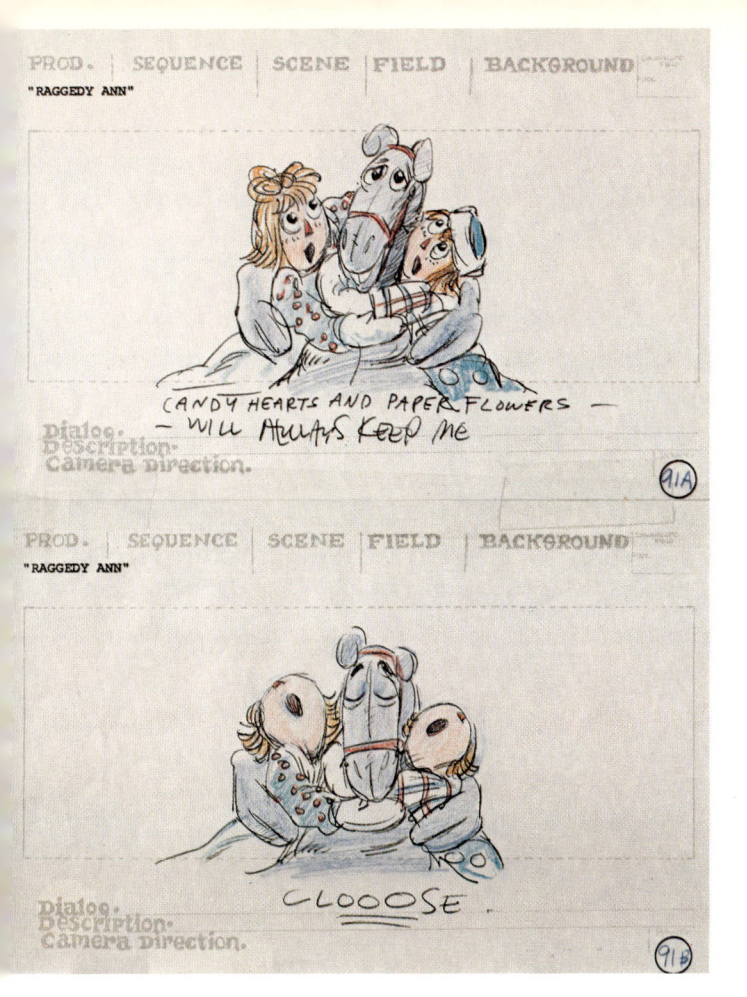

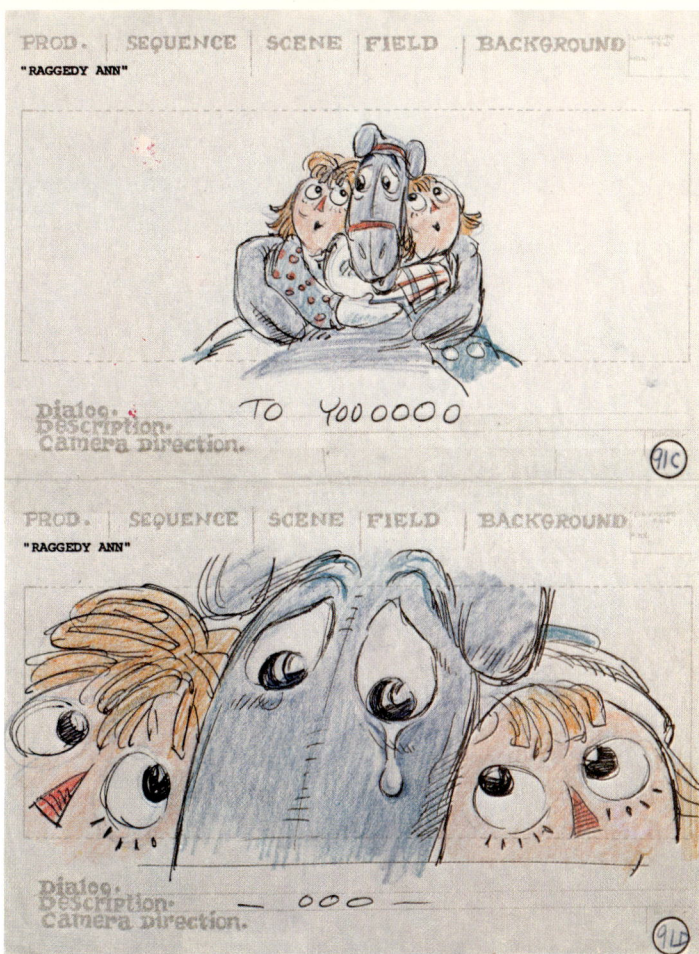

merely the tip of the iceberg—the kick-off—of a two-million-dollar-plus promotional campaign for the film that was to transport the two humble rag dolls into a rarefied realm of fame and fortune inhabited by only one other legendary cartoon star—Mickey Mouse. (The final cost of the feature was over four million dollars.)

The media blitz, sponsored jointly by ITT and 20th Century-Fox, distributors of the feature film, included a tidal wave of television commercials on prime-time network and local broadcast and twenty full-page ads in national magazines, including *Time*, *Newsweek*, and *Sports Illustrated*.

A spokesman for 20th Century-Fox spoke of plans for "charity premieres in major cities" under the sponsorship of Bobbs-Merrill/ITT; group sales to screenings for underprivileged children and for students, teachers, and churches; Eastertime openings in four hundred theaters around the country, with about forty in the New York area alone; and "an avalanche of merchandising tie-ins" that would involve hundreds of nationally famous manufacturers of almost every conceivable product, from recordings and books to toys and dolls to clothing and food—over a hundred manufacturers licensed to make more than five hundred products.

After production on *Raggedy Ann* was concluded, everyone involved in

Richard Williams's story drawings of the film's finale.

the film was faced with the problem of what to do next. Some of the artists found immediate employment. Chrystal Russell and Art Vitello were asked by Dick Williams to work on his new feature, *The Thief and the Cobbler,* and left for London in January; Tissa David (who animated over 1,000 feet, the most footage of any of the animators) went to Hungary for the Christmas holidays, after which she was set to work on Williams's film. She was to be followed by Art Babbitt and Emery Hawkins. Jim Logan assisted on some New York commercials; his plan was then to work for Bakshi's in California. Mike Sporn was slated to work with John Hubley on his TV special based on the comic strip *Doonesbury.*

Some of the young assistants, inbetweeners, and opaquers would be out of work for a long while; some might never work on an animated feature again, or remain in animation at all, for that matter. A few will become animators and will make their own films in their own ways, or they will find work with commercial companies, but somehow they will utilize the experience they gained working on a quality film. They will perhaps enrich the language of the art and improve the industry.

As for Dick Williams, whatever the commercial success of the production, he had learned from the venture. Although this was by no means a normal production, he knew now what it was to do a feature. He knew what to expect of certain animators, what not to expect, and whom never to hire again. He had found some new talents and made some new friends; he had also lost a few.

He feels "by hindsight there was no other way, given the circumstances, to have worked. And though we have made some mistakes, I really don't see how else we could have done it."

Most important, Richard Williams came away from *Raggedy Ann & Andy* with a resolution never to work under anyone else's sponsorship again.

"I can't stand the bit between my teeth," he said. "I have to have total control, and the only way to have it is to do my own productions. I will do *The Thief* now. I'm more convinced now than ever before that I can do it. But I must make sure it is all mine, financially and artistically, even if I have to make commercials for another ten years to complete it."

SELECTED BIBLIOGRAPHY

I hope the following list, though far from complete, may prove helpful to those readers who would like to pursue further the subject of film animation in all its many aspects.

BOOKS

Adamson, Joe. *Tex Avery: King of Cartoons*. Popular Library, 1975. A reference paperback about an innovative Warner Brothers cartoon director.

Anderson, Yvonne. *Teaching Film Animation to Children*. Van Nostrand Reinhold, 1970. An excellent, unpretentious how-to book.

Cabarga, Leslie. *The Fleischer Story*. Nostalgia Press, 1976. A lavishly illustrated history of the Fleischer brothers and their studio.

Field, Robert D. *The Art of Walt Disney*. Macmillan, 1942. Professor Field's year of research at the Walt Disney studio during its "Golden Era" resulted in this fine book.

Finch, Christopher. *The Art of Walt Disney*. Abrams, 1973. Big and beautiful, but spreads itself over too much territory. Best chapter: recounting the creation of *Snow White*.

Graham, Donald W. *Composing Pictures*. Van Nostrand Reinhold, 1970. The great Disney studio instructor expounds on his art theories, including film graphics.

Halas, John. *Computer Animation*. Hastings House, 1974. A collection of writings by twenty-five leading exponents of the new animation technology. Includes the latest methods and criteria for aesthetic appreciation of computer art.

———, and Manvell, Roger. *The Technique of Film Animation*. Hastings House, 1968. A revised edition of a literate coverage of all stages of producing animated films, including special techniques; e.g., pinscreen, computer, puppets, etc.

Heath, Robert P. *Animation in Twelve Hard Lessons*. Heath Production, 1974. Step-by-step programmed instructions that cover the craft of commercial animation (cel) from basic inbetweening to camera trade secrets.

Holloway, Ronald. *Z is for Zagreb*. A. S. Barnes and Company, 1972. An illustrated guide to the famed Yugoslavian cartoon studio and its artists.

Holman, L. Bruce. *Puppet Animation in the Cinema*. A. S. Barnes and Company, 1975. A comprehensive source book on a special subject. Includes techniques, history, a filmography and chronology of representative films.

Madsen, Roy P. *Animated Film: Concepts, Methods, Uses*. Interland, 1969. Concise text, well-structured diagrams and illustrations. Excellent book.

Maltin, Leonard. *The Disney Films*. Crown, 1973. A handy reference work on the films of the "Old Mousetro."

Nicolaides, Kimon. *The Natural Way to Draw*. Houghton Mifflin, 1969. First published in 1941. Helps the artist/animator find and release his individual creative impulse and personality in a drawing.

Perisic, Zoran. *The Animation Stand*. Hastings House, 1976. The unlimited possibilities of the animation camera and rostrum are demonstrated in this paperback.

Reiniger, Lotte. *Shadow Theatres and Shadow Films*. Watson-Guptill, 1970. The great "shadow" animator details a history of her art and reveals its techniques.

Russett, Robert, and Starr, Cecile. *Experimental Animation. An Illustrated Anthology.* Van Nostrand Reinhold, 1976. A much-needed book that presents thirty-eight artist/filmmakers who avoid the traditional production-line procedures of the commercial animation studios.

Schickel, Richard. *The Disney Version.* Simon and Schuster, 1968. Riddled with inaccuracies and hell-bent on proving a low opinion of Disney and all his works, but also contains some acute social commentary about America and acerbic observations about Disney that are worth reading.

Thomas, Bob. *The Art of Animation.* Simon and Schuster, 1959. Disney-sponsored and full of fascinating illustrations and informative insights into the Disney methods of cartoon production.

———. *Walt Disney. An American Original.* Simon and Schuster, 1976. The official studio bio. A warm, remarkably fair retelling of the amazing Disney story.

PERIODICALS

AFI Report. Vol. 5, No. 2. Summer 1974. A special animation issue with articles on Winsor McCay, Max Fleischer, "The Hollywood Cartoon," etc.

Canemaker, John. "A Living Animation Legend: J. R. Bray." *Filmmakers Newsletter,* Vol. 8, No. 3, 1974.

———. "Art Babbitt: The Animator as Firebrand." *Millimeter,* September 1975.

———. "Otto Messmer and Felix the Cat." *Millimeter,* September 1976.

———. "Sincerely Yours, Frank Thomas." *Millimeter,* January 1975.

———. "Vladimir William Tytla: Animation's Michelangelo." *Cinefantastique,* Vol. 5, No. 3, 1976.

Cocks, Jay. "The World Jones Made." *Time,* December 17, 1973. A brief résumé of animation director Chuck Jones's career.

Film Comment. January–February 1975. A special animation issue with articles on the Warner Brothers cartoon directors and on Winsor McCay, Grim Natwick, the Fleischers, TV animation, etc.

Fortune. "The Big Bad Wolf." November 1934. Disney's financial techniques at that time.

Funnyworld. No. 12, Summer 1970; No. 13, Spring 1971; No. 14, Spring 1972; No. 15, Fall 1973; No. 16, Winter 1974–5. Editor Mike Barrier's valuable journal of cartoon art and animation.

Graham, Don. "Animation: Art Acquires a New Dimension." *American Artist,* December 1940. A capsulized explanation of personality animation techniques.

Kasindorf, Martin. "A Kind of X-Rated Disney." *The New York Times Magazine,* October 14, 1973. About Ralph Bakshi and his films.

Millimeter. February 1976. A special animation issue featuring articles on *Raggedy Ann & Andy,* the beginnings of *Fantasia,* teaching animation, Hugh Harman and Rudolf Ising, TV commercials, etc.

Millimeter. February 1977. Special animation issue featuring articles on Len Lye, Oskar Fischinger, John and Faith Hubley, new independent animator/filmmakers, etc.

Time. "Father Goose." December 17, 1954. "Mouse and Man." December 27, 1937. Two *Time* cover stories, both excellent, on Disney at two important periods in his career.

Index

Adams, George Matthew, 70
Adams, Mason, 142
Advertising, 284–285
Aesop's Fables, 50
Albucher, Larry, 208
Alice in Cartoonland, 54
Alice in Wonderland, 94
Ambro, Hal, 229
Animated musicals, 88
Animation, history of, 45–60
Animation drawing boards, 158
Animator, role of, 30, 33
Anticipation, 55, 58, 61
Anzilotti, Cosmo, 18, 242–243
Appet, Lou, 239
Art of Animation, The, 30
Art of Walt Disney, The, 175
Assistant animators, 33, 244–247
Avery, Tex, 60

Babbitt, Art, 91, 100, 101, 145, 146–147, 150, 155, 174–191, 193, 225, 226, 236, 237, 247, 286
Babette, 22–23, 118, 209, 228, 229, 256

Backgrounds, 36, 37, 264–273
Baker, Mark, 138, 139, 143
Bakes, George, 38–39, 243, 244
Bakshi, Ralph, 60, 127
Balazs, Bela, 52
Balzar, Richard, 247
Bambi, 58
Barre, Raoul, 50, 51
Beany and Cecil, 225
Beckerman, Howard, 241–242
Bell, Carl, 93, 94–95, 224–225, 236
Bell, Jan, 224–225, 237
Bennett, James Gordon, 66
Berner, Fred, 18, 242
Bettelheim, Bruno, 75
Blackton, James Stuart, 47
"Blue," 122, 147, 150, 181
Bobbs-Merrill/ITT, 73, 81, 88, 89, 125–130, 215, 285
Boyle, Jack, 51
Bray, John Randolph, 50
Brill, Marty, 142
Brion, Marcel, 50
Bruno, John, 203, 224, 237, 241, 280
"Brutus," 66

Butterworth, Sue, 19, 37, 266, 270, 271
Byrne, Tom, 51

Cabarga, Leslie, 71
Camel with the Wrinkled Knees, 28–29, 56–57, 73, 114, 115, 123, 136, 146–147, 155, 181–190, 257
Camel with the Wrinkled Knees, The, 75
Camerawork, 41, 274–278
Canby, Vincent, 98
"Candy Hearts and Paper Flowers," 78, 87, 143
Cannata, George, 51
Captain Contagious, 115, 120–121, 220, 222–223, 253
Caricatures, 124, 168, 184, 246–249
Cauchemar du Fantoche, Le, 48
Celestri, Gian-Franco, 245
Cels, 16–17, 28–29, 36, 50, 210, 250–253. See also Opaquing
Chang, Harry, 18
Chaplin, Charlie, 52, 239
Charge of the Light Brigade, The, 96, 98
Checking, 41, 254
Chiniquy, Gerry, 19, 219, 220

Christmas Carol, A, 96, 97, 98, 107, 109
Clampett, Bob, 60
Clean-ups, 33
Cockaboody, 125, 173
Cohen, Sheldon, 247
Cohl, Emile, 48, 199, 202
Cole, Corny, 22–23, 31, 110–123, 146–154, 211, 266
Col. Heeza Liar in Africa, 50
Color keying, 255
Color models, 37, 255–258, 261
Conference technique, 30, 145–155
Conn, Didi, 138, 139, 142, 143
Cool Poor Fool, 173
Costs, 127, 285
Country Cousin, The, 175
Cox, Howard, 71, 73
Cox, Richard L., 70
Crane, Doug, 242, 243

David, Tissa, 18, 26–27, 58, 125–126, 145, 151, 154–155, 156–173, 227, 246, 248, 249, 286
Davis, Bill, 208, 209
Davis, Mark, 46
Deep Deep Woods, 26–27, 75, 117, 273
Dinky Doodle, 50
Director, role of, 42. See also Williams, Richard
Disney studio, 20, 21, 36, 45–46, 54, 58, 71, 86, 88, 94–95, 122, 175–177, 204, 229, 238–239
Distortion, 39
Dolls, 73, 75, 208, 209
Donahue, M. A., 70, 71, 73
Dooley, Paul, 142
Downs, Charles E., 220
Downs, Paulette, 220, 237
Dunning, George, 95, 102

Eggs, 173
Enchanted Drawing, The, 47
Enchanted Square, The, 71
Eugster, Al, 51
Everybody Rides the Carousel, 173, 176
Exaggeration, 39, 229
Exposure sheets. See X-sheets

Fantasia, 54, 58, 176
Felix the Cat, 50–54
Feuer, Howard, 138
Field, defined, 40, 41
Field, Robert D., 175
Film footage chart, 43

Finch, Christopher, 88
"First-answer print," 42
Fischinger, Oskar, 54
Flacks, Niki, 142
Fleischer, Max, 50, 71
Fleischer Story, The, 71
Flipping, 158, 159
Flowers and Trees, 58
Follow-through, 57, 58
Frames, 30, 43, 167
Frederick, Robert B., 77
Freleng, Friz, 202
Fritz the Cat, 60
"Funny Picture Man, The," 64
Funny Thing Happened on the Way to the Forum, A, 96, 98

Gaelan, Hetty, 142
Gazooks, 38, 88–89, 214, 243–244
Geneen, Harold, 89
Gennaro, Peter, 283
Gerald McBoing Boing, 60
Gerlach-Barklow, 73
Gertie the Dinosaur, 48, 49
Goldberg, Eric, 245, 246, 247, 248, 249
"Golden Age" of animation, 20
Goofy, 175
Graham, Don, 54, 58
Grandpa, 38–39
Gray, Margery, 142
Greedy, 32–33, 56–57, 118, 119, 150–151, 194–203, 213, 258, 260
Greenberg, Ida, 19, 241, 254–258, 262
Gruelle, Alice Benton, 64, 67
Gruelle, Johnny, 62–70
Gruelle, Justin, 70
Gruelle, Marcella, 64, 66–67
Gruelle, Myrtle Swann, 64, 66, 67, 70–71, 73
Gruelle, Prudence, 64
Gruelle, Richard, 66, 70–71, 73
Gruelle, Richard B., 64, 67
Gruelle, Worth, 63–71, 73, 75
Guerin, Michel, 266, 271

Haden, Klara, 262, 263
Hand, Dave, 30
Happy Prince, The, 270
Harnick, Sheldon, 142
Harris, Ken, 100, 101
Hartman, Steve, 255
Haskett, Dan, 19, 32, 184, 245, 246, 247, 248, 249

Hawkins, Emery, 32, 118, 145, 150–151, 193–205, 248, 286
Heavy Traffic, 60
Heitman, William F., 64
Hellmich, Fred, 145
"Holds," 227
Hollywood Raggedy Ann Studio, 19, 127, 130, 219–239
"Home," 143
Horner, Richard, 77, 79–81, 88, 89, 106, 124, 138, 142, 210, 280
How a Mosquito Operates, 48, 49
Hubley, John, 100, 104, 173, 176, 286
Humorous Phases of Funny Faces, 47
Hurd, Earl, 50

"I Look and What Do I See," 86–87
Image, Jean, 172
Inbetweeners, 36, 244–250
Ink and paint department, 36, 254–263
Irving, George S., 142
ITT. See Bobbs-Merrill/ITT

"Jack the Giant Killer," 66
Jenkins, Ray, 254
Johnny Gruelle Company, 70, 71, 73
Johnston, Ollie, 46, 238, 239
Jones, Chuck, 60, 91, 100, 101
"June Bride—Off for the Honeymoon," 65
Jungle Book, The, 98, 142

Kael, Pauline, 98
Kahl, Milt, 46, 100
Kaiser, Ardyth, 142
Katzenjammer Kids, 202–203
Kausler, Mark, 71
Keaton, Buster, 52, 239
Kelsey, Dick, 94
Kent, Lee, 236, 241
Kern, Jerome, 70
Key method of animation, 33
Kimball, John, 145, 190, 233, 235
Kimball, Ward, 46, 177
King Koo Koo, 24–25, 31, 122, 220, 221, 257
Kneitel, Seymour, 71
Knickerbocker Toy Company, 73, 75
KoKo the Clown, 50
Kuhanek, Bill, 250

Lady and the Tramp, 94–95
Lane, Nancy, 255
Larson, Eric, 238
Laugh-O-Grams, 54

Layout sketches, 30–31
Leica reel, 36, 210
Levitow, Abe, 107, 109
Levitow, Judy, 249
Life Inside and Outside an American Factory, 247
Little Island, The, 94, 95
Little Nemo in Slumberland, 48, 49, 234–235
Littlest Angel, The, 80–81, 87
Live-action, shooting of, 207–208
Locker, Linda, 208
Logan, Jim, 246–247, 249, 286
Loonie Knight, 24–25, 28–29, 116, 215
Loonies, 227
Love Me, Love Me, Love Me, 95–96
Luske, Ham, 30

McCay, Winsor, 48–50, 233, 234–235
McGinty, Officer, 64
Madeline, 60
Magoo's Arabian Nights, 60
Marcella, 207, 211, 215. See also Gruelle, Marcella
Marinelli, Camille, 259
Massie, Nancy, 258, 262, 263
Maxi Fix-It, 37, 209, 230–231
Messmer, Otto, 45, 51–53
Metamorphosis, 199, 202
Mickey Mouse, 54, 58
Mickley, William, 207–208
Millican, Carol, 244
Mingalone, Dick, 208
Model sheets, 33, 34–35, 38, 39, 160, 162–163
Moore, Fred, 30
Motion Picture Cartooning, 258
"Mr. Twee Deedle," 66
Multiplane camera, 58, 275
Music, 84–87, 140–141, 142
"Music in the Disney Films," 88
Myersob, Alissa, 224
My Very Own Fairy Stories, 70

Naisbitt, Roy, 101
Natwick, Grim, 100, 172, 193, 227, 246
New York Raggedy Ann Studio, 18, 127, 130, 240–280
Nicklaus, Carol, 89
Nidah, Frederick, 208, 209
"No Girl's Toy," 87, 102, 105

Of Demons and Men, 173
Old Mill, The, 58

Olivier, Elizabeth, 258
101 Dalmatians, 36, 122
Opaquers, 36, 37, 253–263
Osterman, Lester, 77, 79, 80, 104, 106, 126
Oswald the Rabbit, 54

Painting. See Opaquing
Panavision, 210, 276–277
Parker, Dana, 51
Peel, Spencer, 39, 230
Pegues, Lester T., Jr., 248, 249
Pencil tests, 36
People People People, 173
Pepe, Cosmo, 250–251
Personality animation
  defined, 45–46
  history of, 48–60
Peter Pan, 46, 94, 220
Petrie, Jim, 278–279
Phantom Tollbooth, The, 114
Pinocchio, 176
Pirate sequence, 22–23, 243, 261. See also Captain Contagious
Playroom settings, 37, 108, 112–113, 208, 211, 212, 266–269, 272–273
Pose method of animation, 33
Potterton, Gerry, 24–25, 95, 122, 210, 233, 239, 280, 283
"Punkin Center," 66
Pyle, Willis, 18

Queasy the Parrot, 16–17, 220

"Rag Dolly," 283
Raggedy Andy
  animation of, 16–17, 68–69, 105, 151–155, 160–163
  books on, 67–73
  dolls of, 70, 73, 75
  inspiration for, 67
  voice of, 138, 139
Raggedy Andy Stories, 72, 75
Raggedy Ann
  animation of, 55, 60–61, 68–69, 110, 111, 151–155, 160–170
  books on, 66–75
  dolls of, 70, 73, 75
  inspiration for, 67
  voice of, 138, 139
"Raggedy Ann" (song), 70
Raggedy Ann and Andy in the Magic Book, 73

Raggedy Ann and Raggedy Andy (animation short), 71
Raggedy Ann East. See New York Raggedy Ann Studio
Raggedy Ann's Sunny Songs, 64
Raggedy Ann Stories, 67, 70, 72, 75
Raggedy Ann West. See Hollywood Raggedy Ann Studio
"Raggedy Man, The," 67
Raposo, Joe, 77, 79, 81, 82–89, 106, 107, 109, 124, 130–131, 134, 135, 138, 142, 143, 208
"Reading" the soundtrack, 30, 166–167
Rescuers, The, 210
Return of the Pink Panther, The, 96, 98
Rezek, Al, 210, 250, 251, 274–278
Rezek, Evelyn, 255
Riley, James Whitcomb, 64, 67
Robinson, David, 98
Robinson, Marlene, 224, 241, 280
Rooty Toot Toot, 176
Rose, John C., 71
Roth, Tom, 280
Roughs, 32, 33
Russell, Chrystal, 55, 139, 170, 218, 226, 241, 280, 286

Scarborough, Lester, 249
Scheduling, 126–127, 130, 210, 215, 280–281, 283
Schnerk, Jack, 244
Schwartz, Phil, 240
Selfish Giant, The, 270
Seligman, Max, 166, 207
Set-ups, 40
Silhouette test, 58, 59
Silver, Joe, 142, 194
Sinatra, Frank, 82
Smith, David, 71
Snow White and the Seven Dwarfs, 30, 45–46, 86, 88, 94, 100, 122, 127, 171, 176
Sockworm, 122–123
Sound effects, 278–279
Soundtrack, 30, 42, 58, 135–143, 215. See also Music; Sound effects
Spencer, Evelyn, 255
Spencer, Fred, 30
Sporn, Michael, 18, 241, 244–245, 249, 250, 280, 286
Staircase scene, 232, 234–235
Stang, Arnold, 142
Star grid, 275, 278
Steamboat Willie, 58

Stepping Stones, 70
Storyboards, 20–27, 30, 284–285
Stretch and squash, 56–57, 58, 59, 61
Stuart, Lynn, 142
Stuthman, Fred, 136–137, 142–143, 185
Suddenly It's Spring, 71
Sues, Allan, 142
Sullivan, Pat, 51, 52
Susie Pincushion, 34–35, 209, 256
Sutcliff, Judy, 208, 209
Swift, Allen, 142
Szilagyi, Mary, 244

Taffy Pit, 203. See also Greedy
Telltale Heart, The, 60
Terry, Paul, 50
Terrytoons, 242
Thackray, Patricia, 87, 109, 118
Theory of the Film, 52
Thief and the Cobbler, The, 102–104, 110, 191, 286
Thomas, Bob, 30
Thomas, Frank, 46, 52, 238–239
Thorne, Reverend and Mrs., 207–208
Three Little Pigs, 175
Thurber, Alfred, 51
Topsy-Turvy, 252, 255, 258
Trick films, 47

"Trucks," 40, 170
True Blue Sue, 173
Truth Ruth, 173
Twin Penny Dolls, 220
Tynan, Kenneth, 98
Tytla, Bill, 30, 243–244

United Production Artists (UPA), 60

Vitello, Art, 203, 224, 237, 280, 286
Voices, 135–143, 215
Volland, P. F., 67, 70, 71

Walker, Hal, 51
Walton, Tony, 104
Warner Brothers, 58, 60
What's New Pussycat?, 96
Wilk, Max, 87
Williams, Claire, 206, 207, 213, 214, 215
Williams, Martin D., 63, 75
Williams, Richard
  caricatures of, 247, 248, 249
  drawings by, 38, 39, 68–69, 93–97, 103, 110, 111, 124, 162–163, 246, 247, 248, 284–285
  in the early phases, 125–131, 135–136, 142–143, 145–155

Williams, Richard (Cont.)
  on the film, 15, 61, 75, 109, 111, 122–123, 219, 239, 250, 286
  in the final phases, 283
  at the halfway point, 207, 210, 213–215, 233
  memos from, 13, 145, 155, 213–215, 217, 262
  other people on, 89, 98, 100, 102, 118, 131, 220, 225, 226, 243, 244, 278
  photos of, 18, 19, 37, 42, 90, 92, 99, 101, 103, 105, 107, 191, 213, 226, 236, 244
  role of, 42
  story of, 91–107
Wilson, Amanda, 245
Wise, Cheryl, 278
Women in animation, 170–171, 172–173, 258
Woodin, William H., 64

Xeroxing, 36, 250–251
X-sheets, 30, 164, 167, 170

"Yahoo Center," 66
"Yapps Crossing," 66
Yellow Submarine, 98, 118